Boxing

Boxing

A Concise History of the Sweet Science

Gerald R. Gems

ROWMAN & LITTLEFIELD
Lanham • Boulder • New York • Toronto • Plymouth, UK

Published by Rowman & Littlefield
4501 Forbes Boulevard, Suite 200, Lanham, Maryland 20706
www.rowman.com

10 Thornbury Road, Plymouth PL6 7PP, United Kingdom

British Library Cataloguing in Publication Information Available

Library of Congress Cataloging-in-Publication Data

Gems, Gerald R.
  Boxing : a concise history of the sweet science / Gerald R. Gems.
     pages cm
  Includes bibliographical references and index.
  ISBN 978-1-4422-2990-7 (cloth : alk. paper) — ISBN 978-1-4422-2991-4 (ebook)
  1. Boxing—History. 2. Boxing—Social aspects—History. I. Title.
  GV1121.G47 2014
  796.8309—dc23   2013040171

Printed in the United States of America.

To my father (1918–2005),
regimental boxing champion and still my hero.

CONTENTS

Acknowledgments ix
Introduction xi

CHAPTER ONE   Ancient Boxing I

CHAPTER TWO   The Evolution of Boxing 9

CHAPTER THREE   The Relationship between Boxing and
Social Class 43

CHAPTER FOUR   The Social Construction of Race 73

CHAPTER FIVE   The Concept of Ethnicity 137

CHAPTER SIX   Religion 189

CHAPTER SEVEN   Gender 209

CHAPTER EIGHT   Conclusions 239

Appendix 1: Boxing Sanctioning Bodies 245
Appendix 2: Weight Classes 247
Appendix 3: Boxing Rules 251
Notes 253
Bibliography 311
Index 335
About the Author 345

ACKNOWLEDGMENTS

Thanks to Christen Karniski, acquisitions editor at Rowman & Littlefield, for offering me the opportunity; to Professor Gertrud Pfister for her research assistance and the procurement of European sources and photos; to Professors Jan and Terry Todd for their contribution of photos from their vast collection; to Frank Di Benedetto for the LaMotta-Robinson photo; and to research assistants Aubrie Luesse, Derek Nelson, and Zach Heerspink.

INTRODUCTION

Pierce Egan first called boxing "the sweet science of bruising" in *Boxiana*, his account of the early nineteenth-century prizefighting scene in England, but there has long been a fascination with the brutal confrontation of individuals in a demonstration of physical and psychological superiority. Greek and Roman sculptors depicted the athletic ideals of the ancient era in the form of boxers. Hieronymous Mercurialis used Roman boxers as illustrations in his Renaissance work *De Arte Gymnastica*, in 1573. Egan's *Boxiana* (1812) is copiously illustrated with the boxing heroes of that time, while Thomas Eakins, George Bellows, and LeRoy Neiman have captured the continued appeal of boxers and boxing in the modern era. Their works address the norms, values, and social transformations of society over the past century.

Despite the inherent brutality and countless human tragedies occurring in the ring, some see a work of art in the choreographed performance of ducking, feinting, footwork, and the rhythmic staccato of punches. Sugar Ray Robinson brought a particular elegance to the sport both inside and outside the ring. Muhammad Ali exhibited a flair and exuberance that extended well beyond the battleground. Sugar Ray Leonard borrowed from both in what has been termed "a poetry of physical action."[1]

Maurice Maeterlinck, a Belgian poet, playwright, and winner of the Nobel Prize in 1911 (1862–1949), explained that "in the boxer's stance, one of the most beautiful positions taken by the male physique, all the muscles of the body become legible. From head to toe not a single ounce of strength is wasted. Every ounce is directed toward one or the other of two massive fists, each supercharged with energy."[2]

Writers, both male and female, have been particularly attracted to the human drama that unfolds in the boxing ring. For them, "a great fight is a masterpiece of suspense, in doubt until the closing moments."[3] Each round presents a scene in a drama that might increase or relieve tension, a Darwinian struggle, a physical and a psychological contest, a public display of human limitations that involves strategies and counter-strategies of pure combat without weapons other than one's body. It is a type of nonliterary expression, a craft, and in its best forms an art. "Boxers converse with their physiques how the seemingly inarticulate become poets with their bodies."[4] David Scott, professor of literature, even claims that "boxing has given literature as many great novels as baseball, cinema more classic films than football, and criticism more meaningful essays than tennis."[5]

Robert Musil, an Austrian writer also nominated for the Nobel Prize (1880–1941), explored the celebratory aspects of great fighters. "If one were to analyze a powerful mind and a champion boxer from the psycho-technical point of view, it would in fact turn out that their cunning, their courage, their precision and their combinatory ability, as well as the quickness of their reactions on the territory that they have made their own, are approximately equal. . . . But apart from this there is one other advantage that . . . a boxer [has] over a great mind, and that is that their achievement and importance can be indisputably assessed and that the best among them is really acknowledged as the best."[6]

Some writers have sought a more graphic rather than vicarious experience by entering the combat zone. Lord Byron took lessons from prize-fighter John Jackson. He noted on March 20, 1814, that he had "[s]parred with Jackson again yesterday morning, and shall tomorrow. I feel the better for it, in spirits, though my arms and shoulders are very stiff from it." Later that same year on June 19, 1814, he stated: "My mornings are late, and passed in fencing and boxing, and a variety of most unpoetical exercises, very wholesome, &c., but would be very disagreeable to my friends, whom I am obliged to exclude during their operation."[7] Paul Gallico, one of the premier sportswriters of the interwar era, tested himself against heavyweight champion Jack Dempsey in the ring, which resulted in another knockout for the champ. Heavyweight writers such as Ernest

Hemingway and Norman Mailer sparred with boxers, but George Plimpton's participatory brand of journalism led him to fight a three-round exhibition with light heavyweight champion Archie Moore at the famed Stillman's Gym in New York in 1959. Plimpton prepped for the encounter by reading *The Art and Practice of English Boxing*, published in 1807, and by hiring a professional trainer. The bloodshed began in the first round. It was not Moore's blood. The boxer graciously carried the writer through the remaining two rounds without any serious threat to his life.[8]

Trevor Wignall, a British sportswriter, co-opted Egan's characterization in his own publication, *The Sweet Science*, in 1926, but the term was best popularized by A. J. Liebling, whose *The Sweet Science* went through multiple printings and is considered among the best sportswriting ever produced for the general public. This social history of the "sweet science" is intended as a scholarly synthesis of the sport, not so esoteric as to be incomprehensible to the general public but offering some critical and analytical explanation for the evolution of the sport. Scholars have taken an interest in the sport later than have artists and writers, but they are no less keen on deciphering its racial, ethnic, social, and gendered nuances and meanings. Sociological analyses began in 1952 (Weinberg and Arond) to determine who boxed, when and why they boxed, and what the results were (factual, cultural, medical, and moral). Historians, anthropologists, psychologists, physicians, ethicists, and sociologists have produced a plethora of studies in search of answers since that time.[9]

Over the past half century, boxing has waxed and waned as the sport provided a public stage for the transition in race relations, both in the United States and throughout the world, in the decades following World War II. Italian American boxers symbolized the "great white hope" versus the encroaching social tide of blacks and Hispanics, a battle played out in the ring and on the streets of urban America. Muhammad Ali represented not only a clarion call for individual, religious, and civil rights in the United States but a global test case for newly independent countries in Africa and Asia that had been former colonies of the white, Western powers. The rise of great black, Hispanic, and Asian champions thereafter sustained an interest in boxing throughout the latter decades of the momentous twentieth century, but the fracturing of boxing's administration due to regional and disparate governing bodies, the continued presence of corruption, and the lack of a charismatic heavyweight division have diminished its current relevance. Youth are more drawn to the mixed martial arts and ultimate fighting championships that proliferate in the varied forms of new media.

A. J. Liebling, great chronicler of "the sweet science," predicted as much with the advent of television. "The immediate crisis in the United States, forestalling the one high living standards might bring on, has been caused by the popularization of a ridiculous gadget called television. This is utilized in the sale of beer and razor blades. The clients of the television companies, by putting on a free boxing show almost every night of the week, have knocked out of business the hundreds of small-city and neighborhood boxing clubs where youngsters had a chance to learn their trade and journeymen to mature their skills. Consequently the number of good new prospects diminished with every year, and the peddlers' public is already being asked to believe that a boy with perhaps ten or fifteen fights behind him is a topnotch fighter. Neither advertising agencies nor brewers, and least of all networks, give a hoot if they push the Sweet Science back into a period of genre painting. When it is in a coma they will find some other way to peddle their peanuts."[10] Baseball's minor leagues suffered the same slow death, yet the game survived and prospered by finding new markets and a new and more varied labor force that only increased its global audiences.

Boxing, too, persists despite ongoing attempts to ban it. In the first decade of the twenty-first century, Ken Burns's *Unforgivable Blackness*, a documentary on the life of Jack Johnson; Clint Eastwood's *Million Dollar Baby*; and *The Fighter*, a biography of Micky Ward, were commercial successes in movie theaters, and the television series *The Contender* also proved popular. *The Contender* ran for four years (2005–2009) in the United States and the United Kingdom, was televised in India and on the Spanish-language Telemundo network, and produced spinoffs in Asia and Australia in 2009. In 2012 the International Olympic Committee added women's boxing, an area of growth within the sport and the fitness industry, to its program—indicating that predictions of its demise may be premature. While many see boxing as a primal activity, a residual sport at odds with the civilizing process, I hope this work will provide reasons for its cultural relevance.[11]

ANCIENT BOXING

Individual combat started at the dawn of time as prehistoric beings inevitably fought over food sources, territory, and mates. Evidence of boxing contests in ancient Mesopotamia (present-day Iraq and Syria) appeared about 4000 BCE, and boxers were depicted on Egyptian tombs by 3580 BCE. By c. 1500 BCE, boxers on the Minoan isle of Crete practiced their craft with helmets or headdresses and thongs wrapped around their hands, which served as gloves. A fresco from the Mediterranean island of Santorini in the second millennium BCE (c. 1600) shows two boys boxing, each with a gloved hand. Bare-fisted Egyptian boxers, clad in loincloths, presumably entertained their pharaoh in a relief dated c. 1350 BCE. Such evidence suggests that boxing is one of the oldest sports.[1]

Boxing in Ancient Greece

Sports differ from voluntary play that is unregulated and carefree amusement, as well as from games that are a mental or physical activity with some rules. Sports are serious competitive contests that result in winners and losers. Competition formed the core of ancient Greek life. Greek city-states fought each other for trade and territory, and they united in wars against the encroaching Persian Empire. The *Iliad* and the *Odyssey* recount the ten-year Trojan War fought between Greece and Troy (in modern Turkey), c. 1000 BCE, and its aftermath for one of the heroes. Both include descriptions of boxing.[2]

The Greek Olympic Games, first recorded in 776 BCE and dedicated to, Zeus, ruler of the Olympian gods, featured competition in sports, singing, dancing, literature, and theatrical performances. The Greeks introduced boxing to the program of the twenty-third Olympic Games in 688 BCE. Matches often proved to be bloody and even deadly affairs. The bouts took place in the stadium, although restricted or fenced spaces designated the boundaries. Opponents were drawn by lot. There were no weight classes, rounds, or time limits. Only darkness postponed matches. Greek athletes competed in the nude, and while punches to the groin were deemed illegal they were not unknown and were subject to the discretion of judges who regulated the bouts. Clinches, scratching, and biting were forbidden, and judges enforced the rules with a whip. Matches continued in an elimination tournament until one boxer triumphed over all others. While bigger men enjoyed an advantage, smaller ones might outlast tired opponents, as multiple matches (as many as eight in a six-hour period) were fought in a day. Melancomas from Asia Minor (present-day Turkey), an Olympic champion in AD 49, was especially noted for his ability to avoid punches and outlast his opponents. A knockout, an inability to continue, or a submission signaled by a raised finger determined the winner. The latter was unlikely as boxers often swore to accept death rather than dishonor, and stoicism prevailed in the face of opponents. One contestant swallowed his teeth rather than let his opponent see the damage he had done. Boxers protected their hands with leather thongs that also cut the skin of their foes, and scarred faces, broken noses, and lost teeth marked the combatants. The Renaissance sculpture known as the *Terme Boxer* is indicative of the facial deformities suffered in such matches. Champion boxers enjoyed heroic status and were feted by their city-states and, like other Olympic victors, honored with free meals, cash, and lifelong tax exemptions.[3]

Diagoras, an Olympic boxing champion in 464 BCE, also won the Pythian, Isthmian, and Nemean Games, alternative athletic spectacles dedicated to lesser deities but held in years between Olympiads. Diagoras's size, reputed to be 6 feet 6 inches, gave him a distinct advantage and was the basis for his boxing legacy. In 454 and again in 448 BCE his eldest son triumphed in pankration (added to the Olympics in 648 BCE), a brutal sport that combined both boxing and wrestling. In 448 BCE his second son also won the Olympic boxing crown; his third son surpassed even his father's accomplishments by winning at all four athletic festivals in both 432 and 424 BCE. The family dynasty continued throughout the remainder of the century as his daughter produced one grandson who won the Olympic boxing title in 404 BCE and another who won the boys' boxing crown at the same Olympiad. Competition for boys was added in 616 BCE and judges determined admission to the youth's matches based on physical development rather than chronological age. Those with facial hair had to compete as men.[4]

Among the most celebrated of boxing matches occurred between Kreugas and Damoxenos at the Nemean Games c. 400 BCE. Despite an arduous battle neither contestant had gained a decided advantage. As nightfall approached the boxers agreed to submit to one punch by the opponent which might end the brutal affair. Kreugas was awarded the first blow and struck Damoxenos in the face without success. Damoxenos then told Kreugas to protect his head with his arms and formed his fingers into a karate-like weapon with which he pierced the abdomen of his opponent and pulled out his intestines. Kreugas succumbed to the puncture wound and died on the spot; however, the judges ruled him the victor, as he had punched with one fist while Damoxenos's use of five fingers rather than one was deemed an illegal breach of the agreement.[5]

With time, sports in general and boxing in particular became more specialized. Athletes were required to train for ten months and for one additional month at the festival site prior to competitions and to subject themselves to the approval of the judges, who were chosen as much as a year in advance. Gymnasiums became specialized sites for training with coaches and equipped with specific equipment, such as punching bags (which might be skins filled with sand or water), ear protectors, and padded gloves that softened the blows. By c. 200 BCE fleece-lined leather gloves enclosed the knuckles and extended to the forearm, which allowed for greater defensive techniques to ward off opponents' punches. Practice included shadow boxing and weightlifting with heavy stones. Slaves served as sparring partners.[6]

Still, boxing could be brutal. "This Olympicus . . . once had a nose, a chin, a forehead, ears, and eyelids. Then becoming a professional boxer he lost all, not even getting his share of his father's inheritance; for his brother presented a likeness to him he had and he was pronounced to be a stranger, as he bore no resemblance to it."[7]

The order of events during the Olympic Games started with wrestling, followed by boxing, and finished with pankration; athletes sometimes entered all three contests. The brutal pankration combined both boxing and wrestling and allowed kicking and even strangulation, but prohibited biting and gouging. The breaking of opponents' fingers was considered illegal, but did not stop the practice, which resulted in victory for some perpetrators. The mixed martial arts cage fights popular today would be the closest approximation to pankration.[8]

In 480 BCE Theogenes won the Olympic boxing championship, and four years later triumphed in both boxing and pankration at the Isthmian Games, which took place in the spring before the Olympic Games held in summer. Such multiple successes went unmatched for over two centuries until Clitomachus conquered all foes in wrestling, boxing, and pankration at the Isthmian Games, and won both the boxing and pankration contests at the 216 BCE Olympiad. He vanquished all his opponents three times in pankration at the Pythian Games. Oddly, the Spartans, considered to be the best warriors in ancient Greece, did not produce champions in these events because they refused to participate on the chance that they might be defeated, and a Spartan did not admit defeat.[9]

Sports served several functions for the Greeks. They provided a ritualized ceremony to honor their gods; promoted fitness and military training essential to protect their lands in ongoing conflicts; and extolled individual excellence in face-to-face competition. The latter proved especially true in the combat sports of boxing, wrestling, and pankration. Boxers still test their skills in individual confrontations today, and like the Greeks, each knows the dangers of such battles include the possibility of death.

Ancient Rome

Boxing preceded the founding of the Roman Empire, as images of boxers are evident on Etruscan tombs and vases from the sixth century BCE. An Etrurian wine jar dated 510–500 BCE even details a boxer, a sponge boy, and a presumed referee. Under the Romans, however, sports served utilitarian means, particularly martial sports that would benefit military service and the extension of the Roman Empire.[10]

The Romans even surpassed the Greeks in their ferocity when it came to boxing. They inserted metal spikes in the boxing gloves, known as *caestus*. One scholar notes that bouts with caestus were "more like a knife fight than a boxing match."[11] The Roman poet Virgil, author of the epic *Aeniad*, recounts a boxer's use of borrowed caestus "stained with blood and spattered brains." The boxer demonstrated the power of such a weapon by delivering a blow to the head of a bull, which fractured its skull and resulted in its death.[12]

Like the Greeks, the Romans boxed at funeral games, and in the nude, although combatants sometimes wore loincloths. Emperor Augustus enjoyed watching boxing matches, particularly those that matched his Romans against Greek fighters. Such battles might also be more impromptu affairs as when youth encountered rivals in alley fights. These local confrontations assumed greater significance over the succeeding centuries. In Renaissance Florence, males practiced a form of sparring or slap boxing known as *civettino*. In Venice, small armies of young men attacked their counterparts from other neighborhoods for control of the city's bridges in grand battles known as the "war of the fists." The spirited tussles resulted in injuries, dunkings, and occasional deaths for the amusement of spectators and local recognition until outlawed by the authorities in 1705.[13]

Africa

There is some evidence that the Roman caestus was adopted by fighters in Africa possibly as early as the second century BCE. Oral histories of the Hausa people (modern Sudan and Chad) relate the practice of an ancient form of boxing known as dambe, which is still practiced today. Dambe fighters exhibit the stance and loincloths of the ancients, wrap their punching hand in a cloth thong, and some fighters even added glass to the equipment, similar to the Roman caestus.[14]

Dambe boxing is also practiced in northern Nigeria as well as in Cameroon and Niger, where practitioners wrap a single fist in rope. The sport is part of the fall harvest festival, in which itinerant butchers engage in bouts with the hope of attracting the attention of young women of marriageable age. Bouts last three rounds and opponents must be knocked down to claim victory. Kicking and head butting are permitted, and the use of broken glass with the wrapped fist may be allowed with the mutual agreement of the combatants. The lead hand serves as a shield for defensive purposes, while boxers strike blows with their dominant hand. The popularity of the sport can be measured by the growth of training centers and the recruitment of promising fighters by agents, managers who sponsor the boxers, and promoters who offer as much as $600 to the winners.[15]

In the Angolan region an ancient form of boxing that also includes head butts, kicking, and slapping was practiced; boxers also developed a defensive style, using their agility to avoid blows. At least one scholar claims that such a style was imported to the American colonies with the introduction of African slaves.[16]

In South Africa boxers have practiced a bare-knuckle form of the sport, known as musangwe, for centuries. It served as the traditional means to select the best warriors to protect the Venda tribe, and matches may continue for a period of days. Competitions are arranged by age group, starting as early as nine years of age and conducted at the same location, considered to be sacred ground, over hundreds of years. A former fighter explained that "the blood of our forefathers and their teeth have all fallen here." Matches are an all-male affair, as female spectators are not permitted. Men form a ring around which potential fighters parade, issuing challenges to foes. Upon acceptance the fight begins and continues until blood is shed, a knockout blow is delivered, or one boxer admits defeat by raising a hand, similar to the ancient Greek signal for surrender. Bouts are not commercialized as in Nigeria, as no prize money is offered. Boxers fight for family and village pride as the sport is fostered by generations of participants. The Lundevhe River serves as the dividing line between rivals, with those living north of the waterway opposing those to the south. The bouts also serve as a means of social control in a region beset by poverty, illegal activities, and unemployment. A former champion declared, "Fighting here keeps the young men away from crime. It also teaches them not to beat their women. They must be men to fight other men."[17]

Asia

Boxing appeared in China by about 1700 BCE as a form of military training. During the Han dynasty (206 BCE—AD 220) it became mandatory for soldiers. A tome entitled *The Combat of Two Hands* appeared at the midpoint of the Han regime. Around AD 1300 Chinese boxers adopted boxing gloves centuries before their Western counterparts, but the activity fell into relative disuse until Christian missionaries added boxing to their schools and Westerners in Shanghai resumed the sport during the 1920s.[18]

Muay thai, a form of kickboxing, originated in Southeast Asia. Both Thailand and Cambodia claim to be the progenitor, with records dating back to the thirteenth century, but muay thai was also practiced in Myanmar (Burma). Originally a martial art practiced as a battlefield skill as a means to incapacitate foes, surviving soldiers passed the techniques along to their sons across generations. It became the national sport of Thailand with some rule modifications in the eighteenth century. In 1560 a Thai king purportedly won his freedom from the Burmese after he defeated his captors' best warriors with his muay thai skills. In the late sixteenth century King Naresuan of Thailand promoted and practiced the sport and instituted mandatory training for all soldiers. The sport spread throughout the kingdom, as even peasants took up training with local champions and gained particular esteem. Prachao Sua, known as the Tiger King, ascended the throne at the turn of the eighteenth century; he even competed against village fighters, at least two of whom he reputedly killed in such a battle. In 1767 a Thai warrior named Nai Khanom Tom was captured by Burmese invaders; he gained liberation after the Burmese king witnessed his destruction of eleven foes in arranged matches. Nai Khanom Tom returned to Thailand a hero, where he became a teacher of the martial art and was acknowledged as the "father of muay thai." This era also witnessed the introduction of horsehair bindings wrapped around boxers' hands and forearms, similar to those used by the Romans. The primitive gloves gave way to hemp or cloth which also might be embedded with broken glass. Gambling on matches only enhanced the attraction and prestige of successful practitioners. King Rama VI even awarded military titles to the best boxers by the early twentieth century. Muay thai training remained a military school subject taught until the 1920s.[19]

Similar to the ancient Greeks, muay thai served a religious function with blessings and ritual dances before the commencement of the bouts. By the twentieth century rule changes necessitated a roped ring, the use of gloves, headgear, and groin guards, and timed rounds accompanied by musicians.[20]

Filipinos fought with their bare hands in a combat known as suntukan, which may have evolved from knife fights. They also engaged in personal combat with rattan poles, but both forms of pugilism were outlawed once the Spanish colonized the islands after the sixteenth century. Americans would introduce the Western form of boxing shortly after they occupied the archipelago in the wake of the Spanish-American War of 1898.[21]

While boxing assumed various forms in different regions, it would evolve toward contemporary practices as it was gradually nurtured, developed, and disseminated by the British in the eighteenth century and throughout the British Empire thereafter. Nationalistic challenges to the colonialists would continue throughout the next century as the sport began to assume modern characteristics.

CHAPTER TWO
THE EVOLUTION OF BOXING

While boxing has often been chided as primitive, barbaric, and savage, it has nevertheless met the characteristics of modern sports established by Allen Guttmann in his seminal 1978 work, *From Ritual to Record: The Nature of Modern Sports*. Guttmann asserted that modern sports must be secular in nature, and provide equal opportunities for competition. They are rationalized and have rules and regulations administered by some bureaucratic organization. In modern sports athletes assume specialized roles, and their achievements, or lack thereof, are quantified in numbers or statistics in a quest for records. In his work, *A Sporting Time: New York City and the Rise of Modern Athletics, 1820–1870*, Melvin Adelman adds that modern sports are also commercialized.[1] While the ancient Greeks met some of these characteristics in their sports, such as having rules and regulations and specialized roles, their athletic festivals were religious in nature, meant to honor their gods. They sought a display of human excellence but did not quantify their achievements, so there is little knowledge of actual measured success, only a list of champions. Nor was Olympic competition open to all: a competitor had to be a recognized Greek citizen.

Elements of modern characteristics began to appear in early eighteenth-century England as initial forms of dueling with cudgels and swords transitioned into fistic encounters among combatants, particularly among the lower class who lacked the means for sophisticated weaponry. Fist fights also proved to be a less deadly means to settle altercations and presumed affronts to one's honor. Such confrontations undoubtedly entertained and amused onlookers, and the gentlemen and nobles of the upper classes began to arrange battles between their own liverymen and others. In each case, fights had moved away from the sacred associations of the past and assumed secular and increasingly commercialized characteristics. The *Protestant Mercury* recorded one such bout between the Duke of Albemarle's footman and a butcher in January 1681, in which the butcher emerged as the victor. The paper declared that he had previously won many such affairs and proclaimed him to be "the best at this exercise in England." Tom Tring served in the household of the Prince of Wales for fifteen years in the late eighteenth century. He also enjoyed the good life as an artists' and sculptors' model, exhibiting his mesomorphic frame that reached 6 feet 1 inch and weighed in at 210 pounds. As a boxer, Tring fought sparingly at the request of his royal employer, but in old age he had lost his position and earned an impecunious living as a street porter.[2]

By 1719, James Figg, who was adept at cudgels, sword fighting, and fist fighting, became the acknowledged English champion as boxers began to be rated by aficionados based on their past or overall performances. Figg established a boxing school in a London amphitheater where he provided lessons and promoted bouts. By 1722 women entered into the fray with public challenges, which culminated in Figg's theater for the benefit of paying customers. Elizabeth Wilkinson argued with Hannah Hyfield, and then issued a public notice to settle the matter by boxing on a stage for the prize of three guineas, each woman to hold a coin in her hand and the winner determined by who could hold the coin the longest. Hyfield responded that she would deliver more blows than words this time and deliver a "good thumping." Figg's theater offered both male and female bouts, sufficient in number for a Mrs. Elizabeth Stokes, otherwise known as the "Hibernian Heroine," to claim to be the female champion of the city.[3]

Figg's academy hosted the apparently first nationalistic challenge to English sporting honor, made by a Venetian gondolier of great size who boasted "that he would break the jaw-bone of any opponent who might have the temerity to fight him" and claimed that he had sent many to the surgeon in Italy. Italians and other foreigners in England backed him heartily. Figg produced a challenger in Bob Whitaker, stating that the gondolier could not accomplish his task "if he had a sledge hammer in his hand." Interest in the match proved so great and the cost of tickets so high that commoners were unable to attend the fracas. The Venetian's first blow landed on Whitaker's head and knocked him completely off the stage, but the Englishman jumped back on to continue the struggle. Whitaker charged the foreigner and planted a hard blow to his stomach that knocked him on the seat of his pants and took his breath away. The gondolier barely managed to come to scratch and Whitaker continued to pummel him over the next few rounds until the Venetian was compelled to admit defeat.[4]

Figg quickly displayed his promotional and marketing abilities by promising the crowd that he could produce another fighter who would beat Whitaker within ten minutes in a future match. Whitaker was renowned for his endurance and many thought Figg's claim preposterous, but they showed up to witness the encounter between Whitaker and Nat Peartree a week later. Peartree's own fortitude was marked by the loss of a finger in a previous fight. The fight ensued with Peartree taking careful aim at Whitaker's eyes, succeeding in closing both by swelling in six minutes. Whitaker, temporarily blinded and at the mercy of his opponent, had to admit defeat, regretfully stating "Dam'me, I am not beat; but what signifies when I cannot see my man!"[5]

Despite the advancement of such specialized sites as Figg's amphitheater and the commercialization of the sport, early bouts were little more than street brawls with few rules other than those agreed to by the participants or their benefactors. Gambling became an important component of arranged matches, particularly for the nobility who sponsored their own servants in such affairs and kept boxers among their entourage for such purposes. The interest in boxing even extended to King George I, who had a boxing ring built in Hyde Park in 1723, and young boys emulated their elders in boxing, their bloody noses emblematic of their bravery. Figg died in 1740 and by 1743 Jack Broughton, one of Figg's students, claimed the championship of England and opened his own amphitheater complete with boxes and a gallery, and a large stage. Broughton featured programs with multiple bouts, which captured the attention of the fancy, those swells among the upper classes who often sought their entertainment in the demimonde of the lower class. Broughton's stature enabled him to establish a code of regulations known as Broughton's rules to govern matches. Crowds of spectators attended Broughton's exhibitions and in his matches Broughton "stopped the blows aimed at any part of him by his antagonist, with so much skill, and hit his man away with so much ease, that he astonished and terrified his opponents beyond measure." Broughton had killed George Stevenson in a 1741 bout, and his new guidelines stipulated a greater measure of safety and financial remuneration. Opponents had to "toe the line," which required them to meet at the center of the ring until one was unable to continue and the winner would obtain two-thirds of the purse. Two or three referees might regulate the bout and ensure that no blows were struck below the belt or while the opponent was down. A man was considered down if he was on his knees. A fighter had thirty seconds in which to toe the line after a knockdown. One could not seize an opponent "by the hair, the breeches or any part below the waist." Still, early bouts allowed for wrestling and the throwing of opponents in addition to butting, scratching, kicking, gouging, and biting, as well as the striking of blows with the fist. Broughton held the English title until 1750 when he was defeated by Jack Slack in a match in which the Duke of Cumberland, the son of King George II, lost 10,000 British pounds by betting on Broughton. The duke had offered odds of 10 to 1, but his champion was blinded by a blow during the bout. Broughton's boxing academy was closed and, not coincidentally, Parliament officially outlawed boxing that same year without a great deal of success; yet Broughton's rules continued to serve as the guidelines for bouts for nearly a century.[6]

Fans most appreciated boxers who fought with a sense of honor, adhering to Broughton's guidelines. "Often, though, the spectators got something very different, with much clinching, hugging, feinting, and falling without receiving a blow to bring the round to an end to earn a half minute's rest. Far from being refined out of boxing, wrestling holds and throws became more common from the 1790s. Smart throws were applauded (and pugilistic academies promised to teach them) and it was common to land on top of a thrown opponent, which was not considered illegal, though fighters refraining from doing so earned praise for their restraint and uprightness."[7] Less honorable boxers fell upon their prostate foes with their knees, even kneeing them in the throat in an attempt to gain victory. Others continued to violate the rules by grabbing opponents by the hair, a violation seldom enforced by the referees.

Nationalistic efforts continued to fuel the interest in boxing as Irish boxers confronted English opponents throughout the remainder of the eighteenth century. The Norman rulers of England first attempted to conquer Ireland in the twelfth century; their dominance remained incomplete until the Tudors under Henry VIII and his successors more firmly established a measure of control and enforced the adoption of English law, language, and culture. Periodic rebellions persisted, however, and the repressive invasion of English Puritans under Oliver Cromwell in 1649 solidified control through massacres of the Irish warriors, the confiscation of Irish properties, and the deportation of women and children to America as slaves over the next eleven years. English attempts to wipe out the Catholic religion in Ireland failed however, except in Ulster and the northeastern counties of Ireland, where Scottish and English Protestants had earlier been imported to replace the defeated Irish inhabitants. By the eighteenth century English lords ruled over an impoverished Irish peasantry that had no love for their oppressors, and boxing offered a symbolic means of retaliation.[8]

By 1769 Peter Corcoran arrived from Ireland, to be followed by many Irish boxers thereafter. Corcoran traveled through Birmingham where a butcher, who was also a noted pugilist, took affront with the Irish lad over a piece of mutton in his shop. The argument resulted in fisticuffs and Corcoran won not only the battle but the piece of meat as well. After a stint in the navy where he further demonstrated his strength and martial abilities, Corcoran made his way to London, where he recorded a string of victories in the ring, remaining undefeated until 1776. Corcoran was acknowledged as the Irish champion, but he mysteriously lost to a journeyman Englishman named Peter Sellers. Corcoran knocked down Sellers early in the fight and dominated its first half; thereafter he simply absorbed punches for ten minutes until he surrendered, much to the chagrin of his Irish backers who lost considerable sums on the outcome. Corcoran had been in dire straits before the fight and unable to pay his rent. Two days after the fight his house was filled with amenities and repainted, while he cheerfully cavorted in a nearby tavern. Nationalism had succumbed to want, but Sellers was soon defeated by two other Irishmen, Jack Fearns and a Mr. Harvey, the latter allegedly a rookie to the sport. Both Corcoran and Sellers soon faded to obscurity.[9]

Michael Ryan, a left-handed Irish boxer, earned some fame in both Ireland and England during the latter part of the eighteenth century; reputedly his temper overcame him in a number of bouts, rendering him exhausted. Although a pleasant person outside the ring, affronts to his native land particularly enraged him. He retired to become a boxing instructor and earned a measure of redemption when his son, Bill Ryan, defeated Tom Belcher, the grandson and brother of former champions in 1804.[10]

Irish sentiments revived with the ascension of Andrew Gamble, a stonemason's apprentice from Dublin who honed his fighting skills at home before traveling to England by 1792. Gamble recorded eighteen victories and his bout with Noah James in 1800 earned him a shot at the championship. The contest with James proved a brutal affair with Gamble first splitting the nose of his opponent, and the wound gushed blood thereafter. Gamble then sent a powerful blow to James's neck and broke his collar bone. A subsequent blast later shattered James's jaw; yet he lasted four more rounds before his collapse. The defeated warrior's life seemed so tenuous that Gamble provided a substantial gift to James's wife for his support. Later that year Gamble faced the young Jem Belcher, barely twenty years old, but the grandson of former champion Jack Slack. Belcher had already distinguished himself as a top boxer and would prove his mettle by continuing to fight even after the loss of an eye. The showdown proved anticlimactic as Belcher felled Gamble in only five rounds with blows to the stomach and kidneys that incapacitated the Irish challenger. Gamble's Irish backers lost large sums, and the boxer earned their everlasting enmity for the poor showing. Irish fortunes seemed to rise again with the entry of Jack O'Donnell to the lists. O'Donnell started his boxing career at the age of eighteen and enjoyed initial success. In only his second fight he established his endurance with a win after forty-eight rounds, but a loss in 1803 sent him into a downward spiral and a relatively undistinguished record thereafter.[11]

The spontaneous nature of prizefighting can be discerned from historian Dennis Brailsford's account of an ongoing rivalry between Jem Belcher and a butcher named Bourke. In 1802,

> six weeks after their match in Yorkshire had been prevented, through the joint efforts of the magistrates and the Dean of York, they immediately adjourned to a nearby bowling green and began an impromptu fight. To put matters on a slightly more regular footing their "friends" intervened ("Bourke not being quite sober, and Belcher indisposed") and all agreed to meet next day in Hyde Park to settle the issue. When they

did so, few of the gentry supporters were present, not just on account of the short notice but also because so many of them were out of town in August, which made it the least popular month of the year for serious prize-fighting. Although a large crowd gathered, the purse amounted to no more than 30 guineas a side that could be collected on the spot, and there was no time to erect a stage. The richer patrons of the sport must have been particularly aggrieved, since it was decided afterwards that all bets depending on the intended Yorkshire battle were to hold good for this Hyde Park fight, which, incidentally, Belcher won in the fourteenth round.[12]

Even though they had not been there to witness the event, gamblers were honor-bound to pay their previous wagers from the cancelled bout in Yorkshire.

Boxing had already taken a transnational turn by that time. A 1786 fight at Newmarket was witnessed by the Prince of Wales, the Duke of York, the Duke of Orleans, and a number of French nobles. Five years later the famous Jewish boxer, Daniel Mendoza, embarked on a tour of Ireland, and a French fighter met with defeat in London that same year. Boxing ensued in Scotland by 1793 and Welshman Ned Turner challenged his English counterparts. Irish and English boxers would regularly migrate between the islands thereafter and Glasgow, Scotland became a new venue for commercialization. Boxing even appeared in South Africa soon after the British navy gained control of the colony in 1795. With the end of the Napoleonic Wars in 1815, English fighters continued a surrogate warfare in a Paris exhibition witnessed by the French, Austrians, Prussians, Russians, and their own countrymen. Within three years France offered five sites for boxing exhibitions.[13]

Boxing had already spread westward with the introduction of African slaves to the English colonies in North America. Slave owners on the plantations matched their chattel against those of other owners for amusement, and for considerable sums in wagers. Owners reputedly paid more for slaves who possessed martial skills and who might bring them honor and lucre, not unlike their prized racehorses.[14]

Bill Richmond, a former slave who had been liberated in 1776 with the invasion of the British troops in the American Revolutionary War, became a stable boy for an English officer. At the tender age of thirteen he purportedly whipped three soldiers who had been antagonizing him.

As the valet for General Hugh Percy, Richmond later returned with his master to England, where he gained an education and a trade as a cabinet maker. It was his prominence as a boxer, however, that earned him fame. Black boxers had appeared in England at least as early as 1791 when the African Joe Lashley defeated Tom Treadway in a London bout, and at least four other former American slaves followed in Richmond's wake, but Richmond was the first to contest for the English championship. He began his quest in 1804 and only a year later fought champion Tom Cribb in a disappointing loss. Richmond continued to fight successfully, winning his last fight at the age of fifty-five. He also lived comfortably as a saloon keeper and a trainer of other boxers.[15]

His most famous pupil, Tom Molyneaux (also spelled Molineaux, had followed in Richmond's footsteps. Molyneaux had supposedly won his freedom from bondage when his backer won a large wager in an 1801 plantation bout. Molyneaux honed his skills on the New York docks and boarded ship as a sailor to pursue bouts in England in 1809. There he came under the tutelage of Bill Richmond, and had his first English bout in 1810, in which he "punished his opponent so severely, that it was impossible to distinguish a single feature in his face." Less than a month later Molyneaux took on Tom Blake, known in pugilistic circles as Tom Tough for his endurance and ability to withstand punishment. The American disposed of him with an eighth-round knockout.[16]

Molyneaux then met the English champion, Tom Cribb, on December 18, 1810, in a brutal fight that lasted nearly an hour in a cold rain. In the nineteenth round Molyneaux seemed to have an advantage as he held Cribb incapacitated against the ropes, but a surge of spectators charged the ring, injuring or breaking one of the contender's fingers. Cribb recovered and the fight continued until Molyneaux conceded after thirty-nine rounds. Molyneaux soon asked for a rematch, citing the inclement weather as a factor in his downfall.[17]

In the meantime, Molyneaux thoroughly disposed of another English opponent named Rimmer in twenty rounds. "No pugilist from this time offered a challenge to Molineaux, nor could he get a battle on until Tom Cribb, who had publicly announced his retirement from the ring, was called upon to prevent the championship of England from being held by a foreigner."[18]

Approximately 20,000 spectators traveled to the site of the rematch on September 28, 1811, and "for twenty miles within the seat of action not a bed could be obtained on the preceding night; and by six o'clock the next morning, hundreds were in motion to get a good place near the stage, which even at that early period proved a difficult task." Cribb broke the challenger's jaw in the ninth round and Molyneaux succumbed two rounds later. His career declined thereafter. He argued with Richmond and lost his sponsorship, toured England, traveled to Scotland and Ireland in search of bouts, and became too fond of alcohol. He died in Ireland in 1818. By that time Americans had witnessed their first professional fight when Jacob Hyer defeated Tom Beasley in 1816. Ned Hammond, an English fighter, traveled to the United States to meet Jim Sanford in a bout in New Jersey five years later, as the sport assumed greater global dimensions. The first Australian fighter, Izaac Gorrick, also known as "Bungaree," arrived in England in 1842; by mid-century, technological advances allowed for greater ease of travel as clipper ships plied international waters.[19]

Boxing enjoyed particular popularity in England from the mid-eighteenth century due to the support and patronage of the aristocracy and the wealthy gentry. The Prince of Wales, the Duke of York, the Duke of Orleans, the Duke of Clarence, the Duke of Hamilton, the Duke of Cumberland, the Duke of Queensberry, and Lord Barrymore all provided cachet and promotion to the activity. Frederick, Prince of Wales even provided an annuity to the wife of a boxer killed in a 1788 match that he had witnessed. By the turn of the nineteenth century boxing had great attraction for romantic artists, such as the poet and politician George Gordon, Lord Byron. He and others became practitioners of the sport, taking lessons from the professional fighters who had established "academies" and salons for such purposes. Henry De La Poer Beresford, the third Marquis of Waterford, had taken up boxing while attending Eton and Oxford. While the lower class pummeled each other for the amusement of their superiors, such gentlemen practiced the "art" of self-defense in the event their honor was besmirched.[20]

The nobility were joined by the "fancy" in such undertakings. They composed the element of the bachelor subculture given to slumming, gambling, drinking, and debauchery as a public expression of their masculinity, and sport played a prominent role in their activities. Gambling entailed numerous possibilities, betting on who might draw first blood, how many rounds the fight might go, and so forth. Boxers absorbed ghastly punishment and tested the limits of their endurance, known as "bottom" or "sand" in order not to disappoint their backers. Odds changed with each round as one or another combatant rallied or tired. In an 1833 contest the English champion, James "Deaf" Burke, finally defeated the Irish titleholder, Simon Byrne, after three hours and sixteen minutes that went ninety-eight rounds. Byrne died of his injuries.[21]

After a boxer known as "Brighton Bill" died in a bout with Owen Swift, the Pugilists Protective Association established the London Prize Ring rules in 1838, which further improved on Broughton's rules that had governed the sport for nearly a century. The new regulations stipulated a standard ring of twenty-four feet with two ropes and designated corners for each boxer, and prohibited butting, gouging, scratching, kicking, biting, and the use of hard objects or stones in the fists. All bets had to be paid in cash after the bout, and the victor in the ring would be awarded a colored handkerchief symbolic of his conquest. By 1853, the London Prize Ring rules had become intensely detailed and legalistic, with twenty-nine specific requirements on the conduct and practice of contests.[22]

American fighters also adopted the new rules, but that did not stop the carnage. In 1842 Thomas McCoy, the twenty-year-old son of Irish immigrants, refused to acknowledge the victory of Christopher Lilly, a twenty-three-year-old boxer of English heritage, over a fellow Irishman. At a New York saloon, Lilly struck McCoy, which resulted in a challenge match between the two for $200 each, although backers wagered thousands of dollars on the outcome. McCoy publicly vowed to "win or die" and tied a black handkerchief to his ring post as a symbolic gesture of his earnest endeavor. When Lilly's blows swelled McCoy's eyelids to the point that he could not see, he had his doctor lance them and carried on for 120 rounds "with his eyes closed in funeral black, his nose destroyed, his face gone, and clots of blood choking the throat which had no longer the power to eject them . . . the fight had now lasted two hours and forty-three minutes, McCoy . . . had been thrown or been knocked down eighty-one times, his opponent falling heavily as possible upon him." Upon the last such encounter, McCoy lay lifeless under the bulk of Lilly's body and soon expired. An unconcerned spectator called for McCoy's attendants to carry off his corpse so that the next fight could commence.[23]

Such inhumanity drew severe rebukes from the middle-class media regarding the immorality and brutishness of boxing and calling for authorities to take greater actions to ban the activity. Large numbers of immigrants, however, continued to fuel tensions and rivalries between nativists and the newcomers throughout the 1840s. Potatoes served as the main staple of Ireland, but a fungus attacked the crop in 1845 and continued through 1847. The severe blight resulted in famine and death for as many as a million Irish peasants. Starving survivors fled Ireland for life elsewhere, with 100,000 sailing for North America in 1847. As many as 1.7 million eventually reached the United States over the next decade; they were not warmly received. The Anglo nativists, composed of the English who traced their American history to the early colonists, and Presbyterian Scots-Irish, who fled to the colonies in the early eighteenth century, considered themselves to be the rightful heirs to the American democracy and its opportunities. The peasant Irish were largely uneducated, unskilled, and unwelcome. They were perceived to be beggars, drunkards, and fighters and perhaps worse, Catholics, and consigned to urban ghettos, largely in the cities of the East Coast. Opposition to the newcomers even spawned the creation of a political party known as the Know-Nothings, due to their typical response to questions regarding their clandestine operations.[24]

Germans, too, migrated to the United States in large numbers after a failed revolution in 1848. They were largely skilled craftsmen and educated and fit more easily into the American mainstream, or at least into their own communities where they continued to instill the German language and culture, and introduced beer in family-centered saloons. The Irish, however, lived in squalid conditions, such as the Five Points neighborhood of New York, and faced extreme prejudice. Employment was difficult to obtain and businesses often advertised vacancies with the prohibition that "no Irish need apply." As a result many young Irish men turned to prizefighting in New York, Boston, Philadelphia, and New Orleans. Between 1840 and 1860 the Irish composed 56.3 percent of boxers, and Irish Americans another 15.6 percent, while the American Anglos accounted for 6.15 percent. However, in New York British boxers made up

20 percent of the prizefighters during the 1840s as they too had migrated to the United States in search of opportunity.[25]

The animosity between nativists and immigrants reached national proportions in the 1849 battle between Tom Hyer, the nativist hero and son of the first recognized American champion, and James "Yankee" Sullivan, an Irish immigrant, despite his nickname that perhaps reflected the quest for identity and acceptance. The combatants first had to elude Baltimore police intent on disrupting the affair. The fighters escaped capture and proceeded to a location in the Chesapeake some forty miles distant and covered in snow, which had to be shoveled to set up a ring. Hyer adorned his post with the American flag, while Sullivan chose Irish green. Hyer enjoyed a physical advantage at 6 feet 2½ inches and 175 pounds to Sullivan's 5 feet 10½ inches and 155 pounds, although Sullivan was considered to be a superior wrestler and intended to use throws to weaken his opponent. His strategy proved faulty as Hyer's heavier body continually landed upon Sullivan and he lingered atop his opponent until removed by his seconds (attendants) in the corner. In the fifteenth round Hyer

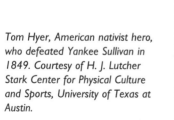

Tom Hyer, American nativist hero, who defeated Yankee Sullivan in 1849. Courtesy of H. J. Lutcher Stark Center for Physical Culture and Sports, University of Texas at Austin.

clinched with Sullivan on the ropes and was apparently able to wrench the Irishman's left arm from its socket by bending it backward. Sullivan came to scratch for the sixteenth round, but Hyer fell upon him heavily again and his seconds admitted defeat. A further altercation ensued in Sullivan's corner when Hyer's party tried to claim Sullivan's colors, a task at which they eventually succeeded. The entire fight took seventeen minutes and eighteen seconds. The media provided complete coverage of the contest and declared Hyer to be not only the champion of America, but capable of taking on any man of his size in Great Britain as well.[26]

Sullivan was succeeded by John Morrissey (who had defeated him in 1853), one of the Irish immigrants who exemplified the American dream achieved through boxing. Politicians employed Irish boxers as "hitters" on election days to "encourage" voters to choose in their favor. Morrissey earned greater fame, however, when he fought John C. Heenan, known as the "Benicia Boy" for his California residence, in an 1858 title bout. Fans and gamblers came from as far as New Orleans and Canada for the contest held in Buffalo, New York. The *New York Tribune* noted

John Morrissey, whose boxing skill enabled him to gain fame, celebrity, and political office. Courtesy of H. J. Lutcher Stark Center for Physical Culture and Sports, University of Texas at Austin.

of the assemblage that "Probably no human eye will ever look upon so much rowdyism, villainy and scoundrelism, and boiled-down viciousness, concentrated upon so small a space." Heenan punished Morrissey for ten rounds, but the latter exhibited greater endurance and outlasted Heenan to become champion. Morrissey then embarked on a career as a gambler, establishing betting parlors and a casino. By 1863 he joined a group as one of the founders of the Saratoga Racetrack in New York and turned his attention to politics, where he became a prominent member of the Democratic Party, serving two terms in the U.S. Congress (1867–1871) and two more terms in the New York State Senate during the 1870s.[27]

Morrissey's bouts were fought under a new set of rules revised by the English Pugilistic Benevolent Association in 1853, which stipulated a ring of twenty-four feet to be laid out on turf with two ropes fastened to eight stakes at intervals of two feet in height. A flip of the coin determined the choice of corners, which were reserved for the corner men who could provide water and a sponge, and carried the fighters back to the corner at the conclusion of each round. Fighters sat on the knee of their corner man while awaiting the call to come to scratch. Corners were to be festooned with the fighter's choice of colored handkerchief which could be claimed by the winner of the match. Two umpires kept time and adjudicated fouls, but they could be overruled by the referee. Spikes in the boxers' boots could not exceed three-eighths of an inch, and fighters had thirty seconds between rounds and eight seconds to come to scratch when called by the referee. In the event that spectators rushed and collapsed the ring, which sometimes occurred when gamblers feared the loss of their considerable wagers, the referee had the power to determine the winner. If a fight could not be concluded in the course of one day, the referee could determine the resumption to take place within the week and all bets held until that time. The referee had the additional power to judge all fouls and prohibit the use of the ropes to strangle an opponent. (The Morrissey-Sullivan bout had been determined on a foul blow, which fostered a wholesale melee in the ring). While the new rules moved toward modernization and began to centralize power within the person of the referee, they still allowed for considerable leeway in the use of wrestling techniques and harmful injuries.[28]

With Morrissey's retirement from the ring John Heenan claimed the title as the American champion, and his challenge to Tom Sayers, the

English claimant, engendered nationalistic fervor on both sides of the Atlantic. Heenan traveled to England for the bout scheduled for April 17, 1860. He enjoyed a distinct advantage in height (5 inches), weight (28 pounds), and youth (eight years younger) over the Englishman, who had more experience. The contest was widely covered by both the American and British media, and the *New York Clipper* claimed to have sold as many as 300,000 copies in a special issue that covered the results. In addition to the popular throngs nearly a hundred British nobles attended the meeting, and recriminations as to the result persisted for years. In the thirty-fourth round with both men swollen and bloodied, Heenan seemed to exert his advantage and the crowd began to encroach upon the ring. The American repeatedly threw Sayers to the ground and landed heavily on his foe. In the thirty-seventh round the referee mysteriously departed, and two rounds later with Heenan attempting to squeeze the life out of Sayers, who could not extricate himself from the ropes with which he had become entangled, a person or persons in the crowd cut the ropes, and both boxers fell to the ground. The fight continued with Sayers being knocked down to conclude the fortieth round, at which time he climbed out of the ring and was covered with a blanket until required to return for the next round. He appeared groggy and avoided Heenan's pursuit until the American rushed him into Sayers's corner, at which point the cornermen interfered and tried to extricate Sayers from the challenger's grasp. Heenan then knocked down the assistant with a mighty punch and added a kick for good measure as his own followers entered his corner for support. Heenan delivered another left to the head of Sayers, felling him and ending the round. Amidst the confusion both fighters came to scratch for round forty-two, and Heenan again knocked Sayers into his seconds and then quickly effected a headlock and the delivery of several severe blows before Sayers's attendant grabbed his arm. Heenan then picked up Sayers and threw him to the ground and fell atop him as others tried to clear the ring. Heenan came to scratch for the call of the forty-third round, but Sayers sat on a chair. When Heenan rushed him he rose to defend himself, but bystanders came between the opponents and no blows were delivered. After two hours and twenty minutes Sayers left the ring and Heenan followed. With no rematch conducted during the next week as prescribed by the rules, Heenan claimed the championship.

In the aftermath, the combatants eventually met with the referee and the editors of *Bell's Life*, which had become the most popular English sports newspaper of the era, to adjudicate the matter. The fighters agreed that each would get a new title belt and a trophy to commemorate their battle and Sayers's old title belt would stay in England—in effect, they agreed to a draw! Sayers decided to retire from the ring in the wake of the decision.[29]

The Civil War disrupted boxing in the United States, yet Heenan returned to challenge then English champion Tom King in 1863. He was soundly defeated, and King duly retired. The transatlantic cable, first laid in 1858, should have provided instant telegraphic results of such nationalistic encounters, but the cable required repair and replacement until 1866 when it achieved more consistent functionality. By 1870 English heavyweights arrived in New Orleans in a transatlantic exchange and Canadian George Godfrey invaded Boston as the British Commonwealth sought to demonstrate its global preeminence in comparison to the growing power of the United States.[30]

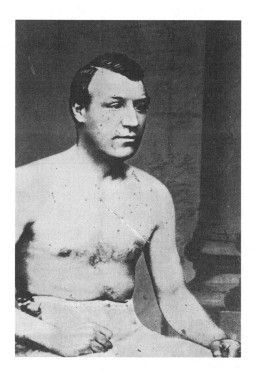

Tom Sayers, English champion. Courtesy of H. J. Lutcher Stark Center for Physical Culture and Sports, University of Texas at Austin.

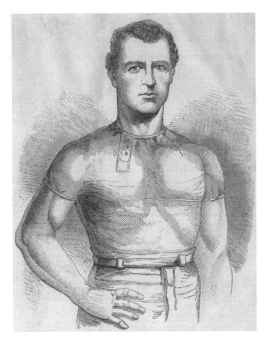

John Heenan in an 1860 challenge match with English champion Tom Sayers. Courtesy of H. J. Lutcher Stark Center for Physical Culture and Sports, University of Texas at Austin.

The British nobility had further involved itself in the regulation of boxing matches when John Sholto Douglas, the Marquis of Queensberry, sponsored a new set of rules. His college classmate, John Graham Chambers, likely drafted the rules in 1865; these were then published in 1867 and were intended to regulate amateur bouts. The new rules introduced the use of padded gloves rather than bare fists, and stipulated that timed rounds of three minutes each with a one-minute rest period in between would replace the untimed rounds measured by a fall or knockdown in the London Prize Ring rules of 1838. A fighter who had been knocked down had ten seconds to regain his composure. Wrestling tactics were eliminated and opponents were to be categorized in three weight classes (lightweight, middleweight, and heavyweight) to further equalize contestants.[31]

Despite the British attempt at fair play, Americans were slow to adopt the Queensberry rules and moralists worked to ban the sport. An 1876 court case in Massachusetts ruled that "Prize fighting, boxing matches, and encounters of that kind serve no useful purpose, tend to breaches of the peace, and are unlawful even when entered into by agreement and without anger or ill will."[32] By 1880 prizefights were banned in thirty states and bouts had to be conducted surreptitiously, such as on barges on waterways or outside the legal boundaries of jurisdiction. The 1880 title fight between Paddy Ryan and the Englishman Joe Goss took place in Colliers, West Virginia, a tiny hamlet on the borders of both Ohio and Pennsylvania, to ease potential escapes if authorities should intervene. Ryan won by a knockout in eighty-seven rounds and claimed the championship. He lost his title two years later to John L. Sullivan in a clandestine bare-knuckle affair held in Mississippi City, Mississippi, under London Prize Ring rules; the bout lasted seventy-five rounds in 100-degree July heat. Ryan reflected on his defeat by stating, "When Sullivan struck me, I thought that a telegraph pole had been shoved against me endways."[33]

Despite the illegality of such contests they generated immense popular interest, stoked by Richard Kyle Fox's weekly publication, the *National Police Gazette*, which catered to the working class and the bachelor subculture with lurid stories of crime, scandal, and debauchery with ample coverage of theatrical and sporting events. The *Gazette*[34] sold 150,000 copies weekly, but that figure reached 400,000 for a special issue of the Goss-Ryan fight, and Fox extended his efforts to promote and publicize sporting spectacles thereafter by offering expensive jewel-studded belts

"Battle of the Giants." Paddy Ryan versus John L. Sullivan. Courtesy of H. J. Lutcher Stark Center for Physical Culture and Sports, University of Texas at Austin.

Richard K. Fox amid trophies and medals. Courtesy of H. J. Lutcher Stark Center for Physical Culture and Sports, University of Texas at Austin.

The $10,000 championship belt offered by Richard K. Fox of the National Police Gazette *for the heavyweight championship. Courtesy of H. J. Lutcher Stark Center for Physical Culture and Sports, University of Texas at Austin.*

for champions of the different weight classes. Fox engaged in an ongoing feud with John L. Sullivan and even went to the extent of importing English heavyweight Alf Greenfield in 1884 in an unsuccessful attempt to dethrone the champion.[35]

The first professional fight in the United States to adopt the Queensberry rules took place that same year when Jack "The Nonpareil" Dempsey knocked out George Fulljames in twenty-two rounds to earn the middleweight championship. Sullivan successfully defended his crown in a bare-knuckle fight against Jake Kilrain in 1889, but lost it in the first heavyweight championship conducted under the Queensberry rules in 1892 to Gentleman Jim Corbett. The English and the Americans recognized different heavyweight champions, symbolic of world supremacy, from 1870 until Corbett unified opinions by defeating Charlie Mitchell of England in 1894.[36]

By that time, neither England nor the United States had any monopoly on boxing. As the imperial ambitions of European powers (soon to be followed by the United States in 1898) extended around the globe, both colonizers and colonized pitted themselves against one another throughout the latter nineteenth century in trials to test the survival of the fittest. The British transferred their sport forms to their colonial subjects, and a Scotsman, James Robertson Crouper, claimed the championship of South Africa in 1883 after defeating Joe Coverwell, a Malay favorite in the colony. Australians adopted the Queensberry rules the following year, and Billy Palmer, a former Australian pugilist turned trainer, became famous as a teacher of defensive boxing techniques. Among his pupils were Peter Jackson, who traveled from the West Indies in 1879 and won the Australian championship in 1886 before embarking on a boxing career in the United States, England, and France; and Bob Fitzsimmons, born in England, raised in New Zealand, and world famous by the end of the nineteenth century as the conqueror of Corbett in 1897. Boxing had become a global enterprise by that time as the sport took root in China, Singapore, and Hawaii. The Spanish-American War of 1898 brought soldiers and American entrepreneurs to the Philippines, where the military taught boxing to the indigenous peoples with weekly commercialized bouts promoted by Frank Churchill and brothers Eddie and Stewart Tait by 1910. Throughout the era the U.S. military and American influence fostered the sport in the Caribbean, Central America, and South America.[37]

The increasing commercialization of the sport led fighters to seek ever greater rewards by building their reputations against lesser opponents in order to market themselves as local, regional, and national champions. Australian Albert Griffiths, who fought under the name of Young Griffo, beat New Zealander "Torpedo" Billy Murphy for the featherweight crown in 1890, but sought greater fortune in the United States in 1893. There he lost to Solly Garcia-Smith, a Mexican American from California and George Dixon, a black Canadian, who reigned over the bantamweights and featherweights of the era. Dixon had traveled to England in 1890 as a nineteen-year-old, where he wrested the bantamweight crown from Nunc Wallace. He returned to the United States the following year, where he gained the undisputed featherweight title against another Australian, Abe Willis. Dixon lost that title to Garcia-Smith in 1897 in a decade that exemplified the multinational scope of boxing.[38]

A host of racial and ethnic migrants learned and bettered their craft in the United States. In addition to George Godfrey and George Dixon, who made the relatively short journey from Canada, Peter Jackson, another top black fighter of the era, took the circuitous route from the West Indies through Australia before arriving in San Francisco. Barbados Joe Walcott arrived in the United States in 1897 and secured the welterweight crown. Swiss-born Frank Erne captured the lightweight championship, while Jack Root (Janos Ruthaly), born in Czechoslovakia, became the first champion of the newly designated light heavyweight division in 1903. Oscar "Battling" Nelson left his native Denmark and turned pro in the United States at the tender age of fourteen. A tough brawler, he lost the lightweight championship to Joe Gans on a foul in the forty-second round in a 1906 fight, but won the title in a 1908 rematch. Stanley Ketchel (Kiecal), the son of Polish immigrants, is remembered as one of the greatest middleweights of all time. Ketchel left his Michigan home as a youth and began fighting as a teenager in Butte, Montana, a tough mining town. By 1908 he had secured the middleweight championship.[39]

While some sought fame and riches in America, some Americans found greater opportunity elsewhere. Kid McCoy (Norman Selby), the colorful American middleweight, embarked on a tour to South Africa in 1896 where he claimed that country's championship, and then proceeded to Australia and the Pacific region. In 1901 he traveled to England, where he scored three knockouts over British opponents and took on a savate martial artist in Paris. Lightweight champ Kid Lavigne and heavyweight Jim Jeffries also made the voyage across the Atlantic. Andrew Jeptha, a South African welterweight who had begun his pugilistic career in 1899, also moved to England in 1902, and enjoyed success in Paris as well by 1908. Aaron Brown, an African American better known as the "Dixie Kid," held the welterweight championship from 1904 to 1908, but gained his greatest fame fighting in Europe.[40] Brown was only one of many African American fighters who sought their fortune in Europe as racial oppression limited their opportunities in the United States and the Jim Crow laws enacted after *Plessy v. Ferguson* in 1896 gave formal and official sanction to segregation.[41]

Barbados Joe Walcott had difficulty finding opponents who would step in the ring with him, and was often forced to fight out of his class, including bouts against heavyweights. Joe Gans, often reviled by the white media, sought opponents in Australia. Another black fighter, Bobby Dobbs, opened boxing schools in France and Germany between 1898 and 1901 and a year later Frank Erne traveled to London and then trained French boxers in Paris as the sport increasingly extended across transnational markets. A dozen boxing clubs opened in German cities by 1903 and German boxers began to test their mettle in the United States and elsewhere within a few years. By 1910 Dobbs had taken his talents to Denmark, where he knocked out Holger Hansen in four rounds before 1,500 fans. Boxing films, developed in the 1890s, made the sport increasingly popular in Europe, and American fighters quickly realized the entrepreneurial opportunities. Sidney Jackson, an American Jewish boxer, traveled as far as Russia where he became an instructor and promoter of the sport.[42]

The influx of American and British boxers and teachers brought a rapid transition from the traditional French form of personal combat known as savate to Anglo-style boxing. Savate may have evolved from battles between rival guilds in the seventeenth century. By the end of the eighteenth century it involved personal duels resulting from challenges to one's honor, fashionable among the gentry. After 1830 private gyms taught martial skills for such encounters and by 1843 a French court case limited such encounters to blows delivered with both the hands and feet, a combination of bare-knuckle fighting and kicking. Organized bouts followed over the next decade and as the population of Paris ballooned be-

*Bobby Dobbs and Holger Hansen in
Copenhagen in July 1910; Dobbs knocked
out Hansen. Courtesy Library of Congress.*

yond a million, overcrowding led to more disputes, consequent duels, and
a prohibition on the use of weapons, which led to greater use and training
in savate. In 1899 the English boxer Jerry Driscoll seemed in control of
a match with Jean Charlemont, Jr., a practitioner of savate, until a kick
to the groin disabled him. Kid McCoy, the American pugilist, emerged
triumphant in a similar match during his Paris sojourn. But after 1904
the French, under British and American tutelage, turned to boxing. By
1907 the Wonderland Francais featured regular boxing bouts sponsored
by French promoters and their American partners. Weekly programs in
Paris, Marseilles, Bordeaux, and Lyon appeared throughout Europe in
Milan, Rome, Amsterdam, Copenhagen, and in the French colonies of
Algeria and Morocco. Madrid, Brussels, and Prague followed with boxing
shows of their own.[43]

France had a particular attraction to African American fighters, musicians, and entertainers, who perceived that country to be more liberal in its
acceptance of non-whites. Top fighters such as Sam McVey (also spelled

Sam Langford, a top black fighter from 1902 to 1926. Courtesy of H. J. Lutcher Stark Center for Physical Culture and Sports, University of Texas at Austin.

Joe Jeannette, a top black fighter from 1904 to 1922. Courtesy of H. J. Lutcher Stark Center for Physical Culture and Sports, University of Texas at Austin.

McVea) headed to Paris in 1907, followed by Jack Johnson, Joe Jennette (also spelled Jeannette), and Sam Langford.

Langford, a Canadian by birth, claimed the heavyweight championship of England, Australia, Canada, and Mexico during his career. McVey's travels took him to England, France, Belgium, Australia, Argentina, and Panama. Both McVey and Jennette became fan favorites in Paris, where French men and women developed a fascination with the black body.[44]

Georges Carpentier, the French star who lost to Jennette in 1914, had remarked that McVey and Jennette "were Negroes of a strikingly different type. Joe Jeannette would pass for a bronze statue. He was not coal black as was Mc Vea [*sic*]; neither was he so forbidding to look at. Mc Vea was frankly a nigger; Jeannette dark chocolate. A more attractive, even handsome, Negro I have never seen."[45] Historian Theresa Runstedtler has termed the American blacks as "figures of fear and desire" during their

Sam McVea, a top black fighter from 1902 to 1921. Courtesy of H. J. Lutcher Stark Center for Physical Culture and Sports, University of Texas at Austin.

Nr. 14. Jahrgang VII.

Preis 20 Heller.

Jllustr. österr. Sportblatt

Herausgeber FELIX SCHMAL und Dr. KARL BITTRICH.

Die Schlusszene eines Boxermatches in London zwischen dem Neger Langford und Lang.

Sportblatt *photo of Sam Langford knocking European opponent through the ropes. Courtesy of Gertrud Pfister.*

French sojourn, and the 1909 bout between McVey and Jennette (which lasted forty-nine rounds) brought ticket requests from "London, Brussels, Liege, Anvers, Geneva, Roubaix, Lille, Troyes, Rouen, Reims, Orleans, and even Bordeaux," with thousands turned away.[46] Bobby Dobbs enjoyed similar acclaim in Denmark the following year, where he easily defeated the local heroes and opened a boxing school in Copenhagen. In Berlin he conquered both German and other American boxers while providing pugilistic instruction to Kaiser Wilhelm's family, and then took his talents to Austria and Hungary.[47] The cultural flow that originated in England was thus reversed by the twentieth century as Americans cultivated the sport in Europe, where race became an exotic, erotic commodity that could be sold in the boxing arena.

The social reformers' ongoing campaigns to eliminate boxing in the United States curtailed matches in the urban centers of the East, but only offered more opportunities for other locales. After the Civil War the booming mining towns of the West, filled with tough young men and a relative absence of women, presented conditions ripe for fighting. Wyatt Earp, famed marshal on the frontier, served as referee in one such match (and others thereafter) in which competing camps raised $50 each and 3,000 spectators cheered their favorites on the Fourth of July. An impromptu bare-knuckle match in New Mexico in 1868 fostered $5,000 in bets, and lasted for 185 rounds and more than six hours of fighting that left both boxers horribly disfigured and the loser dead ten minutes after its conclusion. Other western locations in Nevada and California assumed the role of boxing centers, as did New Orleans in the South. The latter hosted the three-day festival of title bouts known as the Carnival of Champions in 1892. The 1892 battle between Texan Jack Burke and Andy Bowen, a local combatant in New Orleans, was the longest bout in history. Burke broke his right hand in the forty-ninth round. After 109 rounds of uninspired sparring that took seven hours and twenty-five minutes, the referee called it "no contest" at 4:49 in the morning. In 1896 New York attempted to legalize boxing with the passage of the Horton Law that allowed for sparring exhibitions with padded gloves; inadequate regulation and corruption led to its repeal. Nevada legalized prizefights the next year and hosted the largest boxing spectacles over the course of the decade. In 1900 New York passed the Lewis Law, which allowed boxing in private clubs, and the Frawley Law (spanning 1911–1917), which established the first state athletic commission and allowed for bouts without decisions to thwart gambling and corrupt fixes. Sportswriters provided "newspaper decisions" based on their opinions, but fighters' records of that era are marked with many bouts that ended as "no decisions." In 1913 former middleweight, light heavyweight, and heavyweight champion Bob Fitzsimmons applied for a license at the age of fifty-one due to his destitute state but was denied. World War I, in which bayonet training mimicked boxing techniques, resurrected an interest and a need for boxing. New York's Walker Law of 1920 then fully legalized the sport in the state and initiated a state boxing commission to regulate and license promoters, managers, referees, judges, and fighters.[48]

The British had earlier founded the National Sporting Club in London in 1891 with the intention of regulating boxing; a full board of control did not ensue until 1929. The club did, however, extend the number of weight classes to eight in 1909 and club president, Hugh Lowther (Lord Lonsdale), awarded emblematic belts to British titleholders.[49]

Boxing had reached such global proportions by 1913 that representatives from France, England, Belgium, and Switzerland, with approval of the New York commission, formed the International Boxing Union (IBU), which ceased to function when World War I erupted. The organization resumed operations in Paris in 1920, but the International Sporting Club, a British association operating in New York, made an unsuccessful attempt to regulate the sport. Despite the failure of governing bodies and reformers' efforts to ban boxing, the sport flourished. Boxing films and the new medium of radio created athletic celebrities. Promoters and sportswriters heightened public interest by portraying nationalistic and racialized images of foreign or non-white fighters as social Darwinian contests for national supremacy.[50]

The most famous promoter of the early twentieth century, however, proved to be an American, George "Tex" Rickard. His rise to fame started when he left his family and the hardscrabble poverty of his Texas upbringing at the age of ten to become a cowboy. In 1895 he left for the Alaskan goldfields, where he found greater promise as a saloon keeper, gambler, and fight promoter. Rickard left Alaska for the diamond mines of South Africa, but returned to the United States bankrupt and opened another saloon before heading for the Nevada gold fields in 1906, where he resumed his interest in fight promotion. As Nevada was one of the few places that allowed prizefights during the era, Rickard was able to host the 1906 lightweight championship between Joe Gans and Battling Nelson that turned an immense profit and garnered national media coverage. He then hosted the July 4, 1910, heavyweight championship in Reno between Jack Johnson, who was black, and the "Great White Hope," Jim Jeffries, which brought international attention. Rickard's profits enabled him to retire to South America, where he purchased a large cattle ranch in Paraguay. Unsuccessful in his new endeavor, he returned to the United States to once again promote boxing matches and found a slugger of popular interest in Jack Dempsey. Rickard made Madison Square Garden in New York a center of sports spectacles, but his biggest bouts required outdoor arenas to host immense numbers of fight fans. Eighty thousand came to see Dempsey defeat the French hero, Georges Carpentier, in 1921 in a fight that produced a record gate of $1,625,580. Dempsey's wild bout with the Argentinian Angel Luis Firpo in 1923 brought a crowd of 88,000 to the Polo Grounds in New York. Dempsey's two bouts with Gene Tunney drew more than 100,000 spectators and were broadcast nationally on the radio as each contest surpassed $2,000,000 in revenue. "Rickard's marketing genius was to draw in his audience by making each fight he promoted into a narrative, pitting a hero against a villain, turning a boxing match into an elemental struggle between glory and humiliation, triumph and disaster, good and evil. He expanded boxing's appeal far beyond its traditional audience of working-class men . . . respectable and respected public figures—even women—attended the spectacles Rickard staged." In addition to boxing, Rickard introduced ice hockey to the United States and brought horse and dog racing to Florida, where he died of appendicitis in 1929.[51]

Rickard also served as a silent partner in the founding of the *Ring* magazine in 1922, edited by Nat Fleischer. The *Ring* soon offered championship belts in each of the weight classes and became recognized as "the Bible of boxing." Sportswriters hyped their subject throughout the decade, spawning the Golden Age of sport as athletes became celebrities, heroes, and cultural icons. The *Ring* helped to establish boxing as a premier sport during the 1920s and Jack Dempsey enjoyed international fame. The magazine began publishing weight-class rankings in 1925 and selecting its "Fighters of the Year" three years later. It established its own Hall of Fame in 1954 and published historical and nostalgic "all-time best" lists

Tex Rickard, the boxing promoter who produced million-dollar spectacles. Courtesy of H. J. Lutcher Stark Center for Physical Culture and Sports, University of Texas at Austin.

in 1996 to keep the memories of the past and the comparative worth of boxers alive for current fans. Two more boxing halls of fame were founded in the latter twentieth century with similar intentions. The World Boxing Hall of Fame was established in 1980 and is currently housed in the Los Angeles Athletic Club. The International Boxing Hall of Fame opened in 1989 in Canastota, New York, and has become a major tourist site in the village.[52]

The efforts of British colonialists, the American military, Anglo promoters, and the increasingly global reach of the media fostered a widespread interest and growth in boxing in the early twentieth century. In the Pacific a nexus of Asian boxing developed between the Philippines, Japan, Hawaii, Australia, and the West Coast of the United States as upstarts sought greater recognition and bigger paydays, and over-the-hill professionals sought to prolong their careers. Francisco Guilledo, a Filipino better known as Pancho Villa, became the most famous as the world flyweight champion from 1923–1925. American sportswriters characterized Villa's conquests of white opponents as the work of an inhuman demon or a monkey, yet Filipinos idolized him as a hero who negated Anglos' perceptions of racial superiority in a counterhegemonic response to colonialism. American authorities in the Philippines instituted collegiate boxing programs in 1923 with the intent of molding their charges into models of American civilization. Governor General Leonard Wood reasoned that "Boxing develops every muscle in the human body, quickens the brain, sharpens the wits, imparts force, and, above all, it teaches self-control."[53]

U.S. military forces engaged in boxing matches in the Caribbean in conjunction with the Spanish-American War, and British sailors also spread the sport to South Americans, drawing the indigenous populations into the action as well. In Latin America the peregrinations of beleaguered black champion Jack Johnson brought him to Argentina and Mexico, which heightened interest in boxing during the World War I years. When the Argentinian Angel Luis Firpo almost took the heavyweight crown from Jack Dempsey it only intensified interest in the sport during the following decade.[54]

In South Africa the De Beers diamond company organized a boxing club as early as 1878, attracting mine workers to bare-knuckle bouts. The South African Amateur Boxing Association was founded in 1912. Both the black working classes as well as the upper classes began to pursue boxing as a means of social uplift by the 1920s and American missionaries promoted the sport thereafter. Boxing clubs in Johannesburg offered to teach lessons in "civility, discipline, respectability, independence, and self-defence." Indian and other "colored" fighters centered in Cape Town and Durban, where Joe Louis, an African American, would become a heroic symbol for the racially oppressed in the 1930s. Among them, Nelson Mandela took up boxing.[55] In neighboring Rhodesia (Zimbabwe), historian Terence Ranger claimed that "boxing . . . had sprung up and become enormously popular without any direct European instigation, patronage, or influence at all." Government-sponsored bouts served as a means of social control and transferred more deadly tribal rivalries to a surrogate form of warfare.[56]

The British colonial era brought similar developments to Ghana, where the colonial government introduced boxing to the schools as a means of character development and an Anglican bishop invoked the sport as a means of socially controlling youths prone to street fights. By the 1920s newspapers glorified the sport and editors became boxing promoters. Movie theaters featured international bouts. Local bouts became an opportunity for visibility and social display among dignitaries, and women joined the throngs as spectators, wagering sizable bets. John Ebenezer Samuel de Graft-Hayford, a member of a local royal family, entered the professional ring under the alias of Kid Chocolate, while local heroes assumed even more colorful appelations such as "Spider" Neequaye, a former champion at the flyweight and bantamweight categories who founded the Accra Boxing Association, and "Supriser" Sowah, who established one of many boxing clubs in the country. By 1951 the Gold Coast produced a British Empire Champion in featherweight Roy Ankrah.[57]

British immigrants brought boxing to Argentina in the last decade of the nineteenth century, and the first professional match ensued between Paddy McCarthy, an Irish immigrant who served as an instructor at the Buenos Aires Boxing Club, and an Italian fighter, who had a sizable following due to the large number of countrymen who had also settled in the South American nation. Chile soon formed its own boxing federation, and the popularity of Argentinian Angel Luis Firpo would bring international recognition by the 1920s.[58]

Throughout the 1920s and early 1930s Paulino Uzcudun, a Basque heavyweight, carried the flag for Spain as he challenged American supremacy on their home turf. Uzcudun's brawling style left him susceptible to negative stereotypes, and he lost to fascist strongman Primo Carnera of Italy twice (1930, 1933), who was also racialized by sportswriters. Race continued to factor into boxing comparisons as Max Schmeling, a German, attained the championship. Each fought Joe Louis in the 1930s as race meshed with politics to produce symbolic clashes between democracy and fascism that only heightened interest in boxing as Europe moved closer to real carnage throughout the decade.[59]

By that time Panama Al Brown had emerged as the world bantamweight champion (1929–1935, 1938), and Mexican and Caribbean fighters entered the fray at lower weight classes. A Cuban, Kid Chocolate (Eligio Sardinias Montalvo), entered the pro ranks in 1927 as a seventeen-year-old and claimed both the light welterweight (1931–1933) and featherweight titles (1932–1934) by 1932. Sixto Escobar, the first Puerto Rican champion, succeeded Brown as bantamweight champ by beating Baby Casanova of Mexico, who had won forty-two of his forty-three fights by knockouts. Puerto Ricans feted Escobar on his return to the islands and named a stadium after him to commemorate his triumph. His 1937 title defense in San Juan was the first to be contested on the island, and it was claimed that he "brought the game of boxing at [*sic*] Puerto Rico from nothing more than club-fighting to international spotlight, and spawned a whole new generation of fight fans and boxers."[60]

Boxing held such widespread appeal that even amateurs engaged in transcontinental matches. Both the *New York Daily News* and the *Chicago Tribune* offered amateur tournaments as promotional ventures, which became intercity contests known as the Golden Gloves in 1928. A combined all-star team from the two cities fought a French contingent in Chicago's Soldier Field stadium in 1931. Bernard Sheil, the Catholic bishop of Chicago, initiated a comprehensive athletic program throughout all Chicago parishes in 1930 as a means of social control aimed at male youths (see chapter 6). Boxing remained the core of the Catholic Youth Organization (CYO) and it shared fighters with the Golden Gloves and provided athletes to the 1936 U.S. Olympic team. The best boxers competed on the CYO's international boxing squad that traveled around the world, competing in Hawaii and Panama, and against opponents from France, Ireland, Poland, Italy, Germany, and South America.[61]

Despite the Depression, the forces of transport technology, media, and entrepreneurial promoters continued to fuel the globalization process within a capitalist economic framework. Poverty supplied a continuous labor force as the working class chased dreams in a quest for celebrity, a measure of fame, and at least a temporary social mobility. World War II heightened the martial spirit around the globe, and the advent of television offered a vehicle for mass consumption. The British Broadcasting Company televised a championship match as early as March 1939, and NBC broadcast an American bout a month later. The Billy Conn–Joe Louis rematch in 1946 was the first heavyweight championship rematch to be televised. By 1949 fights could be viewed in 16,500 bars and restaurants in New York City. After 1948 the International Boxing Club (IBC), headed by sports promoters James Norris and Arthur Wirtz and lawyer Truman Gibson, attempted to monopolize championship bouts through coercion of boxers and managers and intimidation by organized crime figures such as Frankie Carbo and Frank "Blinky" Palermo. By 1955 televised fights reached an average of 8.5 million homes and earned $90,000 per week for the IBC. The federal government prosecuted the racketeers, sending both Carbo and Palermo to prison in the 1960s, but failed to establish a national boxing commission.[62]

The lack of any centralized boxing authority has led to a multitude of governing bodies, each operating in their own interests. The National Sporting Club that sponsored bouts in England evolved into the British Board of Boxing Control by 1918, and was restructured and renamed the British Boxing Board of Control in 1929. The old International Boxing Union formed in Belgium in 1913 became the European Boxing Union in 1946. In the United States, fifteen state athletic commissions formed the National Boxing Association (NBA) in 1921. With the fall of the IBC in the 1960s a proliferation of governing bodies with regional interests emerged. The National Boxing Association had become the World Boxing Association (WBA) headquartered in Caracas, Venezuela by 1962, reflecting the growth of the sport outside its Anglo origins. The following year the World Boxing Council (WBC) established itself with an office in Mexico City in a move to thwart American dominance of the sport. Factional splits in the WBA resulted in the formation of the International Boxing Federation in 1983 and a further break among disgruntled Latin Americans led to the World Boxing Organization with headquarters in Puerto Rico in 1988. This confusing alphabet soup of governing bodies, each designating their own rankings and champions, has engendered a chaotic state of affairs with at least eighty-one sanctioning bodies at state, regional, national, and international levels. For years boxers denied a license in one state might gain one elsewhere, and rampant corruption in organizations' ranking systems has left the sport in a near-continual state of scandal and incrimination. The International Boxing Hall of Fame recognizes only the WBA, WBC, WBO, and IBF.[63]

Amateur boxing is relatively well organized under the International Boxing Association (AIBA) organized in 1983. USA Boxing, which had already been established in 1977, became a member of the AIBA. AIBA standards also cover boxing in the Olympic Games.[64]

Given the evolutionary history of modern boxing from its roots in eighteenth-century England to its present state, one might discern that the sport is in a backward spiral with a consequent loss of popularity. Still, boxing has a particular appeal in certain regions of the world, and title matches continue to draw fans, television audiences, and immense revenues for promoters.

CHAPTER THREE
THE RELATIONSHIP BETWEEN BOXING AND SOCIAL CLASS

While ancient Greek Olympians may have been of more noble lineage, boxers have generally emanated from humble origins for most of recorded history. Early English pugilists made their living as barkeepers, bakers, butchers, porters, and a host of other blue-collar occupations. Likewise in America, the immigrant slums in urban areas and the mining towns of the frontier produced tough and combative individuals ready to earn a little extra money, defend perceived slights to their honor, or protect their territory from incursions by racial or ethnic rivals.[1]

Early aristocrats in America had settled affairs of honor by dueling, which cost the lives of statesmen such as Alexander Hamilton and his son as well as Stephen Decatur, a hero of the War of 1812; Andrew Jackson proved especially adept in such confrontations before becoming the president of the United States.[2] The rougher sort that inhabited the outer edges of the colonies and later the Western frontier devised their own means of asserting their masculinity, not unlike the pankration contests of the ancient Greek Olympians. While some foes engaged in spontaneous boxing matches resulting from perceived affronts, other battles were staged two to three times per week at public gatherings or after the regular horse races where men gathered for amusement, gambling, and drinking. A typical match started with a public challenge to an individual or to a whole group in a public setting. A traveler described one such affair in Georgia in 1817: "A ring is formed, free for anyone to enter and fight. . . . After a few rounds, they generally clinch, throw down, bite, and gouge, and the conquered creeps out under the ring as a signal of his submission." Combatants engaged in no-holds-barred contests that resulted in noses bitten off, eyes gouged out, and even castrations, although they adhered to a sense of fair play by agreeing to the extent of permissible actions beforehand. Men purposely grew the nails of their thumbs and forefingers long and hardened them in candle fires in order to more expeditiously pluck out an opponent's eye. An Irish visitor in Virginia in 1796 explained that "it is by no means uncommon to meet with those who have lost an eye in combat, and there are men who pride themselves upon the dexterity with which they can scoop one out. . . . But what is worse than all, these wretches in their combat endeavor in their utmost to tear out each other's testicles. Four or five instances came within my own observation, as I passed through Maryland and Virginia, of men confined to their beds from the injuries which they had received of this nature in a fight."[3]

Another traveler described conditions in Pennsylvania about 1806: "Every evening a gang assembled at the numerous taverns to drink, tell stories, and fight. When they had become half drunk, they were noisy and quarrelsome, gouging out the eyes was one of their barbarous practices, and nearly one third of the German population had but one eye. I saw one day a horse with one eye, carrying on his back the husband, wife and child, each with only one eye."[4]

Formal boxing lessons were offered in Boston as early as 1798 and in Philadelphia in 1815. Two townships in Connecticut even settled a boundary dispute by a pair of boxing matches in 1800, with the winning side acquiring the land. Such genteel practice of the "art of self-defense" held little sway in other regions of America. Fistfights were common occurrences throughout the southern colonies and on the frontier well into the early republican era, and such unregulated affairs quickly degenerated into more brutal confrontations. In Ohio, a spectator remarked that no affront was necessary to precipitate a fight; men simply tried each other's prowess to establish their own status and for the amusement of onlookers. Partisans rooted for their favorite, and ardent backers of one or the other might enlarge the battle into a general melee. "A stranger who had kept aloof during a fray of this kind, when it was over, seeing a man with the top of his nose bit off, approached him and commiserated his misfortune. 'Don't pity me,' said the noseless hero, 'pity that fellow there,' pointing with one hand to another who had lost an eye, and showing the eye which he held triumphantly in the other."[5]

As early as 1719 Delaware enacted a law aimed at punishing anyone who intended to "cut off or disable the tongue, put out an eye, slit the nose, cut off the nose or lip, or cut off or disable any limbs or members of any of the King's subjects" under the penalty of death, with little success.[6] Other colonies had to pass similar laws, but the practice persisted.

Conditions in such places, particularly after the Industrial Revolution, relegated previously independent craftsmen to the role of wage laborers, characterized by little or no income, hungry mouths to feed, and competition for limited resources. The poor and the working class had to compete with the multitude of others who shared their lot in life as well as those above them on the social ladder, if they aspired to better themselves. They owned only their own bodies, which they loaned to employers for minimal wages. Often overwhelmed by such stresses, tensions, and hardships, many in the lower class developed a fatalistic attitude, resigned to their misery. Bereft of education or other suitable means of social mobility, defeatism persisted over generations. Historian Elliott Gorn explains, "Pugilism was an autonomous expressive form that symbolically opposed the drift of modern society . . . boxing captured the values, the ethos, the distinct culture of countless working men who felt dispossessed amidst the Victorian era's heady optimism."[7]

The French sociologist Pierre Bourdieu termed that condition to be one's *habitus*, a predisposition toward particular tastes, decision making, lifestyle, and worldview based on one's upbringing and experiences.[8] At the turn of the twentieth century an interviewer questioned a twelve-year-old boy from a working-class, immigrant neighborhood in Chicago about the selection of films at the local nickelodeon. The youth responded that the fairy tales and travelogues were "pretty, all right . . . but it's too slow to make a go of it on dis street. I don't say it's right, but people like to see fights, 'n' fellows getting hurt." Likewise, when the New York censorship board summoned a film exchange manager to explain his offerings, he replied, "They [the public] want red meat and they want it raw."[9] Physicality and physical prowess proved essential to the working-class sense of identity and expression.

When interviewed by a New York sportswriter, light heavyweight champ Billy Conn related his family's attraction to boxing. "My brothers love to fight. My old man loves to fight. And my grampappy loves to fight. My grampappy is the only one of them who can fight a lick. . . . The old man is a fighting man. . . . He's the best fighter in the family. . . . There are plenty of guys he can still fight—for fun that is. He knows where to find his fights around Pittsburgh. I don't know about here. Give him a day or two, I guess, and he'll get guys to slug it out with. My old man once battled it out with my manager, Johnny Ray. . . . When it was finished Pop had a broken nose and Johnny lost a tooth. That made them pals."[10] Jake LaMotta, middleweight champion of the 1940s, reminisced about the end of his ring career: "Here I was an uneducated kid and the better part of a million bucks had gone through my hands and I was only a little better than thirty years old, and now what? What was I going to do? Where was I going?" His contemporary and also champion, Rocky Graziano, asked, "What does Rocky Bob do when he don't fight? Learn a trade? Go on relief? Go back to robbing candy stores and Chinese laundries?"[11]

That reliance on one's toughness remains at the core of working-class life and boxing represents a public display of one's abilities to cope with pressure. Bobby Czyz, former light heavyweight champion, explained, "Good is your ability to give a beating; tough is your ability to take a beating."[12] The latter is an essential requirement of working-class life in or out of the ring.

Italian philosopher Antonio Gramsci explained the working-class dilemma as one in which these people were the first to feel the pain of economic downturns, social oppression, and exploitation; but their inability to understand the cyclical nature of the capitalist economy and their assigned role in its operation left them to lash out in frustration and retaliation. For poor boys boxing offered an escape, both psychologically and physically, where they might control their own destiny based on their physical prowess, one of the few things they held in abundance.[13] Tony Canzoneri, a world champion in the 1920s and early 1930s, began boxing in New Orleans for coins. He put on his first pair of gloves at age eight, which he considered a relatively late start, explaining that he had done plenty of street fighting already.[14] Boxing offered an alternative to the drudgery of industrial labor. Heavyweight champion Rocky Marciano made it plain that he "would rather fight than work in Brockton's shoe factories, where his father and other men of the neighborhood were employed."[15] Decades later when others questioned heavyweight champion Joe Frazier's choice of career and the physical toll it had taken on his life, he responded that "people don't understand what an honor it is to be a fighter. It gave me the best opportunity to prove myself, to stand up and say 'I'm the best. I matter. I am.'"[16]

The interest in boxing is often inculcated at an early age. Carlos Valdez stated that "my dad would buy doughnuts and we would go grandma and grandpa's house to watch boxing, and I loved it. We all loved boxing. My great uncle was a boxer. We had three generations of boxers in the family." The Mexican American children of Austin, Texas, start competitive boxing as early as six years old as long as they can meet the minimum weight of fifty pounds. The team jacket provides an early sense of identity and pride. For the best at their craft the sport offers a chance to travel beyond their narrow world, meet new people, and gain a measure of esteem and local celebrity, distinctions unattainable in a factory job.[17]

Joyce Carol Oates, long a boxing aficionado, claimed that the sport is a "public accounting of the outermost limits of their (boxers') beings."[18] It is a test of physical and psychic capabilities put on display for all to pass judgment. Boxers are thoroughly engaged in what scholars now call body culture. They revel in their body and in its powers, and "in spite of all the pain, and suffering, and the ruthless exploitation it entails, of which fighters are painfully cognizant, boxing can infuse their lives with a sense of value, excitement, and accomplishment."[19] Conrad Sanchez confided that "I would take off my shirt, walk around. I was proud of my body. I had a beautiful body. My body was one big muscle . . . I miss the adrenaline rush. My body craves it."[20] Another Mexican American middleweight claimed, "When you get outa the gym you feel like a brand new person. Some people like t'get high an' *that's my high*."[21] Boxing promoters also rate the bodies of boxers. "Some are considered prime ribs, others pork chops and the least talented scrapple, but rarely are they considered as human beings."[22]

For professional boxers, the sport is also a job, one which permits a greater degree of freedom than the industrialized labor force, although all but the top boxers must work a primary job. A thirty-two-year-old journeyman boxer in Chicago who began boxing at age twelve and had been fighting professionally for eleven years remarked, "I box because it's a payday." Another, a former gang member, stated that "I learned that I can go to the gym, fight, learn the trade an' get paid for fightin' than fightin' in the streets an' gettin' nothing."[23] Even the less skilled and amateur boxers enjoy a measure of respect and celebrity (what scholars term social capital) within the neighborhood for their toughness, work ethic, and discipline. Children follow them through the streets and offer to carry their bags. A relatively unaccomplished fighter could still assert that "everybody knows a boxer is a *tough individual* an' anytime you climb in the ring and put yo' life on the line . . . they give you praise and glory for you to be a warrior." Although the majority of fighters (85 percent in one study) think that they can reach the top of the profession, perhaps the best that most can hope for is a local championship and the sense of accomplishment unavailable in other spheres of life. One such fighter explained that "I was the champion . . . *no one can take that from me—I'll take that to my grave.*"[24]

Among the working class, boxers enjoy an enduring respect for their past displays of physical prowess. "People like to touch fighters, especially retired fighters. Men clap them on the shoulder, linger over a handshake. Women have a habit of laying a hand intimately on a fighter's upper arm. . . . Laying hands on a fighter, lifelong noncombatants can feel the force that has flowed through him in the form of blows given and taken."[25] Jack Dempsey enjoyed such celebrity status long after his ring career ended and his New York restaurant remained a haunt of celebrities for years.

More recently, Wilbert "Skeeter" McClure, a gold medalist at the 1960 Olympics who turned pro as a middleweight in the 1960s, and later earned a doctorate in psychology, still manifested a reverence for fighters of the past. "Athletes of today can't compare to ones of the past . . . The old gyms produced tougher men. Not necessarily better boxers, but tougher. . . . (They) led hardscrabble lives, they were tough men who led tough lives, and they knew that struggle is good for you. They weren't in it for fame and big money."[26]

The esteem in which fighters were held emanated from the long-established homosocial world of the bachelor subculture. While elements of such male congregation and camaraderie might be discerned in the ancient Greek gymnasium, the modern equivalent is evident in the eighteenth-century British "fancy" who crossed class lines in pursuit of a hedonistic lifestyle. With the large-scale emigration to America in the following century, composed largely of young, unmarried males, the fraternization assumed a vibrant transatlantic component.[27]

The young men frequented saloons, pool halls, dance halls, barber shops, and sporting events, engaging in the shared company of other men in a clear rejection of domestic life. In the saloons the patrons practiced a reciprocal ritual known as treating, in which one offered a drink to another and the latter was obliged to reciprocate at the cost of his honor. Honor, loyalty, and expressions of masculinity were highly esteemed among the bachelors. Among the latter, stoicism, or the ability to withstand pain, won the praise of others. Boxers who proved their mettle in long and bloody matches proved especially admirable. Even today, "the specific honor of the pugilist, like that of the ancient gladiator, consists of refusing to concede and kneel down . . . not to bow under pressure. . . . A pug who quits in the midst of battle is branded with the mark of infamy and suffers a veritable symbolic death."[28]

Historian Madelon Powers related the story of a typical Irish saloon in a coal mining community in Pennsylvania in the 1870s. A newcomer to the community walked into the saloon and announced that he'd "sing a song, dance a jig, or fight with any man in the house for the whisky for everybody" in a bid for acceptance. The regular patrons soon produced a challenger, a local miner, and they all retired to the back room for the fight. The young miner landed a big blow to the newcomer's nose, and blood spurted across his countenance—but the newcomer retaliated with a shot to the miner's jaw that knocked him to the floor and abruptly ended the match. The newcomer shook the miner's hand and congratulated him on his prowess, and then all retired to the bar to enjoy the drinks in a newfound camaraderie.[29]

The early bachelor subculture was fragmented by ethnic divisions, and meetings were not always so cordial. During the antebellum era as the multitude of Irish immigrants landed on American shores, nativists opposed their entry into the labor force and the society as an incursion into the abundance that was rightfully theirs. One such encounter in 1855 resulted in the death of Bill Poole, a butcher by trade, but a renowned brawler and leader of a nativist gang in New York. A saloon encounter between Poole and John Morrissey, an Irish immigrant who had won the American boxing championship two years before when he defeated Yankee Sullivan, resulted in insults exchanged and the consequent shooting of Poole by one of Morrissey's associates. Nativists considered Poole to be a martyr to their cause. As many as 250,000 spectators lined the streets after

Bill Poole, nativist gang leader, killed by the Morrissey gang. Courtesy of H. J. Lutcher Stark Center for Physical Culture and Sports, University of Texas at Austin.

thousands viewed his body and 6,000 accompanied him to his grave in a two-mile-long parade that took six hours to reach the cemetery.[30]

Morrissey escaped blame and defended his title against John Heenan in 1858 for $2,500 per side and then parlayed his fame into the American dream. He retired from the ring, opened a casino with his gambling profits, and was one of the founders of the Saratoga race track in New York. He entered politics as a Tammany Hall Democrat and was elected to the U.S. Congress and the New York Senate. The vast majority of boxers, however, were relegated to lesser ambitions.[31]

The Prairie Queen, a Chicago establishment that served as a brothel, offered weekly dog fights and bare-knuckle boxing matches. The winner received a house prostitute for his efforts. A good fighter might earn as much as $500 for a single fight in the 1850s, more than the annual income of a laborer. Such activities allowed some to circumvent the confines of wage labor temporarily, but at the expense of offending Victorian mores of the era.[32]

Chicago banned prizefights in the 1880s (Illinois issued a state ban in 1869) but allowed for exhibitions, with permits issued by police inspector

John Shea, who happened to be a big boxing fan. Parson Davies, a local fight promoter, reserved a ringside seat for Shea and always waited for his arrival before commencement of the bouts. Shea ostensibly performed his duties by ensuring that no brutality ensued and that the laws were upheld, a matter left to his discretion. Such affairs could be less than delicate, as exemplified by a public apology in the *Sporting and Theatrical Journal* by one boxer who threw another from the ring by his heels; although the reporter assured readers that "the audience was a very select one, being composed for the most part of the better class of the fraternity whom lean toward sport while the element who openly show their preference for sport with the mits [*sic*] were there to a man." Patrons at such affairs were not docile onlookers, however. In another Chicago area match two months later, a boxer challenged a heckling spectator to meet him at the saloon afterward.[33]

Frederick Van Wyck, a New York socialite and a member of the sporting fraternity, described the program at one of his haunts. "When you start with a dog fight as a curtain raiser, continue with a cock fight,

Charles "Parson" Davies, a nineteenth-century boxing promoter in Chicago. Courtesy of H. J. Lutcher Stark Center for Physical Culture and Sports, University of Texas at Austin.

then rat baiting, next a prize fight, then a battle of billy goats, and then a boxing match between two ladies, with nothing but trunks on—after that I think you have a night's entertainment that has enough spice—not to say tabasco sauce—to fill the most rapacious needs."[34]

Perhaps the most famous of the saloons in which men congregated was Harry Hill's in New York. Hill, an English immigrant and former boxer, opened his concert saloon in 1854, which prospered until 1886. Hill offered a variety of entertainment that included both male and female boxing matches, dancing, vaudeville, cockfights, and even ratting, in which terriers killed off the rodents at a pace or number in which gamblers could wager. The activities were conducted under electric lights by the latter part of the century and attracted a clientele that ranged from the dockworkers and tough Bowery Boys to judges and congressmen. Moralists judged it to be the "most dangerous and demoralizing place in New York."[35]

The *National Police Gazette,* under the editorship of Richard Kyle Fox, served as the Bible of the bachelor subculture, reaching a national circulation of half a million as it featured sensational and scandalous stories of sex, crime, and sports, especially boxing. Fox proved an avid promoter of the sport and a participant in the male brotherhood. Despite the ban on boxing in many states, Fox portrayed boxers as heroic outlaws.[36]

The *National Police Gazette* promoted Paddy Ryan as its favorite heavyweight in 1880 and printed 400,000 copies of its edition that covered his bout with Joe Goss. Fox's antagonistic relationship with John L. Sullivan led him to sponsor Ryan in their bare-knuckle title match in 1882. Ryan's defeat sent him back to his Chicago saloon, where he promoted local boxing matches. Sullivan garnered more than a million dollars over the next decade, mostly barnstorming the country and challenging local toughs. Sullivan had made a name for himself by walking into an establishment and pronouncing "I can beat any son of a bitch in the house." On his tours he offered cash, as much as $1,000 to anyone who could last four rounds against him. Very few did. He knocked out fifty-nine consecutive challengers and cleared $80,000 on his 1883–1884 road tour, and much more thereafter in endorsements. Sullivan assumed the role of the first great American sports hero, a national celebrity, and a prominent member of the sporting fraternity. Sullivan bought drinks for the house when he entered a saloon and refused any change for the $100

Scenes at Harry Hill's Saloon in New York City. Courtesy of H. J. Lutcher Stark Center for Physical Culture and Sports, University of Texas at Austin.

Harry Hill, proprietor of New York's famous establishment, which catered to the bachelor subculture. Courtesy of H. J. Lutcher Stark Center for Physical Culture and Sports, University of Texas at Austin.

he often placed on the bar, a gesture of his magnanimity. Barrooms across America featured his picture on their walls. Though married, he lived the hedonistic, profligate, and dissolute life of the bachelors who idolized him.[37] A barroom toast went as follows:

> You valiant Sons of Erin's Isle,
> And sweet Columbia too,
> Come, gather 'round, and listen while
> I chant a stave for you.
> Oh! Fill your glass up, every man,
> With Irish whiskey, stout;
> And drink to John L. Sullivan,
> The famous "Knocker-out."
> Chorus:
> Oh! The chorus swell for bold John L.,
> We'll fling it to the breeze,
> Yes, shout it loud, so England's crowd
> Shall hear it o'er the seas;

The great and small, he's downed them all
In many a clever bout;
Hurray for John L. Sullivan,
The famous "knocker-out."
They sent men here from England's shore,
The best they could produce,
The great John L. to try and floor,
But twasn't any use.
Try how they would, they never could
Give Sullivan the rout,
For like a giant there he stood,
This famous "Knocker-out . . ."[38]

Sullivan's following crossed class lines, as detailed by a perhaps tongue-in-cheek account of an 1882 bout in the *Rocky Mountain News*: "Artists, actors, burglars, bankers, bunko-steerers, beer jerkers, blacksmiths, confidence men, cappers, clog-dancers, clerks, capitalists, captains,

John L. Sullivan, America's first great sports hero and the idol of the bachelor subculture. Courtesy of H J. Lutcher Stark Center for Physical Culture and Sports, University of Texas at Austin.

Chinese, Danes, doctors, divines, engineers, firemen, Frenchmen, Germans, governors, harlots, horse-thieves, idiots, Irish, jail-birds, keno men, lawyers, machinists, Mexicans, negroes, officers, politicians . . . were jammed together. . . . From the highest type of respectability to the lowest grade of depravity, every art, profession, vocation, trade and crime had its representatives there, and the capitalist jostled the pickpocket, the judge stood shoulder to shoulder with the sneak-thieves and the senator was cheek by jowl with the thug during the entire evening."[39]

Such fraternity took on added significance in the latter nineteenth century as males contended with a perceived feminization of culture as women entered colleges and professional careers as doctors and lawyers, and engaged in sports previously deemed to be male preserves. A 1904 British study questioned American masculinity by claiming that "the boy in America is not being brought up to punch another boy's head; or to stand having his own punched in an healthy and proper manner." Men donned extensive facial hair in the form of beards and mustaches and took to smoking cigars as visible symbols of their masculinity.[40]

Upper-class males took instruction in fisticuffs, but were quick to draw distinctions from the lower class, labeling their efforts the "art of self-defense." As early as 1867 William Wood published a manual for the proper education of middle-class males in which he stated, "This manly exercise has no necessary connection with the brutal and disgusting exhibitions of the 'Prize Ring.' An accomplished sparrer is as such, no more a vulgar bruiser than an elegant penman is a forger or counterfeiter, or a clever gymnast, who can climb a ladder 'hand over hand,' is a burglar."[41] British courts distinguished between the legal sparring of gentlemen, considered to be scientific training of the body, and the illegal prizefights of sluggers by the 1880s; American courts began to draw the same conclusions a decade later.[42]

At the turn of the twentieth century even President Theodore Roosevelt maintained a boxing instructor, Mike Donovan, in the White House. Roosevelt had been a sickly child, and as a young man spent two years on his ranches in the Dakota Territory in an attempt to fashion an image of greater masculinity as a cowboy. He reveled in telling the story of how he had punched and knocked down someone who had insulted him in a saloon. As president he assumed the same pugnacious stance, extolling and demonstrating American military might.[43]

Even valid members of the sporting fraternity had to defend their honor on occasion. On two occasions during his sojourn in Chicago, heavyweight Joe Choynski was accused of being a "dude" due to the stylish clothes that he wore. In both instances he beat the transgressors into submission in order to "teach them some manners."[44]

Such encounters, within the ring or outside of it, were conducted with bare fists, a mark of masculinity and physicality that symbolized working-class honor. Boxing moved toward a greater measure of modernization and regulation, as well as a response to charges of brutality, with the gradual American adoption of the Marquis of Queensberry rules. Chicago bouts had adopted the Queensberry rules by the 1880s, and *Sporting and Theatrical Journal* offered a $100 gold medal for the state heavyweight title under the British rules. The British introduced leather boxing gloves stuffed with horsehair in 1883. Still, ferocious contests continued. An 1886 gloved match in Boston indicated that a fight between two working-class combatants for $150 "was one of the most brutal witnessed in this city for months. The men pounded each other until both were covered with blood" and ended only when one was knocked out; it took his seconds nearly half a minute to revive him. The fight was conducted at the Athenian Club, whose wealthy members sat in enthusiastic approval, like Romans at a gladiatorial contest.[45]

The Amateur Athletic Union organized boxing championships in 1888, but its version differed markedly from the professional bouts. The American upper classes adhered to the British concept of amateurism, in which any laborer who worked with his hands or anyone who participated in sport for any form of financial remuneration was deemed less than a gentleman and presumably capable of being bribed, and therefore ineligible for competition. The Boston Athletic Association adopted the Marquis of Queensberry rules in 1892, much to the consternation and ridicule of its followers, who considered it to be "gentleman sparring." These gentlemen termed their efforts "scientific boxing," for defensive purposes, "without any intention or desire to injure each other." Matches were to be decided by a system of points without the demonstration of endurance or strength so essential to the professional warriors. The gentlemen amateurs differentiated themselves from working-class "sluggers" by stating that "the science of boxing seeks to enable one to incapacitate an opponent with as little injury to one's self as possible. The science of boxing is an artificial method, and can only be acquired by study and practice." This more refined method of fisticuffs rationalized the sparring encounters of gentlemen as a more cerebral science and the acquisition of a defensive skill, as opposed to the brutal confrontations of the working-class sluggers and attackers whose sole intent was to incapacitate opponents.[46]

The suggested amateur rules denoted a clear upper-class and British notion of sportsmanship. A boxer was permitted to have one "attendant," who was not to speak to him or his opponent while fighting. Wrestling, clinching, butting, blows below the waist, and use of the inside of the hands was forbidden, as was hitting an opponent who had already been knocked down. There was to be a one-minute intermission between three-minute timed rounds. Handshakes were expected to be exchanged both before and after the contest, and spectators were instructed to refrain "from any loud expression or demonstration" during the contest, a clear contrast from the rowdy professional bouts.[47]

Yet at least six fighters died in professional bouts in 1893, and middleweight champion Bob Fitzsimmons faced manslaughter charges in 1895 when he killed a sparring partner, resulting in continued cries for the abolition of the sport. Athletic clubs circumvented laws to ban boxing by offering "exhibitions" to spectators who bought their club "membership" with their paid admission at the door. Despite its illegal status in much of the United States, boxing had become a substantial commercial and global enterprise by the late nineteenth century. An 1887 bout in France offered a prize of $12,000, and by 1889 a match in South Africa and another in Mississippi both provided purses of $22,500.[48]

Jake Kilrain participated in both the French and American matches. He claimed to be the champion due to John L. Sullivan's inactivity. Sullivan had only defended his title twice, both against the British champ, Charlie Mitchell. The second bout was an 1888 match fought in France that ended in a draw. The Mississippi affair was a clandestine arrangement, the last of the bare-knuckle heavyweight championships, fought between Kilrain and Sullivan. It lasted for seventy-five rounds, which took more than two hours in 100-degree temperatures on July 8. Sullivan had spent much of the decade in dissipation, mired in a deepening alcoholism that diminished his skills. In the forty-fourth round his handlers provided a mixture of cold tea and whiskey, which caused him to vomit. Spectators surmised that his stomach was rejecting the

John L. Sullivan versus Jake Kilrain on July 8, 1889 (Sullivan won after seventy-five rounds). Courtesy of H. J. Lutcher Stark Center for Physical Culture and Sports, University of Texas at Austin.

tea, but Sullivan regained his form and his glory, retaining his title by a knockout.[49]

Sullivan held the title for a decade until losing it to "Gentleman" Jim Corbett in 1892 in the first heavyweight title fight under the Queensberry rules that dictated the use of boxing gloves. The battle symbolized the class warfare that permeated the labor struggles between the employers and their employees during the era. Corbett, a more refined bank clerk from San Francisco, had attended college, learned his "scientific" boxing skills at the famed Olympic Club, and his sartorial splendor earned him his nickname. He was backed by the wealthy social set in New York for his bout with Sullivan. The nearly five years that Corbett spent atop the heavyweight division provided the semblance of greater respectability.[50]

The Sullivan-Corbett bout was part of a three-day boxing spectacle, labeled the Carnival of Champions, sponsored by the Olympic Club in New Orleans. Organized as a legal and commercial enterprise that featured championship bouts in three distinct weight classes, held in an urban location rather than clandestine hideaways, and conducted under the

"Gentleman Jim" Corbett, who wrested the heavyweight crown from John L. Sullivan in 1892. Courtesy of H. J. Lutcher Stark Center for Physical Culture and Sports, University of Texas at Austin.

auspices of modern rules and upper-class regulators, it marked a transition in the sport's evolution and greater inclusion in the mainstream society.[51]

Corbett's fights were among the first to be filmed and shown in movie theaters. He proved a favorite among females, who flocked to the matinees that featured boxers in skimpy attire similar to the thong bathing suits of today. "Afternoon presentations, conspicuously, were largely made up of ladies" for the 1897 Corbett title defense against Bob Fitzsimmons. Sixty percent of the Chicago audience was estimated to be women, while large numbers of females attended the Boston and Dallas shows as well. Fight films thus entered the popular culture and attendance by women advanced the perception of the sport as a more respectable mainstream activity. Nevada became the first state to legalize boxing in 1897.[52]

Although San Francisco, New Orleans, New York, and Nevada had emerged as boxing centers, middle-class reformers persisted in their attempts to outlaw the sport. In Chicago multiple boxing promoters competed for clients, and widespread corruption resulted in fixed matches. A Chicago newspaper reported that "men who might conduct boxing shows honestly fear to besmirch their reputations under the present status of the sport, capable referees are being driven into retirement by the rowdy element which seeks to unfairly influence their decisions by boisterous conduct, and the better class of patrons are being alienated. The sport is thus left in the hands of crooks and sure thing gamblers." At one match in a Chicago suburb the 2,200 spectators were subjected to the efforts of nearly twenty pickpockets who worked the crowd during the bout and afterward as patrons waited in crowds for transportation to get home. Given such conditions, reform-minded politicians more stringently enforced the laws prohibiting boxing, although fights at the middle-class clubs might be permitted. The police chief announced that "a scientific match is all right, but when they hire professional sluggers, they violate the state law."[53]

Corruption seemed endemic in the sport. In a 1912 lightweight bout in California, Ad Wolgast defended his title against Mexican Joe Rivers. After the twelfth round Rivers had an advantage and Wolgast only continued when his corner man threatened him with a bottle. In the thirteenth round the fighters landed simultaneous blows with Rivers connecting to Wolgast's jaw and Wolgast delivering an illegal shot to his opponent's groin. Both fighters went to the canvas. The referee counted out both combatants but helped Wolgast to his feet and declared him the winner. The timekeeper declared that the round had officially ended at the count of four, but referee Jack Welch overruled him and gave the fight to Wolgast.[54]

While boxing matches continued surreptitiously or under the watchful eyes of compliant police officers and civic officials in some places, the regular bouts at the athletic clubs were often declared to be "no decisions" as they were officially only "exhibitions" for the paying spectators. Sportswriters then issued their own opinions of the winner in what were termed "newspaper decisions." For example, featherweight champ Abe Attell fought at least 171 bouts, of which 51 were declared no decisions. Johnny Dundee (Giuseppe Carrora), both featherweight and junior lightweight champ, had 330 bouts with 194 no decisions. Welterweight champ Jack Britton had 344 bouts and 190 no decisions. Such machinations and the corruption inherent in the sport hindered the quest for social mobility among many working-class young men who had turned to boxing as a means to supplement their meager revenue. One such young man, Packey McFarland, took a job in the Chicago stockyards, where he managed to knock out a coworker in a lunchtime match. His success led him to seek a professional career as a boxer at the tender age of sixteen. Despite a record of 69 wins with 50 knockouts and 5 draws (as well as 34 no decisions and 37-1-1 record in newspaper decisions) he was never given the opportunity in either the lightweight or welterweight divisions. McFarland quit the fight game and became more successful as a banker and a member of the Illinois Athletic Commission in 1933.[55]

Packey McFarland, one of the best boxers of the early twentieth century, was never given a chance for a title bout. Courtesy of H. J. Lutcher Stark Center for Physical Culture and Sports, University of Texas at Austin.

The most famous and important fights of the early twentieth century were conducted in Nevada or outside the United States. A 1906 inter-racial bout between Joe Gans and Battling Nelson for the lightweight championship took place in Nevada. Jack Johnson, the black heavyweight champion, chased Tommy Burns, the white champ, all the way to Australia to unify the title in 1908, then beat Jim Jeffries, the Great White Hope, in Reno in 1910. He lost his title to Jess Willard in Havana, Cuba in 1915.

With the entry of the United States into World War I in 1917 boxing assumed greater significance and consequent respectability. The trench warfare of the European battlefields might result in hand-to-hand combat or the use of the bayonet. Boxing techniques, such as the jab, the cross, and the uppercut, were very similar to the use of the rifle and bayonet in close-quarter combat and were effective means of teaching recruits. Moreover, men who had become boxers before the war became even more famous as courageous war heroes during the conflagration. Eugene Criqui, a French flyweight, interrupted his successful ring career to join the army in 1914. He was severely wounded in battle and his shattered jaw was replaced with a silver plate and plastic by the reconstructive surgeons of that era. Nevertheless, Criqui resumed his boxing vocation in the war's aftermath, eventually becoming the world flyweight champion in 1923.

Johnny Coulon teaching World War I doughboys to box in Coblenz, Germany. Courtesy of H. J. Lutcher Stark Center for Physical Culture and Sports, University of Texas at Austin.

Georges Carpentier had already received significant laurels as a boxer before the war as a champion in four weight divisions. He had started boxing as a fourteen-year-old in 1908 and had garnered the French welterweight championship by the age of sixteen. He added the European welterweight crown a year later, and the light heavyweight title in 1913. By 1914 he had beaten the best heavyweight in England, but his startling rise took a hiatus with the coming of the war. Carpentier joined the French Air Force, where he won medals for bravery as a reconnaissance pilot before resuming his exploits after the war.[56]

The popular interest in boxing continued after the war, and unable to curtail the sport, New York politicians decided to control it. The New York legislature had permitted ten-round gloved bouts as long as they adhered to the "no decision" restrictions as early as 1911, under the Frawley Act; the death of Young McDonald in a 1917 match due to a blow to the heart gave reformers second thoughts. The promoters of the fight card in the McDonald death had heartlessly continued with the remaining bouts after his tragedy and the legislators let the Frawley Act expire that year. Still, boxing enjoyed legal status in twenty-three states by 1917 and in 1920 the New York legislature enacted the Walker Act, which allowed for decisioned bouts of twelve rounds and established a state boxing commission to regulate and tax the sport. Madison Square Garden soon emerged as the mecca of boxing and the income generated by boxing spectacles led other states to follow suit.[57]

Tex Rickard, the quintessential sports promoter of the early twentieth century who had organized the spectacles in Nevada, moved his operations to New York. There he created some of the greatest sport spectacles and enterprises in American sport history. Rickard allied with Doc Kearns, the manager of boxer Jack Dempsey, to create a national hero. When Kearns was described as "a crook," he responded that "I prefer to be called a manipulator."[58] Jack Dempsey had managed to avoid military service as the sole supporter of his family, and many considered him to be a draft dodger. Dempsey hailed from the mining town of Manassa, Colorado, and had ridden the rails as a hobo, engaging in fights as a brawler to earn some much-needed money. Rickard proclaimed him "the Manassa Mauler" and he became a hero to the working-class fans who shared his rough life. Dempsey had destroyed the giant Jess Willard in 1919 to claim the heavyweight title, and by 1921 Rickard had matched Dempsey

THE LAST OF "GOR-
GEOUS GEORGES" AND
THE FIRST $1,000,000
FIGHT—BOYLE'S
THIRTY ACRES
JERSEY CITY, JULY 2,
1921

Jack Dempsey knockdown of Georges Carpentier at Boyle's Thirty Acres on July 2, 1921. Courtesy of H. J. Lutcher Stark Center for Physical Culture and Sports, University of Texas at Austin.

against Carpentier in a battle that assumed nationalistic and social class characteristics. Rickard promoted the affair as the villainous slacker versus the war hero, the American against the foreigner whom he termed "the Orchid Man," and the rough-hewn Dempsey opposed to the debonair Frenchman. Rickard even built a huge stadium in Jersey City to accommodate the 80,000 spectators who showed up, with nearly $2,000,000 in receipts for the extravaganza. The crowd included more than one hundred members of Congress and assorted other celebrities from Hollywood and Europe. More than 700 journalists from all over the world covered the proceedings with direct telegraph service to London and Paris.[59]

Carpentier broke his vaunted right hand on Dempsey's cheekbone in the second round and could offer little resistance thereafter. Dempsey knocked him out in the fourth round. Though brief, the spectacle only whetted the appetite of fight fans for more of Dempsey, and his management team gladly obliged. Kearns arranged a fight against Tommy Gibbons, a top contender, on Independence Day 1923 in Shelby, Montana, after the small oil town guaranteed $300,000. With fewer than than 1,000 residents, the town built a 50,000-seat stadium, but only a fraction of that number made it to the remote location. Dempsey won a lackluster victory and Gibbons got little, but the town was the biggest loser as all three banks and their patrons went bankrupt. In September 1923 Rickard matched Dempsey against a giant foreigner, Luis Angel Firpo of Argentina, whom he dubbed "the Wild Bull of the Pampas." The encounter took place in New York City's Polo Grounds and resulted in one of the most heralded fights in boxing history. Although it lasted only two rounds, the bout produced nearly a dozen knockdowns. Firpo knocked Dempsey to the canvas to start the fight, and the champion retaliated by pummeling the challenger with seven consecutive drops to the floor. Firpo continued to get up and then blasted Dempsey through the ropes and on to the sportswriters at ringside, who dutifully helped the American reenter the ring before he could be counted out. Dempsey opened the second round with three more knockdowns before the South American finally succumbed.[60]

Dempsey rested on his laurels for three years before Rickard produced another challenger in Gene Tunney, a Marine veteran of World War I. Tunney was a favorite of the upper classes. He read Shakespeare, strategically studied boxing as a science, and eventually married a wealthy heiress and became a millionaire businessman after retiring from the ring. He was a distinct contrast from the brawler Dempsey, and such differences made for easy promotion and good fights: "Where Dempsey was unruly, self-indulgent, passionate and spontaneous, Tunney was controlled, disciplined, methodical . . . and just a little boring." In their first encounter in Philadelphia, more than 120,000 endured a rainstorm while millions more listened on the radio around the world as Tunney won the ten-round decision in an upset. Dempsey fans clamored for a rematch, which Rickard arranged a year later in Chicago's Soldier Field. More than 120,000 fans paid $2,658,660 to see the battle, a record for any sports event up to that time (and for twenty-five years thereafter). Fifty million radio listeners in the United States and another estimated 90,000,000 worldwide followed the battle. They were not disappointed. In the seventh round Dempsey knocked his opponent to the canvas, but failed to retreat to a neutral corner. The state of Illinois had recently enacted the rule that was intended to prohibit fighters from immediate attacks on fallen foes as a move toward better sportsmanship and respectability. As Tunney lay on the canvas the referee motioned Dempsey to the assigned corner until he complied and then began his count. Five seconds had elapsed in the interim and Tunney stood up when the referee reached the count of nine, a total of fourteen seconds. Tunney recovered to win a decision in what has ever since been known as "the long count" fight. "Capone was rumored to have bet $45,000 on Dempsey. . . . It was said that $2 million was wagered on the fight in New York alone." Working-class backers of Dempsey lost untold amounts of their hard-earned cash, and despite a massive petition to over-turn the verdict their prayers went unanswered, symbolizing the fatalism of the masses who felt cheated by the corporate interests that dominated urban life, and now even their leisure interests.[61]

Boxing had particular appeal for working-class youth, and when sportswriter Arch Ward of the *Chicago Tribune* initiated an amateur box-ing tournament as a charity event to challenge the Illinois ban on boxing in 1923, 423 young men applied as entrants, necessitating an expansion of the program. Illinois dropped its ban in 1926. A year later Paul Gallico, sports editor of the *New York Daily News*, organized a boxing tournament that he called the Golden Gloves; 2,300 entered for the chance to win a miniature set of "golden gloves" that verified their toughness. The finals were held at Madison Square Garden, which was filled to capacity with 21,794 fans and another 10,000 turned away. Ward wrote, "Nowhere else in competitive athletics does a boy need the courage required for success in Golden Gloves. . . . The moment he has signed and mailed his entry blank he has proved himself a man. . . . Golden Gloves is no place for the weak hearted." For the working class, physicality and courage more than financial capital proved the measure of one's masculinity.[62]

The two journalists agreed to an inter-city competition in 1928, and soon expanded the program to national proportions with entries from thirty-one states. Applicants from east of the Allegheny Mountains rep-resented New York, while those west of the divide fought on the Chicago team. Applicants during the Depression years would number more than 20,000. Each tournament produced sixteen champions determined by elimination bouts, with the finals fought in Madison Square Garden and the Chicago Stadium. The multitude of applicants required 120 bouts with three rings operating simultaneously for four and a half hours—a boxing fan's dream for less than a penny per bout. Division champions earned a dollar per day for a travel allowance. The number of fighters was greatly supplemented after 1930 with the initiation of the Catholic Youth Organization (CYO) boxing tournament (see chapter 6) that sup-plied boxers to the Golden Gloves and the Olympic teams. A Chicago study of Golden Gloves demographics remarked, "Boxing has long been regarded as a means of self-defense, therefore, it is entirely consistent that the greatest number and also the highest ratio of competitors to the population should be in those areas and among those groups where survival of the fittest was long dependent upon one's ability to defend his rights with fists rather than words." The same study acknowledged the role of the media and the importance of boxing as a means of social control of potentially restless and aggressive youths: "By reason of the promotional activities of leading newspapers and the inclusion of boxing on the sports programs of youth agencies designed to reduce juvenile delinquency in large cities, the number of boys taking up the sport has shown a tremendous increase in the past decade." By 1937 Chicago featured 26 sites offering 379 amateur bouts (that figure does not include the Golden Gloves or CYO bouts) in small clubs, the YMCA, American Legion posts, and those sponsored by a variety of political, ethnic, and civic groups. More than ten commercial gymnasiums in the city and the public park districts offered boxing lessons, and another dozen locations sponsored 103 professional contests that year. There was no shortage of boxers to fill the rings during the 1930s.[63]

The immense interest in boxing, combined with Arch Ward's promotional genius, resulted in the creation of an American national team to challenge boxers from other countries. The first challenge match took place in Chicago in 1933 as the *Tribune* transported a team of Irish fighters to the United States to do battle. The U.S. team took on Poland the next year, and by 1937 it had met France, Ireland, Poland, Italy, and Germany in the ring, with only the latter managing to equal the American wins. During the 1930s such matches took on increasing political symbolism as Italy and Germany espoused a fascist ideology, while the United States fostered democracy. As Mussolini and Hitler fostered the belief in Aryan Supremacy and used boxing to proclaim their race of "supermen" the multiethnic and multiracial American teams demonstrated the values of assimilation and a pluralistic society.[64]

The assimilation of ethnic groups in the United States, however, was an ongoing process, and many still held allegiance to their European roots. In 1934 the star of the American team was a young black fighter named Joe Louis, soon destined to become the heavyweight champion of the world. The Polish team arrived in Chicago, where the multitude of Polish residents still claim it to be the second largest Polish city in the world after Warsaw. While Louis awaited his bout on the night of the scheduled international match, four detectives barged into his dressing room and accused him of murdering his wife in 1929. Louis was taken to the police station for questioning, and Arch Ward managed to get him released after it was ascertained that Louis had no wife and was only fifteen years old at the time of the alleged crime. By that time he had missed his fight, which was exactly what the Polish Americans who bet on his opponent and who had filed the charges had intended.[65]

With few prospects for social mobility, especially during the Depression, many young men sought remuneration as professional boxers. While Joe Louis reached the heights of the profession, only to end up bankrupt, the vast majority of others were relegated to local bouts and little compensation. Several social studies have documented the miserable plight of professional boxers and the distinct link to poverty. A 1932 study of boxers in New York found that of 945 licensed boxers, the average income was $1,500 but most earned less than $600 that year. Out of their winnings the fighters had to pay taxes, expenses, and their managers' take, which was generally one-third of the purse but often amounted to much more as many managers notoriously swindled their fighters out of their hard-earned dollars. For example, Bob Fitzsimmons won world championships in three different weight classes by 1900 yet left the ring destitute. Tommy Loughran, lightweight champion from 1927 to 1929, earned more than a quarter million dollars but ended up broke. Kingfish Levinsky, a heavyweight contender of the 1930s, was a major draw in Chicago, but was relegated to selling ties in later life. Beau Jack, a lightweight champ, was one of the biggest stars drawing the biggest crowds at Madison Square Garden during the 1930s and 1940s but ended up shining shoes, the job at which he started before becoming a boxer. Ike Williams, lightweight champion in the 1940s and early 1950s, never got any money from three title fights, yet he still had to pay the taxes after his manager absconded with the purses. Even the best fighters, such as Joe Louis and Sugar Ray Robinson, who both earned more than $4 million in their bouts, ended up bankrupt. Louis had to humiliate himself as a pro wrestler and then as a wrestling referee to subsist, and ended up as a doorman in Las Vegas. He still owed the Internal Revenue Service $1,250,000 in 1956. The same sad story continued throughout the remainder of the century as world champions such as Wilfredo Benitez, Alexis Arguello, and Roberto Duran all ended up in bankruptcy.[66]

A 1952 study of boxers found that most fighters came from the working class, and only 8.8 percent reached the level of contenders, 84.2 percent were relegated to local bouts, and only 7.1 percent earned national recognition. But boxers fought for more than money. For the working class, physical prowess counted more than money or intelligence, and even mediocre fighters gained respect and a measure of local celebrity in their blue-collar neighborhoods. Education seemed of little value if unaccompanied by opportunities:

> They say that too much education softens a man and that is why the college graduates are not good fighters. They fight emotionally on the gridiron and they fight bravely and well in our wars, but their contribution in our rings has been insignificant. The ring has been described as the refuge of the under-privileged. Out of the downtrodden have come our greatest fighters. . . . An education is an escape, and that is what they are saying when they shake their heads—those who know the fight game—as you mention the name of a college fighter. Once the bell rings, they want their fighters to have no retreat, and a fighter with an education is a fighter who does not have to fight to live and he knows it. . . . Only for the hungry fighters is it a decent gamble.[67]

Colleges had fielded boxing teams as early as 1919, but most schools discontinued the sport after a student died after a 1961 bout. Few college boxers saw the sport as a means to a career. Roland La Starza, a heavyweight challenger in the post–World War II era, drew criticism for his education. A sportswriter asked, "Can La Starza, contaminated by two years of college education, become heavyweight title holder, succeed to the throne held by Sullivan, Corbett, Jeffries, Dempsey, Tunney, and Louis but never by a college man?" He further criticized La Starza's caution in the ring: "He, like many another college man, can't see the need for taking punches or needless risks." La Starza was battered by Rocky Marciano in a heavyweight title fight and he left the ring to become an actor in Hollywood. Another who pursued professional accolades in the early 1950s was Chuck Davey, a four-time All-American from Michigan State University. Davey attracted attention because of his college pedigree, his good looks, and early success as a pro, but he got little respect from working-class opponents. Twenty thousand spectators attended his welterweight title bout in Chicago against Cuban Kid Gavilan in 1953 and another 35 million watched the bout on the new television technology that would transform sport throughout the remainder of the century. The colorful Gavilan, who popularized his "bolo punch," a remnant of earlier days as a worker cutting sugar cane, knocked Davey down four times before ending the bout with a knockout. The boxers who emanated from the laboring class and who had faced the deprivations of poverty took particular joy in defeating those who led a more privileged life and who were deemed to be their social superiors.[68]

Perhaps one of the reasons that boxing has managed to survive—and at times flourish—despite the many attempts to abolish the sport is its cultural and social meanings, particularly for the working class. Boxers fight for more than money, as very few can make a living at the sport. They wake early to do their road work, jogging miles to build up their cardiovascular system. Training takes place in dirty, smelly, often unventilated gyms where boxers engage in a monotonous repetition of perfecting the jab, cross, hook, and uppercut, rhythmically hitting the speed bag, pounding the heavy bag, catching the medicine ball and doing endless sit-ups to strengthen the abdomen, skipping rope at three-minute intervals, and sparring with other boxers. The hot, sweaty environment and practice of their craft is not unlike the steel mills, blast furnaces, factory floors, or construction sites in which the working class has labored to make a living.

Loic Wacquant, a French sociologist, traveled to Chicago and joined a boxing club in the 1990s in an attempt to discover the attraction of the sport for its practitioners. He found that in addition to the possibility of financial gain, boxers also valued the self-discipline, strong work ethic, and skill development that fueled their self-worth in an environment and an economy that offered little else. Historian Elliott Gorn surmised that "pugilism was an autonomous expressive form that symbolically opposed the drift of modern society . . . boxing captured the values, the ethos, the distinct culture of countless working men who felt dispossessed."[69] Lou Stillman, owner of the famous eponymous gym in New York where countless boxers trained, decided to sell out in 1959 due to an improvement in the economy; he reasoned, "There's no more tough guys around, not enough slums. That's why I'm getting out of the business. The racket's dead. These fighters today are all sissies."[70] A current trainer of boxers in a poor neighborhood in Boston agreed that fighters must have a physical and psychological hunger: "You don't have two parents at home, food in the fridge, and come in here and make it."[71]

The body culture, within which boxers and the working class in general establishes its identity, can earn one a small measure of celebrity within the neighborhood and even greater acceptance within the cult of masculinity. Such a status allows a boxer to "construct a heroic, transcendent self which allows him to escape the status of a 'non-person.'" In other words, boxing allows its participants to become "somebody," though that sphere of realization is limited. Even middle-class suburbanites who have other avenues in which to establish their masculinity have sought such recognition.[72]

Tim Struby, a middle-class, college-educated professional, gave up his suburban existence for the better part of a year and joined an urban gym at age thirty-one to prepare for the New York Golden Gloves tournament in 2001. He wondered if he had "the discipline to wake up at 6:30 every morning, stiff and sore, to run in the cold rain"; to do "pull ups, dips, crunches, lunges, dead-lifts and bench and shoulder presses." Even though he became a fixture at the gym, his acceptance had to be earned. He engaged in a daily regimen of "stretching, shadowboxing, four rounds on the heavy bag, sit-ups, speed bag, jump rope. . . . My left shoulder aches with dull pain. I'm exhausted." For weeks no one paid any attention to him, until he entered the ring for a sparring match and suffered a knockdown. He later endured a broken jaw. An experienced boxer let him know that "it's a secret world fighters have. Knowing what it's like to hit and get hit. We're different." Struby had won acceptance and he learned that "boxing gyms are strange—they're all about race and class, but they're the least biased place in sports."[73]

After nine months of training Struby awaited his Golden Gloves opponent in a small Catholic school gym, but it felt like Madison Square Garden. "They say the walk from locker room to ring is the longest of your life, a watered-down version of a trip to the electric chair. . . . The crowd, maybe 400, sounds like 40,000." Once the fight commences Struby learns another lesson. "Hitting is addictive. When I land a solid punch, I'm invincible. It's like mainlining macho." But he did not throw enough punches and his opponent gained the decision, which taught him a final lesson: that is "that you don't quit. Lose every fight, you still get respect; give up, don't bother showing your face."[74] It is a lesson that every working-class fighter knows only too well as they fight life's battles in and out of the ring on a daily basis.

THE SOCIAL CONSTRUCTION OF RACE

Race is an abstract concept used to differentiate human beings without any real basis in scientific support. The Human Genome Project, a cooperative venture by research institutes in the United States, Europe, and Asia, began it investigations into the genetic codes of all humans in 1990 and finished its analysis in 2003. It determined that humans throughout the entire world have 99.9 percent identical genes and that humans differ from chimpanzees by only 1.2 percent.[1] In other words, underneath the variety of skin colors, humans are all virtually the same in terms of biology and physiology. Racial categories were developed, or socially constructed, by early scholars who chose to study the differences rather than the similarities between themselves and the groups with whom they came in contact. Such studies were already underway when Charles Darwin published *On the Origin of Species* in 1859, which created a scientific revolution that included the social Darwinism movement that concentrated on explanations for human evolution and the nature of civilization. European and American scientists, almost invariably white, Anglo-Saxon Protestant males, assumed that they held the position at the top of the human pyramid by virtue of their education, standard of living, and conquest of the supposedly inferior groups in the ongoing contest of the survival of the fittest, just as Darwin rationalized the evolution of the world's flora and fauna by adaptation in which only the strongest survived.

By the mid-nineteenth century pseudoscientific studies and biological theories rationalized human differences as divergent evolutionary paths. Phrenologists studied the structure and bumps on human skulls and claimed that these indicated levels of intelligence, while some determined brain size as the measure of thinking ability. Others, known as physiognomists, purported that one's character could be foretold by facial features. The Italian scientist Cesare Lombroso won fame as an early forensic pathologist by asserting that criminality could be determined by the primitive shape of one's forehead (similar to apes) or the size of one's ears, and that such traits could be inherited, making a case for the eugenics movement. Racial stereotypes abounded and in 1857 the U.S. Supreme Court ruled that "Negroes (were) beings of an inferior order with no rights which any white man was bound to respect."[2]

The Chinese were excluded by law from the United States as being undesirable, and many of the southern and eastern European immigrants that flooded American shores after 1880 were not considered to be white. Scholars developed the concept of whiteness by the 1890s as a means to differentiate a variety of groups and their levels of acceptance, but whiteness meant more than just skin color. It included presumed levels of intelligence, adherence to middle-class standards of morality, lifestyle, and values, as well as acceptance of republican virtues and the Protestant religion. In 1874 William Wells Brown, an African American doctor, described the Irish immigrants of the era, who were not considered to be white: "These people are remarkable for open, projecting mouths, prominent teeth, and exposed gums, their advancing cheekbones and depressed noses carry barbarism on their very front. . . . Degradation and hardship exhibit themselves in the whole physical condition of the people . . . giving such an example of human degradation as to make it revolting. They are only five feet two inches, upon an average, bow-legged, bandy shanked, abortively featured, the apparitions of Irish ugliness and Irish want."[3] That perception was reinforced more than two decades later when another writer in the popular *Atlantic Monthly* magazine stated that "a Celt . . . lacks the solidity, the balance, the judgment, the moral staying power of the Anglo-Saxon."[4] Other Europeans fared no better in the estimation of nativists. It was stated that "only hunkies worked blast furnaces which were too damn dirty and too damn hot for a white man," a reference to the large number of Slavs in the steel mills. Italians lacked whiteness due to "swarthy" skin color and their alien religion. They received lower wages than the Irish or blacks. Jews, too, by virtue of their religion and their poverty were deemed to be unacceptable. In 1893 a *New York Times* article stated that "this neighborhood, peopled almost entirely by the people who claim to have been driven from Poland and Russia, is the eyesore of New York, and perhaps the filthiest place on the western continent. It is impossible for a Christian to live there because he will be driven out, either by blows or the dirt and stench. Cleanliness is an unknown quantity to these people. They cannot be lifted up to a higher plane because they do not want to be."[5] It is little wonder that African Americans and poverty-stricken Europeans turned to boxing as a means to test the tenets of the social Darwinian belief system.

In 1911 the U.S. government published a three-year study of immigrants by the congressional Dillingham Commission that concluded that there were forty-five separate races with varying degrees of whiteness and acceptability for citizenship. In the following decade the United States would institute immigration quotas, greatly restricting the number of foreigners permitted. Only after World War I did sociologists begin to develop the concept of ethnicity as distinct from race. Ethnicity classified people by similarities in language, culture, customs, and a common history rather than by skin color. Such a designation allowed for the attainment of whiteness and greater acceptability within American mainstream society, and the practice of American sport forms by the children of immigrants signaled their transition to Americanization. Boxing in particular offered an entrée to American sporting culture and the Irish, who had immigrated earlier than most other groups, became eager participants. As evidenced by the careers of John Morrissey and John L. Sullivan, successful boxers enjoyed celebrity status and a measure of social mobility. The Irish were soon followed by the Jews, Italians, African Americans, and Hispanics.

The History of Black Boxers

Plantation owners in the American South had used slaves in boxing matches against those of other estates for their own amusement and for gambling purposes. The interracial confrontations had been evident as early as the bouts of Bill Richmond and Tom Molyneaux with white British fighters in the early nineteenth century. While British followers of the sport referred to the color of the American blacks, nativist concern regarding the possible loss of the championship to a foreigner posed a greater threat than any racial comparisons and African American fighters continued to ply their trade in England throughout the nineteenth century.[6]

With the rise of social Darwinism, sport assumed greater importance in its comparison of physical abilities. As early as 1835 John Cox Stevens, an American businessman and sportsman, offered a purse of $1,000 for the winner of a ten-mile race and another $300 if the winner could complete the distance in less than an hour. The *American Turf Register and Sporting Magazine* advertised "The Great Race" and termed it a "great trial of human capabilities." The race drew an international field of competitors and was won by Henry Stannard, an American farmer, in 59:48. Such endurance events would test individual and presumably national fitness throughout the remainder of the century, but boxing provided an evaluation of not only endurance, but one's strength, power, and toughness as well. The championship symbolized the ultimate prize in the demonstration of masculinity, and upon the achievement of such an honor John L. Sullivan publicly announced that he would not allow any blacks to challenge for the title. Although Sullivan met the acknowledged black champion of the era, Canadian George Godfrey, in 1880 (before Sullivan's 1882 win over Paddy Ryan), the proposed bout was interrupted by police, and Sullivan never answered repeated challenges by Godfrey thereafter. When Jim Corbett wrested the championship from Sullivan in 1892, he too adhered to the restriction, ensuring that whites would retain the claim to physical superiority.[7]

Corbett's decision was based on more than conjecture. The racist stereotypes associated with non-whites were tested in the ring. It was believed that black boxers could not sustain a stomach punch. The *Sporting and Theatrical Journal*, a popular weekly of the bachelor subculture, informed its readers that "colored pugilists are twice as bad as white ones while the fight lasts, but they are usually quick quitters."[8] Corbett knew better. In 1891, before winning the title, he had fought a grueling sixty-one round match with Peter Jackson that took four hours and ended in a draw. Born in St. Croix in the Virgin Islands in 1860, Jackson had traveled to Australia and won the Australian championship in 1886. He then defeated George Godfrey in San Francisco in 1888 to claim "the colored championship of the world." Corbett declined to give Jackson a rematch once he won the title from Sullivan, but Jackson defeated the English champion in 1892. Thereafter he traversed the United States in search of

Peter Jackson, top black heavyweight of the 1890s, never given a chance at the championship. Courtesy of H. J. Lutcher Stark Center for Physical Culture and Sports, University of Texas at Austin.

opponents, fought in England and Paris for three years, and contracted tuberculosis. In 1898 he lost for the first time in nearly fifteen years to Jim Jeffries, who would later defeat Bob Fitzsimmons, a pupil of Jackson's in Australia. Jeffries then claimed the heavyweight championship of the world, but refused to fight again against any blacks.[9] By that time the U.S. Supreme Court had already sanctioned the legal separation of the races in its 1896 *Plessy v. Ferguson* case that supported Jim Crow laws.

Boxing hastened such a ruling and exemplified the racial animosity prevalent throughout the South, as was evident in the aftermath of a prominent interracial bout in 1892. One of the bouts offered by the New Orleans Olympic Club in its three-day Carnival of Champions that year featured the featherweight title fight between white Jack Skelly and black Canadian George Dixon. Born in Halifax in 1870 to a black mother and reputedly white father, Dixon—known as "Little Chocolate" to fight fans—had begun fighting at the age of sixteen, but his career mush-roomed after taking up residence in Boston. By 1890 he had already de-feated the British champion in London, the first North American to win the title from an Englishman on his home soil. He defended his title later that year against Johnny Murphy in a forty-round battle in Rhode Island. "Dixon as a black man fighting in front of white audiences was often at a disadvantage . . . (in the fight against Murphy) Dixon won the fight, but had to fight near the center of the ring to stay away from the ropes where fans could hit his legs with blackjacks and slug shots. Black boxers were encouraged to fight like lions against each other but like lambs against Caucasians. . . . They were often coerced into losing deliberately to white opponents, or at least doing nothing that would cause a white foe undue distress."[10]

Dixon paid little heed to such admonitions. In 1891 he knocked out Australian champ Abe Willis to earn both the undisputed featherweight

George Dixon, world featherweight champ during the 1890s. Courtesy of H. J. Lutcher Stark Center for Physical Culture and Sports, University of Texas at Austin.

crown as well as the bantamweight title. The New Orleans bout with Skelly offered a purse of $7,500 and raised side bets of $5,000. Dixon was able to use his influence as champion to secure seating for more than 400 black spectators, who were not disappointed. The New Orleans *Times-Democrat* provided headline coverage on the front page and round-by-round details of Dixon's eight-round triumph. "What with bruises, lacerations, and coagulated blood, Skelly's nose, mouth and eye presented a horrible spectacle, and as the poor fellow staggered about almost help-less, even some of the most blasé fans at ringside were heard to shudder, and some even turned their heads in disgust as they saw Dixon savagely chopping away at that face already disfigured past recognition, and heard the ugly half-splashing sound as his blood-soaked glove again and again revisited the bleeding wounds that drenched them."[11] The *Chicago Tribune* reported: "White fans winced every time Dixon landed on Jack Skelly. The sight was repugnant to some of the men from the South. A darky is alright in his place here, but the idea of sitting quietly by and see-ing a colored boy pummel a white lad grates on Southerners."[12] The black citizenry of New Orleans celebrated Dixon's win for two days, which only further antagonized whites.

An editorial in the *Times-Democrat* chastised the Olympic Club when it stated

> it was a mistake to match a negro and a white man, a mistake to bring the races together on any terms of equality, even in the prize ring, and especially a mistake to arrange a fight where representatives of the two races were placed in antagonism; for among the ignorant negroes the idea has naturally been created that it was a test of the strength and fighting powers of Caucasian and African. No one can doubt who saw the reception of Dixon when he arrived and the interest and enthusiasm felt over the fight by the colored population of this city, that they re-garded "the little darky" as the champion of their race; and that because of his victory they are far more confident than they ever were before of the equality of the races, and disposed to claim more for themselves than we intend to concede. . . . We of the South who know the fallacy and danger of this doctrine of race equality, who are opposed to placing the negro on any terms of equality, who have insisted on the separation of the races in church, hotel, car, saloon and theatre; who believe that the law ought to step in and forever forbid the idea of equality by making

marriages between them illegal, are heartily opposed to any arrangement encouraging this equality, which gives negroes false ideas and dangerous beliefs. They have their legal rights, they should have no more; and the white race of the South will destroy itself if it tolerates equality of any kind.[13]

Dixon had struck a blow for racial equality and a challenge to social Darwinism. He further tested societal restrictions by taking Kitty O'Rourke, the sister of his white manager, as his second wife. As the premier small fighter of the late nineteenth century, Dixon's boxing provided a stage for social transformation—much as that same stage offered Muhammad Ali the ability to challenge American society in the 1960s—but Dixon fought beyond his prime, retiring in 1905 with as many as 800 fights and dying destitute at the age of thirty-seven two years later.[14] He died too soon to effect any permanent change, and New Orleans banned all prizefights after a local favorite, Andy Bowen, a light-skinned mulatto who passed as white, died after being knocked out by Kid Lavigne in an 1894 bout.[15] As the outraged writer of the *Times-Democrat* editorial requested, in 1896 the U.S. Supreme Court delivered its ruling on the *Plessy v. Ferguson* case that had originated in New Orleans when Homer Plessy, a mulatto who was seven-eighths white, refused to sit in a segregated railroad car. In Louisiana and elsewhere any drop of African American blood resulted in one's classification as "black." The court ruled that separation of the races was legal as long as facilities for both were equal. That ruling generated a host of segregation laws throughout the United States that would remain in effect until legally overturned by the Supreme Court in the *Brown v. Board of Education* case in 1954.

Such conditions caused many black fighters to seek better opportunities in Europe (see chapter 2), but Joe Gans succeeded Dixon as the next great black fighter to challenge the notions of white supremacy. Gans, known as "The Old Master," was the premier fighter of his times, the first black born in the United States to win a world title, and considered by some to be the best ever. He developed the footwork, defense, and punching combinations that formed the basis for modern boxing techniques. Born in Baltimore in 1874, his father delivered him at the age of four to a foster mother, a laundress named Maria Gant, who raised him. Writers would later misspell the surname to saddle him with the sobriquet of Gans. Joe gained employment at the fish market as an oyster shucker, and he was exposed to the fights on the Baltimore docks. Black boys were often subjected to the spectacle of battle royals, which consisted of white men rounding up black youths and corralling them in a ring, often blindfolded, in which they fought to the finish for the amusement of the whites. The last one standing was declared the winner and might be lucky to garner some coins for his efforts. Gans's success in such endeavors gained the notice of a promoter, Al Herford, who became his manager and allowed Gans to enter the ranks of the professional fighters. He fought at least sixty bouts and probably many more that went unrecorded as he learned his craft and before he reached national attention. By 1900 he had earned the chance to face Frank Erne for the lightweight championship. Unfortunately for Gans, he suffered a debilitating cut above his eye that blinded him, likely caused by a head butt in the twelfth round. Some reports stated that the eye had been dislocated from its socket. In either case, Gans had to retire and the match was awarded to his

Joe Gans, world lightweight champ from 1902 to 1908. Courtesy of H. J. Lutcher Stark Center for Physical Culture and Sports, University of Texas at Austin.

opponent. His decision haunted him and reinforced the stereotype that black fighters were "quitters" when faced with adversity.[16]

Gans's character was further besmirched in December of that same year when he faced featherweight champion Terry McGovern in Chicago for a purse of $7,500 and gamblers wagered another $75,000 on the outcome. Despite a reputation for his endurance, Gans suffered multiple knockdowns and succumbed to a knockout punch in only the second round. George Siler, the referee for the bout, wrote, "I do not wish to accuse any fighter of faking but if Gans was trying to win last night I do not know much about the game. Gans, of course, is entitled to the benefit of the doubt as to whether or not numerous body blows which Terry pumped into him in close quarters during the early part of the fight weakened him. But the fact remains that the few blows he delivered were the weakest ever seen from a man of his known hitting ability." Even McGovern claimed that he was surprised by the abrupt ending of the expected battle. Boxing witnessed the increasing intervention of gamblers, and numerous scandals of fixed fights had already brought dishonor to the fight game that year. There had been rumors of a fix and even black gamblers in the city placed their money on McGovern. The day after the outcome the boxers, their managers, and the referee were all hauled into court to testify. No witnesses to the fix could be obtained, and the charges were dismissed. Nevertheless, the city banned future prizefights in Chicago. Despite the legalities and his reprieve, Gans's reputation suffered and the stereotype of black cowardice remained. His biographers reasoned that Gans's manager, never known for a high sense of ethics, arranged the fix with McGovern's camp in the hope that such a poor showing would earn Gans a shot at the lightweight title. The friendship displayed between the supposed opponents both before and after the affair seems to provide circumstantial evidence of such an arrangement.[17]

Over the next six years Gans labored assiduously to restore his honor. In 1902 he got a rematch with Frank Erne and knocked him out in 1:40 of the first round to become the lightweight champion. Terry McGovern served in Gans's celebration entourage after the fight. Notwithstanding the amity of former opponents, the battle took place in Canada across the river from Erne's residence in Buffalo due to the racial tensions of the times and the outcry after the Dixon-Skelly match in New Orleans a decade earlier. Despite attempts by the white media to disparage Gans, he successfully defensed his title seventeen times over the next few years.[18] The most important challenge came in 1906 when he faced Battling Nelson, a transplanted Dane, who also claimed to be the champion; "Nelson was one of the roughest, toughest men to ever enter the ring, no doubt about it. He could box a little but rarely did. He preferred to brawl." Organized by the first great boxing promoter of the twentieth century, Tex Rickard, the fight took place in the boomtown of Goldfield, Nevada.[19] Gans, left destitute by his previous management, was even more bereft by his new white management team. He had to settle for only a third of the $30,000 purse, and his new managers wagered $45,000 on him and threatened to kill him if he lost. It seemed more than an idle scare tactic to Gans, for at least sixty-two African Americans were lynched that year. Despite suffering a broken hand in the thirty-third round, Gans punished Nelson in a brutal fight that lasted forty-two rounds before the Dane delivered yet another obvious foul to Gans's groin, and the referee declared Gans the winner. Around the country whites retaliated against blacks and two weeks later a full-blown race riot erupted in Atlanta that cost the lives of a dozen African Americans and the destruction of black homes and businesses.[20]

Gans invested his winnings in a Baltimore hotel that he named the Goldfield in honor of his Nevada victory. There he nurtured ragtime musicians who would go on to create their own fame and celebrity that transcended racial boundaries. Gans contracted tuberculosis, and despite two subsequent losses to Nelson in 1908 he fought once more in 1909, defeating Jabez White, the British lightweight champion. He died the next year having spent half his years in the ring, but not before he trained heavyweight Jack Johnson for the biggest racial encounter of the era, one that would affect American society for decades. Francis Grimke, pastor of the Presbyterian Church in Washington, D.C., had already acclaimed Gans's importance after his victory over Nelson: "It is generally conceded . . . that Booker T. Washington has done much good and will do much for the colored race for its uplifting, its education, for making its members citizens in a true sense of the word; but with all that, in the entire course of his life work he never did one-tenth to place the black man in the front rank as a gentleman as has been done by Joe Gans."[21]

Grimke's allusion to Booker T. Washington, the acknowledged leader of the African American community in the United States, symbolized the transition in race relations at the turn of the century. Washington, born a slave in 1856, gained an education and founded the Tuskegee Institute in Alabama, which offered vocational training for blacks. White philanthropists favored his accommodationist approach to race relations, proclaimed in his Atlanta Compromise speech to a mixed audience in 1895 in which he acquiesced to segregation, suffrage restrictions, and limited opportunities for blacks. He stated that "agitation of questions of racial equality is the extremist folly,"[22] and "in all things purely social we (black and white) can be as separate as the fingers, yet one as the hand in all things essential to mutual progress."[23] Such admonitions won him favor among influential whites who supported Tuskegee. He became the first black man invited to the White House as a guest of President Theodore Roosevelt and the most powerful African American in the country.

As in the ring, younger blacks disdained such notions and W. E. B Du Bois emerged to challenge Washington's leadership after the turn of the century. Born free in Massachusetts and educated in the North, Du Bois was the first African American to earn a PhD from Harvard. He took a more militant approach to the oppression of blacks and his 1903 publication, *The Souls of Black Folk*, criticized Washington's conciliatory approach to race relations. In a 1906 speech Du Bois proclaimed that "we want full manhood suffrage and we want it now. . . . We want discrimination in public accommodation to cease. . . . We want the Constitution of the country enforced. . . . We want our children educated. . . . We are men! We shall be treated as men. And we shall win!"[24] Such aggressive challenges to white hegemony soon came to a head in the person of Jack Johnson.

Johnson, born in 1878 in Galveston, Texas, to a father who had been slave and a mother who became a defining influence in his life, grew up in the era of Jim Crow segregation laws, miscegenation bans on interracial marriage, the growing influence of the Ku Klux Klan, and widespread lynching of African Americans. Whereas Booker T. Washington continued to call for gradual change in race relations, Jack Johnson forced abrupt and direct confrontation in such matters, not only in the United States, but on a global scale. Through Johnson, boxing served as a metaphor for the social, racial, and political struggles of the period, which placed him in the vanguard as a catalyst for the New Negro movement that transpired after World War I.

Like many other black boys in the South, "Lil Arthur" (his given birth name was Arthur John Johnson) was subjected to battles royal. He was bullied by others and defended by an older sister until his mother admonished him that he would receive worse from her unless he learned to defend himself. Johnson learned so well that many boxing historians consider him to be the greatest defensive fighter of all time. Still a teenager, Johnson embarked on a career as a professional boxer in 1897, one that overturned notions of white superiority and challenged the social mores of cultures on four continents.[25]

His first bout of any consequence took place in Galveston in 1901 when he fought Joe Choynski, a noted heavyweight of the era but on the decline at that time. Still, Choynski made quick work of Johnson, knocking him out in the third round, after which both were promptly arrested by police for violation of the state's ban on prizefights. Both fighters spent twenty-four days in jail. There Johnson learned the finer points of boxing from his mentor and began his peripatetic wandering across America as a wiser, more seasoned fighter. In 1902 in Los Angeles he knocked out Jack Jeffries, brother of the reigning heavyweight champion, and by 1903 Johnson was acknowledged as the black champion of the United States. Such newfound status enabled him to pursue a profligate lifestyle of spendthrift gambling, womanizing, sartorial splendor, and fast cars. The colorful Johnson engaged in an ongoing repartee with opponents and fans, often antagonizing both. More disconcerting to whites, however, was his relationships with white women, to whom he had turned after a number of failed relationships with black paramours.[26]

Throughout his tenure as heavyweight champion Jim Jeffries adhered to the ban on black challengers; he retired undefeated in 1905. The vacancy resulted in the declaration of Marvin Hart as titleholder, but Hart lost his first defense to Canadian Tommy Burns (Noah Brusso), who weighed only 175 pounds. Upon winning Burns vowed to take on all comers regardless of race. He subsequently held the title for two years, traveling to Europe to meet challengers and proving himself the best. By 1908 Burns's tour had taken him to Australia. Johnson had traveled to Australia the year before, where his conduct with white women outraged the local white populace. Johnson returned to the United States for a match with the former champion Bob Fitzsimmons, whose impoverished state required him to accept a bout with the black fighter. It did not last long, with Johnson securing a second-round knockout. Johnson then followed Burns to England but could not secure a match until both appeared in Australia, Johnson for the second time. There a local promoter, Hugh McIntosh, offered Burns the sum of $30,000 to meet Johnson, who had to settle for only $5,000. Even though Burns's manager served as the referee it proved a mismatch with the white champion outweighed by more than twenty pounds. Johnson toyed with Burns, taunting and punishing him throughout the bout until the police stepped in to end the carnage in the fourteenth round. Johnson was declared the winner and the Anglo world would never be the same.[27]

Whites felt besieged by the challenges to their assumed superiority. In 1905 the Japanese had defeated the Russian Empire in a war, and Johnson noted the racial transition: "Do you think it is to go on forever, this domination of the millions of people of color by a handful of white folks? I think it is not . . . the time will come when the black and yellow man will hold the earth, and the white man will be regarded just as the colored man is now."[28] Films of Johnson's victory had reached Africa and Asia and indigenous residents reveled in his victory, fostering fears of racial conflict. Johnson soon embarked on a theatrical tour of Australia, then returned to Chicago, his new adopted home where he acquired a fine house for himself, his mother and sisters, and consorted with a bevy of white prostitutes. "His white women represented the ultimate conquest for the black man and the greatest insult to white notions of security and dominance in race relations. It signified the inability of white men to protect their most precious treasure."[29]

Johnson's conquests in and out of the ring engendered a search for the "Great White Hope," anyone who might reclaim white honor and reestablish the racial hierarchy, but Johnson destroyed five white challengers in 1909. The most accomplished fighter, fearsome middleweight champion Stanley Ketchel (Stanislaus Kiecal), known as "The Assassin," is still presumed by many boxing historians to be the best ever in his weight class. The two champions had allegedly made a pact to do no undue harm and split the purse, but Ketchel deviated from the script and actually knocked Johnson to the canvas in the twelfth round. The enraged Johnson retaliated with a thundering blow that not only knocked out his smaller opponent, but dislodged his front teeth. Canadians tried to find a worthy white contender, even South Africa offered two of its heavyweights to

Jack Johnson's knockout of Stanley Ketchel. Courtesy of H. J. Lutcher Stark Center for Physical Culture and Sports, University of Texas at Austin.

confront the black champion to no avail, and the search continued as "Johnson assumed the trappings of royalty. The African American prince reversed social and economic roles by hiring white managers, chauffeurs, valets, and women who waited upon him and served his needs. . . . He sped . . . around the country in racing cars, oblivious to the laws. In 1910 he even challenged (but lost) to Barney Oldfield, one of the premier professional auto racers of the era."[30]

Johnson's confrontations with the white power structure elicited calls from the media that finally coaxed the seemingly invincible Jim Jeffries out of retirement to vanquish the repugnant black pretender. Jeffries responded to his followers that "I realize full well just what depends on me, and I am not going to disappoint the public. That portion of the white race that has been looking to me to defend its athletic superiority may feel assured that I am fit to do my very best."[31] When the fight was banned from California, Tex Rickard staged it in Reno on July 4, 1910. Twenty thousand spectators and more than 500 reporters descended on the desert community to witness the spectacle. The winner would garner 75 percent of the astronomical $101,000 purse as well as income from the movie rights and the inevitable vaudeville tour.

Once the bout commenced, it soon became apparent that Jeffries could not match his former glory, and Johnson controlled the outcome. He bloodied the Great White Hope and broke his nose as he ridiculed the former champion and his cornerman, "Gentleman Jim" Corbett, who had bet $5,000 on Jeffries. In the fifteenth round Jeffries fell to the canvas, the first knockdown of his career. Johnson then knocked him through the ropes, but ringside patrons assisted him back into the fray. After the third knockdown Jeffries's handlers conceded rather than suffer the indignity of a knockout to their hero. Novelist Rex Beach lamented, "Today we saw a tragedy. A tremendous, crushing anti-climax had happened and we are dazed. . . . He (Johnson) demonstrated further that his race has acquired full stature as men; whether they will ever breed brains to match his muscle is yet to be seen." Whites thus had to accept physical, if not intellectual equality.[32]

In the aftermath of the fight race riots erupted throughout America, with lynchings of blacks and deaths on both sides. Johnson earned

Jack Johnson delivering a left to Jim Jeffries. Courtesy of H. J. Lutcher Stark Center for Physical Culture and Sports, University of Texas at Austin.

Jack Johnson versus Jim Jeffries. The defeat of the Great White Hope set off race riots throughout the country. Courtesy of H. J. Lutcher Stark Center for Physical Culture and Sports, University of Texas at Austin.

$140,000 from the fight and returned to a hero's welcome in Chicago, hailed as a black messiah. A crowd of 10,000 met him at the train otation in New York. Johnson embarked on a vaudeville tour amidst death threats and further infuriated whites when he married Etta Duryea, a white woman. Even after his marriage Johnson maintained a relationship with Belle Schreiber, a white mistress who had worked at the Everleigh Club in Chicago, the world's most famous brothel. Despite a ban on black patrons Johnson had managed to convince at least nine of its employees to leave with him, a decision that cost all of them their jobs.[33]

Johnson took his tour to England, where the racial struggle continued. The governments of England, South Africa, and fifteen U.S. states as well as the District of Columbia had banned the showing of the fight film, and he was unable to secure any bouts. Johnson had become an international sensation by that time and his travels and assaults on the racial status quo brought worldwide media attention. He returned to the United

States for a match with "Fireman" Jim Flynn (Andrew Chiariglione) on July 4, 1912, which Johnson won on a foul, and resulted in a federal ban on interstate commerce in fight films.[34]

Johnson found another source of income in the Café de Champion, the lavish cabaret complete with an orchestra that he opened in Chicago just south of the vice district. The new enterprise attracted a mixed crowd of blacks and whites drawn to the youthful exuberance and vibrant nightlife of the growing African American community in the city. Such interracial interaction would continue to be fueled by the jazz age following World War I; mainstream white society viewed such "slumming" as a dangerous sign and a breakdown in the segregation of the races. The cabaret took on greater notoriety when Johnson's white wife committed suicide only eighteen months after their marriage. He remarried only two months later to Lucille Cameron, a white teenager who worked at the club. Her mother raised a national furor when she claimed that Johnson had abducted the young woman, a charge that the daughter denied. Black businessmen prevailed on Johnson to clarify his alleged ability to have any white woman that he wanted. Johnson couched his defense not as a moral issue, but one of basic human rights: "I have the right to choose who my mate shall be without the dictation of any man. . . . So long as I do not interfere with any other man's wife I shall claim the right to select the woman of my choice. Nobody else can do that for me. That is where the trouble lies."[35]

While Johnson felt persecuted, the U.S. government tried to portray a more benevolent vision to the world. The 1912 Olympic team that summer featured an African American sprinter, Howard Drew; a gold medal swimmer in Duke Kahanamoku from Hawaii; and two Native Americans from the Carlisle Indian School—Louis Tewanima, who won a silver medal in the 10,000 meter run, and the star of the Games, Jim Thorpe, who captured the gold medals in both the pentathlon and decathlon. The multiracial contingent presented the perception of an inclusive and unbiased democracy to the world. The reality, however, was much different. The American Indians did not even gain citizenship until 1924, and at least sixty-two African Americans were lynched that year. Jack Johnson faced that possibility every day.[36]

The government had tried to indict Johnson for violation of the Mann Act, also known as the White Slave Traffic Act, designed to prohibit the transportation of females across state lines for immoral purposes. When Lucille Cameron refused to provide any damning testimony, the government turned to the jealous Belle Schreiber. Although the law intended to address commercialized vice rather than complicit sexual behavior between consenting adults, the state utilized Schreiber's testimony of her liaisons with Johnson as evidence against him. The city closed Johnson's cabaret and jailed him until he could produce an adequate bail. The trial began in May 1913 and Johnson realized that the deck had been stacked against him. Even so, it took the jury four ballots to convict him, and Johnson was sentenced to 366 days in prison and a $1,000 fine. He did not wait to be incarcerated, and fled to Canada and onward to Europe, where he hoped to continue fighting.[37]

Johnson made three title defenses in Paris, but little money in 1914 and the eruption of World War I meant even fewer possibilities. He traveled to Argentina in 1915 where his theatrical performances and a bout against a minor foe drew little interest, and he moved on to Barbados and Cuba. Johnson agreed to a title bout with Jess Willard, a large, lumbering cowboy from Kansas, scheduled for forty-five rounds on April 5 in Havana. At 6 feet 6 inches and 238 pounds, Willard had little distinction other than his size, but both men and women cheered wildly for the challenger: "From the moment the two entered the ring it was more than a battle between prize fighters in the eyes of those who saw the contest. To them it was a struggle between the white and black races and an opportunity to reassert the superiority of the Caucasian over the African."[38] A white journalist reported that "the fight was all Johnson's during the first twenty rounds . . . on occasions Johnson played with him, once standing with guard down and letting Willard swing at him, only to dodge and laugh at the awkwardness of his opponent."[39] Another stated that "Johnson punched and pounded Willard at will for the first twenty rounds, but was unable or unwilling to go on" and sent his wife home after the twenty-fifth round. In the next round Willard landed a powerful right hand that sent the champion to the canvas, where, knees bent and right forearm shielding his eyes from the sun, Johnson took a ten count, then "quickly got up." Bat Masterson, famed frontier lawman who attended the affair, wrote that it was a "puzzle to fans."[40] The Associated Press reporter claimed, "There is much discussion tonight and probably will be for a long time, among the followers of the fighting game as to whether Johnson was really knocked out. In the sense of being smashed into unconsciousness he certainly was not put out. . . . A second or two after Jack Welsh, the referee, had counted ten, Johnson quickly got up."[41]

Mrs. Jennie Rhodes, Johnson's sister, soon claimed that the fight was a fake. Johnson corroborated her story a year later by stating that he accepted a large cash payment and a U.S. government promise of leniency upon his return to the United States. Most historians discount Johnson's version; regardless, he lost on both counts, for there was no quick return to his homeland or any leniency. Jubilant whites taunted blacks in the aftermath, requiring police intervention, and with the war raging in Europe, Johnson's life became no easier. His theatrical tour in London lost money and the government expelled him. He took up residence and bullfighting in Spain. When the United States entered the war Johnson offered his services in return for a pardon, but the government had no interest. He had to pawn his wife's jewelry and moved to Mexico, where he opened a saloon in Tijuana.[42]

In 1919 Chicago erupted in a race riot that lasted two weeks and cost thirty-eight lives and immense destruction of property. The event started when a black youth mistakenly crossed over into the white section of a segregated public beach. White youths threw rocks which hit him in the head and caused his drowning. When his black friends sought the help of the white policeman they found little solace. White gangs invaded the black neighborhood bent on destruction, but recently returned black veterans from World War I, armed with their weapons, no longer backed down. Jack Johnson had made a statement; so would they. The resulting carnage bloodied both sides, with more than 500 injured.[43]

When Johnson's patron, President Venustiano Carranza of Mexico, was assassinated in 1920, the new administration sought better relations with the United States. Johnson lost his saloon and any opportunities for fights. Tired of wandering, he submitted to U.S marshals on the California border on July 20, 1920. The enforcement of his sentence resulted in a year's imprisonment at Fort Leavenworth. Upon his release he continued to fight, but never gained another title match. Jess Willard reinstated the color ban, and his conqueror, Jack Dempsey, adhered to it, denying Harry Wills, the next great black heavyweight, any shot at the title.[44]

Lucille Cameron divorced Johnson in 1924 and he married a third white wife, Irene Pineau, in 1925. Johnson fought—and won—his last bout at age fifty-three, and another exhibition in 1945 at age sixty-seven as a fundraiser for World War II. A year later his life ended almost predictably in a speeding car crash, but Johnson left an enduring legacy as a social force. He forced white Americans to take notice, he confronted racial stereotypes, and he gave millions of African Americans hope, pride, and a sense of self-esteem. Others soon took up the crusade for human and civil rights in the hopeful New Negro movement and the creative Harlem Renaissance that produced distinguished figures in art, literature, music, theater, dance, and sport. Marcus Garvey explained the influence of the boxer in a 1922 speech when he stated, "The age for turning the right check if you are hit on the left is past. This is a Jack Johnson age, when the fittest will survive." Garvey even promoted a separate black economy and a return to Africa, but like Johnson he ran afoul of the federal government, which deported him back to his native Jamaica.[45]

The stereotypes and caricatures attributed to non-white "others" extended beyond racist depictions of African Americans. In 1904 St. Louis hosted the Olympic Games, which included a bizarre experiment known as the Anthropology Days organized by anthropologist William J. McGee and James Sullivan, head of the Amateur Athletic Union. They recruited a variety of indigenous groups from various regions of the world who were housed in "native" villages as exhibits in the accompanying World's Fair grounds. The participants engaged in several athletic competitions, as well as mud slinging, pole climbing, and a tug-of-war for the purpose of comparing their physical performances with those of whites to judge natural superiority. Some of the so-called competitors did not take the events seriously, and most of the events were "won" by American Indians who were already familiar with American sports due to their required education in American government boarding schools. Nevertheless, the Americans proclaimed the superiority of white Anglos in comparison to "others."[46]

Some European immigrant groups also labored under the designation of non-whites, including southern Italians and Sicilians who sought a better life in the Americas. While most sought refuge in the United States, others traveled to Brazil and Argentina. British immigrants had introduced boxing to the latter country in 1895, and the first professional bout between Paddy McCarthy, an Irish immigrant, and Italian Abelardo Robassio, occurred in 1903. Both British and American teachers offered instruction at the Buenos Aires Boxing Club, which held weight-class championships by 1910. In 1914 Jack Johnson knocked out fellow American Jack Murray in a pro bout in Argentina during his global wanderings. By 1917 Angel Louis Firpo, an Argentinian Italian, had begun his professional career as a boxer. Within a relatively few years he had secured the South American heavyweight championship and headed for bigger paydays in New York, where the American media characterized him as a giant at 6 feet 2 inches and 220 pounds. After a series of knockout victories promoter Tex Rickard matched him against former champion Jess Willard, who was even bigger than Firpo. A massive crowd estimated as high as 85,000 witnessed Firpo demolish the American with an eighth-round knockout. Firpo followed that encounter with a string of four more knockouts against less-distinguished foes before Rickard matched him with Jack Dempsey for the world championship on September 14, 1923.[47]

The American media referred to Firpo as the "Wild Bull of the Pampas," and generally denigrated him as a savage. A supposed psychological study claimed that "the man is a combination of a Patagonian giant and a Genoese wild man. Like his progenitors, who were some of the most famous of Italian vendettists, he has the ability to curb his strength and his passions and disguise his feelings until the proper moment for action is arrived. . . . He is absolutely cold blooded."[48] Such racist promotions drew 88,000 to the fight scene to witness perhaps the greatest brawl in boxing history.[49]

The encounter featured eleven knockdowns in only two rounds. Near the end of the first round Firpo knocked Dempsey through the ropes, where he landed on the sportswriters seated at ringside. The reporters duly helped the champion back into the ring before he was counted out and the referee conveniently overlooked their assistance, which were grounds for disqualification, and allowed the fight to continue. Dempsey roared back to finish the challenger with a knockout in the second round. When Firpo fell in defeat a journalist stated, "If Luis Angel Firpo had the brain power in proportion to his tremendous strength, there is no denying that he and not Jack Dempsey would be world's heavyweight champion this morning. Endowed with the mentality which would enable him to think and think quickly in emergencies, Firpo could afford to be slow moving and cumbersome. But Firpo, with all his great strength to give and take punishment, lacked that one essential—a fighting brain."[50] Such a rationalization relegated Firpo, and the Italians who cheered for him, to the level of primitive people, still unworthy of full inclusion in white, Anglo society. A successful businessman who became a multimillionaire after his retirement from the ring, Firpo would belie such depictions.[51]

The racial challenges to white supremacy continued across the Atlantic and in the United States over the course of the next two decades. Black Americans had been traveling to Paris throughout the nineteenth century, and by 1900 the city included many Africans from the French colonies. Blacks perceived the French capital to be more liberal and receptive to a pluralistic society and African American boxers and entertainers increasingly sought refuge and opportunity there during the early twentieth century. A writer of the era claimed, "They earn more in a week there than they used to in many months over here." The French fascination with the black body drew patrons to cabarets, theaters, and boxing matches. When World War I erupted, black Americans offered their services to the French military, and the French called upon their colonial subjects in Africa for additional support. At least 134,000 Africans fought for the French, and 30,000 lost their lives.[52]

Louis Amadou M'Barack Fall, better known as "Battling Siki" from Senegal, interrupted his budding boxing career to answer the call. Siki fought bravely at Gallipoli and in Europe, earning both the Croix de Guerre and the Legion of Honor for his exploits. Siki spent five years in the French army and when not engaged in combat he was able to hone his boxing skills against Americans in the military camps. Upon his release he pursued his vocation as a light heavyweight with great success. Siki defeated Hans Breitenstrater, a German heavyweight, and Giuseppe Spalla, the Italian heavyweight champ, in 1921, but when matched against war hero and national idol Georges Carpentier on September 24, 1922, he experienced the limits of French tolerance. A 1919 chronicler of boxing stated that "it is no exaggeration to say that every time Georges Carpentier enters a ring to do battle there are thousands of fair bosoms aflutter with hope and fear throughout France. Take a night at a Cirque de Paris, when perhaps Georges is to do battle for the honour of the white race against a giant negro. . . a sigh of admiration tinged with fear as he faces the black colossus." Carpentier defeated Battling Robinson, a black American, in his first bout after the war; Siki presented a more formidable challenge.[53]

Siki fought sluggishly and suffered two knockdowns in the first three rounds, but after Carpentier taunted him, he attacked with fury. Siki knocked out Carpentier in the sixth round; however, the referee ruled that he had tripped his opponent and disqualified him. The verdict brought volatile reactions, and the president of the French Boxing Federation, who was in attendance, reversed the decision. Siki had become the first black to gain a championship since Jack Johnson. Ho Chi Minh, then residing in France and later destined to lead Vietnam in wars against that colonial power and the United States, published an article on the symbolic importance of Siki: "From the colonial viewpoint, a Carpentier-Siki match is worth more than one hundred gubernatorial speeches to prove to our subjects and protégés that we want to apply to the letter the principle of the equality between races."[54] The white French media, however, chafed at the loss and characterized Siki as the "French Jack Johnson," a reference to Siki's blonde Dutch wife. They portrayed him as a primitive savage and a wild man, despite the fact that he spoke five languages. Siki responded, "I am not a cannibal . . . I speak and I write French like the average French person . . . I should say that since my great victory over Georges Carpentier, I perceive that I am very much a son of France." To the declaration that he was "a chimpanzee who has been taught to wear gloves," he replied, "That kind of hurts me. I was never anywhere but in a big city in my life, I have never even seen a jungle."[55]

Siki later claimed that the Carpentier fight had been fixed by the champion's manager, but he decided not to adhere to the agreement. Siki's lifestyle outside the ring resembled that of Jack Johnson as he dressed lavishly, ambled through Paris with his Great Dane dogs and other exotic pets, and got in brawls. The French Boxing Federation revoked his license for detrimental actions and he could no longer fight in France. Siki accepted a fight with an Irishman, Mike McTigue, in Dublin on St. Patrick's Day 1923, shortly after Ireland won its independence from Great Britain. On such an occasion and in such a place Siki's only chance would have been a knockout; unable to accomplish that, McTigue was awarded a disputed decision and the light heavyweight title. Siki's only recourse was to seek opportunities in the United States, and he arrived in New York in September of that year.[56]

Americans disparaged his boxing style. Nat Fleischer, the dean of boxing writers, stated that he "was guided by one simple rule—to slug, slug, and keep slugging from bell to bell, until either he or the other fellow dropped for the count."[57] British writer Louis Golding concurred:

Siki knockdown of Carpentier for the light heavyweight championship. Courtesy of H. J. Lutcher Stark Center for Physical Culture and Sports, University of Texas at Austin.

"Big, strong, and ugly, there was a terrific power in those long, pendulous arms of his which could be unleashed with devastating effect when he was roused. Skill and science were beyond the scope of his limited intelligence, but many a slugger has risen to the heights of the game."[58] Siki had to suffer through such racist depictions, for he knew that his exoticism sold tickets. His strolls through New York included his pet lion, but in a message to the *New York Tribune* "he meant to show American fight fans . . . that he was 'no freak imported from the jungles of Africa as a circus attraction.'"[59]

Siki spent two years in the United States, where he married an American woman who was an octoroon but described as white, which hardly endeared him to the white mainstream after Jack Johnson's assault on the miscegenation standards of the era. Like Johnson, he doled out large amounts of cash to the poor, yet the media characterized him as foolish rather than charitable. He drank too much, got in brawls, and was banned from fighting in several states. On December 16, 1925, three assailants gunned him down in the Hell's Kitchen neighborhood, allegedly for reneging on fixed fights. The police were not overly concerned with finding his killers, and no one was ever convicted of the crime. He had won nearly 80 percent of his bouts in Europe, but less than 17 percent in the United States. The *New York World* account even discounted his linguistic achievements on his death when it editorialized that "he could speak nine languages, and his total vocabulary in all, it is said, was 157 words, counting profane expletives." Scholar Gerald Early described him as a marginal man, one bereft of a country, and out of place wherever he went. "No wonder he wound up a boxer. What else could he have been?"[60]

While Siki invaded the United States from his European base, the Americans encountered another threat from Asia, one of their own making. In 1898 when the United States declared war on Spain after the U.S.S. *Maine* exploded in Havana harbor, American military forces quickly subdued Manila, capital of the Philippines, a Spanish colony in the western Pacific. The United States disregarded the fact that a rebel army of nationalist Filipinos had already surrounded the Spanish occupiers and established a revolutionary government. When the United States gained the entire archipelago of more than 7,000 islands in the treaty that ended the war, it faced a diverse population often at odds with the American occupation forces. Americans described the population in racial terms:

"The inhabitants of the Philippines included . . . Kanakas and Malays who are half-civilized and in rebellion; canny Chinese and shrewd Japanese and—in the interior—thousands of naked negritos, wild and untamed as the red aborigines."[61]A guerrilla war ensued for years in the islands, and a strident anti-imperialist movement opposed the conquest of the territory. An extensive sport program enacted by the colonial administration proved effective in channeling Filipino nationalism toward regional rivals such as the Japanese rather than the American rulers. Even before the colonial administrators took control of the islands' governance, U.S. Army soldiers had already introduced the locals to baseball and boxing.[62]

Within a decade Manila featured weekly bouts promoted by American entrepreneurs. Among them, Frank Churchill had a keen eye for talent. Churchill had been a prospector in Alaska before taking a job in the customs house in the Philippines. He worked as a carnival barker and in advertising before finding treasure as a boxing promoter. His key discovery was the son of poor plantation workers, whom they named Francisco Guilledo but who assumed the moniker of Pancho Villa, the Mexican outlaw who had terrorized the southwest United States during World War I. Villa fought in the flyweight class, allegedly winning all but one of his bouts before making his U.S. debut in 1922 at the age of twenty-one. He had been matched thirteen times against Mike Ballerino of the U.S. Army, a future world champion, and never lost.[63]

His success as the first Asian to gain a world title belied the opinion of an American executive who complained about his Filipino workers to an American general:

> My personal belief is that the reason for this resentment against foreigners is that we set too fast a pace for them. A Filipino does not want to work and resents either consciously or unconsciously the fact that he has to work. We tend to speed him up, we tend to accelerate the process of evolution. The Filipino knows nothing of evolution and cares less. If he did know anything of evolution his natural impulse would be to attempt to retard it. . . . The average Filipino is, of course, to a degree lazy and dishonest and absolutely lacking in initiative or executive ability, but he is good natured, extremely amenable to discipline and easy to handle generally, provided he is not interfered with and misled by the shrewder though incompetent political type.

In the United States and Hawaii Filipinos were exploited as cheap labor, attacked as non-white foreigners, and often segregated.[64]

Villa damaged such perceptions and destroyed a host of white fighters on his climb to the world flyweight championship, and always displayed the utmost sportsmanship in the ring. Nevertheless, the white media took issue with Villa's extravagant lifestyle, which resembled that of Jack Johnson. Villa's fights drew record crowds and grossed nearly $300,000 during his two years in the United States, much of which he spent on white women. Like Johnson, he carried large bills and spent them freely. Even though the flyweight title did not carry the same symbolic value as the heavyweight championship, white writers characterized Villa as a demon and an inhuman savage, "his brown sweating body flashing back and forth like a caged monkey . . . it was impossible for anything human to get around so fast."[65] He remained an idol in the Philippines, but his glory proved short-lived. In 1925 he contracted a tooth infection which resulted in the further extraction of three teeth by a San Francisco dentist, and the development of a throat malady that killed him. More than 100,000 turned out in Manila to view his body as the stores closed and the streets were draped in black. Almost a century later he remained a national hero:

> Into his person he collected all the swank and swagger of the period and the whole country felt a vicarious pride in his rise from rags to riches—and in his magnificent wardrobe, his collection of silk shirts and natty hats, his pearl buttons and gold cufflinks, and his princely retinue. He had a valet to massage him, another valet to towel him, another valet to put on his shoes, another valet to help him in his trousers, and still other valets to comb his hair, powder his cheeks, and spray him with perfume. He was, perhaps, more idolized as a magnifico than as a boxer; and when he died the nation's heart broke.[66]

The Associated Press recognized his immense talent when it named him the flyweight of the century in 1999.

The challenges of Johnson, Siki, and Villa coincided with the rise of the Ku Klux Klan in America; even great black heavyweight fighters like Harry Wills, though a devoutly religious family man who met the standards of the respectable white middle class, had no chance for a title shot. At the lower weights, which carried less symbolic value, Theodore "Tiger" Flowers managed to become the first African American to win the middleweight championship in 1926 when he defeated Harry Greb. Born in Georgia, the young Flowers was forced to fight in the humiliating battle royals, similar to the experience of Jack Johnson and other black boxers. He married at a young age in 1915, and his wife encouraged the pursuit of a boxing career. A contemporary of both Siki and Villa, Flowers fought 157 bouts between 1918 and 1927. Like Villa he was praised for his sportsmanship and although he was deferential to whites, the media claimed that he displayed the "berserk ferocity of the African jungles" when in the ring.[67]

Outside of the ring he proved anything but threatening to whites or anyone else as an honest, humble, and polite gentleman. He invested his money and owned a fourteen-room house with servants in Atlanta, and made charitable gifts to churches and the poor. He served as a trustee at a church, abstained from alcohol, practiced vegetarianism, and joined the Elks, Masons, and Knights of Pythias fraternal organizations. To whites, he represented the ideal black man and was even called "the whitest black man in the ring." For blacks, he transcended racial and class lines and allowed all black Americans to obtain a greater measure of racial pride. For even the worst racists, there was little to criticize.[68]

Flowers had found it difficult to get matches against white fighters, but once he won the middleweight title he defended it ten times from April to December of that year, including a rematch with Harry Greb. Flowers lost the championship to Mickey Walker in his last title defense in a very controversial decision. Although he dominated the contest in Chicago the fight and the title were awarded to Walker, a judgment that was investigated but never overturned by the Illinois Athletic Commission. Walker refused to grant Flowers a rematch. Flowers died the following year after undergoing an operation to repair scar tissue around his eyes. His biographer asserted that the death seemed mysterious and that his white manager was suspected of chicanery in an attempt to gain access to Flowers's money.[69]

The concept of race gradually evolved into more definitive classifications of ethnicity after World War I, yet Italians remained suspect and not fully accepted in the white mainstream society by the 1930s. Benito Mussolini had taken over Italy in 1922 and his fascist dictatorship aimed to elevate Italy into a world power. Sport offered a comparative basis for evaluation of his endeavor. In 1930 Primo Carnera, a giant (6 feet 7

Tiger Flowers, the first African American middleweight champ. Courtesy of H. J. Lutcher Stark Center for Physical Culture and Sports, University of Texas at Austin.

inches and 265 pounds) former circus performer turned boxer, made his first tour of the United States. Carnera's mesomorphic body resembled a Greek statue and he embarked on a whirlwind schedule that included twenty-four bouts in only thirty-seven weeks, attracting huge crowds. He garnered more than $100,000 in his first ten fights alone. On his return in 1932 he killed his opponent, Ernie Schaaf, in a bout held at Madison Square Garden, the American temple of boxing. He assumed the role of the fascist superman and he had a large following among Italian American fans; however, the American media presented him as the gargantuan, deviant "other," one with criminal ties to gangsters and a fascist unworthy of Americanization.[70]

The Italian government considered not only immigrants, but their American-born children, to still be citizens of Italy and subject to military service, and many had returned to fight in World War I. Mussolini sponsored Italian language schools in the United States in Catholic parishes and offered summer camps in Italy for American-born offspring. Many Italian Americans admired him for bringing greater respect to their homeland. An Italian American girl expressed her guarded admiration of Mussolini: "You have got to admit one thing, he enabled four million Italians in America to hold up their heads, and that is something. If you had been branded as undesirable by a quota law you would understand how much that means." For downtrodden Italians living in America Mussolini resurrected Italian pride and enhanced Italian self-esteem. In 1933 he sent famed aviator Italo Balbo and a squadron of seaplanes to the Chicago World's Fair to demonstrate Italian technological excellence and counteract the gangster image in America. Balbo reminded Italians to be proud Americans, but not to forget that they were also Italians, thus reinforcing the dilemma of cultural identity.[71] Another Italian American male was more adulatory in his pronouncement that "Mussolini was a hero, a superhero. He made us feel special, especially the southerners, Sicilians, Calabrian. . . . We had the equivalent of your pep rallies for football teams."[72]

In 1933 Carnera knocked out Jack Sharkey in the sixth round to gain the heavyweight championship of the world, and "returned to Rome to a hero's welcome and, on the eve of Italy's invasion of Abyssinia (Ethiopia), was feted by the Italian dictator as an icon of Italian prowess." Carnera's reign, however, proved short-lived, as he won two title defenses but lost the crown to Max Baer in 1934 and was unceremoniously knocked out by the rising star, Joe Louis, in 1935. Carnera enjoyed great strength but very limited boxing skills, and sportswriters exposed many of his victories as fixed bouts arranged by American gangsters.[73]

Primo Carnera versus Max Baer. Courtesy of H. J. Lutcher Stark Center for Physical Culture and Sports, University of Texas at Austin.

Boxing took a curious turn in Germany after World War I as the avante-garde adopted the sport as part of their reaction to modernization and the development of a body culture that fostered naturalism. Boxing offered a means for national rejuvenation. Within such an atmosphere Max Schmeling emerged as a darling of the artistic community. The art journal *Querschnitt* featured naked boxers with more than fifteen illustra-tions of Schmeling, artists painted him, and sculptors molded his body into works of art during the years of the Weimar Republic. According to one writer, "For some, the boxer-hero served to compensate for a sense of historical loss and disempowerment."[74]

The rise of fascism in Europe took on greater meaning for American fight fans in the 1930s as Mussolini ruled Italy, General Francisco Franco took control of Spain, and Adolf Hitler ascended to power. The latter envisioned a resurgent Germany as the world leader and athletic prowess served as a symbol of national power. Max Schmeling had captured both the German and European heavyweight championships by 1928 and embarked for the United States to seek greater fortune. In 1930 he became the first boxer to win the heavyweight crown by virtue of a foul, which disqualified his opponent, Jack Sharkey. Schmeling lost the rematch in a controversial split decision in 1932. He then forced the tough Mickey

Max Schmeling, who symbolized the social transitions in Germany during the interwar era. Courtesy of H. J. Lutcher Stark Center for Physical Culture and Sports, University of Texas at Austin.

Walker to quit after eight rounds, but lost to Max Baer in 1933; Baer, who was Jewish, wore the Star of David on his trunks to emphasize the growing plight of Jews in Germany. Although Schmeling was never a member of the Nazi Party, the American media associated his German identity with the policies of Hitler. After another disappointing loss Schmeling returned to Germany.[75]

As Schmeling regained his form in Europe, Joe Louis fashioned a phenomenal rise to stardom in the United States. Born Joe Louis Barrow, the seventh of eight children, to poor Alabama sharecroppers, he lost his father at the age of two when the sire had to be institutionalized due to mental illness. His mother remarried and moved to Detroit, where Joe eschewed the money she provided for music lessons in favor of boxing tutorials. When he began to fight competitively he dropped his surname so that his mother would not recognize him in the media coverage. He proved too good for the subterfuge to last very long. In 1934 he won the Amateur Athletic Union and Golden Gloves national championships and attracted the attention of John Roxborough, a local black lawyer and numbers runner, and Julian Black, a Detroit businessman and gambler, who agreed to sponsor his professional career. They did so, however, under strict guidelines. Louis was to comport himself as the anti–Jack Johnson, never gloating over a beaten foe, never being seen with a white woman, and portraying himself in a humble, religious manner. Louis obliged and quickly won all twenty-two bouts over the next year, eighteen by knockout. His trainer, Jack Blackburn, had told him, "It's mighty hard for a colored boy to win decisions. The dice is [sic] loaded against you. You gotta knock 'em out. . . . Let your right fist be your referee." Louis learned his lessons well.[76]

The Great Depression hit all Americans hard, black Americans particularly so. Joe Louis provided a psychological antidote. The black media provided more coverage of Louis than any other African American public figure. More than forty songs echoed his prowess, and blues artist Memphis Minnie asserted that she'd forego eating in order to bet more money on a Joe Louis fight. A study of black schoolchildren in Georgia found that they could not identify the National Association for the Advancement of Colored People (NAACP) leader, W. E. B. Du Bois, or even the U.S. president; but all knew Joe Louis. Italy's aggressive designs on Ethiopia came to fruition in 1935 as Italian Americans sided with their ancestral homeland and black Americans favored the African nation. The bout between Louis and Primo Carnera in June of that year thus took on added political significance. When Louis conquered the Italian giant in only six rounds it set off celebrations in the black communities, incurring retaliation by Italian Americans in Harlem where residents were later attacked.[77]

A writer for the International News Service reported the results in racist terms, equating Louis to an animal: "Something sly and sinister, and perhaps not quite human came out of the African jungle last night to strike down and utterly demolish a huge hulk that had been Primo Carnera, the giant."[78] Other sportswriters had characterized Louis as a "shufflin' shadow," a "chocolate cobra," and a "black panther," ultimately settling on the moniker of the "brown bomber," a nickname provided by a black journalist.[79]

Louis's stature only increased when three months later he knocked out the former heavyweight champ, Max Baer, in only four rounds in a fight witnessed by 88,000 fans and a gate of more than $1 million during the Depression. The victory engendered wild celebrations throughout black communities. In Chicago, novelist Richard Wright witnessed the scene: "Negroes poured out of beer taverns, pool rooms, barber shops, rooming houses and dingy flats and flooded the streets. They chanted 'Louis!' Louis! Louis!' throwing their hats in the air . . . They shook the hands of strangers. They clapped one another on the back. It was like a revival. Really, there was a religious feeling in the air. . . . They went stark, raving 'joy mad,' clapping their hands and forming long, undulating snake lines." Louis followed that impressive performance with a stoppage of Paulino Uzcudun, a tough Basque fighter who had been the European champion and had never been knocked down. Louis needed just four rounds to end the Spaniard's career.[80]

Another black writer from New York explained the growing importance of Louis for the black psyche. "What he is doing as a fighter will do more to show up the fallacy of 'inherent inferiority' of Negroes than could be done by all the anthropologists in the nation—so far as the ears and eyes of the white masses are concerned. One flash of his mighty brown arm is a better argument than a book—to a great majority of men. His personality is more impressive than a thousand sermons, for he will be felt where no sermon would ever be heard." Actor Ossie Davis remembered

Joe Louis knockout of an opponent hanging on the ropes. Courtesy of H. J. Lutcher Stark Center for Physical Culture and Sports, University of Texas at Austin.

that "Joe was our avenging angel. . . . He was spiritually necessary to our sense of who we were, to our manhood."[81]

While Louis ascended the heavyweight ranks, both Max Schmeling and Jim Braddock were resurrecting their boxing careers. Braddock's rise, decline, and rebirth are chronicled in the popular *Cinderella Man* movie, and on June 13, 1935, he gained the championship in a decision over Max Baer. Schmeling returned to the United States to meet the undefeated Louis, who had won all twenty-seven of his fights, twenty-three by knockout. The encounter had gained increasing political significance as the American media continued to portray Schmeling as a tool of the Nazis, and the U.S. Olympic team was in the midst of a potential boycott of the Games which were to open in Berlin a month after the bout. Even within the United States, the populace was divided as most Americans favored Louis but German Americans and many Southerners rooted for Schmeling. A journalist for the *Philadelphia Tribune* prematurely rejoiced by informing his black readers that after Louis's triumph they could expect great societal change. "Brothers, the battle is over. . . . Soon you will be able to travel all over the Southland, marry women of other colors if you so desire, go any place and do anything." The Nazi Party was unhappy with Schmeling because he had an American Jewish manager, Joe Jacobs, and for agreeing to fight a black man with potential repercussions for the party's Aryan supremacy doctrine if he lost. The international interest in the confrontation could be judged by worldwide radio broadcasts in English, Spanish, and German.[82]

Louis entered the fight an overwhelming favorite, and few gave Schmeling a chance. A smaller than expected crowd of about 40,000 showed up to watch what was expected to be a short fight; 60 million Americans tuned in on the radio. Louis started impressively, but Schmeling had studied Louis's previous fights assiduously on film and found a weakness: he dropped his left arm after delivering a blow. The German

Schmeling knocking down Joe Louis. Courtesy of H. J. Lutcher Stark Center for Physical Culture and Sports, University of Texas at Austin.

began exploiting that susceptibility to a right hand and connected in the fourth round, knocking Louis to the canvas for the first time in his professional career. Louis fought the remainder of the bout in a daze as Schmeling continued to pound with his right. Louis hung on until the twelfth round when his opponent landed a series of bludgeoning right hands that put Louis down for the count, his first defeat, which gave Schmeling the right to challenge Braddock for the world championship.

Singer Lena Horne and her band had been listening on the radio; she said that she "was near hysteria toward the end . . . and some of the men were crying." Likewise, poet Langston Hughes stated that he saw "grown men weeping like children and women sitting on the curbs with their heads in their hands."[83] The rest of black America reacted in several ways, some violently, but most fell into a gloom and depression captured by Maya Angelou: "My race groaned. It was our people falling. It was another lynching, yet another Black man hanging on a tree. One more woman ambushed and raped. . . . This might be the end of the world. If Joe lost we were back in slavery and beyond help. It would all be true, the accusations that we were lower types of human beings. Only a little higher than apes."[84]

The German radio announcer declared Schmeling "the greatest heavyweight of all time," and American media castigated Louis. A writer for the *Atlanta Journal* stated that "Louis did what all the negro prize fighters before him have done. He quit." Schmeling returned to Germany to a hero's welcome. The Nazis credited German discipline, intelligence, and courage for his triumph, providing greater impetus for the dissemination of Hitler's philosophy in the Olympic Games to be held in August 1936. Hitler predicted that his Third Reich would last a thousand years and he had plans drawn up for a monumental stadium to seat hundreds of thousands as a permanent site in Germany for the Olympic Games. The Nazis initiated the torch run from Greece to Germany in 1936 to symbolically link the grandeur of the ancient civilization to Hitler's fascist society. The Games would offer Hitler the opportunity to show the world the validity of his doctrine of Aryan supremacy, as the German Olympic committee banned Jews from its national teams. A host of African American athletes led by the indomitable Jesse Owens, who won four gold medals, discredited the fascist ideology in the track and field events, but Germany won the overall medal total, enabling the Germans to adhere to their claim of racial superiority.[85]

That claim would be tested again as Schmeling sought the world heavyweight championship, then in the hands of Jim Braddock. The champion rightfully should have offered the next title fight to Schmeling, the top contender, but his managers reasoned that Louis would be a better draw. They met in Chicago on June 22, 1937, which resulted in Louis's ascension to the throne with an eighth-round knockout. Black Americans rejoiced in wild celebrations throughout the United States, but the new champion did not consider himself to be the valid holder of the crown until he had regained his honor by defeating Schmeling. Louis won three title defenses, two by knockout, before he and Schmeling could agree on terms. Like it or not, Louis would represent all Americans in the rematch, which the media characterized as a political struggle. In Germany the Nazis increased their persecution of Jews, and annexed Austria. In May 1938 Hitler visited Rome to confer with Mussolini, and the fascist imperial government in Japan had already invaded China, Italy had taken over Ethiopia, and General Franco's fascist forces were engaged in an ultimately

Neighbors congratulating Joe Louis's mother after his victory over Jim Braddock. Courtesy of H. J. Lutcher Stark Center for Physical Culture and Sports, University of Texas at Austin.

successful takeover of Spain. As European governments acquiesced to fascist demands, it seemed as though the United States was the last hope as a stalwart defender of democracy. Joe Louis represented that hope.

The two symbolic combatants met on June 22, 1938, along with more than 66,000 spectators in Yankee Stadium, while another 60 million Americans listened in on the radio, and countless others heard the global broadcast in German, Spanish, and Portuguese. The contest had barely begun when Louis unleashed a fusillade of heavy blows on Schmeling, who finally landed one of his own and clinched for a respite; Louis resumed his onslaught. Halfway through the first round the challenger hung on the ropes but stood upright when the referee began a knockdown count, only to have Louis send him to the canvas with a devastating right. He got up again at the count of four, only to have Louis pummel him into final submission in only 2:04 of round one. Schmeling had landed only two blows of his own when his handlers threw in a towel and entered the ring, an automatic disqualification. The German broadcast of the fight to the homeland soon terminated abruptly.[86]

The celebration throughout America—particularly in black communities—started immediately. An onlooker in Harlem stated, "They rejoiced with all their might. . . . There was never anything like it. . . . Take a dozen Harlem Christmases, a score of New Year's eves, a bushel of July 4th's and maybe—yes maybe—you get a faint glimpse of the idea."[87] Black poet Langston Hughes paid homage to Joe Louis and his meaning for African Americans:

> Joe Louis is a man
> For men to imitate—
> When this country needed him,
> He did not stall or fail.
>
> Joe took up the challenge
> And joined up for war.
> Nobody had to ask him,
> "What are you waiting for?"
>
> As a private in the army
> Of his talents he gave free
> Two mighty boxing matches
> To raise funds for liberty

That's more than lots of others
Who still try to jim-crow Joe
Have either heart or mind to do—
So this is to let them know

That Joe Louis is a man for any man to imitate.
If everybody was like Joe Louis there'd be no
"Too little" or "too late."[88]

The real war erupted in 1939 when Hitler's forces invaded Poland, and the United States entered the global fray in 1941 shortly after the Japanese attack on Pearl Harbor in Hawaii. Joe Louis joined the still-segregated U.S. Army in 1942 and donated his winnings from two title defenses that year to the Army and Navy Relief Funds for survivors of servicemen killed in the war. He spent the remainder of the war giving boxing exhibitions for the troops in Europe, England, North Africa, Alaska, and the mainland United States and lobbying behind the scenes for better treatment for African American servicemen. Upon his discharge in 1945 the government awarded him the Legion of Merit. He resumed his career after the war, for despite his charity, the federal government charged him with the back taxes on his winnings. Louis held the title for nearly a dozen years, making twenty-five successful defenses. His 1946 rematch with Billy Conn, the first heavyweight title bout to be televised, netted almost $2 million. Louis lost a fifteen-round decision to Ezzard Charles in 1950 and was knocked out by Rocky Marciano a year later, two of the only three losses in his long career. His life went downhill thereafter with taxes and gambling debts, multiple marriages, and drug addiction. In later years he acted as a doorman at a Las Vegas establishment. When he died in 1981 he was buried in Arlington National Cemetery; it was Max Schmeling who paid for his funeral.[89]

The heroics of Joe Louis brought a sense of pride to African American communities, but did not change the social prohibitions in the South. Texas had banned interracial fights in 1933, a statute that remained for twenty years until overturned in a suit filed by "Sporty" Harvey, a black boxer. The preeminence of Joe Louis inspired other black fighters, however. Henry Armstrong (born Henry Jackson in 1912, the eleventh of fifteen children) began his professional ring career before Louis, but did not gain preeminence until the late 1930s, capturing the featherweight, welterweight, and lightweight championships within a span of ten months in 1937 and 1938. In 1937 he fought twenty-seven times, winning all of them and recording twenty-six knockouts. No one had or has ever held three titles simultaneously. Armstrong exemplified the growing confidence of black athletes in a white world and the power of boxing to symbolically, at least, right past wrongs when he stated that "you can't Jim Crow a left hook."[90]

On August 27, 1943, near the end of his long career, Armstrong lost a unanimous decision to a new star, Sugar Ray Robinson. Born Walker Smith, Jr. in Detroit in 1921, he idolized his neighbor, Joe Louis, and carried his bag to the gym as a young boy. His mother and father later separated, resulting in a move to New York in 1932. He embarked on a boxing career after dropping out of high school; too young for his first bout, he had to borrow the identification card of another boxer named Ray Robinson. He gained the appellation of "Sugar Ray" when a sportswriter described his performance as "sweet as sugar." His amateur record reached an astounding 85-0 as he won the New York Golden Gloves titles at the featherweight (1939) and lightweight (1940) divisions and then turned professional. He won his first forty pro fights, twenty-nine by a knockout. He lost a decision to Jake La Motta in a rematch in 1943, but beat him again only three weeks later. Robinson was drafted into the U.S. Army the next day, but spent much of his time giving boxing exhibitions, for which he insisted upon integrated audiences. The army administration provided helpful assistance to allow Robinson to fight throughout the year. The media chastised him for missing the boat for scheduled exhibitions with the Joe Louis troupe in Europe while he was hospitalized due to a fall, but he was honorably discharged in 1944. In 1946 he fought sixteen times, ending the year with a victory over Tommy Bell for the welterweight championship. By 1950 he had won another forty-eight consecutive bouts and toured Europe, adding the world middleweight championship in his sixth bout with Jake La Motta in 1951.[91]

Robinson made his first defense of the welterweight crown against Jimmy Doyle in Cleveland in 1947. He claimed that he had a premonition the night before the fight of killing Doyle in the ring and tried to call off the fight, but was urged to continue by the boxing commission and a variety of clergymen. In the eighth round, "Robinson lashed with one punch, a left hook. It caught Doyle on the point of the chin. He

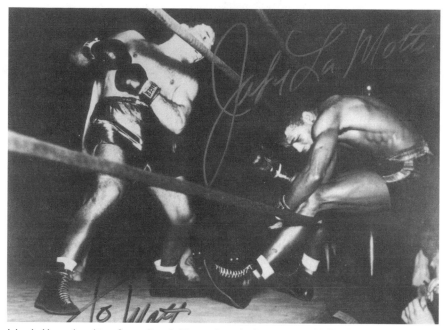

Jake LaMotta knocking Sugar Ray Robinson through the ropes in 1943. Courtesy of Frank Di Benedetto.

tipped backward, stiff and flat as a toy soldier. His head bounced on the ring floor twice. That didn't help him. But neither did that terrifying left hook or those dozens upon dozens of blows that Robinson struck from the opening gong to the fatalistic conclusion." Doyle died the next day and Robinson donated proceeds from his next four fights to set up a trust fund for Doyle's mother.[92]

When a congressional investigative commission later asked Robinson if he knew that he had Doyle in trouble, he responded "Sir, they pay me to get them in trouble." Though more caring than the comment appeared, Robinson, like all pro boxers, knew that their profession was a brutal and potentially lethal one. His six bouts with Jake La Motta were among the most brutal of that era. In 1951 Robinson lost for only the second time when Randy Turpin, a black Englishman, decisioned him in London. Two months later Robinson avenged the loss and regained the middle-weight title by stopping Turpin in the tenth round before more than 61,000 fans at the Polo Grounds in New York.[93]

Robinson won two fights in 1952 before challenging Joey Maxim for the light heavyweight championship in June of that year. In the sweltering summer heat of New York the temperature reached 104 degrees in Yankee Stadium. Robinson was well ahead on all the judges' cards, but he could not beat the heat. Suffering from heat prostration, he could not answer the bell for the fourteenth round and Maxim was declared the winner, effecting only the third blemish on Robinson's record. Robinson explained, "I was incoherent from that heat prostration. I passed out. But I went longer than the referee. Goldstein passed out before I did. He passed out in the tenth round." [94] After twelve years as a pro Robinson quit the ring to pursue dancing and acting ventures; unable to sustain his lavish lifestyle, he returned in January 1955. While Joe Louis offered the American public an abstemious anti–Jack Johnson version of a champion, Robinson presented a more flamboyant example: "The mass media of his glory days . . . frequently described him as handsome, charming, debonair, glamorous, and graceful." Like Jack Johnson, he had multiple wives; unlike Johnson, none were Caucasian, which did not arouse the ire of whites. He traveled in a pink Cadillac and owned several businesses in Harlem. His entourage included several servants, a barber, a chauffeur, a masseuse, a golf pro, a dwarf who acted as camp jester and interpreter, three trainers, his wife and other relatives, as well as 100 pieces of luggage. The car held particular significance for a downtrodden people: "That car was the Hope Diamond of Harlem. Everybody had to see it or touch it or both to make sure it was real. And to most of them it literally was the *Hope* Diamond because if skinny little Walker Smith could come off the streets to own a car like that, maybe they could too." Robinson enacted his newfound black agency by negotiating his own contracts, requiring promoters to pay him what he knew he was worth, and refusing to fight if his demands were not met.[95]

After a two-and-a-half-year layoff and at the age of thirty-four, the speed, punching power, and brilliant footwork with which Robinson had dazzled fans and bewildered opponents was no longer what it had been. He won two short title fights by knockouts against Bobo Olson in 1955 and 1956 to regain and retain the middleweight championship, but then lost it to Gene Fullmer in 1957, who won a fifteen-round decision. In the rematch five months later, Robinson scored a fifth-round knockout to regain the title. In September of 1957 he lost it to Carmen Basilio by a split decision in Yankee Stadium in a fight that *Ring* magazine declared the Fight of the Year. The same two opponents met six months later and again *Ring* judged it to be the best fight of 1958: Robinson won by a split decision and held the title for two years. After two losses to Paul Pender in 1960 Robinson managed one more title match with Gene Fullmer in December of that year, which ended in a draw. Fullmer retained the title and Robinson soldiered on until 1965 without further glory until the age of forty-four. He had been the world champion six times in a twenty-five-year career that included more than 200 bouts. He had knocked out more than half of his opponents, and sixteen of his nineteen losses occurred after his initial retirement.[96]

With life in the ring behind him, Robinson turned to business ventures and founded the Sugar Ray Youth Foundation in Los Angeles to help disadvantaged youth. Throughout his career Robinson had favored the least fortunate. He explained, "I was born poor. I learned early what it was to need help. If God blessed me with the talent to make real big money then he also entrusted me with the responsibility to care for those without talent."[97] He lived a full life and said that he had no regrets, but so many bouts had taken their toll. In his later years he developed Alzheimer's disease and died on April 12, 1989—but not without leaving a lasting legacy. His reign as champion coincided with a growing civil rights movement. "He was a hero to a generation of young black men . . . Muhammad Ali called him 'my idol' and borrowed his dancing style. Sugar Ray Leonard borrowed his name. In an era when African Americans were supposed to be humble, docile, and restrained, Robinson embodied black pride and success." The Associated Press named him the greatest boxer of the twentieth century in 1999.[98]

Robinson ushered in the civil turbulence of the 1960s and race played perhaps the most prominent role in the social upheaval. The black migration from the South to urban centers in the North that had started in World War I continued over the next half-century. World War II, allegedly fought to ensure liberty and democracy, seemed hypocritical to blacks who lacked basic rights and opportunities in the United States. Segregation was legal until the Supreme Court overturned the policy in the *Brown v. Board of Education* case in 1954. Southerners did not acquiesce to the ruling willingly, and black Americans, eventually led by Reverend Martin Luther King, embarked upon a civil rights movement to enact social change. Sport had been in the forefront of the movement—not only boxing, but professional football and basketball had integrated their ranks soon after the war, and Jackie Robinson desegregated Major League Baseball in 1947. While such athletes exemplified the potential of sports and promoted racial pride, the vast majority of blacks and an increasing number of Hispanics lived in dismal conditions with inadequate education in overcrowded and deteriorating cities. Failure to meet their basic needs resulted in urban strife, riots, and even armed resistance marked by the formation of the Black Panthers in 1966, who espoused socialistic practices at odds with the dominant white society. One black athlete became a symbol for the era: "Black discontent magnified itself in the person of Muhammad Ali. Both loved and reviled, Ali transcended sport and became a focal point of many tensions of the era. With Ali, sport became a stage for the cultural warfare taking place in America, as rebels battled traditionalists in a struggle to define the nature of sport and the larger society. . . . Athletes tested authority with new styles and innovations and provoked radical change in the norms, standards, and mores of mainstream American society. This movement, termed the "Athletic Revolution," found its leader in Muhammad Ali."[99]

Born Cassius Clay in Louisville, Kentucky, in 1942, Ali took up boxing at a young age and progressed rapidly. He won the light heavyweight gold medal at the 1960 Olympic Games and embarked on a professional career as a heavyweight. In the ring he clowned, danced, and destroyed his opponents with fast hands and feet. Outside the ring he recited poetry, bragged that he was "the greatest," conducted ranting interviews, and predicted the rounds in which he would dispose of his opponents. The ultimate showman, he attracted legions of new fans who either loved or hated his antics; regardless, his skills could not be denied. In 1964 he faced the seemingly invincible Sonny Liston for the heavyweight championship. The sullen Liston, a convicted felon, bludgeoned the previous champion, Floyd Patterson, on two occasions that ended in two first-round knockouts. Gamblers listed Clay as a 7 to 1 underdog. He astonished fight fans by winning the title when Liston could not answer the bell for the start of the seventh round. After the fight Clay announced his name change and his conversion to the Nation of Islam, a separatist Black Muslim faith, which many whites viewed as a mysterious and anti-American threat to the established order. While he had amused fans and the media, some of whom even lauded him for his patriotism before his religious conversion, that changed abruptly with his announcement. "For the first time here was a black American sports hero who would not allow himself to be defined according to white racist stereotypes. . . . Clay was going to create his own identity and shove it down their throats."[100] The next year he knocked out Liston in the first round of their rematch, solidifying his hold on the title.

Tours to Africa and Asia increased his global reach and brought previously uninterested groups, particularly Muslims, to become boxing fans and Ali supporters. Ali stated, "I can't name a country where they don't know me. If another fighter's going to be that big, he's going to have to be a Muslim, or else he won't get nations like Indonesia, Lebanon, Iran, Saudi Arabia, Pakistan, Syria, Egypt, and Turkey—those are countries that don't usually follow boxing." A member of a Pakistani family living in Scotland proclaimed that "Ali belonged to *us* and we would observe with a mixture of awe and envy, especially at how white people *respected* Ali the Muslim. . . . [He] was a source of inspiration and solace in the racist climate of the time."[101]

Using the heavyweight throne as his pulpit, Ali became more defiant and more influential. "Unlike previous black champions like Joe Louis or Floyd Patterson, he extolled his blackness and demanded respect from white fans and the white controlled media. . . . To many he seemed the devil incarnate, and for others he represented black retribution." By 1967 he remained undefeated in the ring having beaten nine challengers, seven by knockout. Like Jack Johnson, the federal government indicted him for actions outside of the ring when he refused induction into the army at the height of the Vietnam war. He claimed conscientious objector status based on his religion and that he had no quarrel with the Viet Cong who "had never called him a nigger." The government levied a fine of $10,000 and sentenced him to five years in prison. While he awaited his appeal to the Supreme Court, state boxing associations stripped him of his boxing license, which curtailed his employment in the ring: "Stripped of his title and unable to pursue his livelihood, he assumed the role of a principled martyr who placed his values above lucre, fame, and glory. His enforced absence only made him more celebrated as the antiwar movement escalated."[102]

By 1967 even Dr. Martin Luther King, Jr. opposed the war, which had enrolled a vastly inordinate number of working-class youth, both black and white—as many as 30,000 to 40,000 per month—to fill the growing need for combatants. In an April 1967 speech delivered at the Riverside Church in New York, King stated:

> We have been repeatedly faced with the cruel irony of watching Negro and white boys on TV screens as they kill and die together for a nation that has been unable to seat them together in the same schools. . . . Half of all Negroes live in substandard housing and he has half the income of white. There is twice as much unemployment and infant mortality among Negroes. [Yet] at the beginning of 1967 twice as many died in action—20.6 percent—in proportion to their numbers in the population as a whole.[103]

Denied the opportunity to pursue his profession, Ali became a public speaker—often on college campuses—and assumed the role of a leader in the athletic revolution. As early as 1965 black football players organized a boycott of the AFL all-star game due to several grievances, including lower wages than their white counterparts, a lack of black coaches, and the "stacking" of black athletes in positions that required skills but lacked any leadership opportunities. Black players on college football teams revolted and went on strike due to the lack of black coaches and educational facilities, resulting in boycotts at thirty-seven schools and three head coaches being ousted from their positions. In 1968 Harry Edwards tried to organize all black athletes into a boycott of the Olympic Games. The athletes' demands included the restoration of Ali's title. Although Edwards's efforts ultimately failed when students left for summer vacations, the Olympic sprinters Tommie Smith and John Carlos produced the infamous Black Power salute broadcast around the world, for which they were sent home the next day. The following year Curt Flood, an all-star outfielder for the St. Louis Cardinals, refused a trade to the Philadelphia Phillies, which challenged the reserve clause that had held players in bondage since the nineteenth century. The reserve clause in players' contracts dictated that all players were exclusively employed or reserved to the team that signed them to a contract and could not be traded or employed by any other team without the consent of the original team. Such conditions kept players' salaries low and denied them the right to negotiate a release or free agency to pursue employment with another team.[104]

Black discontent exploded in violence in Los Angeles, Cleveland, Newark, and Detroit. Black Power advocates called for greater social, economic, and political power. Ali had even formed his own corporation to control the economic aspects of his boxing enterprises. Whites feared that the Nation of Islam would take over boxing if Ali held the title, and efforts were made to boycott his fights and commercial broadcasts. Ali retaliated by taking his next three fights to Europe, where he made even more money than in America. That expansion of black economic power was curtailed with Ali's indictment. While the Nation of Islam advocated a separate black nation, the militant Black Panther Party confronted the white power structure in violent encounters. Ali remained at the forefront of the antiwar controversy. In 1966 he reaffirmed his opposition to the war, but did so relative to his stand on racial equality and social justice when he stated, "If I thought the war was going to bring freedom and equality to 22 million of my people they wouldn't have to draft me, I'd join tomorrow."[105]

After more than three years the Supreme Court overturned his conviction, but Ali had already discovered a means to return to the ring by fighting in Georgia, a state without a boxing commission. After stopping two white opponents he met Joe Frazier, the recognized champion, in Madison Square Garden in 1971, the first of their three encounters, considered among the best in boxing history. The initial event proved to be the most publicized and the most lucrative in American sports history up to that time. Frazier had garnered the title while Ali was on hiatus, and both entered the contest undefeated. Ali mocked Frazier as the champion of whites, and the animosity as well as the contrasting fighting styles made for heroic battles over the nature of blackness and the rights to authenticity. Frazier's brawling, never-retreat attitude complemented Ali's slick footwork and boxing skills as they traded both physical and verbal blows over their claims to black manhood. In the first encounter Frazier retained his title with a unanimous decision after fifteen rounds.[106]

Ali then traveled the world with victories in Switzerland, Japan, Canada, Ireland, and Indonesia, and traded wins with Ken Norton before obtaining a rematch with Frazier in New York on January 28, 1974. This time Ali won the unanimous decision, but Frazier had already lost the title to George Foreman the previous year. Ali's triumph enabled him to challenge Foreman for the championship in a bout held in Kinshasa, Zaire, for a $10 million purse with global significance, as the fight was broadcast to more than 120 countries. The site held significance for all black people as the first African nation to host a fight of such magnitude. The two competitors represented polar opposites of the cultural wars then taking place in the United States. Ali represented the racially proud, antiestablishment, antiwar martyr, while Foreman served as the darling of the conservative white establishment. While other black athletes at the 1968 Olympic Games protested and delivered the Black Power salute to the televised world, Foreman captured the gold medal among the heavyweight boxers, then paraded around the ring waving a small, American flag, a symbol of meritocracy. He gave thanks for the opportunity that sport had provided for him and its deliverance from the streets and a life of crime.[107]

Foreman had dispensed with the tough Joe Frazier in only two rounds, and some sportswriters feared that the giant might actually kill Ali in the ring, as the big slugger sported a 40-0 record with thirty-seven knockouts. Ali, however, enjoyed the psychological advantage. He arrived first in Zaire (now the Democratic Republic of the Congo) and convinced the populace that Foreman was a Belgian, the former and brutal colonizers of the country. When Foreman showed up with two Belgian shepherd dogs it only reinforced the perception of a transgressor. Ali would command home court advantage in a seemingly neutral country. Once the fight commenced Foreman pounded away as expected, while much to the chagrin of his trainers, Ali languished on the ropes protecting himself from the thunderous blows with his gloves around his head and elbows tucked closely to his sides in what he termed his rope-a-dope strategy. By the eighth round Foreman had exhausted himself without securing the presumptive knockout and Ali then unleashed his own arsenal of weapons that turned the tide, knocking out the champion and reclaiming the throne. Ali soon basked in worldwide acclaim as a Muslim champion, and a black champion that represented a vast number of the world's population. He clearly transcended race, religion, and his American citizenship to become a global icon. He published an autobiography the next year, and a film of his life, titled *The Greatest*, followed in 1977.[108]

Such acclaim set the stage for the final bout with Joe Frazier on October 1, 1975, held in Manila, capital of the Philippines, which brought Ali's traveling spectacle to Asia for the championship bout and the rubber match after each had beaten the other in previous contests. It proved to be a contest of indomitable will as much as fighting ability, as each combatant tried to impose himself on the other in a furious struggle that pushed both men to their physical and psychological limits. They battered one another for fourteen rounds; Frazier could not muster the strength for the final encounter of their brutal dance. Ali admitted that if Frazier had not conceded it was doubtful that he could have continued either. *Ring* magazine extolled the vicious clash as the Fight of the Year, but it took a great toll on both participants. Frazier would fight only two more times, while Ali engaged in ten bouts before retiring.[109]

Ali left much more than a sterling boxing record as his legacy. He served as a symbol of a divided America during the 1960s and beyond. He challenged the federal government and many of its citizens to honor its basic beliefs and accordant rights to freedom of speech, freedom of religion, and human dignity.

> His stance was an inspiration for many black activists in America and this black civil rights movement was the catalyst for other human rights movements in America and around the globe. Black Power energized and educated black Americans, introducing many to the concept of political pluralism. It spurred new interest in African liberation struggles and the plight of the powerless world wide. Newly sensitized to the political nature of oppression, Black Power converts set out to remedy the situation by forming numerous political action caucuses and grass roots community associations. These, in turn, served as often utilized models for the various ethnic, gender and class consciousness movements of the seventies and eighties.[110]

A generation after his confrontation with the white power structure, in an age when glamorous black athletes had won widespread acceptance and opted for the lucrative endorsements of commodified capitalist culture rather than Ali's adherence to principle before profit, America realized his true worth as a rebel with a cause. He was chosen to light the Olympic flame at the 1996 Olympic Games hosted by Atlanta as a global symbol of a nation better for his being. In 1999 both *Sports Illustrated* and the British Broadcasting Company named him the sportsman of the century. Maya Angelou captured his global appeal when she stated that Ali "belonged to everyone . . . his impact recognizes no continent, no language, no colour, no ocean. He belongs to us all."[111]

The social progress gained by Ali's efforts seemed to take a reverse turn in the tragic career of Mike Tyson. The distinguished writer and avid boxing fan Joyce Carol Oates described Tyson as a "prehistoric creature rising from a fearful crevice in our collective subconscious," and "a tragedy in progress."[112] She further contended that "he seemed to invite his fate outside the ring, with sadomasochistic persistence, testing the limits of his celebrity's license to offend by ever-escalating acts of aggression and sexual effrontery."[113] Tyson's life seemed doomed from the start. Born in the Bedford-Stuyvesant slum of Brooklyn in 1966, his birth father seemed nonexistent and played no further role in his life. At age nine he and his mother moved to the equally deprived neighborhood of Brownsville, and Tyson began roaming the streets engaged in a life of crime. "The stealing, lying, and violence that eventually led to his institutionalization were similar to the antisocial behavior of Italian fighters like Jake La Motta and Rocky Graziano whose boyhood and adolescent lives Tyson's greatly resembles. Had it not been for their fighting skills, the very combination of derring-do, cynicism, and barbarity that guaranteed their survival in the short term would have killed them all as young men. Instead they were channeled into the entertainment industry largely intact."[114]

By the age of twelve Tyson had been committed to the Tryon Reformatory in upstate New York. There he came to the attention of a physical education teacher who introduced him to the aged, sage, and ascetic boxing trainer, Cus D'Amato, who ran a gym in the nearby town of Catskill. D'Amato had trained heavyweight champion Floyd Patterson and light heavyweight champ Jose Torres, but had eschewed the limelight for more than a decade. Upon witnessing the vast potential of Tyson in the ring, D'Amato asserted that this was the one he had been waiting for his whole life. D'Amato gained custody of Tyson, who officially became his ward upon the death of Tyson's mother in 1983. D'Amato and Camille Ewald, his common-law wife, served as surrogate parents thereafter, instilling a level of discipline, an education based on the boy's interest in boxing, and thorough instruction in the fight game with the intention that Tyson would surpass D'Amato's earlier pupil, Floyd Patterson, as the youngest person ever to achieve the heavyweight championship.[115]

Tyson showed his potential in a sterling, but brief, amateur career that featured spectacular knockout victories. He embarked on his professional crusade with the same malicious intent in 1985. "Once Tyson became a professional fighter, 'Iron Mike' was born. This was Tyson as the austere warrior: coming into the ring crouching and weaving like Jack Dempsey, throwing punches like Henry Armstrong, swaggering like John L. Sullivan, eyeing his prey as scientifically as Joe Gans."[116] He seemed like an invincible force that embodied the qualities of the greats of the past. D'Amato died in November of that year, by which time his young protégé had already amassed eleven knockout wins. Eight of his foes did not finish the first round and only one lasted for as long as four rounds. So powerful were his punches that early opponents claimed that it felt like they had been hit by a blackjack or a sledgehammer. Tyson would go on to defeat twenty-seven opponents, all but two by knockouts, before he met Trevor Berbick for the heavyweight championship on November 22, 1986, in Las Vegas. Berbick lasted two rounds as Tyson fulfilled his and D'Amato's dream by gaining the crown as a twenty-year-old. With the death of D'Amato, Kevin Rooney became his trainer and Jim Jacobs and Bill Cayton continued as his comanagers who attempted to shield him from the corrupting influences and political intrigues of the sport. Tyson had only to concentrate on perfecting his boxing skills, but the relative harmony would dissipate with the death of D'Amato.[117]

Tyson married aspiring actress Robin Givens in February 1988. She and her mother, Ruth Roper, formed Mike Tyson Enterprises to control Tyson's immense and growing finances. Givens also introduced her husband to the real estate mogul Donald Trump, who saw the potential for Tyson fights in his casinos. The ill-fated and stormy marriage lasted only eight months, still long enough for Tyson's image to be irrevocably damaged. Givens provided a televised interview to Barbara Walters, accompanied by a sedated Tyson, that portrayed the wife-mother team as a saintly combination with the best intentions who had to contend with a manic-depressive husband who beat his wife. Newspapers, magazines, and television shows assiduously reported conjugal flare-ups throughout the union, in which the Givens-Roper duo pushed Tyson away from his estranged handlers. Kevin Rooney was fired that year, despite the fact that Tyson had gone undefeated with thirty-five straight victories. Convicted felon turned boxing promoter Don King saw his own opportunity and convinced Tyson that his wife had been engaging in an extramarital affair with Trump, destroying any possibility of an amicable resolution to differences. King also employed two of Tyson's acquaintances to alienate him from his former boxing partners by claiming racist intentions and their own personal benefits. Don King soon controlled the promotion of Tyson's future fights and the rights to the marketing of spin-off ventures.[118]

Tyson commanded a global audience and British sportswriter Hugh McIlvanney asserted that King "has precipitated decay in practically every fighter with whom he has been associated."[119] The case proved no different for Tyson. His new managers under the employment of King, John Horne and Rory Holloway, had little experience in the sport. They promoted a thug image popular with young inner-city African Americans and an increasing number of white suburbanites and fostered by the hip-hop culture and its recording artists. Tyson had been charitable before he encountered Horne and Holloway, routinely presenting street dwellers with $100 bills to assuage their misery. His largesse and his entourage only grew under King, Horne, and Holloway. Tyson bestowed turkeys on the poor and bought jewelry and cars for his friends. He even offered his slightly damaged Bentley to Port Authority police officers after a minor traffic accident. Although a haphazard driver who usually employed a paid chauffeur, Tyson bought himself a host of luxury vehicles that included a Rolls Royce, two Porsches, two Ferraris, two Mercedes, a Range Rover, and a Lamborghini, as well as a mansion befitting the heavyweight champion. He hired Scott Ledoux, already retired and down on his luck with two kids and a recently deceased wife, as a sparring partner. Ledoux lasted only one encounter, but Tyson kept him on the payroll at $1,000 per week.[120]

Tyson's beneficence was seemingly matched by his primitive savagery. He stated, "I try to catch my opponent on the tip of his nose, because I want to punch the bone into the brain."[121] He routinely insulted opponents, telling Donovan "Razor" Ruddock that he would "make you my girlfriend."[122] His demeanor became more surly and belligerent. His ring record reached an unblemished 37-0, but wild partying and womanizing began to erode Tyson's feared skills. When Don King arranged a bout against journeyman James "Buster" Douglas in Tokyo in February 1990, Tyson hardly bothered with training as he and King anticipated a more lucrative encounter with Evander Holyfield. Such hedonism and disregard for the opponent cost Tyson dearly. He managed to knock Douglas down in the eighth round, but the challenger dominated the next two rounds, knocking Tyson to the canvas in the tenth where he was unable to get up by the count of ten. Don King protested the result, claiming that the referee had given Douglas the favor of a long count in the eighth-round knockdown as his enumeration differed from that of the official timekeeper by two seconds, but the referee's decision stood. Tyson had never been knocked down before and the result is considered to be perhaps the biggest upset in boxing history as Tyson had been a 42 to 1 favorite, according to Las Vegas oddsmakers.[123]

Douglas lost his title in his first defense to the undefeated Evander Holyfield, who had already captured the cruiserweight crown; before Tyson could challenge the new champ his aberrant behavior sent him to prison for three years. In 1991 Tyson attended the Miss Black America beauty pageant in Indianapolis, where he met Desiree Washington, an eighteen-year-old contestant, who agreed to accompany him to his room at nearly 2 a.m. Tyson contended that the two engaged in consensual sex, while Washington cried that she had been raped. A jury sided with Washington in a still-disputed trial that had limited testimonies. While in prison Tyson, who had been raised Catholic, converted to Islam and initiated a program of self-education in which he read extensively, including literary classics. Seemingly a new man, Tyson forged a comeback upon his release. His first bout with Peter McNeeley proved an utter mismatch, but garnered record revenues in cable television and global pay-per-view sales. In 1996 he captured the World Boxing Council version of the heavyweight championship by stopping Frank Bruno in three rounds and followed that with the World Boxing Association title with a first-round knockout of Bruce Seldon, setting the stage for a battle with Evander Holyfield.[124]

The two met on November 9, 1996, and despite being a distinct underdog, Holyfield prevailed in an eleventh-round technical knockout. Tyson complained that Holyfield had headbutted him throughout the fight without penalty. The inevitable rematch occurred on June 28, 1997, and grossed more than $100 million in revenue. When Holyfield again butted Tyson, causing a cut to the eyelid, he clinched and retaliated by biting his opponent's ear. Referee Mill Lane stopped the fight, but eventually allowed it to continue, and Tyson repeated his action, biting off a piece of Holyfield's right ear, effectively disqualifying him. The media castigated him relentlessly as sportswriters called him "a nightmare in a suit," a "psycho-pup," and a "mad pit bull." Others characterized his behavior as "dirty, disgusting, repellent, bestial, loathsome, vile, animalistic, vampiristic, deranged, maniacal, cannibalistic, murderous, cowardly." The outcry resulted in the forfeiture of part of his $30 million purse and the temporary loss of his boxing license.[125]

Tyson resumed his career in a knockout of Francois Botha in South Africa in 1999, but his attempt at a comeback was again derailed by incarceration for attacking two motorists after an auto accident the previous year, for which he served another nine months in jail. Still, he remained a top drawing card. He engaged in five more bouts without defeat, but a failed drug test resulted in a retroactive no-decision against Andrew Golota. By 2002 he managed yet another championship battle, this time with Lennox Lewis, which garnered over $106 million in pay-per-view subscriptions. The interest proved anticlimactic as Lewis scored an eighth-round knockout. Tyson faced additional turmoil outside the ring as his second wife (from 1997 to 2003) Monica Turner, a pediatrician and mother of two of his children, filed for divorce. Despite more than $300 million in ring earnings, he had to file for bankruptcy in 2003. He owed $12 million in taxes, and he learned that Don King had been deducting large sums from his account while he was in jail for business expenses and to employ King's wife and daughter in menial roles. Such burdens forced Tyson to continue to box despite his apparent loss of ability. He retired after two consecutive knockout losses in 2004 and 2005. Two years later Tyson admitted to an addiction to cocaine, and his troubles continued. In 2009 a daughter (one of eight children) died as a result of a household accident. Shortly thereafter he married Lakiha "Kiki" Spicer, the mother of two of his children, a union that seems to have brought some peace to his tragic life, which continues to fascinate the general public and resulted in renewed celebrity status as a pop-culture figure. Tyson has appeared in movies, television shows, and on the stage. His one-man show, directed by Spike Lee and entitled *Mike Tyson: Undisputed Truth*, has been acclaimed by critics. "Tyson turns out to be a compelling storyteller—funny, self-aware and fully capable of filling a vast stage . . . while holding a large audience at full attention in a way that many experienced actors never quite master. . . . And if ever there were proof that American life is not only FULL of second acts—but capable of supplying at least a dirty dozen of them—this is your show of shows. Only in America." Tyson claims to have made personal apologies for his past transgressions and states that he can now live in peace with himself and others—but he cannot erase his past. He might have been the greatest heavyweight of all time, yet he was recognized as "one of the most compelling anti-heroes in the history of the sport." He not only squandered his chances, but reignited some of the racist stereotypes that Ali had so courageously dispelled.[126]

The Rise of Caribbean and Asian Champions

The 1920s brought a wide array of foreign boxers in search of laurels and big paydays to the United States as it became the global nexus for fight promotions engineered by the likes of Tex Rickard and other entrepreneurs in the expansive economy of the era. One of the early stars, Panama Al Brown (Alfonso Teophilo Brown), arrived in New York in 1922. Born in Colon, Panama, he had learned to box by watching Americans in the Canal Zone, and an agent noticed his unique frame and abilities. At 5 feet 10 ½ inches and less than 120 pounds, Brown possessed a 76-inch reach, greater than many heavyweights. Whites derisively characterized him as a "tall, skinny freak." He worked as a New York busboy while fighting as a flyweight, but found his greatest success as he grew into a bantamweight, and was the first Hispanic to win a boxing championship when he captured the vacant title in 1929. He would hold it until 1935, practicing his craft on a global scale by fighting often in Canada, Europe, and even in North Africa. In a career that lasted until 1942, Brown compiled a 131-19-13 record and was never stopped in any bout—although he refused to fight his close friend, Kid Chocolate of Cuba.[127]

American troops occupied Cuba after the Spanish-American War and maintained a large degree of control over the island until 1934. Cuban interest in boxing increased after the famed Jack Johnson–Jess Willard match held in Havana in 1915. By 1922 the local newspaper, *La Noche*, organized an annual boxing tournament for newsboys. Eligio Sardiñas, the youngest of six children, was born in 1910 to a washerwoman, the daughter of slaves, and her laborer husband who died five years later. An older brother apparently boxed under the name of Chocolate, and Eligio assumed the moniker of Kid Chocolate. Entering the tournament as a twelve-year-old combatant he went undefeated for two years, beating a fifteen-year-old for the seventy-pound championship and amassing an unblemished record as an amateur fighter. He turned professional in 1927 at age seventeen, and after a string of victories in Cuba, headed for New York.[128]

There he enjoyed immediate success and drew large crowds of fans, but his black skin relegated him to a residence in Harlem. He returned to Cuba often and on one such occasion in 1929 the multitude of local fans awaiting his triumphant return to Havana caused a pier to collapse. He enjoyed similar esteem in New York, where restaurant owners disregarded their segregation policies to welcome him to their establishments. He dated dancers from the famed Cotton Club and heaped candy upon children in Harlem. At the renowned Apollo Theater, African Americans gave him a standing ovation and adopted him as their own. In 1931 he captured the world junior lightweight championship and added the world featherweight crown the following year. The Associated Press, United Press International, and radio broadcasts kept his homeland fans abreast of his accomplishments. According to one writer, "In an era when athletic achievement was viewed across the globe as a proxy for the overall capacity of national or racial groups, Kid Chocolate's success loomed large for a nation seeking to establish its capacity for self-governance in the face of North American political tutelage and the racist ideology used to justify it."[129]

After 1933 his skills and successes diminished, leading eventually to retirement in 1938; "Like Jack Johnson he had squandered his money on a lavish lifestyle that included six cars, but the Cuban government, then under the nationalistic dictator Fulgencio Batista, provided him with a house and a lifetime pension for bringing honor to Cuba." On his return to his native island he became an instructor at the national boxing academy. Even after the communist revolution of 1959 overthrew the government, Fidel Castro reinstated his pension. He remains a national hero to this day in Cuba.[130]

The United States obtained and subjugated Puerto Rico in the wake of the Spanish-American War, bringing its attitudes toward race to the island. An American anthropologist who studied the Puerto Ricans for three years came to the conclusion that they were "primitive, illiterate, idolatrous, destitute, superstitious, and dark-skinned."[131] Whereas the indigenous people had eighteen different terms for skin color and judged others by their character, Americans seemed fixated on skin color. The YMCA instituted an extensive program of sports, restricting those "too dark and of Negro blood" from using the facilities. Such arbitrary decisions relegated some Puerto Ricans to lower-class status and produced conflicting identities.[132]

During the 1930s Puerto Rican athletes began to establish reputations beyond the shores of the island territory, enhancing their national identity and a greater sense of self-esteem. Puerto Rico entered the Central American and Caribbean Games competition, similar to a regional Olympics, in 1930 as a separate nation, distinct from though not completely separate from the United States. Boxing, legalized in 1927, provided Puerto Ricans with their first athletic hero. Sixto Escobar, the first Puerto Rican champion, succeeded Panama Al Brown to the bantamweight title when he staked a claim to the crown by scoring a ninth-round knockout over Mexican boxer Baby Casanova in 1934 and solidified that hold with a win over Pete Sanstol a year later. He unified the disputed title with a victory over Tony Marino, whom he had knocked down five times in the second round en route to a thirteenth-round technical knockout. Puerto Ricans feted Escobar upon his return to the islands and named a stadium after him to commemorate his triumph. His 1937 title defense in San Juan was the first to be contested on the island, and it was claimed that he "brought the game of boxing at [sic] Puerto Rico from nothing more than club-fighting to international spotlight, and spawned a whole new generation of fight fans and boxers."[133]

One of the "new generation," Jose Torres—who became an Olympian silver medalist as a middleweight and light heavyweight world champion, as well as president of the World Boxing Organization—stated that Escobar helped Puerto Ricans overcome their inferiority complex during an era "when the island suffered an identity problem; when it had a confused culture; when we saw any non-Puerto Rican individual as superior to us." Puerto Rico beamed at Escobar's accomplishments and their restoration of national pride. His obituary in 1979 named him "the father of modern Puerto Rican boxing" and "a national shrine."[134]

Carlos Ortiz added to the Puerto Rican laurels in the post–World War II era as he ruled the lightweight division from 1962 to 1968. He had turned pro in 1955 before the age of twenty and fought until 1972, compiling a ring record of sixty-one wins against only seven losses and one draw. Jose Torres, born in Puerto Rico in 1936, joined the U.S. Army at the age of eighteen, where he learned how to box, and turned pro in 1958. In 1965 he knocked out Willie Pastrano to become the first Hispanic boxer to ascend the light heavyweight throne. He retired four years later after suffering only three defeats in his pro career, but enjoyed a distinguished livelihood as a New York state athletic commissioner from 1984 to 1988 and presiding over the WBO from 1990 to 1995.[135]

Sixto Escobar's contemporary, Alberto "Baby" Arizmendi, born in Mexico in 1913, began boxing as a child as an antidote to polio. He allegedly had 140 amateur bouts before turning pro at the age of thirteen in 1927. Although he moved to Los Angeles and later served in the U.S. Navy, he is recognized as the first Mexican champion, king of the featherweights in 1932. His boxing career continued to 1942 in which he amassed a record of 84-26-14.[136]

Kid Gavilan (Hawk), born Gerardo Gonzalez in Cuba in 1926, entered the professional ranks as Arizmendi left. A practitioner of the bolo punch over his fifteen-year career, he gained the world welterweight title in 1951. A year later he successfully defended his crown in the first integrated match in Florida. A colorful favorite, he helped to usher in the television era of the sport during the 1950s, retiring in 1958 with a record of 108-30-5 and recognition as one of the greatest welterweights to grace the ring.[137]

Gavilan was followed by Emile Griffith, born on St. Thomas in the U.S. Virgin Islands, as a welterweight champion. Griffith began his pro career in 1958 and won the title in 1961. Over the next four years he lost and regained the championship four more times as he engaged in a bitter rivalry with Benny Kid Paret that eventually resulted in Paret's death in 1962. Griffith moved on to temporarily conquer the middleweights in 1966, a title that he lost and then regained the following year. He continued to ply his trade for another eleven years before finishing with an 85-24-2 record.[138]

Among Asian fighters, Pancho Villa represented the best of a host of early Filipino fighters who traveled to the United States in the early decades of the twentieth century. Speedy Dado, born Diosdado Posadas on Christmas Day 1906, challenged for both the featherweight (1933) and bantamweight (1935) titles, but came up short on both occasions. Dado fought mostly in California, where a large Filipino community provided fan support over his long career (1925–1940). He compiled a 97-42-16 record, the vast majority of his defeats coming after 1933. Dado also served as a chauffeur for the movie star Mae West, who took a special interest in fighters.[139] Ceferino Garcia also served West as both chauffeur and bodyguard. He proved even better than Dado by winning the middleweight championship in 1939 in a long career that lasted from 1923 to 1945. Garcia adopted the bolo punch, developed by Filipino fighters as early as the 1920s and marking their particular national identity (later used by Cuban boxers as well), to become a fan favorite in the Filipino community. Hawaiian plantation owners imported large numbers of Filipino laborers, and when the territory legalized boxing in 1930, boxing promoters counted on their interest in boxing to turn a profit. At least a dozen Filipino boxers traveled the boxing circuit between California and Hawaii during the following decade, and when Garcia gained the championship in 1939 his first title defense occurred in Manila, further integrating the Philippines within the global boxing network. Garcia claimed that he had been inspired by the reception of Pancho Villa that he witnessed as a boy, and that he would not return to his homeland until he had become a champion as well. His return was treated as a national holiday and he rewarded his fans with a knockout victory over the American challenger, Glenn Lee.[140]

Gabriel "Flash" Elorde followed Garcia as a stalwart Filipino champion after World War II. His pro career started at the age of sixteen in 1951 and lasted for twenty years. It took him only one year to capture the national bantamweight championship in his homeland and he then accumulated the Asian titles in the bantamweight, featherweight, and lightweight classes. From 1960 to 1967 he ruled as the super featherweight champion of the world. Elorde proved to be a popular and philanthropic champ, using his winnings to construct a chapel, an orphanage, and other school buildings in the Philippines. In gratitude for his efforts he was presented with numerous national awards and a papal medal from Pope John Paul II.[141]

The rivalry between the United States and Japan became evident shortly after the modernization of the Asian country in the late nineteenth century. The Japanese had already adopted baseball in the 1870s and challenged American teams by the 1890s. After Japan defeated China in a war in 1894–1895, the Japanese considered themselves to be rightful heirs to the Pacific region, and that perception only increased when Japan quickly vanquished Russia in 1904–1905. Americans voiced their disagreement in racial terms: "All of us who have lived in the Far East know that in practice these yellow and brown peoples must be guided and often driven in a forward direction so that they do not obstruct the progress of the world nor infringe on the rights of other nations."[142] As early as 1910 General Leonard Wood determined that the Japanese would challenge the United States for hegemony in the Pacific. He stated, "Japan is going ahead in a perfectly methodical philosophical way to dominate the Far East and as much of the Pacific and its trade as we and the rest of the world will permit. When she has a good excuse she will absorb the Philippines unless we are strong enough to prevent it." Sport became one means to test pretensions of racial and cultural superiority.[143]

American administrators in the Philippines utilized sport as a means to channel the Filipinos nationalistic impulses against the Japanese rather than the American rulers by inviting Japanese baseball teams to compete against the locals. They expanded such efforts in 1912 by reorganizing the Manila Carnival from a business exposition into an athletic spectacle that assumed the role of a Far East Olympics. As the Japanese contended for regional honors they also entered the international Olympic Games in Stockholm, Sweden in 1912. World War I interrupted the Games, but the Japanese won their first medal in 1920. Five years later the Japanese Amateur Athletic Federation made a concerted effort to present a more formidable team with governmental support, which produced four medals, including two gold medals. Both the 1932 and 1936 Japanese Olympic teams won eighteen medals as they not only challenged notions of their inferiority, but began to expand their dominion throughout Asia.[144]

Japanese boxers also challenged Western powers. In 1933 the French champion Emile Pladner traveled to Japan where he met five local fighters in bantamweight bouts over the course of a month, winning four and ending with two draws. One of these matches, against the undefeated Horiguchi "Piston" Tsuneo, drew 30,000 spectators. World War II derailed the Japanese bid for power, but in the aftermath of the war Japanese boxers started to exert themselves in the lower weight classes.[145]

Yoshio Shirai began his career in 1943, during the war. He defeated Dado Marino, a Filipino Hawaiian, in Tokyo in 1952 to gain the flyweight title, the first Japanese fighter to earn a world championship. Masahiko "Fighting" Harada also gained the flyweight crown in 1962.

He moved up to the bantamweight class and captured that title in 1965 by defeating the previously unbeaten Eder Jofre (47-0-3), holding it for three years.[146] Harada lost his position to Pone Kingpetch, the first Thai fighter to claim a world title.

The post–World War II era witnessed the rise of several Asian champions, yet race had been a compelling factor since the early nineteenth century. Boxing, more so than any other sport, provided a social experiment in the Darwinian test of the survival of the fittest. As scientists pondered the concept of race and human differences, boxing allowed for direct comparisons, ultimately negating the Anglo perception of superiority in the ring, the only place where people of color might challenge white hegemony without the threat of punishment or incarceration. African American fighters held the heavyweight championship—symbolic of the world's toughest man—from 1937 to 1952, until Rocky Marciano assumed the role of the Great White Hope as champion. Marciano's tenure as champ even solidified Italian Americans' claim to whiteness, which had been in question since their massive migration in the 1880s.[147]

CHAPTER FIVE
THE CONCEPT OF ETHNICITY

The Dillingham Commission (1907–1910), a federal commission on immigration to the United States, determined that there were forty-five different races, based on biological or physical differences among populations. In the next two decades the sociologists at the University of Chicago and anthropologist Franz Boas at Columbia University discredited much of the presumed "science of racialization," opting for a new concept of ethnicity, which categorized peoples by their shared cultural practices, such as language, foods, social cohesiveness, and identity rather than skin color or biological characteristics. Under the previous system any dark-skinned person might be classified as a member of the black race. Ethnicity allowed for different designations based on one's cultural background, so although some Americans, Europeans, Africans, Bahamians, Puerto Ricans, Dominicans, Haitians, and so on might all be black, they represent a variety of different lifestyles and social practices. Despite the clarification many stereotypes persisted, and the study and evolution of the concept of ethnicity continues throughout the twenty-first century.[1]

A variety of ethnic groups contested with each other to meet the standards of whiteness prescribed by the white, Protestant, middle class—the dominant group in American society that set the norms, standards, and values for inclusion and acceptance. Sports provided an exposure to middle-class values, such as a strong work ethic, discipline, competition, and respect for authority. Ethnic children were introduced to American sports and games in the schools, parks, playgrounds, settlement houses, and neighborhood clubs; they often maintained their ancestral lifestyle at home, where parents were slow or unable to grasp the English language, adhered to their preferred foods and customs, and continued to practice alternative forms of religion. Such dual lives placed second-generation ethnics in a liminal position, known as "hyphenated" Americans (Italian Americans, Polish Americans, Jewish Americans, etc.), in which they lived in two worlds, no longer entirely foreign, but not yet fully American.[2]

Throughout the twentieth century, scholars proposed various theories about the assimilation process that immigrants faced on the road to Americanization. Some claimed that the gradual inclusion of ethnic immigrant groups produced an American melting pot, in which all eventually assumed an American identity. Others claimed that American society more closely resembled a salad bowl, in which groups retain their individual characteristics as they assimilate. By the latter decades of the century, a recognition of the United States as a pluralistic or multicultural society emerged that encompassed some differences but general agreement on core values and a national identity.[3]

For many, sport eased the acculturation process. Immigrant children adopted American games and created neighborhood teams to compete against children of other ethnic or religious groups. When gambling on such ventures required the best athletes to win, ethnicity gave way to talent in the quest for an advantage. Similarly, school teams sought the best players regardless of social class or ethnicity. Colleges and universities even offered the best athletes athletic scholarships, with the possibility for higher education and consequent social mobility. The University of California initiated the first college-level boxing club in 1916, but most ethnic fighters gained their first experience in the streets, parks, and gyms of the inner city.[4]

Urban rivalries between nativist and ethnic groups became apparent as early as the 1830s in American cities, and increased markedly as Irish immigrants poured into such enclaves in the following decade. Street battles and individual combats became commonplace in the Five Points district of New York. German immigrants battled police in Chicago in 1855 when the mayor attempted to shut down the saloons where they enjoyed their leisure time. The ethnic group members formed gangs to protect themselves and their territory, with the toughest resident serving as the gang leader. The best fighters became integral to such endeavors and valued for their martial skills. Politicians noted the ability of "shoulder hitters" to coerce seemingly undecided voters to cast their ballots appropriately on election days, and these fighters became prominent allies to the political machines in big cities. The Irish proved particularly helpful in that, unlike other immigrant groups, they spoke English. Historian Melvin Adelman discovered that most of the prizefighters (56.3 percent) in New York between 1840 and 1860 were Irish, many of whom had learned their craft in their homeland. Irish Americans comprised another 15.6 percent of the boxers. In the 1850s a good fighter in Chicago could earn as much as $500 for a single bout, exceeding the annual wage for most workers.[5]

Historian Steven Riess has suggested that it is possible to trace the social mobility of ethnic groups in the United States through boxing. The Irish dominated the sport until the 1920s, with nine of the nineteen world champions in the 1890s and thirteen of forty-seven between 1900 and 1920. The Irish produced 40 percent of the top contenders from 1909 to 1916. They were superseded by the Jews in the 1920s and the Italians in the 1930s. In those two decades Jews accounted for fifteen of the champions, and Italians comprised twenty-four titlists. African Americans had won five championships between 1890 and 1908; by the 1930s they comprised 22.5 percent of all boxers, and 50 percent of all contenders by 1948. After that point Hispanic fighters began to assume a larger role in the ring, especially in the lower weight classes. African Americans prevailed in the higher weight classes (middleweight and above). Riess warns that "most pros didn't make a lot of money, had short careers, and ended up in occupations relative to their social origins and educational level." A survey of boxers between 1900 and 1960 showed that 32 percent ended up in working-class jobs, while the rest attained lower middle-class levels on the social strata. Jewish fighters, however, surpassed other ethnicities, as only one of the thirty-six studied remained mired in the working class. Whereas 17 percent of the study group remained in the sport as trainers or managers, 27.8 percent of Jews became entrepreneurs. A comparison with pro basketball players of the 1930s showed that 75 percent had attended college, and 20 percent of pro baseball players did so by 1941.[6]

Irish Boxers

The Irish arrived in the United States in large numbers during the 1840s when the potato crop failed, leaving a multitude of peasants cold, hungry, and mired in poverty. They set sail for America but found themselves unwelcome by the residents, who hung out signs that stated "no Irish need apply" for the jobs they offered. For many young men boxing offered a release for their pent-up energies and a means to defend their personal and ethnic honor.

The best of the many Irish boxers offer a glimpse of the promise and the portentous reality of life as a boxer. All earned fame and celebrity, and a few gained a measure of wealth, yet many died young and impoverished. The Irish nearly monopolized the heavyweight championship throughout the nineteenth century as "Yankee" Sullivan (James Ambrose, born in Ireland), John Morrissey (born in Ireland), and American-born John Heenan rose to prominence in the middle decades of the era. By the latter decades American-born fighters began to establish their dominance. John L. Sullivan, born in Roxbury, Massachusetts, claimed the heavyweight title by defeating Irish-born Paddy Ryan and Jake Kilrain (John Joseph Killian, born in New York). Sullivan lost his title to yet another Irish American, James J. Corbett, in 1892. Corbett reigned as champion for nearly five years and provided a greater level of respectability to the sport. The son of middle-class Irish immigrants, he learned to box at the San Francisco Olympic Club and worked as a bank teller; hence the nickname "Gentleman" Jim. His good looks drew a bevy of females to the sport as fans, spectators, and movie patrons. Like Sullivan, he used his position to embark on a theatrical tour and a post-fight career as an actor.[7]

Mike Donovan, born in Chicago in 1847, served as Corbett's trainer for the Sullivan bout. Donovan claimed the middleweight championship after serving with the Union forces in the Civil War. His active career lasted thirty years until 1896, in which time he often fought much larger men and lost only four times. He graduated to boxing instructor at the New York Athletic Club in 1884, a post he held for thirty-eight years. Known as "the professor," his emphasis on defense rather than brawling promoted boxing as a scientific sport and made him an acceptable tutor to upper-class men who engaged in the "art of self-defense" as a marker of their masculinity. He also served President Theodore Roosevelt as a sparring partner in the White House.[8]

Like Donovan, Bob Fitzsimmons often fought larger men, becoming the first to win titles in three different weight classes. Born in England, the son of a former Irish soldier, Fitzsimmons was raised in New Zealand and won the national amateur championship in 1880 before traveling to Australia in search of professional laurels. His pro career began in 1885 and moved to the United States in 1890, where he defeated Nonpareil Jack Dempsey (John Kelly) for the world middleweight championship in 1891. Though undersized, he challenged for the heavyweight title in 1896, but lost the match on a foul. The next year he knocked out heavyweight champ Jim Corbett in the fourteenth round, although he weighed only 167 pounds for the bout. He lost the title to Jim Jeffries in 1902 and

Bob Fitzsimmons, who fought from 1884 to 1915 and held titles in three weight classes. Courtesy of H. J. Lutcher Stark Center for Physical Culture and Sports, University of Texas at Austin.

suffered another loss to Jeffries a year later. One of Fitzsimmons's opponents died in 1903 after a first-round knockout, which resulted in a trial in which he was exonerated. Later that year he beat George Gardner in a twenty-round decision to earn the light heavyweight crown. Destitute, he continued to fight until 1914, almost a thirty-year ring history, but finally succumbed to pneumonia in 1917 at the age of fifty-four.[9]

Nonpareil Jack Dempsey, born in 1862 in Ireland as John Kelly, traveled to the United States as a boy. He began his American pugilistic career as a wrestler, but preferred boxing by 1883. He claimed the national middleweight championship only a year later. In 1890 he defeated Australian Billy McCarthy for the world middleweight title, but lost it to Bob Fitzsimmons a year later. He died in 1895, a victim of tuberculosis at the age of thirty-two, ending a short but brilliant career. He lost only three times in sixty-four bouts and was widely recognized as one of the premier fighters of the era, hence the nickname "Nonpareil." A slew of boxers who followed him adopted the Dempsey moniker.[10]

Jack McAuliffe, born in Cork, Ireland in 1866, traveled to New York where he became a boyhood friend of Nonpareil Jack Dempsey. McAuliffe would attain his own distinguished ring laurels, beginning his quest a year after Dempsey entered the professional ranks. McAuliffe, known as the "Napoleon of the Ring," won the lightweight championship in 1886, and retired in 1897 as one of the few fighters never to have suffered a loss. McAuliffe fought several exhibition bouts thereafter but devoted himself to a new career in vaudeville and married two stage actresses as a result.[11]

Jimmy Barry, an Irish American contemporary of McAuliffe, emerged as one of the few other fighters who retired undefeated. Born in Chicago in 1870, Barry began boxing as a professional in 1891 and overcame his slight 105-pound frame with an aggressive style and a powerful punch. Barry obtained the paperweight, flyweight, and bantamweight titles and a perfect record of 59-0 with forty wins by knockout. Six of his battles involved brutal ethnic encounters with Casper Leon (Gaspare Leoni), the first of the great Italian fighters. When the British disputed his claim to the paperweight title, he traveled to London to fight Walter Croot in 1897, a fight that resulted in the death of the English fighter. Barry was arrested but exonerated, yet psychologically damaged as a result, fearing to knock out any further opponents with nine bouts afterward resulting in draws until he retired in 1900. With the American entry into World War

I, however, Barry offered his services to the country and was assigned to teach bayonet training, as parrying in combat proved similar to sparring in the ring and won greater acceptance for the utilitarian value of boxing.[12]

Philadelphian Jack O'Brien, born James Francis Hagen in the City of Brotherly Love in 1878, fought as a middleweight and as an under-sized light heavyweight from 1896 to 1912. Well-tailored and articulate, O'Brien spoke as well as he boxed. He admired the British, stating that "I have always loved to hear the verbiage that flows from an English-man, whether he be an Oxfordian or otherwise." O'Brien traveled to the United Kingdom and France in 1901, where he accumulated sixteen consecutive victories, claiming the middleweight championship when he knocked out Dido Plumb at Newcastle. The following year he suffered a loss to Al Limerick, who weighed in at 220 pounds. He then succumbed to Bob Fitzsimmons, but managed to defeat Tommy Burns, the future heavyweight champion. In 1905 he lost his middleweight title to Hugo Kelly (Ugo Micheli), but continued to challenge the best fighters of the era. In 1907 O'Brien lost a twenty-round bout for the heavyweight cham-pionship to Burns on points; on March 26, 1909, he was knocked out by middleweight great Stanley Ketchel (Kiecal). O'Brien reasoned that "I had heard that Ketchel's dynamic onslaught was such it could not be withstood, but I figured I could jab his puss off." O'Brien was forced to concede that Ketchel was "a tumultuously ferocious person." Less than two months later, O'Brien took on heavyweight champion Jack Johnson, who outweighed him by more than forty pounds, which resulted in a de-batable loss as neither fighter exerted himself; both needed the money to support their lavish lifestyles. In the wake of the Johnson fight the aging O'Brien began to wane. From 1910 to 1912 he lost five of his six bouts and finally retired.[13]

"Terrible" Terry McGovern, born in Pennsylvania in 1880 but raised in Brooklyn, never attended school. He became a newsboy, a job that often required vendors to protect their turf from others who sought a bet-ter or more populous market for their own sales. McGovern turned pro at the tender age of seventeen, and within two years he knocked out the reigning British bantamweight champ, Tom (Pedlar) Palmer, to claim the title. Palmer had been undefeated, and the match drew a crowd of 10,000 in England; he lasted less than a full round under McGovern's onslaught. In 1900 McGovern gave up the bantamweight crown, but gained the featherweight title with an eighth-round knockout of George Dixon. In his very next bout he knocked out the lightweight champ, Frank Erne, in the third round of a non-title match. That year he also engaged in the famous fixed fight with Joe Gans (see chapter 4), although McGovern apparently had no part in the duplicity that killed boxing in Chicago for twenty years. McGovern sat out for a year between February 22, 1902, and February 6, 1903, but could not regain his old form. He lost twice to Young Corbett II (William Rothwell) in featherweight title bouts when his opponent caused him to lose his composure with infuriating ethnic slurs related to McGovern's Irish ancestry. McGovern finally retired in 1908, but ring damage had taken its toll on his mental faculties. He died of pneumonia and kidney failure in the charity ward of a Brooklyn hospital in 1918.[14]

Johnny Kilbane fared better. A crafty boxer rather than a heavy puncher, Kilbane, born in Cleveland in 1889, entered the professional ranks in 1907. He fought for the featherweight title by 1910 in a bout he lost to Abe Attell. He defeated Attell in a twenty-round match in 1912 to gain the title by decision, which he held until 1923. Attell retired to become a henchman for Arnold Rothstein, and both became key figures in the Black Sox scandal of 1919 when the Chicago White Sox, American League baseball champions, were bribed into throwing the World Series to the Cincinnati Reds. Kilbane retired to a more respectable life as a boxing referee, and the operator of his own gym. During World War I he served as a boxing instructor for military personnel, and in 1941 he was elected a member of the Ohio state legislature. At the time of his death from cancer in 1957 he held the position of clerk of the municipal court in Cleveland.[15]

Patrick "Packey" McFarland also fared much better than most fighters. Born in Chicago in 1888 and a resident of the tough Stockyards neighborhood where fights were common, he turned pro at the young age of sixteen in 1904. He proved so good as a lightweight and welterweight that champions refused to fight him; hence he never won a title and retired in 1913. He returned to fight once more in 1915 to finish with an official record of 69-0-5 with fifty knockouts. An astute businessman, McFarland had saved $300,000 and became a brewer and a banker, and later a director of the Catholic Youth Organization and a member of the Illinois Boxing Commission before a heart attack took his life in 1936.[16]

McFarland met Jack Britton, a fellow Stockyards resident in Chicago, in the ring on three occasions. Born in 1885 as William Breslin, by 1904 Britton had embarked on a boxing career that lasted twenty-five years and 344 fights, twenty of them with Ted "Kid" Lewis (Gershon Mendoloff), with whom he exchanged the welterweight title several times. For years the two combatants carried on an antagonistic relationship in which they refused to talk to each other or to shake hands. Like many boxers of the early twentieth century who engaged in the illegal activity, bouts had to be arranged as "exhibitions" for paying club members who paid their dues at the door. As "exhibitions," gamblers had to rely on the consensus of sportswriters to declare the winner, unless the match was decided by a knockout with an obvious winner. More than 150 of Britton's victories were rendered as "newspaper decisions." Britton finally surrendered the welterweight crown to Mickey Walker in 1922, but continued to fight for seven more years due to his financial losses in the Florida land boom of the 1920s. He finally retired at the age of forty-four to become a boxing instructor at a New York athletic club.[17]

Mickey Walker, known as "The Toy Bulldog," proved to be one of the most popular heroes of the Golden Age of Sports in America. Walker's demeanor became evident when he was expelled from his Catholic elementary school in Elizabeth, New Jersey. After defeating a shipyard coworker, who also happened to be a professional boxer, Walker assumed a new career. With no training as a boxer and no amateur experience, Walker relied on his skills as a tough brawler. After gaining the welterweight crown at the age of twenty-one in his 1922 bout with Jack Britton, Walker sought laurels at higher weight classes. Although he weighed less than 150 pounds he challenged Ireland's Mike McTigue for the light heavyweight championship in 1925, which ended in a no-decision outcome. (Two years later Walker knocked out McTigue in a rematch.) His exploits attracted the attention of "Doc" Kearns, the manager of heavyweight champ Jack Dempsey, who negotiated further championship encounters for his new charge. Kearns and Walker freely spent the latter's winnings in bars and brothels, with little training. In 1925 Walker faced the equally tough "human windmill" Harry Greb, with the latter winning a decision. When they happened to meet at a bar later that night the fight continued in a back alley and Walker reversed the decision by sucker punching his opponent. When Tiger Flowers (see chapter 4) beat

Greb to become the champ, Walker beat him for the middleweight title in a controversial decision in Chicago.[18]

After defeating McTigue in the 1927 bout Walker resumed his quest for the light heavyweight title against Tommy Loughran in 1929, but lost by decision. Two years later he fixed his sights on the heavyweight crown, giving up nearly thirty pounds to fight Jack Sharkey. Although the fight ended in a draw, Sharkey got the title fight and defeated Max Schmeling for the title. When Walker fought Schmeling in Madison Square Garden in 1932, the German hero won convincingly with a technical knockout—but no one could question Walker's courage and ability to withstand pain. At the height of the Depression, Walker represented the pain felt by many Americans as they tried to overcome overwhelming odds. Like them Walker never quit and kept coming back for another try. In 1933 he lost a light heavyweight decision to Maxie Rosenbloom in a championship bout. A year later Walker revenged that loss, but his hedonistic lifestyle took a toll on his skills and his finances. When he retired in 1935 he had little to show for his years in the ring. An acting career proved short-lived and he resorted to operating a bar and took up a new avocation as an artist. His wild lifestyle and drinking habits resulted in six marriages, two of them remarriages to his first and second wives, before his death from Parkinson's disease.[19]

Tommy Loughran, born to an Irish immigrant family in South Philadelphia in 1902, followed in the mold of previous tough Irish boxers. He turned pro at seventeen but was beset by fragile hands that plagued him throughout his career. He fought defensively and counterpunched, unlike many of the sluggers that proved more attractive for fans. Still, Loughran proved highly skilled, and fought not only the best of the light heavyweights, but took on the heavyweights as well. In 1922 he fought a draw with Gene Tunney. He battled four times with Mike McTigue, capturing the light heavyweight crown in 1927, and fought six times against Hall of Famer Harry Greb. Loughran also owned victories over Georges Carpentier, and future heavyweight champs Jim Braddock and Max Baer. In 1929 Yankee Stadium accommodated 45,000 fans to watch Loughran's unsuccessful challenge for the heavyweight title in a bout against Jack Sharkey. In 1929 and again in 1931 *Ring* magazine chose Loughran as its Fighter of the Year. In 1934 he lost in another heavyweight title fight to Primo Carnera, who not only towered over him but outweighed him by eighty pounds. In 1934 he traveled to South America where he fought six bouts, as he could no longer garner top honors in the United States. Loughran retired in 1937, then opened a restaurant, worked at a recreation center, and joined the marines when World War II erupted. In the 1950s he became a commentator for televised boxing matches, as the new form of media transformed American sport and leisure lifestyles.[20]

Throughout the 1950s boxing proved particularly amenable to the new technology because the relatively primitive equipment limited coverage to sports with a narrow visual focus. Arthur Daley, a sportswriter for the *New York Times*, stated that "the ring is small enough to always be in focus. The contestants are the absolute minimum of two. It's the ideal arrangement because every seat in front of a video screen is a ringside seat. And the price is perfect—free." Initially, television proved a boon to boxing, and sponsorship of the Gillette (the razor blade company) *Friday Night Fights* became a weekly institution for many American males. The Pabst Blue Ribbon brewery soon offered a similar version on Wednesday evenings. Nearly 90 percent of American households owned a television by 1960. The advent of the television, however, eventually caused the closure of the neighborhood boxing clubs and the gyms that supplied the fighters.[21]

Jim Braddock, an Irish American whose life was chronicled in the 2005 movie *Cinderella Man*, was born in 1905 in the Hell's Kitchen neighborhood of New York, where he got an early introduction to fighting in the neighborhood battles. The family moved to New Jersey where his boxing skills earned him two state championships before he turned pro in 1926. Braddock then went undefeated in his first twenty-six bouts, but in 1929 his career crashed along with the stock market. Like millions of Americans he suffered through the Depression, sporadically finding work on the New Jersey docks. He persevered through the adversity, managing to resurrect his boxing career with a string of victories after 1933 that got him a title fight for the heavyweight championship with Max Baer in 1935. Despite heavy odds, Braddock triumphed once again, then took a two-year hiatus while he toured the country. Upon his return to the ring in 1937 he lost his title to Joe Louis. Braddock's manager, Joe Gould, negotiated a contract for that fight that provided Gould with 10 percent of Louis's winnings for the next decade, somewhat akin to winning the lottery. Braddock's loss made him the last Irish American to hold the heavyweight championship; though he did not fare as well as Gould, he retired to a successful life as a businessman.[22]

Billy Conn followed Braddock as the top attraction among Irish American fighters, beginning his pro career inauspiciously in 1934 before he reached the age of seventeen. Conn had dropped out of school in the eighth grade to take up boxing. With no amateur experience beyond street fights, he lost six of his first fourteen bouts before reversing his fortunes by going undefeated in his next twenty-seven bouts. By 1939 he had garnered the light heavyweight championship, yet Conn is best remembered for a 1941 loss to heavyweight champ Joe Louis. More than 54,000 gathered at New York's Polo Grounds to watch Conn stunningly outbox the champ, who held a nearly thirty-pound weight advantage, for twelve rounds. Conn held a lead on the judges' scorecard, but when he became overconfident and decided to slug it out with Louis he was knocked out with two seconds left in the thirteenth round. Conn responded to sportswriters in a post-fight interview: "What's the good of being Irish if you can't be dumb?"[23]

Conn did not fight between 1942 and 1946 due to World War II, during which he joined the army and accompanied Bob Hope's troupe on a tour of military bases. He did, however, get into a fight with his father-in-law, "Greenfield" Jimmy Smith, who objected to Conn's marriage with his daughter. Conn broke his hand in the encounter, preventing any impending battles. After the war Conn and Louis engaged in a rematch for the heavyweight title in 1946 in a lackluster bout dominated by Louis, who enjoyed another twenty-five-pound advantage. Conn retired after two more wins in 1948. In later years he suffered from dementia, but reasoned, "People think you're nuts to be a fighter, and they're right, but it's better than working in the mills." Such was the logic of many poor Irish fighters who gained fame and celebrity via boxing versus those who toiled in anonymity fighting the heat and stench of the blast furnaces, and occasionally each other, for less pay than the best boxers.[24]

In the postwar era few Irish Americans reached the elite levels of professional boxing, although many former boxers continued to serve as managers, trainers, and promoters. The Irish, in general, had become part of mainstream American society and sought the more lucrative and less painful occupations as educated white-collar professionals. Sean O'Grady, born in 1959, began boxing at age six. His father, Pat, a trainer, managed his son's career, which reached its pinnacle with the World Boxing Association (WBA) lightweight championship in 1981; O'Grady held the title for only six months. He retired at age twenty-four with a college degree and a record of 81-5-0 (seventy knockouts) and pursued an acting career, becoming better known as a television boxing analyst over the next decade.[25]

The Irish homeland, particularly Northern Ireland, continued to produce several boxers of note. John J. "Rinty" Monaghan, born in 1920 in Belfast, embarked on a boxing career by age twelve. Seventeen years later he was recognized as the world flyweight champion, a title he held until retirement in 1950. Dave McAuley, also from Northern Ireland, held the International Boxing Federation (IBF) flyweight crown from 1989 to 1992. Wayne McCullough, another Ulsterman, won a silver medal in the 1992 Olympic Games and succeeded to the 1995 World Boxing Council (WBC) bantamweight championship before a brain tumor shortened his career. Barry McGuigan (born Finbar Patrick McGuigan in Ireland), who held the WBA featherweight title from 1985 to 1986, began fighting in 1981. His career lasted nine years with a fine record of 32-3-1 with twenty-eight knockouts, but he knew little else. When asked why he had become a boxer, he responded, "I can't be a poet. I can't tell stories."[26]

Until the Irish economy surged in the late twentieth century the poor still had limited options, but young men had recognized that toughness had brought Irish boxers at least a measure of respect for the previous two hundred years. In the United States boxing had provided more immediate recognition and social mobility for a lucky few.

Jewish Boxers

German Jews had migrated to the United States in large numbers during the purge of 1848 in the wake of the failed revolution. Many had prospered by the time their Eastern European brethren began arriving in the latter nineteenth century. Joe Choynski (1868–1943), born in San Francisco, was the son of a Jewish teacher and newspaper publisher who had attended Yale University. Joe, however, dropped out of school and opted for the blacksmith's trade. Undersized at less than 180 pounds, he never reached championship status as a heavyweight, but fought the best in the division between 1885 and 1904. Choynski knocked out future great Jack

Johnson in 1901 at the start of the latter's career ,and then tutored him on the finer points of the pugilistic craft as they languished in jail for twenty-four days for their illegal bout in Texas. Upon retirement he stayed active in the sport as an instructor and promoter.[27]

Harry Harris (1880–1959), a Chicago-born Jew, had a twin brother, Sammy, who also took up the sport, but Sammy died at the young age of twenty-one. Harry began his pro debut at the age of fifteen. At 5 feet 8 inches and only 105 pounds, he was known as the "human hairpin," but his long reach gave him an advantage in the ring. Harry captured the bantamweight championship in 1901, ending his eleven-year career in 1907 having never suffered a loss by knockout, and finding a less-strenuous occupation managing theaters and a more lucrative one on Wall Street.[28]

Abe Attell (1883–1970), the sixteenth of nineteen children, was one of a family of boxing brothers born in San Francisco and fought under the nickname of "The Little Hebrew." Abe proved the best of the brothers (although Monte Attell gained the bantamweight crown in 1909, and Caesar fought as a featherweight), winning the featherweight championship in 1904, which he unified without dispute in 1906. Attell defended his crown on twenty-one occasions, losing it in 1912. While that title provided him a measure of fame, he reached lasting ignominy after his 1917 retirement as one of the key figures in the Black Sox baseball scandal of 1919 as the intermediary and fixer for the top gambler, Arnold Rothstein, who bribed the White Sox to throw the World Series to the Cincinnati Redlegs.[29]

Israel "Charley" Goldman proved more typical of the Jewish youth who turned to boxing. Born in Poland in 1888, he started boxing professionally by the age of sixteen, earning five dollars per bout and sometimes boxing twice per night or on consecutive nights in New York clubs. Because boxing was technically illegal and clubs offered bouts as "exhibitions" for their members, who paid at the door, Charley allegedly held membership in hundreds of such clubs. At the end of his active days in the ring he became a trainer of numerous world champions, most notably Rocky Marciano.[30]

English Jews returned to prominence as World War I approached. Aschel "Young" Joseph fought for more than a decade (1903–1914) and captured the European welterweight title, which he held in 1910–1911. He was overshadowed by Ted "Kid" Lewis (1893–1970), born Gershon Mendeloff, the only son of eight children born to Russian Jewish immi-

Abe Attell. Courtesy of H. J. Lutcher Stark Center for Physical Culture and Sports, University of Texas at Austin.

grants. The wayward son Anglicized his name to pursue boxing, a pastime to which his parents objected. Nevertheless his success gained him the world welterweight title from 1915 to 1916 and again from 1917 to 1919. Lewis both won and lost his championship to Jack Britton, whom he fought a remarkable twenty times. Upon his retirement in 1929 he owned homes in both Great Britain and the United States. Lewis is often credited with being the first fighter to adopt the now required protective mouthpiece.[31]

His American contemporary, Battling Levinsky (born to Russian immigrants in Philadelphia as Beryl "Barney" Lebrowitz, 1891–1949), began his boxing career as Barney Williams in 1909. The Anglicization of names gives some indication of the perceived negativity or inferiority of ethnics in the dominant culture and the parental/religious disapproval of boxing. He learned his craft as a jeweler's apprentice whose duties included safeguarding the store. In a career that lasted until 1930 Levinsky amassed

289 official bouts, and probably many more than that. Along the way he held the light heavyweight championship from 1916 to 1920.[32]

Mushy Callahan (Vincent Scheer, 1905–1986) also chose an Irish name in the United States. By that time the Irish had procured a dominant role in the American boxing scene. As Callahan he held the junior welterweight championship from 1926 to 1930, and retired two years later to become a well-known boxing referee. Callahan also worked in Hollywood as a trainer and boxing instructor for actors. He renounced Judaism and converted to Catholicism. His son became a Jesuit priest. He lost his title to the last of the great English fighters of the era, Jackie "Kid" Berg (1909–1991), who held the crown in 1930–1931. Born Judah Bergman to Russian Jewish immigrants, Berg offended his parents by his fighting, but presented his Judaism by wearing the Star of David on his trunks and engaging in a staged pre-fight but public prayer ritual that highlighted his difference and helped at the turnstiles until his 1945 retirement. He managed to turn his winnings into a suburban home and a middle-class lifestyle. His parallel life included film work as a stuntman, service in the Royal Air Force, and a London restaurant.[33]

Benny Leonard, born Benjamin Leiner to Russian immigrant parents in New York in 1896, became the most revered and influential of the Jewish boxers in the early twentieth century. As a youth his street fights in the tough Lower East Side of New York brought paying spectators. He reputedly served as a protector of the elderly and synagogue-goers. The Anglicization of his name resulted from an attempt to hide his boxing ventures from his religious parents, but his father acquiesced when he brought home $20 from a fight, as much as the parent made for a week's work as a sweatshop tailor. Leonard turned pro at fifteen in 1911 and secured the lightweight championship in 1917, a post he held until 1925. During his tenure as champ, Leonard wore the Star of David on his trunks as "revenge for the bloody noses, split lips, and mocking laughter versus little Jewish boys who had to run the neighborhood gauntlet." Out of respect for his mother he refused to fight on Jewish holidays. He drew some of the largest gates during the 1920s, and historian Peter Levine claims that young Jewish women bet hundreds of thousands of dollars on his victories. Leonard earned more than $500,000 by his retirement in 1925; the stock market crash of 1929 caused him to resume boxing until 1932, despite the loss of sight in one eye.[34]

Benny Leonard. Courtesy of H. J. Lutcher Stark Center for Physical Culture and Sports, University of Texas at Austin.

Leonard brought immense pride to Jews as he battled the presumably dominant Irish boxers and other ethnics who preyed on Jewish neighborhoods. He did much to not only reverse perceptions of Jewish debility, but serves as a public symbol of assimilation. In World War I he served as an officer and a boxing instructor, fighting exhibition bouts to raise funds for war bonds. He directed the physical training program for Camp Hakoah, a Jewish camp named for the famed European soccer team that conquered gentile teams in the 1920s, and he promoted religious harmony when he was recruited by Bishop Bernard Sheil as a boxing instructor for the Catholic Youth Organization in the 1930s. In World War II he joined the U.S. Maritime Service. He died of a heart attack in the ring while refereeing a bout in 1947. Acknowledged as one of the greatest fighters of all time, upon his initial retirement in 1925 the *Jewish Daily Bulletin* declared that he was, perhaps, greater than Einstein, for he was known and understood by millions, whereas few were capable of understanding Einstein[35]

One of Leonard's admirers, Jackie Fields, earned his own accolades as welterweight champion from 1929 to 1930 and 1932 to 1933. Born Jacob Finkelstein in 1908, the son of a Chicago butcher, he stated that "in the ghetto, you had to fight." His father's poor health resulted in a move to Los Angeles in 1921 where his street fighting skills were refined by a trainer at the Los Angeles Athletic Club. He won the 1924 Olympic gold medal as a featherweight by defeating a fellow American, Joe Salas. Fields was only sixteen years old at the time. He turned pro the next year and was able to pay off his mother's home in a year. By 1929 he held the welterweight title and accumulated $500,000, but the onset of the Depression wiped out his bankroll. A 1932 car crash detached his retina and cost him the sight in one eye. Nevertheless, he returned to the ring for an additional year to recoup his losses. In retirement Fields became a studio manager for 20th Century Fox, edited films for MGM, and in the 1940s sold jukeboxes and liquor. In 1957 he invested in a Las Vegas casino and also served as a member of the Nevada State Athletic Commission.[36]

Jews also succeeded at the heavier weight classes in the 1930s. Max Baer became a popular fighter due to his colorful playfulness in and outside of the ring. Although not raised as a Jew, he affected a Jewish persona, wearing the Star of David on his trunks as a marketing gimmick. He assumed a greater symbolic Judaism in his 1933 victory over Max Schmeling, who was saddled with the taint of Hitler's Naziism. When he knocked out Primo Carnera a year later, Baer became a short-lived heavyweight champion until Jim Braddock defeated him in 1935. More than 88,000 crowded into Yankee Stadium to witness the Baer-Joe Louis battle, ending in a quick knockout win for Louis after four rounds. Baer continued to box until World War II, when he served as an instructor in the air force and took on movie roles afterward.[37]

Maxie Rosenbloom, a contemporary of Baer, shared his disdain for training and attraction to nightlife. Still he fought nearly 300 bouts, holding the light heavyweight championship from 1932 to 1934; only nineteen of his wins came by knockout. A superb defensive boxer with a feeble punch, he became known as "Slapsie Maxie" for his open-handed cuffs to opponents. Rosenbloom retired in 1939 and teamed with Baer in a nightclub comedy act. He also acted in films. Historian Jeffrey Sammons contends, however, that the antics of Rosenbloom and others only reinforced Jewish stereotypes that slowed acceptance within the mainstream society.[38]

A strong strain of anti-Semitism persisted during the interwar era with the rise of the Ku Klux Klan, restrictive quotas imposed on Jewish students at Ivy League universities, a ban on Jews at some Adirondack resorts, and the religious differences that marked Jews as "others" not yet fully assimilated in the American culture. The last of the great Jewish champs, Barney Ross, exemplified the painful transition to Americanization.[39]

Born in New York in 1909 to Russian Jewish Orthodox immigrants as Beryl (Barnet) Rosofsky, four of his siblings died in infancy. His scholarly father started as a peddler and opened a grocery store in the Jewish ghetto when the family moved to Chicago in 1911. In 1923 robbers killed his father in a holdup, and his mother suffered a nervous breakdown. Ross forsook religious studies and turned to his own life of crime, serving gangsters as an errand boy. Influenced by the success of Jackie Fields, he took up boxing, where even amateurs could pawn their medals and trophies for added income. He fought in bouts almost every night, sometimes twice in one night. He remarked that "I won almost all of them. . . . I didn't keep any of the medals or watches I won—I traded all in for cash the day after each bout." When newspapers began reporting his successes, he Anglicized his name to shield his fighting from his religious mother. He intended to retrieve his sister and two brothers from the orphanage to which they had been assigned after his father's death. In 1929 he won the Chicago Golden Gloves (a premier amateur tournament) featherweight championship and followed that with a victory over the New York champ in the annual inter-city competition.[40]

Ross turned pro that year and his mother became his biggest fan, reportedly leading the march of fans from the Jewish ghetto to Chicago Stadium for his local fights. In 1933 he acquired the lightweight championship as well as the junior welterweight title by defeating Italian favorite Tony Canzoneri in Chicago. When he beat Jimmy McLarnin for the welterweight crown in 1934 a crowd of thousands accompanied by a band met him at the Chicago train station, and city hall accorded him a public tribute. *Ring* magazine named him Fighter of the Year in both 1934 and 1935. Ross traded the title with McLarnin over the next year, but he held it continuously from 1935 to 1938. During those years, as Hitler's persecution of the Jews became more pronounced, the Star of Davis that Ross wore on his trunks became a symbol of ethnic solidarity, and he donated large sums to Jewish charities. He also refused to fight on Jewish High

Barney Ross, who held simultaneous titles in three weight classes during the 1930s. Courtesy of H. J. Lutcher Stark Center for Physical Culture and Sports, University of Texas at Austin.

Holy Days. He retired after losing his title to Henry Armstrong in 1938, only his fourth loss in seventy-nine bouts. When World War II erupted he joined the marines, winning the Silver Star for his heroic valor in the battle for Guadalcanal. He also contracted malaria, and the pain from his wounds resulted in a morphine addiction that required years of hospitalization. He used his celebrity to promote political causes, especially Zionism. In the post–World War II years he engaged in gun-running activities and offered to fight in Palestine for the new Jewish state. His life was chronicled in an autobiography and two movies that depicted his success, despite overwhelming odds, in winning whiteness within the dominant culture. No longer just a Jewish hero, he had become an inspiration to all Americans.[41]

Italian Boxers

More than 4 million Italians migrated to the United States from 1880 to 1924. Like Jewish and black residents, Italians suffered distinct discrimination and continued to be stereotyped as gangsters. They were the second most lynched group after African Americans, and were paid less than the Irish and black laborers who built the New York City subway. Most of the immigrants came from southern Italy and Sicily, and beholden only to their family and *paesani* from their own village, they had no conception of an Italian identity. Sports provided a primary means of acquiring a uniform national identity in their quest for acceptance and respect in America.[42]

Among the first of the Italian fighters, Casper Leon (Gaspare Leoni) promoted his island identity in the ring as the "Sicilian Swordfish" due to his angular frame. Born in Palermo, Sicily, in 1872, he migrated to the United States where he took up boxing in 1891. By 1894 he was able to challenge Jimmy Barry for the 105-pound title, losing that encounter after twenty-eight rounds. The pair fought to a draw the next year at 110 pounds. Over the next three years Leon fought twelve other championship bouts at the paperweight, flyweight, and bantamweight levels, winning the American bantamweight crown in 1896. In each case he challenged the social Darwinian notion of Anglo superiority by confronting Anglo and Irish fighters.[43]

Leon also drew attention to the arrival of ethnic Italians on the American sport scene. The children of immigrants were drawn to American sports and games, which proved problematic for their parents who saw such activities as frivolous when they could be working and contributing to family needs. Such Old World concerns lessened as boxers began to bring home more money than their father earned, although that might also upset traditional family hierarchies. In the poverty-ridden ghettos in which many Italians resided, much-needed income eventually superseded tradition in the process of Americanization.

Despite Leon's triumphs, many early Italian fighters continued to Anglicize their names to fit the popular belief in the superiority of Irish boxers. For some, managers suggested the easier pronunciation as a marketing device. Giuseppe Carrora won the junior lightweight (1921) and featherweight (1922) championships as Johnny Dundee, the "Scotch Wop." Andrew Chiariglione fought for twenty-six years (1899–1925) as Fireman Jim Flynn in the heavyweight ranks, and Giuseppe Di Melfi became the Young Zulu Kid. Giovanni Cervati fought as a featherweight under the name of Little Jackie Sharkey from 1914 to 1926, while

Angelo Geraci won the bantamweight title as Bushy Graham in 1928, and Raffaele Capabianca Giordano became Young Corbett III, claiming the welterweight crown in 1933.[44]

Many Italians settled in Louisiana, where they faced harsh conditions and were treated as blacks. The biggest lynching of Italians occurred in New Orleans in 1891 when eleven Italians were killed on March 14 for the alleged but unsubstantiated murder of the police chief. [45] Growing up under such conditions, Italians often had to fight, and the Louisianans produced some early champions. Pete Herman (Gulotta) worked as a shoe-shine boy in his youth, enforcing payment with his fists if necessary. Fighting allowed his father to retire from his manual labor job and enabled the son to earn enough money to open a restaurant in New Orleans, but it also cost him his eyesight. He fought at least 330 bouts from 1912 to 1922, claiming the bantamweight championship by the age of twenty in 1917 before joining the navy as a boxing instructor during World War

Pete Herman (Gulotta), Italian bantamweight champ from New Orleans from 1917 to 1919, in 1921. Courtesy of H. J. Lutcher Stark Center for Physical Culture and Sports, University of Texas at Austin.

I. An Italian sportswriter claimed that the Italian boxers of the era "were fighting not only their rivals in the ring but also the cold hostility of the crowds of that period who could not bring themselves to believe that a 'wop' could fight with gloved fists."[46]

Nativist sentiments prevailed during the era and sportswriters characterized the Argentinian Italian heavyweight, Luis Angel Firpo (see chapter 3), in racist terms when he challenged Jack Dempsey for the title. A supposed psychological study claimed, "the man is a combination of a Patagonian giant and a Genoese wild man. Like his progenitors, who were some of the most famous of Italian vendettists, he has the ability to curb his strength and his passions and disguise his feelings until the proper moment for action is arrived. . . . He is absolutely cold blooded."[47]

When Dempsey rallied to win the wild spectacle, a journalist characterized the challenger as a brute: "If Luis Angel Firpo had the brain power in proportion to his tremendous strength, there is no denying that he and not Jack Dempsey would be world's heavyweight champion this morning. Endowed with the mentality which would enable him to think and think quickly in emergencies, Firpo could afford to be slow moving and cumbersome. But Firpo with all his great strength to give and take punishment, lacked that one essential—a fighting brain." Scholars ranked racial groups according to desirable characteristics and fitness for American citizenship, advocating eugenics for some, and the federal government soon enacted immigration quotas.[48]

Boxing fans were drawn to interethnic contests as battles for the survival of the fittest, and Italian fighters began to compete against Jews for supremacy in the post–World War I years, particularly in the lower weight classes. Sammy Mandell (Mandella) turned pro as a fifteen-year-old in 1919 and captured the lightweight crown when he defeated another Italian, Rocky Kansas (Rocco Tozzo), in 1926. Mandell held the title until 1930, defending it against other top Italian lightweights Billy Petrolle and Tony Canzoneri. Frankie Genaro (Di Gennaro) won the flyweight gold medal at the 1920 Olympic Games and proceeded to take the professional title in that class in 1923. He lost it to another Italian, Fidel LaBarba, who had won the 1924 Olympic championship. The participation of Italians on the American Olympic team symbolized the gradual transition from a European to an American identity, and promoted the perception of meritocracy in the United States. LaBarba fought to protect his turf as a

Los Angeles newsboy and worked nights as a pin boy in a bowling alley. He started boxing as a pro while still in high school, which enabled him to help his siblings. He later used his ring earnings to study journalism at Stanford, which provided him with social mobility and a post-boxing career as a writer—but the cost was considerable. Like Pete Herman, he lost an eye due to boxing.[49]

Midget Wolgast (Robert Loscalzo), the son of a professional boxer, turned pro at the age of fifteen in 1925 and in 1930 won the flyweight championship, which he held for five years. Battling Battalino (Christopher Battaglia) also took the world featherweight title in 1930 despite breaking both hands in the fight. Battalino asserted that he had no interest in school and only wanted to fight like his hero, Johnny Dundee. His father objected to his fighting and even threw him out of the family home for a while. He claimed that he made as much as $1,500 on "amateur" fights before turning pro. Without an education, he had little choice but to continue to fight, which he did until 1940. He weathered the Depression due to his boxing skills, but had little to show for it after helping out friends with loans that went unpaid.[50]

Tony Canzoneri fought for coins as a boy in New Orleans and learned his ring craft when he moved to New York. He escaped poverty and became a hero to Depression-era Italian Americans by winning the featherweight (1927–1928), lightweight (1930–1933, 1935–1936), and junior welterweight (1931–1933) championships. In the course of his ring career he defeated thirteen world champions, using his earnings to buy a home for his parents and a 144-acre farm for himself in upstate New York. He also owned a store and a bar and grill in New York City. When his boxing career ended in 1939, he lost his money investing in Broadway shows and died a pauper in a seedy hotel at the age of fifty-one.[51]

Canzoneri lost his lightweight title to another Italian, Lou Ambers (Luigi D'Ambrosio), who had been one of his former sparring partners. Ambers learned his boxing skills in Herkimer, New York. He graduated from the amateur ranks to the professional circuit in 1932 at the height of the Depression. He stated, "I never made up my mind to get married until I had my mother comfortably fixed. I bought her a nice house, and completely furnished it, in the swank section of Herkimer . . . my (immigrant) father . . . lost his (saloon) business and his savings and was obliged to move us to a poorer section of the town. My parents had seven sons and

Fidel LaBarba, 1924 Olympic gold medalist and world flyweight champ by 1926. Courtesy of H. J. Lutcher Stark Center for Physical Culture and Sports, University of Texas at Austin.

three daughters." As a youth, his boxing earnings from "amateur" bouts covered the family's weekly expenses. Ambers nearly quit boxing after an Italian foe, Tony Scarpati, died after their bout in 1936. Ambers became a restaurateur after his ring career ended in 1941.[52]

Throughout the 1930s Italians continued to garner boxing titles. Harry Jeffra (Ignacius Guiffi) fought from 1933 to 1950, winning the bantamweight (1937–1938) and featherweight championships (1940–1941). Sammy Angott (Engotti) also had a long career from 1935 to 1950, hailing as the lightweight champ between 1940 and 1944. Fred Apostoli spent six years in an orphanage as a child and exchanged his job as a bellhop in a San Francisco hotel for a boxing career in 1934. By 1937 he had gained a version (International Boxing Union) of the middleweight title and beat Young Corbett III the next year to win the world title. He joined the navy during World War II as a gunner on a cruiser and was wounded in the Pacific. *Ring* magazine named him the Fighter of the Year in 1943 for his exemplary conduct. [53]

While such young Italian Americans of the second generation brought pride and recognition to their ethnicity, the Italian who claimed the heavyweight crown, Primo Carnera, caused a dilemma in identity and continued mistrust of Italian Americans' allegiance. A former circus strongman turned boxer, Carnera first arrived in the United States on December 31, 1929. Over the course of the next ten months he won twenty-three of twenty-four fights, twenty-two of them by knockouts. At 6 feet 7 inches and 270 pounds, the muscular mesomorph presented an imposing figure in the ring. When he arrived in Chicago in September of that year the *Tribune* urged, "Every man, woman, or child with a drop of Italian blood in their veins should see the Greatest Italian Fighter of all times."[54] Carnera shuttled between Europe and the United States over the next three years, rolling up a string of victories, mostly by knockout. In 1933 he fought Ernie Schaaf in a bout at Madison Square Garden witnessed by 20,000, which ended in another knockout. Schaaf died a few days later. In his next fight Carnera wrested the heavyweight championship from Jack Sharkey with another knockout victory. He became a hero to ethnic Italians. Future champion Rocky Marciano marveled at his sight as a boy in Brockton, Massachusetts; Carmen Basilio recalled, "I used to hear my father and all his old Italian buddies talking about Primo Carnera all the time." Others questioned Carnera's ties to gangsters and the dubious nature of some of his fights.[55]

Carnera returned to Rome to a hero's welcome and dictator Benito Mussolini praised him as a fascist superman. Mussolini considered Italians in America and their children to still be Italian citizens and worked earnestly to cultivate their loyalty to the homeland. Many Italians in the United States had returned to Italy for military service in World War I and they might serve Mussolini's ambitions to create an Italian empire once again, as he invaded Ethiopia in 1935. By that time Carnera had lost the title to Max Baer, yet the following that he generated among Italians in the United States and his implicit ties to the fascist government in Italy resulted in continued uncertainty about Italian American loyalty. Such doubts would continue until massive numbers of Italian Americans joined the military services during World War II, and many made the ultimate sacrifice.[56]

Willie Pep (Papaleo) joined the military even though he was the sole supporter of his family. He won the Connecticut state championship as a flyweight in 1938 as a sixteen-year-old, and turned pro in 1940. His immigrant father protested when he Anglicized his name as a marketing device, but he came to appreciate the son's earning power. The elder Papaleo earned $15 per week as an employee of the Works Progress Administration (WPA), a Depression-era government program that put the unemployed to work. When Willie earned $50 by fighting two bouts in one night and presented his father with $40 from his winnings, the father responded with approval, stating: "If you fought tonight and you got forty dollars see if you can fight twice a week from now on."[57] In 1942 Pep won the world featherweight title at the age of twenty en route to sixty-two straight wins. His consummate defensive skills, crafty footwork, and ability to slip punches made him hard to hit. After a loss to Sammy Angott, Pep reeled off another seventy-three bouts without a defeat. In 1947 he suffered serious injuries in a plane crash that killed others. He endured casts for five months, and returned to boxing to defend his title. He fought four vicious fights with Sandy Saddler between 1948 and 1951, accounting for three of his losses in a remarkable 229-11-1 record. Pep continued to fight at age forty-three before finally retiring in 1966. Both the Associated Press and *Ring* magazine named him the greatest featherweight of all time. Despite such honors, the intervening years, gambling, and six marriages had taken a toll. Pep suffered from Alzheimer's disease, and died in a nursing home in 2006.[58]

Italians produced two of the more memorable middleweight division fighters in the middle decades of the twentieth century, Rocky Graziano (Thomas Rocco Barbella) and Jake LaMotta. Both displayed the angst of the Italian underclass, but were perceived differently by fans and the general public. Writer Gerald Early asserted that "Graziano was the bad boy who became one of the most beloved athletes and personalities in America. . . . LaMotta was . . . the bad boy who grew up and became a bad man." *New York Times* reporter Arthur Daley described LaMotta as one "who falls several light years short of qualifying as one of nature's noblemen . . . He wouldn't add to the décor of a room even if stuffed and placed over the mantelpiece." Sportswriter Jimmy Cannon called him "the most despised man of his generation."[59]

Only half of the ten Barbella children survived childhood. The fathers of both Graziano and LaMotta pushed them into neighborhood fights at a very young age, and both men adopted a brawling style that transported their rage to the ring. LaMotta explained that they were "always in fights. Stealing stuff. In fact, we both ended up in reform school in Coxsackie, New York, at the same time." Graziano explained, "I quit school in the sixth grade because of pneumonia. Not because I had it, but because I couldn't spell it. We stole everything that began with an 'a'— a piece of fruit, a bicycle, a watch, anything that was not nailed down." His thievery resulted in three trips to the reformatory, and he spent six of his first twenty years in jail.[60] A policeman predicted his future: "Well, there goes another little guinea on his way. Good looking kid. But I can tell his kind. Look in his eyes, you see the devil himself. Ten years from now, the Death House at Sing Sing."[61]

Graziano began fighting under assumed names and won the city Amateur Athletic Union (AAU) championship in 1939, but was drafted into the U.S. Army where he knocked out a captain in an altercation for which he spent ten months in Leavenworth prison and was given a dishonorable discharge. His fists saved him from further incarceration.[62]

Graziano maintained the physicality and camaraderie of street life, and he adhered to an Italian sense of communalism. When he began making considerable sums he bought a used Cadillac and loaded it with $1,500 worth of Christmas gifts, which he delivered to the poor children of his old New York neighborhood. He dispersed another $5,500 to their impoverished parents.[63]

The neighborhood arranged a motorcade with blaring horns down decorated streets with flowing banners after he won the world middleweight championship in 1947. Graziano stated, "They make me feel like some kind of king"; he would soon become more than just a local celebrity.[64] He exchanged the title in three bouts with Tony Zale, all ending in knockouts and considered to be among the more brutal in boxing history. Graziano was known as a heavy puncher, knocking out fifty-two opponents and finishing his career with a record of 67-10-6. He retired in 1952 and enjoyed a new and successful career as a popular actor, comedian, and television personality. He also had a number of pizza restaurants and enjoyed a long marriage to his Jewish wife that produced two daughters. In other matters he adhered to his ancestral lifestyle, speaking Italian and growing tomatoes and basil in his swank New York penthouse to remind him of the Little Italy of his youth. He maintained that "my idea of a good time is getting away from those skyscrapers to some Little Italy neighborhood, with a bunch of Italian guys in a bar like downtown Puglio's on Hester Street or the Leading Tavern in the Bronx, and laugh it up over old stories, while we load our stomachs with things like cheese, prosciutto, salami, pasta e fahzool, sausage and peppers, tripe, capozelle, everything flavored with garlic, big Italian salad, Italian bread, and strong wine." His life was chronicled in an autobiography that was made into a movie.[65]

Jake LaMotta also retained his love for Italian cooking throughout his long life. La Motta favored sausage and peppers and cooked his own eggplant parmesan and pasta. His life paralleled Graziano's in many other ways as well. LaMotta's father, an immigrant peddler, rebuked his son when he came home crying after being bullied on the streets. He gave him an ice pick and told Jake to "dig a few of them! Hit 'em with it, hit 'em first, and hit 'em hard. You come home crying anymore, I'll beat the shit outta you more than you ever get from any of them! Ya understand?" Jake remembered, "Until the ice pick, I was always the kid getting it in the ass. If it wasn't my old man belting me around, it was these kids after me, or a teacher slapping me silly—always someone asking me what right I had to be alive. The ice pick showed me what it felt like to make the other guy as afraid as I had always been." His father then forced him to fight other neighborhood kids for money to help pay the rent. He also had to fight to protect his turf as a shoe shine boy. LaMotta managed to get a ninth grade education, but a failed jewelry store heist earned him a year and a half stay at the Coxsackie reformatory. Upon his release he took up formal boxing, winning all twenty-one of his amateur bouts, and supporting his mother and four siblings by pawning the watches he won.[66]

Upon turning pro he was able to buy a house for his extended family and an apartment building to sustain his separated father. In the ring he unleashed his pent up rage in furious assaults on opponents, earning the nickname "The Bronx Bull." "LaMotta was an outstanding middleweight renowned for his incredible stamina. He was less than 5 feet 7 inches tall, but his torso was constructed along the lines of a tank. He was relentless in attack and apparently impervious to pain."[67] He fought the great Sugar Ray Robinson six times, winning the second bout—he was the first to defeat perhaps the greatest boxer of all time. Still he could not get a title shot until he agreed to throw a fight against Billy Fox in 1947, allowing the gangsters who controlled the sport to win large sums on the outcome. LaMotta also had to pay $20,000 for the opportunity to fight for the title at a later date. Graziano had also been suspended for failing to report bribes of as much as $100,000 to throw fights; both adhered to the Italian code of silence. LaMotta explained:

> Besides coming from the neighborhood I came from, I could never be a screw. You know, a stool pigeon or a rat. You could never do that in my business. Because of your ego, your manhood, your pride, whatever, you could never do anything like that. Even if you were being hurt, and it was all wrong. You had to fight your own battle. The mob was on the other side. And I was on my own, so I had to take it on the chin. . . . Besides, there were a lot of guys at that time who couldn't get any fights because they were black. And they were good. They were very good.[68]

When LaMotta finally got his chance he conquered Frenchman Marcel Cerdan in 1949 to take the middleweight championship. He lost the title to Sugar Ray Robinson in 1951 and retired in 1954. His postring career was no less traumatic. He moved to Miami to open a bar and liquor store, but went to prison for child sex trafficking (which he denied) and cocaine issues. He lost his considerable savings and became a nightclub bouncer and a comedian. His routine addressed his numerous marriages. "My first wife divorced me because I clashed with the drapes. My second wife used to ignore me all the time. And if there's one thing I can't stand, it's ignorance. I was in so much hot water I felt like a tea bag. My third wife divorced me because the only thing I said to her was, 'Darling, your stockings are wrinkled.' Now how the hell did I know she wasn't wearing any?"[69] He lost two sons, one to cancer and the other in a plane crash. His autobiography became an award-winning movie, *Raging Bull*, in 1980. He married his seventh wife in 2013 at the age of ninety.[70]

Joey Maxim (Giuseppe Berardinelli, 1922–2001) also started as a middleweight, winning the 1940 Golden Gloves and national AAU titles in that division. He turned pro in 1941, served in the U.S. Army during World War II, and grew into a light heavyweight. He won that championship in 1950 and held it for two years until losing it to Archie Moore. He had the distinction of being the only fighter to gain a technical knockout over Sugar Ray Robinson in their 1952 bout. He retired in 1958 after a long ring career.[71]

His contemporary, Carmen Basilio, was the son of immigrant share-cropping onion farmers in Canastota, New York, one of ten children. His father returned to Italy and fought in the Italian army during World War I. Basilio began boxing on his high school team. He stated that "it was the only reason I went to high school." When the school dropped the sport, he dropped out of school. Basilio joined the Marine Corps at the age of seventeen and joined its boxing team. He began his pro career in 1948 but developed slowly with uneven results until he found a trainer and manager. Noted for his toughness and his assiduous dedication to training that produced remarkable endurance, he slowly gained recognition, capturing the welterweight championship in 1955 and defending it in the 1956 Fight of the Year (*Ring Magazine*) against fellow Italian Tony DeMarco (Leonard Liotta). He lost it to Johnny Saxton in a disputed decision, possibly engineered by the corrupt International Boxing Club that controlled the sport during the era, but regained the crown in the Fight of the Year. He then moved up to the middleweight class and defeated Sugar Ray Robinson to gain that title, which he lost to Robinson the following year. He retired in 1961 to become a physical education instructor at Le Moyne College in Syracuse, New York, and an activities director and public relations representative for a local brewery.[72]

Basilio's military service—like that of the multitude of Italian American youth who lived a hyphenated American existence—proclaimed his loyalty, but he continued to express his allegiance to his Italian family. When his mother objected to his choice of a boxing career, he replied, "'I am going to pay off your mortgages and you aren't going to owe anybody anything.' If I didn't do anything the rest of my whole career I did that for my mother and father. I took them out of debt. When I made enough money boxing I walked into the house, and I laid down the mortgage and the deeds. My dad had tears in his eyes."[73]

Joey Giardello (Carmine Tilelli) followed the path of Basilio as the next Italian to win the middleweight title. He stated that as a youth, "I had many fights in the street . . . I couldn't stand some guy picking on a little kid. There was a crippled kid who lived across the street from us. Nobody could touch him while I was around." He joined the army at sixteen by using a cousin's name, which he kept when he became a professional boxer at eighteen in 1948 without any amateur bouts. He remained a top contender for several years but could not get a title fight. An indication of the rampant corruption in the sport at that time occurred in a 1952 bout which Giardello won by split decision in New York. A state boxing commissioner then arbitrarily changed the score to give the opponent the victory. Giardello had to take the case to court to get his victory reinstated. He refused a $12,000 bribe but failed to report it. Similar to the Italian code of honor expressed by LaMotta, "the code of ethics he learned in the streets of Brooklyn prohibited any form of squealing, about fixes or anything else." Unlike Basilio, he hated training, but fought with a fury once in the ring. He finally got a chance for the title in a 1960 fight with Gene Fullmer, a brutal, dirty encounter that ended in a draw. After defeating Sugar Ray Robinson in 1963 he got another shot at the crown and defeated the Nigerian Dick Tiger, who regained the championship from Giardello in 1965. In his post-ring career Giardello sold insurance and became involved in the Special Olympics and other services for children with disabilities. One of his own sons was born mentally impaired.[74]

After Giardello beat Tiger for the championship his former manager declared him to be "the last of the great white fighters."[75] The fighter who really solidified whiteness for Italians was Rocky Marciano (Marchegiano). While the first generation of Italian immigrants were not treated as whites, their children lived in two worlds as the hyphenated Italian Americans, trying to assimilate in schools and the larger society, while adhering to their ancestral language, foods, and customs at home. Among them were Joe DiMaggio, the great baseball player for the New York Yankees; Frank Sinatra, the popular singing icon and movie star;

and Rocky Marciano, undefeated heavyweight champion from 1952 to 1956. Together they achieved acceptance for Italians in the mainstream culture. Marciano did so as the unsolicited representative of whites against the rising tide of black boxers.

Marciano was born to Italian immigrants in Brockton, Massachusetts, on September 1, 1923. His father served in the U.S. Marine Corps in World War I and had been gassed and wounded in the battle for the Argonne Forest. He returned to Brockton to work in the shoe factory. It was not a fulfilling life. The parents and six children (one died in infancy) lived in a small house with no heat, no hot water, and no bathtub. Rocky, the eldest, swore that he would never work in a shoe factory. As a youth he loved baseball, and played both baseball and football on the Brockton High School teams until dropping out of school as a sophomore. Working-class Italian families valued the extra income of their working children rather than education, which was deemed unavailable and a waste of time in the old country. Rocky toiled away at odd jobs until drafted into the army in 1943, where he served with the combat engineers. After his release he got a tryout with a Chicago Cubs minor league team, but failed to make the cut. He then turned his attention to boxing, which he had taken up while in the military service.[76]

As a boxer, he lacked finesse but threw powerful punches, preferring to brawl with opponents until he landed a crushing right hand. He entered the professional ranks in 1947, and two years later he nearly killed Carmine Vingo, who suffered a fractured skull and a severe concussion. Vingo had become the twenty-fifth straight opponent to fall to Marciano, and all but two had been by knockouts. Marciano paid his hospital expenses and also provided a hefty sum for his family. Vingo would recover to become a close friend.[77]

Marciano became a hero in his hometown and the community presented him with his first car. Residents bet heavily on his matches, and he began to attract national attention with the growth of television. *Time* magazine described his popularity in begrudging terms as "a simple, good natured fellow. . . . He was brilliant in sports as he was dull in books, and sports mean more to most boys . . . the rippling muscularity of his workouts bespeak an unclouded mind in a body sound as a brick. . . . To hero-hungry fans from Brockton and across the nation, Rocky is far more than a winner . . . he is Hercules, Ivanhoe, Paul Bunyan." His eighth-round knockout of an aging Joe Louis in 1951, Marciano's idol as a youth, signaled the end of an era and the media promotion of the Italian as a new "white hope." Louis had knocked out a string of Italian heavyweights—Al Ettore, Nathan Mann (Manchetti), Tony Galento, Gus Dorazio, Tony Musto, and Tami Mauriello—before Marciano reclaimed Italian and white honor. Sugar Ray Robinson had also defeated the best of the Italian middleweights in Rocky Graziano, Jake LaMotta and, later, Carmen Basilio. Interracial and interethnic encounters still drew the attention of fans as the civil rights movement began to stir American society in the 1950s and boxing promoters sought such confrontations in the ring.[78]

The next year Marciano knocked out Jersey Joe Walcott in the thirteenth round to win the heavyweight championship in a bout that was telecast nationally to thirty-one states. His 1953 defeat of Roland La Starza by technical knockout, and his 1954 knockout of Ezzard Charles were both declared the Fight of the Year by *Ring* magazine. His last fight against Archie Moore on September 21, 1955, took place in Yankee Stadium before more than 61,000 spectators. Countless others listened on the radio, and a closed-circuit telecast reached ninety-two cities. He retired from the ring in 1956 with a record of 49-0, the only undefeated heavyweight champion in the history of the sport. Forty-three of his victories were acquired via knockouts. In retirement, despite his obsessive frugality, he lost a lot of money by loaning it without retribution. He dealt only in cash as he distrusted banks, lawyers, and accountants. He had paid off his parents' mortgage, bought their home appliances, and sent them on trips to Italy. Of his own aspirations he stated, "The one thing I want to do is make a tour of Europe, especially Italy . . . and get acquainted with relatives. . . . The biggest thrill I can think of would be an audience with the pope."[79]

Marciano died in a plane crash on August 31, 1969, but he left a lasting legacy. Despite the fact that he consorted with underworld figures and that his manager, Al Weill, served as a promoter of matches for the notorious International Boxing Club, Marciano was respected for his integrity and honesty. There is no concern that he ever engaged in fixed matches. He wore his ethnicity proudly. Although he allowed Weill to slightly change his surname, he insisted that it retain its Italian character. Famed boxing trainer Lou Duva said Marciano "was a real Italian . . . Italian food was his thing. We'd rather go into a little Italian restaurant, him and I, and grab a good Italian meal, rather than go to a fancy place where you had to put on a tux or be catered to." Angelo Dundee asserted that Marciano "meant a lot to Italian Americans, naturally. . . . He was loved and respected." His unblemished record can only be equaled, never surpassed, which entitled him, and symbolically all Italians, a place not just among ethnic heroes but among the American pantheon as well.[80]

Although Marciano is assured the highest honor among Italian boxers, ethnic Italian fighters remained a continued presence throughout the twentieth century. Willie Pastrano's pro boxing career began in 1951 as a sixteen-year-old in his native New Orleans. He fought in every weight class from welterweight to heavyweight, winning the light heavyweight championship of the world in 1963, which he held for two years.[81]

Nino Benvenuti, born in Italy, won a gold medal in the 1960 Olympics at Rome, then turned pro, capturing the European middleweight championship, and in 1965 the WBA version of the light middleweight title. He beat Emile Griffith for the world middleweight crown in 1967. Vito Antuofermo was also born in Italy, but migrated to Brooklyn as a boy. He captured the world middleweight crown in 1979.[82]

Ray "Boom Boom" Mancini represented the third generation of Italian Americans. His grandfather had emigrated from Sicily in 1913. His father, Lenny, had been raised by an uncle, Firpo, named for the Argentinian Italian heavyweight, after his father went to prison as a bootlegger. As a Youngstown, Ohio, millworker the father had worked twelve hours per day, six days per week for twenty cents per hour, and running liquor during Prohibition seemed like a quicker and easier way to make a living. As caretaker, Firpo arranged street-corner battles between neighborhood kids, including Lenny, and gambled on the outcomes. Lenny left school after the fifth grade. He joined the Civilian Conservation Corps, a New Deal work program for Depression-era youth that built the National Parks system and enabled young men to send their paychecks home to their needy families. Lenny made extra money as a fighter in camp boxing matches. He turned pro in 1937 and reached contender status until World War II and the wounds he suffered derailed his quest for the lightweight championship.[83]

His son, Ray, born in Youngstown in 1961, resumed the crusade. Ray emulated his father and took up boxing at fourteen. Two years later he had won the regional Golden Gloves championship, and began his professional pursuit of the lightweight title in 1979 at a time when the industrial economy of the Midwest was in shambles. The steel mills and local plants of Youngstown experienced massive layoffs. The city struggled. Ray became their working-class hero. One unemployed steelworker stated, "I can tell you honestly, he's about all we've got that's good here. There's not much else to go on."[84]

Historian Marcus Lee Hansen predicted as early as 1938 that the offspring of immigrants would flee from their ethnicity in the quest for assimilation, yet the third generation would experience a resurgence of ethnic identity. One might argue that the Mancini family retained its Italian identity throughout the century. Ray revered his father and never missed Sunday mass. He wore red, white, and green trunks, the same colors as the Italian flag, to symbolize his Italian identity as he moved up the lightweight ranks. When he beat Jorge Morales for the North American Boxing Federation (NABF) version of the lightweight crown in a nationally televised fight in 1981, he rejoiced by kissing his beloved father on the mouth. Although he lost a tough fight to Alexis Arguello for the World Boxing Council (WBC) version of the title later that year; he rebounded to knock out Pepe Frias for the WBA title in 1982 in a memorable war that lasted only two rounds. Youngstown organized a parade in his honor, gave him the keys to the city, and named a street after him. Ray honored his father by placing the title belt around Lenny as the motorcade made its way through the city. Ray took his parents to Sicily to see their relatives, where the townspeople of Bagheria awakened at 4 a.m. to see his fights on television. They treated his arrival as if it were a papal visit.[85]

Mancini brought his next title defense to Warren, Ohio, which brought approximately $8 million in revenue to the deflated local economy. After stopping Ernesto Espana in six rounds, he then took on Deuk-Koo Kim, the South Korean fighter touted as the Asian champion in Las Vegas on November 13, 1982. In a brutal encounter, Kim pledged to win or die, a tragic prophecy as he suffered a terrible beating that ended in the fourteenth round. He died four days later with dreadful consequences for all involved. Kim left behind an unborn child; his mother and the referee of the bout both committed suicide; and Mancini would be haunted for the rest of his life. The aftermath changed the sport, as well, as the various boxing governing bodies reduced championship bouts from fifteen to twelve rounds after a study showed that the most damage to boxers occurred after the twelfth round.[86]

Mancini continued to hold the title until 1984 when he lost it to Livingstone Bramble. Mancini lost a rematch with Bramble and then waited four years before losing a split decision to Hector "Macho" Camacho. With a knockout loss to Greg Haugen in 1991 Mancini finally called it quits and pursued an acting career.[87]

With the downfall of Mancini, Vinny Pazienza carried the Italian flag in a long career (1983–2004) in which he fought in fifteen different title fights, winning the IBF lightweight championship (1987–1988), the WBA light middleweight crown (1991–1992), and the International Boxing Council (IBC) super middleweight laurels (1994–1997). Arturo Gatti, born in Calabria, Italy in 1972, moved to Montreal, Canada, where he followed an older brother into boxing. An exciting battler, he fought in several weight classes, winning titles as an IBF super featherweight (1995–1998), WBC super lightweight (2004–2005), and International Boxing Association (IBA) welterweight (2006). The success of Paulie Malignaggi (WBC light welterweight champ, 2004; IBF light welterweight champ, 2007–2008; World Boxing Organization/North American Boxing Association [WBO/NABO] light welterweight champ, 2009; and WBA welterweight champ, 2012) indicates that Italians continue to hold some stature in the sweet science, although their dominance has been superseded by others.[88]

Black Boxers

By the mid-twentieth century Africa began producing a corps of top fighters. Hogan Kid Bassey (Okon Bassey Asuquo) from Nigeria spent eleven years in the ring (1949–1959) as a featherweight. He worked his way through the local ranks to gain the Nigerian national championships in the flyweight and bantamweight divisions in 1949 and 1950. By 1955 he had earned the British Empire featherweight title, and won the world featherweight championship in 1957, holding it for two years.[89]

Dick Tiger (Richard Ihetu), another Nigerian, followed Bassey into the professional ranks in 1952. A decade later he defeated Gene Fullmer for the WBA middleweight championship, and claimed the WBC version of that title the following year. *Ring* magazine declared him the Fighter of the Year in 1962 and again in 1965. In 1965–1966 he held both the WBA and WBC forms of the middleweight titles before moving up to the light heavyweight class in the latter year. Upon defeating Jose Torres in 1966 Tiger became the light heavyweight champion of both the WBA and WBC for two years. He retired in 1970 to become a security guard at the New York Metropolitan Museum of Art, succumbing to liver cancer only a year later.[90]

Cornelius Boza-Edwards, born in Uganda in 1956, transferred to Las Vegas to pursue greater boxing rewards, which he achieved as the WBC super featherweight champ in 1981. Another Ugandan, John "The Beast" Mugabi, represented his country on the 1980 Olympic team, winning a silver medal as a welterweight. As a professional he fought as a middleweight, starting his career with twenty-five straight knockouts. He held the WBC light middleweight championship from 1989 to 1990, finishing with a record of 42-7-1 with thirty-nine victories by way of knockout.[91]

Ghana has also produced a bevy of top boxers, most notably Azumah Nelson, born in Accra in 1958. He fought professionally from 1979 to 2008, holding the WBC featherweight championship from 1984 to 1988, and then retaining the WBC super featherweight title from 1988 to 1994 and again from 1995 to 1997. Ike Quartey, another Ghanaian, had twenty-six siblings, one of whom won a silver medal as an Olympic boxer in 1960. His father, officially a court bailiff, was also noted as a tough street fighter. Quartey began boxing at age seven and entered the amateur ranks by fourteen. As a professional from 1988 to 2006, he held the WBA welterweight crown from 1994 to 1997. Such countries as Nigeria, Uganda, and Ghana have developed a boxing tradition and Africa continues to produce world-class fighters in the twenty-first century.[92]

African Americans have produced a bevy of champions throughout the past century. In addition to those discussed in chapter 4, black Americans dominated the welterweight and middleweight ranks during the 1980s. "Marvelous" Marvin Hagler plied his trade from 1973 to 1987, ending his career with a record of 62-3-2 with fifty-two knockouts as a middleweight. He won the national AAU middleweight championship as an amateur in 1973, and proceeded to rule the professional ranks from 1980 to 1987 as WBA, WBC, and IBF (1983–1987) middleweight champion. He was named Fighter of the Year in 1983 and again in 1985.

Both the Associated Press and *Ring* magazine named him among the greatest middleweights of all time. He retired to a movie career in Italy.[93]

Hagler's contemporary, Thomas "Hit Man" Hearns, won the Golden Gloves and AAU light welterweight championships in 1977 and began his pro career that same year. He continued to fight until 2006, becoming the first boxer to win titles in four weight divisions and then the first to accomplish that feat across five weight classes. He held the welterweight championship from 1980 to 1981 (United States Boxing Association and WBA), the WBC super welterweight title from 1982 to 1986, the NABF middleweight crown in 1986, and won both the WBC middleweight and light heavyweight laurels in 1987. The following year he gained the NABF and WBO super middleweight titles and followed that with the WBA light heavyweight championship in 1991. He then moved up to the cruiserweight division, taking the NABF version of the title in 1994, the World Boxing Union belt in 1995, and the International Boxing Organization (IBO) championship in 1999. *Ring* magazine named him Fighter of the Year in 1980 and 1984, and in 1994 he was deemed to be the greatest junior middleweight of all time. He finished with a record of 61-5-1 with forty-eight knockouts, but did lose a 1985 bout for the middleweight championship to Hagler by a technical knockout.[94]

In a decade that produced many outstanding boxers, Sugar Ray Leonard emerged as the most prominent. Born in 1956, he began to attract notice as the 1973 national Golden Gloves lightweight champion, and followed that performance with the Golden Gloves and AAU light welterweight title the following year. He repeated the latter win in 1975, then took the Olympic gold medal in 1976 at Montreal in the same weight class. He adopted the nickname of "Sugar Ray" Robinson and the flashy style and showmanship of Muhammad Ali, with Ali's former trainer, Angelo Dundee, assuming the same role for Leonard. As a professional he took the WBC welterweight title from Wilfredo Benitez in a 1979 technical knockout. He lost it in the first of three memorable battles with Roberto Duran in 1980 and regained it in the famous "no mas (no more)" fight in which a frustrated Duran refused to continue after the eighth round in the rematch. Over the next two years Leonard accumulated the WBA light middleweight and welterweight championships. He unified the WBC and the WBA welterweight titles by a fourteenth round technical knockout of previously unbeaten Tommy Hearns in the 1981 Fight of the Year.[95]

Leonard retired due to a detached retina in 1982; the respite proved temporary. He returned two years later, and then took another three-year hiatus. In 1987 he upset Marvin Hagler to take the WBC middleweight crown in another Fight of the Year that grossed more than $100 million. He captured the WBC light heavyweight and super middleweight belts a year later. In 1989 he fought to a draw in a rematch with Hearns, and then earned a unanimous decision in the final bout against Duran. Leonard lost to Terry Norris in 1991 and returned for one final bout, a loss to Hector "Macho" Camacho in 1997. After leaving the ring he became a boxing promoter and a television analyst for bouts. He was the first boxer to earn more than $100 million in purses, and both *Ring* magazine and the Associated Press named him among the greatest welterweights of all time.[96]

Among the stellar African Americans who succeeded the stars of the 1980s, Roy Jones, Jr. amassed a record of 56-8-0 with forty knockouts as a cruiserweight from 1989 to 2012. Jones began boxing as a ten-year-old and he had garnered the national Golden Gloves championships in 1988 and 1989. He represented the U.S. Olympic team in 1988 in Seoul, Korea, where his silver medal finish was highly disputed, so much so that officials awarded him the most outstanding boxer trophy despite the official loss. As a professional boxer, Jones became the first to hold six world championships across four different weight classes: IBF middleweight (1993–1994), IBF super middleweight (1994–1996), WBC light heavyweight (1997), WBA and WBC light heavyweight (1997–2000), IBO light heavyweight (2000), National Boxing Associaiton, World Boxing Federation (WBF), and IBA light heavyweight (2001), WBC light heavyweight (2003–2004), WBA heavyweight (2003–2004), WBA and North American Boxing Association (NABA) light heavyweight (2006), and IBC light heavyweight (2007). He won the WBA heavyweight championship in 2003 despite a nearly thirty-pound weight disadvantage against John Ruiz. The multitalented Jones also pursued a variety of other interests as he played professional basketball, and became a rapper, a promoter, and an actor.[97]

Floyd Mayweather, Jr. (Floyd Sinclair) continues to collect championships. Born in 1977, he began boxing as a seven-year-old. By 2012 he had won eight world titles in five weight classes (WBA super featherweight, 1998–2002; WBC lightweight, 2002–2004; WBC super lightweight, 2005–2006; IBF welterweight, 2006; WBC welterweight, 2006–2008, 2011; WBC super welterweight and light middleweight, 2007; WBA super welterweight, 2012) and had become the highest paid athlete. As of 2013 he remained undefeated with a record of 43-0 with twenty-six knockout victories.[98]

Equally remarkable, Bernard Hopkins continued to fight over a twenty-five-year career that started in 1988, becoming the oldest champion in modern boxing history when he defeated Tavoris Cloud to claim the IBF light heavyweight title on March 9, 2013, at the age of forty-eight. He had previously held the world middleweight crown from 1995 to 2005, successfully defending that championship twenty times over the course of the decade.[99]

Hispanic Boxers

Hispanics have suffered under the same strictures as earlier immigrant groups by being labeled as inconclusively white. The Spanish-American War of 1898 resulted in the U.S. occupation of Puerto Rico, and the racial differences became immediately apparent: "A comparative social study determined that 'in the United States, a man's color determines what class he belongs to[;] in Puerto Rico, a man's class determines what color he is.' Puerto Rico had eighteen different terms to designate one's skin color, while the United States saw only black and white."[100] Residents of the islands had been granted citizenship in 1917, and gained commonwealth status in 1952; neither assured them the rights and privileges of whiteness. By the mid-twentieth century the migration of Puerto Ricans to and from New York became known as the Nuyorican community. As it was for ethnic groups of previous generations, boxing seemed to be one avenue for social mobility. Wilfred Benitez was born in the Bronx in 1958 and relocated with his family to San Juan as a boy, where he became a boxing idol. Turning pro in 1973, he became the youngest champion in boxing history when he won the WBA junior welterweight title in 1976. He later added the WBC welterweight crown in 1979 and the WBC super welterweight belt in 1981. He continued to fight until 1990, amassing $7 million in winnings—all for naught. Boxing offered temporary gains in economic capital, but ultimately produced false hope. Severe brain damage required round-the-clock care by family members.[101]

Wilfredo Gomez followed Benitez as the next prominent Puerto Rican champion, starting his pro career in 1974. From 1977 to 1983 he held the WBC super bantamweight title, and added the WBC featherweight championship the next year. He held the WBA super featherweight crown in 1985–1986, finishing his career in 1989 with a record of 4-3-1 with forty-two knockouts.[102]

Edwin Rosario, like his predecessors, turned pro at a young age, entering the paid ranks at sixteen in 1979. By 1983 he held the WBC lightweight title, and later added the WBA version (1986–1987 and 1989–1990). In 1991 he won the WBA light welterweight championship. He compiled a record of 47-6 with forty-one knockouts before his early death in 1997. Felix Trinidad, born in Puerto Rico in 1973, fought professionally from 1990 to 2008. It took him only three years to gain his first championship, holding the IBF welterweight title for seven years. He added the WBC welterweight version from 1999 to 2000, as well as the WBA (2000, 2000–2001) and IBF light middleweight belts (2000–2001). In 2001 he moved up to win the WBA middleweight championship. He retired in 2008 with a record of 42-3.[103]

Hector "Macho" Camacho proved to be the most ostentatious of the Puerto Rican champions. A flashy and colorful showman, he exhibited flair both inside and outside the ring. He started boxing in New York, winning multiple Golden Gloves titles before embarking on professional laurels in 1980. He remained undefeated until 1991, winning championships across seven weight divisions, including the WBC super featherweight (1983–1984), WBC lightweight (1985–1987), and WBO junior welterweight (1989–1991 and again in 1991–1992). He continued to box at the age of forty-eight in 2010 and was never stopped in the ring, compiling a record of 79-6-3. While in Puerto Rico in 2012, however, he was shot outside a bar, leaving him brain dead. His wake, held in Puerto Rico, attracted the past and present boxing luminaries of the territory, and at his funeral, held in Spanish Harlem, thousands of fans mourned his passing.[104]

Puerto Rico has had a long history of producing stellar athletes since the 1930s, especially in baseball and boxing. The endemic poverty of the commonwealth relative to the mainland United States has pushed many young men into the ring in search of a better life, but far too many have lived a short one. This is exemplified by Joseph Moncure March's poem:

A fighter's life is short at best.
No time to waste;
No time to rest.
The spotlight shifts:
The clock ticks fast:
All youth become old age at last.
All fighters weaken.
All fighters crack.
All fighters go—
And they never come back.
Well—
So it goes:
Time hits the hardest blows.[105]

Despite such hardships—or perhaps because of them—"indigenous boxers and baseball players promoted a nationalistic pride that separated them from other American citizens. They accentuated that difference in the selection of their own flag, their own anthem, and their own Olympic team. They revel in their athletic heroes, who have demonstrated an excellence worthy of any independent nation."[106]

Mexicans have labored under similar plights as Puerto Ricans in their questionable whiteness and relegation to poverty. But poverty elicits toughness, a quintessential necessity for boxers, and Mexican fighters have been renowned for their tenacity and fortitude in the ring for more than a century. Mexicans engaged in early bouts along the border in the southwestern United States during the nineteenth century, and by the 1930s Los Angeles had become a mecca for interracial and interethnic bouts.[107]

By mid-century Jose Napoles emerged as a top welterweight. Born in Cuba in 1940, he defected to Mexico in the wake of the Cuban Revolution led by Fidel Castro. In 1969 he won the world (WBA and WBC) welterweight championship, which he held for a year, and then regained it in 1971, defending it through 1975. In 1969 he was chosen as the Fighter of the Year and became a national hero in his adopted country. Mexican fighters also began to wear trunks that displayed their national colors of green, white, and red.[108]

Ruben Olivares, born in Mexico City in 1947 as one of twelve children (half of whom died), felt the pangs of early poverty. Street fighting was endemic in his neighborhood, similar to the urban ghettos of America in the early twentieth century. Often suspended from school for fighting, he decided to make it his career choice. Beginning in 1965 he opened his ring quest with twenty-three straight knockouts and sixty-one consecutive wins as a bantamweight. He possessed a vicious left hook and opponents claimed that he hit like a heavyweight. His three fights with fellow Mexican Jesus Castillo (1970–1971) produced more than a million dollars in revenue as they exchanged the bantamweight title, with Olivares owning a 2 to 1 advantage. Olivares held the WBA and WBC bantamweight championship twice (1969–1970 and 1971–1972), and won the featherweight title as well (WBA, 1974; WBC, 1975). He fought until 1988 with a record of 89-13-3. The Associated Press named him co-bantamweight of the century. Olivares shared that distinct honor with Carlos Zarate, another devastating puncher as a bantamweight. Zarate held the championship from 1976 to 1978, and again in 1979, accumulating a record of 66-4 with sixty-three knockouts, a 90 percent rate, among the highest ever recorded in boxing.[109]

Salvador Sanchez also started young and left behind a great, but short career in boxing. Born in 1959, he entered the pro boxing ranks in 1975 and garnered the WBC featherweight crown by 1980. The following year *Ring* magazine named him the Fighter of the Year. He had already recorded a mark of 44-1-1 when he died in a car crash at the young age of twenty-three in 1982.[110]

Among the greatest of Mexican champions, Julio Cesar Chavez began boxing in 1980 at the age of seventeen. He went undefeated for the next fourteen years, with only a draw after eighty-seven straight wins, and two more victories before losing his light welterweight title to Frankie Randall in 1994, a setback he soon avenged. His 1990 title bout with Meldrick Taylor was declared not only the Fight of the Year but the Fight of the Decade. He won titles in three weight divisions: WBC super featherweight (1984–1987), lightweight (WBA, 1987–1989, and WBC, 1988–1989), WBC light welterweight (1989–1994, 1994–1996), and IBF light welterweight (1990–1991), before his retirement in 2005 with a record of 107-6-2.[111]

Mexican fighters continue to challenge for multiple championships. From 1993 to 2012 Juan Manuel Marquez achieved a mark of 55-6-1, winning seven world titles across four weight classes (IBF and WBA featherweight, 2003–2005; WBO featherweight, 2006–2007; WBA and WBO lightweight, 2009–2012; WBO light welterweight, 2012 to the present). He has attracted worldwide attention in his rivalry with Filipino great Manny Pacquiao. Their four matches have resulted in three disputed decisions. The first, in 2004, ended in a draw. In 2007 Marquez lost on a split decision, and in 2011 on a majority decision; he reclaimed his honor with a knockout victory in 2012. He now resides in California.[112]

Mexican American fighters continue to express their ancestral pride. Abel Davilla of Texas stated, "When I started to feel that my Mexican American heritage really meant a lot was when I started to move to San Antonio and people told me that you fight like a Mexican. If you're Latino, you'll fight like you've never fought before, as hard as you can. If you do that—win, lose, or draw—you feel great." Conrad Sanchez stated that "it is part of our history; you're Mexican, you fight—like a rooster." Like the Jews and Italians before them, the Mexican fighters subscribe to a communal society in which they are beholden to a larger group, and feel responsible for the representation of *latinidad*. Artist LeRoy Nieman described such a communal experience like a religious ritual: "When the Latin fighter comes into the ring, there is a procession that comes down the aisle. They are holding belts up like saint relics; they're coming down and it is a ritual procession. It's like they're going to say mass or something: its religious . . . it's a sacrifice. And the crowd picks up on that—the crowd is in a frenzy—and they're ready to fight. And God is with them. It's beautiful."[113] John Ruiz, although born in Massachusetts in 1972, bestowed a great sense of accomplishment and honor when he became the first Hispanic to win the heavyweight championship in 2001 (WBA, 2001–2003).[114]

Perhaps the Mexican American who has elicited the greatest recognition—at least until marital woes, alcohol, and drugs tarnished his image—was Oscar De La Hoya. De La Hoya was born in California in 1973 after his parents migrated from Mexico. Both his father and grandfather had been boxers. He vowed to win a gold medal for his mother, who died before she fulfilled her dream, at the 1992 Olympics. He then turned pro and won his first thirty-one bouts, acting as his own manager from 1993 to 2008. In his storied ring career he accumulated a host of championship titles: WBO super featherweight (1994); WBO lightweight (1994–1996); IBF lightweight (1995); WBC light welterweight (1996–1997); WBC welterweight (1997–1999); WBC welterweight (2000); WBC light middleweight (2001–2003); WBA light middleweight (2002–2003); WBO middleweight (2004); and WBC light middleweight (2006–2007). His pay-per-view fights tallied $680,600,000. In 1995 he earned Fighter of the Year honors, and also established a charitable foundation that provided for a charter high school, a cancer center, and a children's medical center to serve the Hispanic community of East Los Angeles. His success in the ring, his youth, and his good luck enabled him to enjoy crossover celebrity status in the mainstream culture. In 2000 he branched out to release a Latin pop album and one of his songs received a Grammy nomination. In 2002 he founded Golden Boy Promotions, which made him a major player in the arrangement of boxing spectacles, the first Hispanic to own such a company. In 2007 De La Hoya bought *Ring* magazine, considered to be the bible of boxing. In addition to his promotional ventures he has become a real estate developer, a model entrepreneur for the Latin community.[115]

The Hispanic population outside of North America has also produced several champions. Carlos Monzon, born into poverty in Argentina in 1942, began his professional boxing career in 1963. He languished in local bouts until fifty straight wins brought him contender status in 1970. That year he won the WBA middleweight championship, which he held for seven years. He also acquired the WBC version (1970–1974, 1976–1977). In 1972 he was honored as the Fighter of the Year, and remained undefeated for thirteen years (1964–1977) until he retired. He developed a lavish lifestyle, cavorted with the elites of society, and had a reputation as a Casanova despite a marriage. He later killed his common-law wife and died at the age of fifty-two in a car crash.[116]

Alexis Arguello entered the world in poverty in Managua, Nicaragua in 1952, one of nine children born to a shoemaker and his wife. He learned to fight early, stating that it was "neighborhood against neighborhood, we'd fight just to see who was the best." He began his ring quest in that city in 1968; politics interfered with his ambitions. He wanted to win a championship for his country, but Nicaragua became mired in a civil war between the Sandinista movement which overthrew the Somoza dictatorship and fought the U.S.-backed Contras from 1979 to 1990. Arguello would eventually be banned from the country, and his property confiscated.[117]

Arguello's first fifty-one bouts took place in Central America; in 1974 he traveled to California to defeat Ruben Olivares in a featherweight title bout (WBA, 1974–1977). From 1978 to 1980 he held the WBC super featherweight championship and then moved up to take the WBC lightweight crown (1981–1983). He continued to move up in weight and challenged Aaron Pryor for the junior welterweight title in 1982, a fight deemed to be the Fight of the Decade and the eighth best title fight of all time. Both *Ring* magazine and the Associated Press named him the greatest junior lightweight of all time. Arguello retired in 1995 with a record of 89-8 and became a boxing judge until 2001. In 2008 Nicaragua honored him as its flag bearer at the Olympic Games in China. He died a suicide in 2009 at the age of fifty-seven.[118]

Panamanian Roberto Duran battled his way out of extreme poverty to become a national treasure. Beginning as a seventeen-year-old, he started his venture by going 72-1 over the first thirteen years of his long career. He reached championship status by capturing the WBA lightweight title in 1972, which he held for seven years. He accrued the WBA version in 1978, and then won the WBC welterweight crown in 1980 from Sugar Ray Leonard. He returned to Panama on the presidential plane, feted with champagne, and slept in the presidential palace. He stated, "I understand the importance my life holds for people who are poor and have nothing."[119]

But the rematch later that year resulted in the infamous "no mas" contest in which Duran quit in the eighth round. Panamanians who revered him were shocked in disbelief, and Duran struggled for the remainder of his career to win redemption. Graffiti in Panama labeled him "a traitor" and he stated that "the only thing they didn't call me was a *maricon* (homosexual). The most common cry was 'Vende patria.' (You sold out your country.)" He held the WBA light middleweight laurels from 1982 to 1984 and the WBC middleweight championship from 1989 to 1990. His 1989 defeat of Iran Barkley for that title was honored as the Fight of the Year. Duran retired in 2001 at the age of fifty; by that time the Associated Press had already named him the greatest lightweight of the twentieth century and *Ring* magazine confirmed him as the greatest lightweight of all time in 2001.[120]

Although he never entered the professional ring, Cuban heavyweight Teofilo Stevenson rates mention as one of the greatest amateurs of the era. At 6 feet 5 inches and 220 pounds, he dominated amateur boxing for a decade, winning three gold medals at the Olympic Games in 1972, 1976, and 1980. He declined a million dollar offer to turn pro and face Muhammad Ali, choosing to remain loyal to the Communist revolution in Cuba. He died in 2012 of a heart attack, honored as a national hero.[121]

Asian Boxers

Asian fighters have been prominent, particularly in the lower weight divisions, for decades. Thai fighters emerged as champions in the post–World War II era. Chartchai Chionoi fought from 1959 to 1975, gaining the flyweight championship (WBC, 1966–1969, 1970; WBA, 1973–1974) before completing his career with a record of 61-18-3.Saensak Muangsurin had a shorter, but no less productive, career. Fighting from 1974 to 1981, he managed to win the WBC light welterweight title in only his third professional bout in 1975. He held the title for a year and then regained it from 1976 to 1978. He fought only twenty bouts in his career, but twelve were world title bouts.[122]

Khaosai Galaxy (born Sohla Saengham in 1959) became a world champion kickboxer, but also took up boxing in 1980. He held the WBA super flyweight title from 1984 to 1992. His name change ensured an even greater public visibility in the Thai celebrity culture, and his ring record of 47-1 with forty-one knockout victories earned him the nickname of the "Thai Tyson." His twin brother won the WBA bantamweight championship in 1988, making them the first set of twins to both hold world titles.[123]

Sot Chitalada followed Galaxy as a champion among the flyweights (WBC, 1984–1988, 1989–1991), ending in 1992 with a record of 26-4-1. Saman Sorjaturong (born Saman Sriprated in 1969) also reigned over the light flyweight class as WBC (1995–1999) and IBF (1995–1996) champ, finishing his ring career in 2005 with a final mark of 46-8-1. Veeraphol Sahaprom, born in 1968, got a relatively late start as a pro boxer in 1994, having practiced the muay thai form before that. He lasted until 2010, finishing with a record of 66-4-2. He won a world title in only his fourth pro bout and reigned as bantamweight champion from 1995 to1996 (WBA) and 1998 to 2005 (WBC). Thai boxers continue as stalwarts at the lower weight classes as Pongsaklek Wonjongkam (Phongskorn Wonjongkam) captured the WBC flyweight championship in 2001 and held it until 2007, and then regained it from 2010 to 2012.[124]

Korea had been under Japanese sovereignty since the early twentieth century. It remained so until the end of World War II when the peninsula was divided between the political factions of North and South Korea, which resulted in the Korean War (1950–1953). Boxing became emblematic of the martial spirit instilled in the Korean population and a means to assert national identity. Numerous Koreans, both male and female, have held world titles for a brief period of time. Among the most enduring, Ki-Soo Kim became South Korea's first world champion as a light middleweight (WBA and WBC) from 1966 to 1968. He finished his boxing career a year later with a record of 33-2-2.[125]

Chong-Pal Park began fighting as a professional when he was only seventeen in 1977. Seven years later he obtained the super middleweight title (IBF, 1984–1987; WBA, 1987–1988), accumulating a 46-5-1 record before his retirement in 1988. Jung-Koo Chang produced a stellar record of 38-4 between 1980 and 1991. He held the WBC light flyweight title from 1983 to 1988. His contemporary, Myung-Woo Yuh, held the WBA version of the light flyweight division from 1985 to 1991, and again from 1992 to 1993, suffering only one loss against thirty-eight victories.[126]

Joo-Hee Kim, born twenty years after Kim Messer, reached the heights of women's boxing as a flyweight, beginning her career in 2001. Over the past dozen years she has lost only one bout (17-1-1) while winning the World Professional Boxing Federation, Women's International Boxing Association, Women's International Boxing Federation, Global Boxing Union, International Female Boxers Association, and WBA championships, upholding a proud heritage for Korean fighters.[127]

Masamori Tokuyama, born Chang Soo Hong in Tokyo in 1974, is of North Korean ancestry. He began fighting in 1994 and often used the ring as a political stage, displaying the North Korean flag and playing its national anthem. Because of his association with the Communist state he was banned from competing in the United States, so all of his bouts took place in Asia. After his retirement in 2006 he adopted South Korean citizenship in 2007, but continued to reside in Japan. In 2000 he won the WBC super flyweight title, which he held until 2004 and regained from 2005 to 2006. Japan named him its fighter of the year in 2002.[128]

Since the late Meiji Period (1868–1912) in which Japan modernized and adopted Western technology, the country began to compete with other nations for hegemony in the Pacific. Japan defeated China in the Sino-Japanese War of 1894–1895 and then vanquished Russia in 1904–1905. Athletic challenges in the form of baseball games against American teams began in the 1890s. In 1912 Japan sent its athletes to the Olympic Games for the first time, and their swimmers and track stars challenged Western notions of superiority thereafter. The emergence of Japanese boxers in the 1930s was interrupted by the advent of World War II, and resumed in the Cold War era (see chapter 4).

Hiroshi Kobayashi, among the first of the Japanese fighters to gain worldwide notice, attained the WBA (1967–1971) and WBC (1967–1969) super featherweight championships at the same time that Shozo Saijo captured the WBA featherweight title (1968–1971), and Masao Ohba held the WBA flyweight (1970–1973) crown. Ohba owned a 35-2-1 record when he died in a car crash in 1973 at the age of twenty-three, while still champion.[129]

Japanese fighters had a brief hold on several weight classes, and Kuni-aki Shibata secured the WBA (1968–1971, 1973) and WBC (1970–1972) flyweight class for the better part of five years. He then moved up to take the WBC super featherweight championship in 1974–1975. Yoko Gushiken followed with the WBA junior flyweight title, which he held from 1976 to 1981. Jiro Watanabe controlled the upper limit of the division as WBA (1982–1984) and WBC (1984–1986) super flyweight title holder.[130]

In the early part of the twenty-first century Japanese boxers, both male and female, continued to challenge and hold the championship belts in numerous lower weight classes. Yutaka Niida entered the professional ring in 1996 and remained for a dozen years, heading the WBA minimum weight class for most of that time from 2001–2003 and 2004–2008. Female boxing has become popular in Japan over the past two decades, which will inevitably lead to future Japanese champions.[131]

Filipinos, like the Japanese, have been continual contenders in the lower weight classes, but managed to make a splash in the middle ranks as well. The Philippines has produced more than thirty world champions since 1960. Among them, Erbito Salavarria held the WBC (1970–1971) and WBA (1975–1976) flyweight crowns in a career that lasted from

1963 to 1978. The Penalosa family is particularly distinguished in this regard. Dodie Boy Penalosa followed his father into the professional boxing circuit, and produced two sons who have continued in their footsteps. Dodie Boy Penalosa fought from 1982 to 1995, holding the IBF light flyweight (1983–1986) and IBF flyweight titles (1987) during that time. His younger brothers Jonathan and Gerry (Geronimo) Penalosa upheld the family tradition. Jonathan won the WBC flyweight championship in 1989, which he held until 1992, and Gerry fought from 1989 to 2010, collecting the super flyweight belts from the WBC (1997–1998, 2000–2002) and the WBF (2004) and the WBO bantamweight title (2007–2009).[132]

Luisito Espinosa was born in Manila and stepped into the pro ring in 1984, later moving to San Francisco. In 1988 he won the California state bantamweight championship and followed that with the WBA world title in the same class the next year, keeping it until 1991. From 1995 to 1999 he held the WBC featherweight crown. Like Espinosa, Nonito Donaire was also born in the Philippines but immigrated to California, where he began to box in 2001. By 2007 he had earned recognition as the Boxer of the Year by gaining the IBF (2007–2009) and IBO (2007–2009) flyweight championships. He moved up to win the WBA super flyweight belt in 2009, and then conquered the bantamweight ranks of both the WBC and WBO in 2011, proceeding to take the IBF (2012) and WBO (2012–2013) super bantamweight titles as well.[133]

The most acclaimed of all Filipino boxers has been Manny Pacquiao, born in 1978, who began fighting as a sixteen-year-old in 1995. His successes drew global attention and recognition as, pound for pound, Pacquaio is the best boxer in the world—the first to garner eight world championships in eight different weight classes. Pacquiao initiated his dominance by claiming the WBC flyweight championship in 1998, followed by the IBF super bantamweight (2001) and the IBF featherweight (2003) crowns, as well as the WBC super featherweight title in 2005. He moved up to the lightweight division to take the WBC version in 2008, then the IBO light welterweight and WBO welterweight belts in 2009, and the WBC light middleweight championship in 2010. Pacquiao was named Fighter of the Year in 2006, 2008, and 2009; the Boxing Writers Association subsequently honored him as the Boxer of the Decade. In addition to his own fights, he began promoting other bouts in both the Philippines and the United States. His interests led him to roles as a singer and movie and television actor. His popularity reached mania proportions in his home country and he started his own political party. Filipinos elected him to the national legislature in 2009. Pacquiao stated, "All my life I have had to fight. At first as a child I had to fight just to get something to eat." About his political aspirations, he declared, "I believe this world needs new heroes. The biggest fight in my life is not boxing but it is now to end poverty in my country." To that effect he established a foundation to address such social issues affecting the Filipino populace.[134]

Like members of other ethnic groups, boxing has enabled Pacquiao and the minority of others who have enjoyed success in the ring to gain greater visibility, a measure of socioeconomic capital, and celebrity status. For more than a century boxers have been defined by their race and ethnicity. In the worst of cases interethnic battles have promoted deep-seated nationalism, racism, and ethnocentric pride; but in the best instances, the bouts have taught fans to admire the shared tenacity, spirit, and physical excellence possessed by all cultures. In the best examples, such as Pacquiao's, one can witness the common humanity and an idealistic concern for others that transcends the boxing ring.

CHAPTER SIX

RELIGION

Religion carries little significance in boxing today, but it played a more important role in the past. For thousands of years religious wars marked the vicissitudes of peoples throughout the world. Such differences carried over to the surrogate wars in the boxing ring for centuries as boxers were saddled with religious identities and the stereotypes that accompanied such designations.

English Jewish Boxers

Jews have historically faced persecution and were expelled from England as early as 1290. They were not allowed to serve in Parliament until 1858. Religious differences marked Jews as "others," unwilling or unable to assimilate into the mainstream Christian cultures wherever they settled in the Western world. Often stereotyped as cerebral but weak, effeminate, and cowardly due to religious prohibitions regarding bloodshed, sport provided one avenue to greater assimilation. Jews held a prominent position among boxers in England by the late eighteenth century. Foremost among the Jewish boxers was Daniel Mendoza, followed by "Dutch" Sam Elias and Barney Aaron.[1]

Mendoza (1764–1836), born to a Sephardic Jewish family, grew up in Whitechapel, a poor district, where he found work in various occupations as a glass cutter, laborer, grocer, and even an actor. He claimed that he became a boxer because he was "frequently drawn into contests with butchers and others in the neighbourhood, who, on account of my mistress being of the Jewish religion, were frequently disposed to insult her."[2] His boxing career enabled him to become a tavern keeper with his wife, Esther, whom he married in 1787, and support eleven children. He fought more than thirty bouts between 1787 and 1806. Only 5 feet 7 inches in height and weighing but 160 pounds, but possessed of great endurance and courage, he developed superior defensive skills and enjoyed a large following among the Jews in England who wagered freely on the outcomes of his matches. In four of those encounters Mendoza fought Richard Humphries, with Mendoza winning three bouts. The first confrontation in 1788 drew thousands of spectators. The umpires ruled that Humphries, who had become entangled in the ropes, was to be considered as down and could not be hit. Humphries went on to win that match; Mendoza acquitted himself well and published *The Art of Boxing* a year later. Their battles proved significant on two counts, one entailing an ongoing clarification of the rules regarding hitting an opponent who was already down, as Humphries developed the strategy of taking a knee when needing a rest in subsequent matches. The second and greater matter of significance involved the symbolic importance of Mendoza, who represented all Jews in England and the respect gained by his successes. In the third bout with Humphries, which took place in 1790, Pierce Egan reported that "Mendoza, in being a JEW, did not stand in so favourable a view, respecting the wishes of the multitude towards his success, as his brave opponent." Mendoza so pummeled Humphries in that contest that his opponent needed medical attention.[3]

Mendoza became so famous that he opened a theater in 1791 for public sparring exhibitions attended by both men and women, and he served as a boxing instructor. He defeated Will Ward in 1792 to become the heavyweight champion of England, a title he carried until 1795. Admiration of his abilities won him the patronage of the Prince of Wales. Dennis Brailsford, a historian of early English boxing, claimed that he "was a popular and admired champion" and that "the racialist comments which such pugilists inspired . . . generally held rather less malice than comments directed at politicians or the royal family; but *The Daily Register* noted typically that Mendoza's boxing school was 'consistently with his character as a Jew,' near the Bank!" which suggests that stereotypes still prevailed.[4] Egan, however, gives full respect by stating that "Mendoza was

Richard Humphreys (aka Humphries) versus Daniel Mendoza in Odiham, Hampshire, England, on January 9, 1788. Courtesy of H. J. Lutcher Stark Center for Physical Culture and Sports, University of Texas at Austin.

considered one of the most elegant and scientific Pugilists in the whole race of Boxers, and might be termed a complete artist." He not only brought pride to the Jews, but was acknowledged by Christians as well. In 1806 Mendoza came out of retirement to avenge his personal honor in a dispute with Harry Lee over the payment of bail money, a fight which ended with Mendoza victorious after fifty-three rounds. He reputedly lost another grudge match in 1820 and died penniless in 1836, leaving behind his autobiography, *The Memoirs of the Life of Daniel Mendoza* (1816).[5]

Mendoza also supported another Jew, "Dutch" Sam Elias (1775–1816), acting as his second in the latter's fistic encounters. Dutch Sam, at only 5 feet 6½ inches and 130 pounds, was discovered beating a larger man in a roadside fight and encouraged to take up prizefighting. His opponents often outweighed him by ten to nearly forty pounds, yet he proved to be one of the best prizefighters in England from 1801 to 1810. Egan termed him a "phenomenon" who was also known for his sportsmanship and honesty. He declined to hit a disabled opponent and refused to take a bribe of 1000 British pounds for a big match. He trained sparingly, but like Mendoza, he displayed a crafty style of defense and possessed a devastatingly hard punch. He is credited with inventing the uppercut, which he popularized and used to great effect. His most famous bouts occurred with Tom Belcher, brother of the British heavyweight champ, and grandson of Jack Slack. The boxing Belchers traced their lineage back to Jim Figg. Dutch Sam won two of three encounters with Tom Belcher. The first in 1806 lasted fifty-seven rounds and was the first loss on Belcher's record. Two rematches in 1807 ended in a draw after thirty-four rounds, and Sam conquered Belcher in the finale in thirty-six rounds. Sam retired in 1810, but returned for one final bout to avenge his honor in 1816, which he lost. Much dissipated by drink, he died that same year. His son resurrected his glory by fighting as Young Dutch Sam. The son (1808–1843) began fighting at the age of fifteen and retired undefeated, widely recognized as the world welterweight champion in the 1820s and 1830s.[6]

Abraham "Aby" Belasco, born in 1797, was the most successful of four brothers who became boxers. He took up the sport in 1817, and one of his encounters in 1820 featured the use of gloves, although he conducted the rest of his business in bare-knuckled fashion. At 5 feet 7 inches and about 150 pounds, Belasco lacked size but possessed talent and strength. Phil Sampson proved to be Belasco's biggest rival. The two met four times, the last a result of a religious issue when Sampson insulted Belasco and the Jewish community. Belasco felt duty bound to address the affront to Jewish honor. He responded:

> Had Sampson challenged me in terms which one brave man usually addresses another, I should have contented myself with simply accepting his offer to meet me in the prize ring . . . within one or two months. As, however, he has been pleased to give vent to his impertinence, in his letter . . . by refusing to make the match with one of "our people," I feel called upon myself to state, that I consider it no disgrace to belong to a community which boasts of a Mendoza and a Dutch Sam, and ranks among its members of the present day, gentlemen in the sporting world, not less remarkable for their honorable and gentleman-like conduct than for their liberality to men in the prize ring.[7]

Belasco met his antagonist on August 19, 1823, and though he lost the fight, he acquitted himself well enough to gain respect. A commentator on the bout reported "To speak of the Jew as he deserves . . . it is true Belasco has been defeated, but he stands higher in the estimation of his friends than ever; let no more slurs be thrown upon him . . . He had to contend against height, length, weight, and youth . . . He has not disgraced 'his people.' . . . To the credit of both men it may be stated that they now shook hands and became friends." Belasco consequently served as a second for Sampson in a later match. Belasco retired in 1824 and died soon thereafter.[8]

Barney Aaron (1800–1850) won his first fight at nineteen and became a standout among English lightweights in a career that lasted until 1834; his son, born in 1836 and fighting as Young Barney Aaron, won even greater esteem. The son migrated to the United States in 1855 and took up boxing the following year. In 1857 he dethroned American lightweight champ Johnny Moneghan to become the first Jew to hold a title in the United States. Young Barney lost the title a year later, but regained it in a sixty-eight round victory in 1867 before retiring to open a New York gym.[9]

Jews would wait another generation before they produced another champion. In both the United Kingdom and the United States many Jews adopted the more liberal Reform version of Judaism, assimilating more quickly within the mainstream societies and gaining social mobility. Still they were not fully accepted in Anglo social circles. Banned from the elite businessman's clubs and Anglo country clubs, they formed their own. The violent pogroms in the Russian empire after 1880 and spreading through Europe thereafter produced a diaspora with many, often Yiddish-speaking, Orthodox Jews fleeing to England and the United States. The sensational Dreyfus affair in France, in which a Jewish army officer was unjustly accused of treason, continued over a dozen years (1894–1906) and resulted in the imprisonment—but ultimate vindication—of Alfred Dreyfus. The media attention to the multiple and ongoing trials, however, promoted a virulent anti-Semitism that reinforced negative stereotypes. Such racism extended throughout Europe and the Americas as naysayers purported Jews to be part of an international financial conspiracy. Jewish youth faced by violent ethnic rivals learned to defend themselves, and some made a temporary living through their physical prowess.[10]

Between 1894 and the 1930s Jewish entrepreneurs in London opened at least five boxing halls in the East End Jewish community. The boxing venues accorded Jewish youth the chance to develop their skills in regular programs that were well attended by patrons in the neighborhood. The Jewish upper class, however, took a dim view of the activities, which caused a fracture within the Jewish community of Great Britain. The elites complained about overcrowding, gambling, and the negative influences of popular culture, especially boxing, which resulted in "Jews not associating themselves with Jewish life' and drifting physically and culturally closer to mainstream society. . . we find young men growing up almost with a loss of moral sense." They found further fault with inter-ethnic competitions for "it was certain that whoever finally triumphed in the ring, the real battle would be fought out afterwards."[11]

Political pressure resulted in increasing regulation and the eventual closure of the Jewish boxing halls during the interwar years, greatly limit-ing the opportunities for poor Jewish youth to develop their skills and to enjoy the partisan fans that supported them in such venues. As Jewish boxers declined in the aftermath, Jewish fight aficionados moved into roles as managers and promoters within the sport. Jewish boxers were replaced by newer immigrants, particularly those from the Caribbean islands within the British Commonwealth. Engagement in boxing did, however, promote greater assimilation of the Jewish immigrant working-class community within the mainstream Anglo culture and greatly ne-gated stereotypical notions of Jewish debility.[12]

European Jews, however, suffered greatly during World War II as the Nazis corralled millions in concentration and extermination camps. In some, Jewish males were forced to fight each other or the Nazi guards in the boxing ring for the amusement of the camp commanders. The bet-ter boxers were rewarded with food, upgraded sleeping quarters, and less work. They might manage to prolong their inevitable demise, while other Jews were simply used as human punching bags by the sadistic soldiers.[13]

American Jewish Boxers

In the United States Jewish leaders assumed a decidedly different ap-proach, pursuing fuller assimilation within the mainstream culture. They established the Educational Alliance and the Henry Street Settlement House in New York, which offered citizenship classes and social services, but also provided boxing lessons for Jewish youth. By the 1890s Jewish boxers became heroes in their ethnic neighborhoods with the emergence of Danny "Dolly" Lyons and Joe Bernstein, who won accolades as the "Pride of the Bowery." Charley (Israel) Goldman was born in Warsaw but found his career in New York. Starting as a sixteen-year-old, Goldman fought in the professional boxing ranks from 1904 to 1918. Although he didn't reach championship status, he later became trainer of several world champions, including Rocky Marciano. In Chicago, Sigmund Hart became a fan favorite and the Harris twins won even greater acclaim when Harry Harris won the bantamweight championship (see chapter 4).[14]

Boxers found employment outside the ring in Chicago when William Randolph Hearst introduced his *Chicago American* newspaper as a competitor to the established *Chicago Tribune* and the *Chicago Record Herald* at the turn of the century. Hearst hired Max and Moses Annenberg to forcefully introduce and sustain the sale of his paper on Chicago's street corners. The Annenbergs managed to do so with heavy-hitting boxers and violent gangsters who used more than their fists to gain compliance. Robert McCormick, publisher of the *Tribune*, hired Moses away from Hearst to perform the same duties for his newspaper. Boxing became a necessity for newsboys who had to fight not only for customers, but for the territory to market their product.[15]

Louis Wirth chronicled the developments of the Jewish community in Chicago. As eastern European Jews settled in the city during the late nineteenth century, they obtained their rabbis from their homelands and maintained their orthodoxy, while the established German Jews had opted for a Reform version of Judaism. Their appearance in long coats and boots, their beards, their Yiddish language, and their religious practices clearly set these later immigrants apart from the mainstream Anglo culture and the earlier German Jews who had largely assimilated and prospered: "The orthodox sections of the Jewish population, and particularly the Russian and Polish groups . . . were less absorbed into the larger life of the city; they continued to speak their familiar Yiddish; they lived close together; they gathered around their synagogues in daily prayer; they had their cheders (religious schools) that transmitted the heritage to the younger generation, and what members deserted the group were more than compensated for by the constant influx of orthodox and pious immigrants from Europe."[16]

Lest the newcomers endanger their own social and economic capital, the German Jews founded their own settlement houses in urban neighborhoods to provide Jewish youth with an alternative to the Protestant YMCA and the social agencies run by Christian organizers. The Chicago

Hebrew Institute, established in 1903, became a model for all others, organized and managed by some of the city's top businessmen. Featuring some of the best athletic facilities in the nation, it offered a comprehensive program of sports, entertainment, English language and vocational courses, and dances, as well as a Zionist club. Under the direction of Harry Berkman, the sports program intended to acculturate young Jews with the intent to "improve physical bearing . . . and the loss of objectionable mannerisms peculiar to our people; and provide rapid assimilation through contact with other athletes. These results once accomplished much of the prejudice against our people will be removed, and the Jew will then possess those traits and characteristics held in common by the other peoples of the community, and still not lose his inborn Judaism, of which he is so justly proud."[17]

The German Jews spent lavishly to accomplish their goal with the children of their more orthodox Eastern European brethren. They added a gymnasium and hired Ernst Kartje, a professional wrestler, to coach its team; three-time Olympian and gold medalist Jimmy Lightbody was employed as the track coach; and Danny Goodman, a professional boxer, joined the gym. Goodman allegedly fought about 350 bouts in his career from 1904 to 1919, and he bragged that he had fought and defeated forty-two black opponents in the Social darwinian struggle of the survival of the fittest. Jewish fighters might become standard bearers for the Zionist cause. The facilities also proved attractive to non-Jews as well as Catholic, Protestant, and secular teams that requested their use, and weekly attendance of 11,000 soon surpassed that of the nearby and nationally famous Hull House settlement. The Hebrew Institute subsequently played host to numerous city-wide competitions that fostered greater integration among the disparate ethnic and religious groups then inhabiting the city.[18]

Judge Abraham Lincoln Marovitz provided one case study in the successful assimilation process. The son of an itinerant tailor, born in 1905, Marovitz sold newspapers before Jewish benefactors sponsored his membership in the Chicago Hebrew Institute. He employed his boxing skills at a young age to augment the family income. Alfred Austrian, a prominent Chicago attorney, became a fan; when Marovitz lost his job due to his religious beliefs, Austrian hired him as an office boy and even paid his tuition through law school, which eventually resulted in a distinguished legal career as a federal judge.[19]

Boxing proved especially helpful to Jewish boys, who were often accosted by ethnic rivals. Jackie Fields, who would become an Olympic and world champion, explained the situation in his Chicago neighborhood: "We had Stanford Park three blocks away where you had to fight your way to the swimming pool because the Italians, the Polish, the Irish, the Lithuanians were there. The Jews were surrounded by all of 'em. So in order to go the pool you had to fight. 'What are you doin' here, you Jew bastard? 'Hey, kike.' You know. We'd start fighting right away."[20]

Jews in Philadelphia faced similar confrontations. Benny Bass, who would become the world featherweight champion, claimed that at the age of fourteen his Irish neighbors forced him to fight every one of them in daily battles over the course of three months. Despite a swollen nose and black eyes Bass asserted that he won ninety-two straight victories, which prompted him to enter an amateur boxing tournament, where he "beat up on Bohemians, Germans, Italians, Greeks, more Irish, a few English and some folks from his own race."[21]

A 1927 study by Frederic Thrasher revealed more than 1,300 gangs in Chicago, at least 300 of which were organized by politicians. He stated that "about one-fourth of the membership of the WWWs (a Jewish gang) is composed of professional prize fighters, and more than once this gang has struck terror into the hearts of overaggressive Polish groups." The WWWs as well as the TTT gangs dispelled the notion of Jewish cowardice and became known as among the toughest in the city. The boxers protected other Jewish youth on their passage to the synagogues as they were too often confronted with antagonistic Poles along the way.[22]

The Miller brothers gained a considerable reputation in the Jewish community by providing such services. Dave Miller eventually established a gym that catered to boxers, providing them with meals, clothes, and sponsorship. His stable of fighters included three Golden Gloves champions and a young Barney Ross, who would become a world champion. Others who emanated from the Jewish ghetto in Chicago included Charley White, Jackie Fields, Kingfish Levinsky, and Davey Day (Daitch). Levinsky was the son of a fish peddler. He grew into a colorful heavyweight managed by his sister, Lena, and became known for his clownish antics in the ring. Yet he fought all the top heavyweights of his era from 1928 to 1939, including Primo Carnera, Max Baer, Jack Sharkey, and Joe

Louis. By 1928 Jews comprised a larger number of professional prizefighters than any other ethnic group.[23]

Jewish presence in the ring diminished as educational opportunities increased and entrepreneurial success offered greater social mobility in succeeding generations. In the latter decades of the twentieth century few Jews appeared in the ring. Dana Rosenblatt, a middleweight champion (WBU, 1994–1995, and IBO super middleweight, 1999–2000) enjoyed a distinguished career from 1992 to 2002, finishing with a record of 37-1-2. More recently, Jewish immigrants such as Dmitriy Salita, born Dmitriy Lekhtman in the Ukraine in 1982, have followed the pattern of Jewish boxers from a century ago. His family left the Ukraine due to oppression and persecution, but he found conflict in the United States as well. Classmates tormented him and he got suspended from school for fighting. His martial skills eventually led him to a professional boxing career and he adopted his mother's surname as well as the "Star of David" nickname to promote his orthodoxy. He strictly observed the Sabbath and all Jewish holidays as well as dietary laws, but the effects of American popular culture are evident in his procession to the ring, which is accompanied by rap music in Yiddish. His undefeated welterweight record was interrupted in 2009 after thirty-one straight victories when he was knocked out by Amir Khan in a WBA light welterweight title fight.[24]

The most influential of Jewish boxers, however, never pursued a professional career in the ring. Nat Fleischer became a sportswriter and editor for a number of newspapers, but in 1922 he embarked upon a new enterprise as publisher of the *Ring* magazine. The *Ring* became known as "The Bible of Boxing," an authoritative source on the sport. In 1926 Fleischer and others founded the Boxing Writers Association. In 1941 he also began publishing an annual record and encyclopedia of the sport. In addition to such ventures, Fleischer wrote numerous books on boxing, including early histories, greatly raising the profile of the sport.[25]

Over the course of the early twentieth century, sports and boxing in particular allowed Jews to overcome negative stereotypes: "Religion continued to be a conspicuous distinction . . . but Jews were no longer considered un-American . . . they had gained a measure of acceptance, recognition and respect."[26]

Catholic Boxers

Although many states banned boxing at the turn of the twentieth century, it continued in clandestine fashion. In 1911 New York passed the Frawley Act, which legalized the sport and permitted the state to regulate and tax it, providing considerable income to its coffers. But when a fighter was killed in the ring in 1917, the law was allowed to expire. Boxing took on greater significance when U.S. military forces entered World War I. Boxing instructors soon performed a valuable service, as boxing and bayonet training required similar techniques. Boxing was especially important among British troops, who conducted tournaments throughout the war. With the conclusion of the war the American military and the YMCA organized the Interallied Games, an athletic spectacle similar to the Olympic Games among eighteen different nations, which included boxing matches. The British forces took a minimal part in the contests, but then offered their own military boxing tournament in England in December 1919. Gene Tunney, later to become heavyweight champion, won a gold medal for the Americans; the British won the overall standings. The American-European rivalries that existed before the war thus continued to be played out in sport thereafter.[27]

With the renewed interest in boxing New York passed the Walker Law in 1920, which once again legitimized the activity. Though still banned in Illinois, military bases in the Chicago area became centers for boxing action. In 1924 the *Chicago Tribune* flaunted the law by holding bouts, which were duly reported in its editions and sold to a growing fan base, largely composed of ethnic Catholics in the city who followed an assortment of their ethnic heroes. The paper's acquisition of radio stations throughout the remainder of the decade gave it even greater voice in the boxing debate. Even Jewish rabbis who held Benny Leonard in high regard favored legalization, and the Illinois legislature finally approved the sport in 1926.[28]

The Catholic Church faced a number of issues at the time, including the large number of European ethnic immigrants susceptible to the popular socialist and anarchist ideologies prevalent in their homelands; the reluctance, and even refusal, of those ethnic Catholics to submit to the Irish American hierarchy within the church; and rebellious, working-class youth who were increasingly attracted to the gangs and gangsters of the urban ghettos. University of Chicago sociologists had determined as early as 1925 that "gangs have exercised considerably greater influence in forming the character of the boys . . . than has the church, the school, or any other communal agency."[29] Catholic parishes were organized along ethnic lines with little social interaction beyond their boundaries, and transgressions upon another's turf invited confrontation and combat. George Mundelein, named archbishop of Chicago in 1916 and its cardinal in 1924, had little success in trying to unify his disparate factions. On the national level the Ku Klux Klan march on the University of Notre Dame in 1924 and the stinging defeat of Al Smith, a Catholic, in the 1928 presidential campaign gave ample evidence that the papal constituency was not yet fully welcome in the American polity. Moreover, some of the Catholic groups adhered to a strident anti-Semitism, spurred on by the radio preacher Father Charles Coughlin, and as late as 1933 African Americans still considered Catholics as "perhaps the most prejudiced group in the United States." Such isolationism, division, and discord did little to enhance prospects for acceptance and respect.[30]

Boxing, however, offered some means of accommodation as it attracted the poor, working-class youth most susceptible to juvenile delinquency and whose habitus determined that they seek status and personal honor through the expression of physical prowess. A Chicago sportswriter stated that "nowhere else in competitive athletics does a boy need the courage required for success in the Golden Gloves (amateur boxing tournament). The moment he has signed and mailed his entry blank he has proved himself a man." Such competitions brought wayward youth under the guidance and regulation of middle-class administrators, but despite the best efforts of the regulators and middle-class reformers, boxing offered ample opportunity for gambling as fans supported their ethnic and religious heroes. Even amateur stars such as Leo Rodak, and Max Marek, who defeated Joe Louis before he turned pro, had their own booster clubs.[31]

Paul Gallico, the sports editor for the *New York Daily News*, initiated an amateur boxing tournament known as the Golden Gloves in 1927 that drew 2,300 entrants and nearly 22,000 fans to Madison Square Garden. Another 10,000 rioted when they had to be turned away. The *Chicago Tribune* followed with its version a year later, and the two conducted an intercity competition that same year. By 1932 the tournament had expanded to national proportions. Catholic parishes supplied a plethora of contenders, and the collaboration only increased when Arch Ward assumed the duties as sports editor in 1930. Ward crafted his journalism skills as a student press agent for Knute Rockne at Notre Dame before becoming a sportswriter for the *Tribune*.[32]

Ward's close relationship with Bishop Bernard Sheil, the protégé of Cardinal Mundelein, reaped great rewards for both. Under Sheil's direction the archdiocese embarked on a new venture aimed at providing social services to its growing ethnic, working-class constituency while effecting greater cohesion within the church and with mainstream American culture. Sheil saw sports as the answer to the problems besetting the church. As a former major league pitching prospect and chaplain at the Cook County Jail, he had an idealistic faith in the powers of sports as a means of character development. The enterprise, known as the Catholic Youth Organization (CYO), started in 1930 with the following intention: "We'll knock the hoodlum off his pedestal and we'll put another neighborhood boy in his place. He'll be dressed in C.Y.O. boxing shorts and a pair of leather mitts, and he'll make a new hero. Those kids love to fight. We'll let them fight. We'll find champions right in the neighborhood."[33]

Drawing upon Ward's expertise, Sheil organized an amateur boxing tournament in 1931 similar to the Golden Gloves, but the program soon expanded to include both males and females in a multitude of sports that surpassed the athletic offerings of the city's public schools. The 1931 basketball tournament drew more than 120 teams and eventually encompassed 600, the largest league in the world. The 1931 boxing tournament drew 18,000 fans to Chicago Stadium, providing a consistent source of revenue to the Church in the hard times of the Depression. Boxing proved so popular that individual parishes began offering regular bouts as fundraisers. CYO boxers received free equipment, instruction, and medical care. The championship competition presented an athletic spectacle in which combatants passed through an honor guard of 1,000 CYO Boy Scouts. Champions were awarded with a gold medal commissioned by the papal sculptor, four-year college scholarships, and a guaranteed trip to California to compete against a Los Angeles team. The traveling team journeyed in style, as each member received a new suit, socks, shoes, shirts, underwear, ties, and hats while lounging in a chartered railroad car. They had a special diet and bottled water and stayed in one of the finest hotels in Los Angeles. Not surprisingly, the 1932 tournament included entrants from every Catholic parish, as the CYO became the new gang that attracted youth who sought a better life without surrendering their working-class values.[34]

Sheil welcomed not only Catholics, but all creeds and races to his program; yet when a 1932 survey of participants indicated that 40 percent did not practice their faith, he instituted a pledge required of all participants in 1934: "I promise upon my honor to be loyal to my God, my country, and to my Church; to be faithful and true to my obligation as a Christian, a man and a citizen . . . [I] promise to avoid profane, obscene and vulgar language and to induce others to avoid it. I bind myself to promote clean, wholesome, and manly sport . . . to be a man of whom Church and country may be proud."[35] Catholics were expected to partake of the sacraments, and failure to earn passing grades in school would result in a six-month ban from CYO activities. Sheil intended to impart both religious and middle-class value systems.[36]

Sheil came under fire from critics for associating the Church with boxing; he took to the radio to rationalize that the Church's spiritual mission included physical well-being and that the sport enhanced physical, mental, and moral qualities while promoting "health, strength, and vitality, of alertness, endurance, courage, and self-control accruing from . . . training and actual participation."[37] Sheil viewed his policies and the CYO program as consistent with papal directives such as Pope Leo XIII's *Rerum Novarum* of 1891 that asserted the responsibility to address the needs of the working class; Pope Benedict XV's 1919 *Maximum Illud*, which called for the inclusion of blacks; and the most recent *Quadragesimo Anno* of Pope Pius XI in 1931 that called for social activism to achieve a just society.[38] By 1935 the *New World* Catholic newspaper proclaimed the CYO to be a League of Nations, as its boxers spanned a multitude of races and ethnicities.[39]

The CYO soon reached beyond its local confines to become a national and international enterprise, assisted by the publicity of Arch Ward at the *Chicago Tribune*. The CYO and the Golden Gloves shared the same corps of fighters, and Sheil's Western ventures did not impinge upon Ward's intercity matches. Intercity rivalries fostered a greater civic identity that united disparate ethnic groups in a common cause and drew them closer to a larger social community. Catholic patrons in Chicago assured financial success for both programs during the Depression. Sheil and Ward even combined their two teams for an international challenge match against a French team at Chicago's Soldier Field in 1931, which was attended by 40,000 spectators who were treated to a grand pageant that included a band, fireworks, and an American Legion escort for the fighters that promoted American patriotism rather than an insular ethnic identity. The alliance bridged the archconservative ownership of the newspaper and the liberal hierarchy of the Chicago archdiocese to include significant, wealthy social and political groups within the city and throughout the United States. With such backing, the CYO garnered attention and support as politicians sought an affiliation. In 1932 its championship team, including the runners-up who served as alternates, traveled to Panama, where it spent ten days as it took on the U.S. Army boxers in the Canal Zone. In succeeding years both the Golden Gloves and the CYO extended their international competitions, with the latter traveling to Hawaii. Three of the CYO boxers made the U.S. Olympic team in 1936, while others turned pro. For the latter, the CYO secured rights to their professional contracts to protect them from criminal or predatory managers. The CYO paid their expenses, invested their winnings with one-third of their purses placed in retirement accounts, and found jobs for boxers who retired from the ring.[40]

Tony Motisi dropped out of school, but fought on the CYO international team and stated that the trip to Hawaii was the thrill of his life. He turned pro thereafter. Max Marek made the 1932 Olympic team and went to Notre Dame on a CYO scholarship before pursuing his ring career. Tony Canadeo used his boxing scholarship to attend Gonzaga, where he earned All-American honors as a football player. Jimmy Christy graduated from street fights to become a CYO champion and then entered the professional ranks. He entered the military during World War II as a fighter pilot, which cost him his life. Christy had been a favorite of Sheil, and he had instilled a sense of duty and patriotism in all of his boxers. As the Nazis asserted their power in Europe Sheil declared:

> We have a need of a youth which will carry on the good fight not merely in the field of boxing and athletics, but in the greater field if [*sic*] life on a far flung front. . . . We are faced by foes . . . confronted by enemies that are shaped in the form of an ideology and a philosophy alien to

an American and a Christian standard of living . . . ruling powers have attempted to crush religion under the heel of militant nationalism. We must fight against any subversive influences . . . eight years ago the Catholic Youth Organization enlisted in this campaign . . . through the channels of this vast organization, American children are being guided and trained in the American manner.[41]

Chicago hosted a number of radical labor groups' athletic competitions, including the communist Counter Olympics of 1932, that might have drawn ethnic youth to their ideologies if the CYO had not offered a counter to that threat at the height of the Depression when many Americans questioned the capitalist system. Sheil introduced his program with boxing, which remained the core of CYO activities for decades, because of its appeal to the working class; yet he preached education, inclusion, and the adoption of middle-class values. He even hired Jewish champions such as Benny Leonard and Barney Ross as boxing instructors. In so doing Sheil served as an intermediary between social classes, as well as between religious, ethnic, and racial groups. He did so without forcing the working class to surrender its cherished physicality as a means to social mobility and a measure of celebrity. Even those who did not attain championship status won recognition and respect in their neighborhoods, transforming their ethnic identity to an American one in the process.[42]

Sheil's social activism on the behalf of the working class, Jews, and African Americans won him recognition, and politicians sought his counsel. He was the first gentile to win the B'nai B'rith humanitarian award, and he served both presidents Franklin Delano Roosevelt and Harry Truman, as well as numerous labor organizations. The CYO program had greatly aided

[the] integration of ethnic factions within a centralized Catholic bureaucracy, and both African Americans, Jews, and the larger working class consolidated their political allegiance within the established system under the Democratic wing. The international competitions of both Sheil and Arch Ward focused the attention of the working class outward, developing a greater sense of Americanization, nationalism, and patriotism. World War II quickly solidified that emerging identity and by 1944 twelve hundred CYO boxers had joined the fight against fascism, with twenty five making the ultimate sacrifice.[43]

Muslim Boxers

There have been several Muslim boxers, though few have made an issue of their religious beliefs. Mustafa Hamsho, born in Syria, settled in Brooklyn and had a long career (1975–1989) as a middleweight contender, losing two title fights to Marvin Hagler. An Indonesian Muslim, Muhammad Rachman, held the IBF (2004–2007) and WBA (2011) minimum weight championship over the course of his career. "Prince" Naseem Hamed, a British-born Muslim, had a colorful career between 1992 and 2002. He reigned as the featherweight champion (WBO, 1995–2000; IBF, 1997; WBC, 1999–2000), compiling a career record of thirty-six wins against only one loss. Amir Khan, another British-born Muslim of Pakistani descent, first captured the WBA light welterweight crown (2009–2011, 2012) at the age of twenty-two.[44]

A number of African American fighters have converted to Islam in the course of their careers. Among them, Muhammad Qawi, born Dwight Braxton, got a late start in boxing but had a long tenure in the ring from 1978 to 1998, competing in his last bout at the age of forty-five. He converted to Islam in 1982 and competed as a top cruiserweight, holding the WBC light heavyweight title from 1981 to 1983 and the WBA cruiserweight belt from 1985 to 1986. Bernard Hopkins, another convert, is among the most remarkable fighters of all time (see chapter 5), having held the middleweight title for ten years and winning the light heavyweight championship at the age of forty-eight in 2013.[45]

Undoubtedly the most controversial convert to Islam was Muhammad Ali, whose religious stance cost him his title, the prime years of his career, and nearly cost him a prison sentence (detailed in chapter 4). His adherence to Islam and its perception by mainstream American society formed the core of the issue, as he refused to fight in the Vietnam War, following the example of his religious leader, Elijah Muhammad, who served a prison term rather than submit to military service in World War II. The black Nation of Islam had been a rather obscure sect until a former boxer, Malcolm X, became a very public spokesman in the 1960s; the conversion of Ali brought the movement international attention. Mike Tyson secretly converted to Islam while serving his jail sentence (1992–1995), a decision that has apparently brought some solace to his troubled life, but did not announce the conversion until 2010.[46]

Anthony Mundine, an Australian Aborigine who also converted to Islam, has become the most controversial of Muslim boxers with the retirement of Tyson. A former world-class rugby player, Mundine has had considerable success in the ring as well, winning the WBA super middle-weight title twice (2003–2004, 2007–2008). He accepted his new religion in 1999 and after the September 11, 2001, attacks on New York City his comments implied that the United States had brought such tragedy upon itself, which resulted in vitriolic responses, often aimed at his religion. One of the biggest Australian celebrities, Mundine has branched out into other popular culture expressive forms as a television actor, singer, and music video actor. In one of his music videos he burned the Union Jack, which hardly endeared him to the British Commonwealth. A steadfast proponent of Aboriginal rights, he has been critical of governmental policies in this regard. He has also questioned the indigenous authenticity of an opponent, Daniel Geale, to whom he lost his IBF middleweight championship in 2013. Such escapades have made him a polarizing figure, but boxing fans continue to subscribe to his pay-per-view fights in record numbers.[47]

Muslim women boxers have attracted a good deal of attention in India, where Hindus are the majority and religious quarrels have resulted in riots and attacks on minority groups. While boxing has benefits for self-defense, women's participation would seem to violate Muslim tenets.

The female boxers who have drawn scholarly notice reside in a poverty-ridden neighborhood of Kolkata. Although M. C. Mary Kom, a Christian, has won women's world championships five times at the 46- and 48-kilogram weight divisions, as well as an Olympic bronze medal at the 2012 London Olympics, the Muslim women claim that their inspiration was Laila Ali, the Muslim daughter of Muhammad Ali. In order to train, Muslim women confront religious and societal norms related to clothing and sport participation. The women do not wear a hijab or bur-kha when practicing; they wear shorts and spar with male boxers. Some do not fast during the holy month of Ramadan due to their energy needs. The female boxers, however, assert that theirs is not a religious quest but a nationalistic one: "We don't look at ourselves as Muslims or Hindus, we look at ourselves as boxers who are here to win laurels for our country."[48]

A Hindu female boxer indicated that her family was not supportive of her pursuit of boxing; their attitudes changed once she started winning tournaments. The women are proud of forging new identities and skills as athletes, find their sport liberating, and emphasize their nationalistic intent. The Muslim minority has been suspect in their national loyalty since the early 1990s when Hindu fundamentalists assumed power. Boxing provides Muslim women with a means to dignity and self-respect, even if that practice differs from the mainstream majority.[49]

Religion, especially when linked to race and ethnicity, has been a catalyst for marketing and promotion of boxing for centuries. While religion appears to be on the wane in Western nations, it can still generate a base antipathy among fans and followers, although those inside the ropes can have little concern for such a matter. While some still extol their religiosity in their boxing attire or in their persona, it means little once the bell rings.

CHAPTER SEVEN
GENDER

Gender, like race and ethnicity, is a socially constructed concept learned over time. A person is assigned a biological gender at birth based on their sexual genitalia, but he or she must then learn, perform, express, and identify with the behaviors or conduct associated with that gender over time. Such behaviors differ by culture and evolve within cultures so that the concept of gender is a fluid one. For example, Western male athletes have often represented a masculine ideal in the presentation of their physical bodies, their aggressive nature, and their competitive zeal. But in Asian societies physicality has historically been the province of lower-class servants, and in ancient Greece homosexuality was a normal practice evidenced by the homoerotic inscriptions on Olympic steles. Gender thus has to be performed within the prescribed guidelines of a particular culture and a particular chronological period. Those who do not identify with and conform to such norms project alternative forms of gender, sometimes labeled as aberrant or deviant.[1]

Boxing has always had a distinct historical link to masculinity. The ancient Greeks (chapter 1) fought for more than civic pride. Their matches offered a public display of physical domination, and losers were shunned. While men may have practiced a homosexual lifestyle, the combative skills necessary for boxing, wrestling, and pankration marked them as distinctly different physically and psychologically from women (although Spartan girls were trained in traditionally male activities). Similarly, the gladiatorial contests of ancient Rome required a demonstration of martial skills that might result in life or death for male participants. Boxers performed for the entertainment of their social superiors. Little had changed in eighteenth-century England as the aristocracy retained boxers among their liverymen, whom they sponsored in boxing matches. When the American Commodore Matthew Perry sailed to Japan in an effort to open its markets to Western traders in 1853, American sailors boxed to impress the Japanese with their martial spirit. The Japanese demonstrated their masculinity with an exhibition by sumo wrestlers. Such characteristics seem to cross cultures and time periods; for example, the African Ashanti tribe of Ghana has long celebrated a warrior ethic. In many cultures a demonstration of aggression and violence was "the appropriate discourse for the practice of power invested in the male sporting body [which] is a military discourse of war and combat—of struggle, confrontations, strategies and tactics. By implication, these military characteristics of manly sports make men fit for work [business], battle and imperial projects."[2]

In the modern world, boxing has long been associated with one's social class (see chapter 3). That relationship assumed greater relevancy as industrialization robbed some men of their previously independent status. Many men derived their identity and their social standing by their physicality. None questioned the strength of a blacksmith or an independent craftsman who controlled his own working hours. When the factories came to town and displaced such livelihoods, it created an identity crisis and a loss of self-worth for many. When the lack of economic capital diminished one's social capital, boxing enabled working-class males to maintain a sense of physical power. Some took to the ring while others assumed an associative role as fans, followers, and spectators enjoying masculine camaraderie.[3]

The patriarchal nature of most societies empowered males with leadership roles in government, the military, business, religion, the family, and virtually all aspects of the community. The nineteenth century, however, witnessed a feminist challenge to such male domination. Women began to assume new roles beyond their traditional domestic sphere. Young women entered the factories as wage laborers, became schoolteachers and nurses, and by the latter decades of the century, social workers in the urban settlement houses. Activists held their first Women's Rights Convention at Seneca Falls, New York, in 1848 and proposed equal rights for females, including suffrage and property ownership. By mid-century, women encroached on the male domain of sports. Female equestrians drew particular attention in 1857: "Our daughters as well as our horses, girls of tender age, girls of larger growth, and even wives as well as fillies, pacers, and breeding mares, are brought on to the course for exhibitions, and gazed at, and criticized by thousands, and praised and flattered, and caressed for the same reasons as the animals which they drive, beauty of skin, and form and limb, and grace of action." Croquet and skating became popular recreations, but women soon progressed to archery, and then tennis, cycling, golf, and even baseball, which required dress reform. By the end of the century women played basketball and volleyball, two new sports invented by the YMCA. Women of the lower ranks even engaged in clandestine boxing matches.[4]

The Woman's Christian Temperance Movement (WCTU) worked to ban alcohol, a staple of masculine behavior. Perhaps its most ardent crusader, Carrie Nation, attacked and vandalized saloons with a hatchet during the first decade of the new century, including that of boxing idol John L. Sullivan in New York. The WCTU also campaigned to prohibit the sport of boxing and the sale and the presentation of boxing films as well. Boxing, they claimed, represented the barbarity and immorality of masculine culture. Men largely saw such incursions into the male domain as upsetting to traditional gender and social roles, and an affront to their honor. Arthur Worthy, who boxed under the pseudonym of the Battling Boy from Borneo, took such matters into his own hands by using his wife as a sparring partner. Consequently he was arrested for battery, reinforcing the case of the WCTU.[5]

For virtually all men in the Anglo world regardless of their social class, the concept of honor also impacted their sense of masculinity. A man who had been offended, especially in a public manner, was required to assuage such an affront to maintain the respect of other men. Dueling became commonplace for those who could afford weapons. For the rougher classes, fists would suffice. By the mid-nineteenth century men issued their challenges publicly and directly in the newspapers, placing their intended target's honor at stake.[6]

In such confrontations a man might reclaim his honor even if defeated, providing that he demonstrated his courage. One might do so by stoic endurance despite pain, injury, or a lost cause. A man might be knocked down several times with no chance of winning, yet he returned to the fray only to prove his mettle to others. Some even chose death before dishonor.

Such was the case in 1741 when Jack Broughton killed George Stevenson, which resulted in Broughton's new rules. The first recorded ring death in the United States occurred in 1834; many others followed. In the twentieth century alone, several championship bouts have resulted in deaths. Such televised horrors as the Emile Griffith–Benny "Kid" Paret match that ended in the latter's death resulted from a question of masculinity in 1962. When Paret publicly addressed and disparaged his opponent's gender, Griffith delivered a savage beating that put Paret in a coma from which he did not recover. Only a year later Davey Moore lost the featherweight title he had held since 1959 to Sugar Ramos when he fell against the third rope, which snapped his neck. Despite calls for a boxing ban and condemnation by the pope, a fourth rope was added to the ring as a safety measure. The Ray Mancini–Duk Koo Kim tragedy followed in another televised championship bout in 1982 when Kim expired days after a fourteenth-round knockout. In 2005 Leavander Johnson died of brain trauma five days after his lightweight championship bout with Jesus Chavez. Joyce Carol Oates appropriately noted that boxing was "not theatrical, not a staged drama, but a spectacle of unfeigned damage and pain."[7]

Boxing has historically served as a ritual of masculinity. The practice of the sport, no matter how inept, served as proof of one's courage and virility. Aggression and violence, pain and injury, even the possibility of death were accepted risks. Boxing was and is war, an individual combat in which competitors try to impose their domination on another. Such intentions hold true whether they take place in street fights or within the regulated confines of the ring.

Boxers assume monikers that reinforce their masculinity, such as Roberto Duran, who had "hands of stone," Hector "Macho" Camacho, Fernando "the Aztec Warrior" Vargas, or Jesus "El Matador" Chavez. Sportswriters and fans often referred to Mike Tyson as "the baddest man on the planet" until his precipitous fall from such lofty recognition. Opponents typically extoll the damage that they will inflict on each other before and even during the contest. Muhammad Ali even predicted the rounds in which he would do so. The very demeanor which marks boxers as warriors would not be considered acceptable behavior in more polite circles of society.[8]

For many, boxing serves as a form of community, one in which boxers often assume traditional masculine roles as providers and protectors (see chapter 6): "For some,—the orphans of the city streets—the gym provides a sense of community, the only true family some of them ever had."[9] A female attendee at a local gym in Austin, Texas, commented on the sense of community that centered on the place: "It was beautiful to see people find a goal, something they can accomplish. They were just happy to get together to do things. It was a mix of African Americans and Hispanics, not too many Anglos. We got to know them and we'd make them *tortillas* and teach them Spanish. After the boxing we'd all go to Hill Side, where they had bands like Ruben Ramos, and we'd sit on the grass, enjoy the music, and have some refreshments." For such participants a psychic bonding in a shared interest brings a cohesion and acceptance perhaps not experienced in other spheres of life.[10]

Rocky Graziano enjoyed playing the role of benefactor, dispensing Christmas presents to neighborhood kids and their parents with his winnings (see chapter 5). Likewise, Ray Mancini felt obligated to redeem his father's interrupted quest for a world championship. Upon fulfilling his goal Ray's father stated, "I wish my father was alive to see this." Ray claimed that "it made me feel like a good son." The Italian community extended beyond the immediate family as his hometown of Youngstown, Ohio, reveled in his accomplishment, while their own lives suffered in an economy mired in recession (see chapter 5). The larger Italian community extended well beyond Youngstown. Frank Sinatra informed the young slugger that "I've been following you. You're making *us* real proud." When Ray took the family to Italy he was feted like a long-lost family member: "The Italians considered him one of their own, a favorite son."[11]

While the gym can be a community for boxers, they have to conform to the traditional acceptable form of heterosexual masculinity. Boxing gyms are often dank, dirty, sweaty places, although more sterile fitness clubs now offer boxing lessons to attract a white-collar clientele. "This is because boxing continues to hold a deep appeal for the masculine psyche, the charmed circle of the squared ring exerting a fascination that for some can be exorcised only through the physical involvement within it . . . the ring represents a theater in which a personal and physical challenge has to be met under the unrelenting gaze of one's fellows."[12] That mandate continues to hold true within boxing circles, and only recently has an active professional boxer admitted to an alternative masculinity. Emile Griffith acknowledged his sexual orientation in 2005, decades after his ring career; Orlando Cruz, a Puerto Rican featherweight who boxed in the 2000 Olympics and later turned professional, was the first to confess his homosexuality while still active in the ring. He felt doubly pressured not only by the hypermasculine environment of boxing culture, but also by the macho culture of his ethnicity. Although his decision to reveal himself would have been unthinkable only a few years ago, he celebrated the general acceptance of his sexuality by wearing a symbolic kilt in a 2013 fight that displayed the Puerto Rican flag on one side and the colors of the gay community on the other.[13]

While Cruz has seemingly overcome the obstacles presented by his gender identification, women still battle with stereotypes in the boxing world. They have traditionally been unwelcome and unwanted in such a male domain, even though women have been boxers for centuries. Numerous bouts between women took place in eighteenth-century England. London bouts in the first two decades of that era proved ferocious enough to draw blood, and one observer indicated that a featured attraction at one arena included two women "engaged in a scratching and boxing match, their faces entirely covered in blood, bosoms bare, and the clothes nearly torn from their bodies. For several minutes not a creature interfered with them . . . and the contest went on with unabated fury."[14]

In 1722 Elizabeth Stokes claimed to be the female champion of London, and women's matches continued throughout the decade. A money prize of three guineas was offered for the contest between Elizabeth Wilkinson and Hannah Highfield at Hockley in the Hole in 1727. The following year Mrs. Stokes came out of retirement to answer a challenge in the *Daily Post*. "I, Elizabeth Stokes, of the City of London, have not fought . . . since I fought the famous boxing woman of Billingsgate 9 minutes, and gained a complete victory, which is six years ago; but as the famous Stoke Newington ass woman (Ann Field) dares me to fight her for 10 pounds, I do assure her I will not fail meeting her for the said sum, and doubt not that the blows which I shall present her with will be more difficult for her to digest than any she ever gave her asses." By mid-century James Figg's Amphitheater accommodated both male and female bouts.[15]

Although the British Parliament officially outlawed boxing in 1750, the brutal bouts continued. In 1768 it was reported that "Bruising Peg" had defeated her opponent. A detailed account of a 1794 battle stated:

Great intensity between them was maintained for about two hours, whereupon the elder fell into great difficulty through the closure of her left eye from the extent of swelling above and below it which rendered her blind through [sic] having the sight of other considerably obscured by a flux of blood which had then continued greatly for over forty minutes . . . not more than a place even as large as a penny-piece remained upon their bodies which was free of the most evident signs of the harshness of the struggle. Their bosoms were much enlarged but yet they each continued to rain blows upon this most feeling of tissue without regard to the pitiful cries issuing forth at each success which was evidently to the delight of the spectators since many a shout was raised causing each female to mightily increase her effort.[16]

In 1807 the *Times* reported on another battle between Mary Mahoney, who worked at the market, and Betty Dyson, a fish peddler, referring to both women as "Amazons" in a fight that lasted beyond forty minutes, in which both were "hideously disfigured by hard blows." The newspaper found it to be disgusting, but provided coverage nonetheless. In 1822 ethnic animosities boiled over again as Martha Flaharty and Peg Carey fought for a prize of nearly eighteen British pounds. To ensure that fellow workers could view the combat, they started at 5:30 in the morning before their normal labors began. Flaharty downed a pint of gin beforehand to steel herself, which apparently helped her to salvage a win despite being badly injured.[17]

American women tested their opponents by the mid-nineteenth century. Shortly after the Civil War, in 1865 Maggie Shoester fought Annie Wood in the presence of a referee in a match that approximated the recent carnage on the battlefields. "Both participants were punished within an inch of their life, both their homely visages barbarously mutilated and disfigured with . . . all sort of fantastic bloodstains and blotches." The middle-class male critic who reported the action considered it a disgrace.[18] A similar bout in Chicago so offended Victorian sensibilities that the state outlawed the sport in 1869. "Prize fights between men are beastly exhibitions, but there is an unutterable loathsomeness in the worse brutality of abandoned, wretched women beating each other almost to nudity, for the amusement of a group of blackguards, even lower in the scale of humanity than the women themselves."[19] Despite Chicago's prohibitions, female boxers found ready acceptance at Harry Hill's Exchange, a well-known saloon favored by the bachelor subculture (see chapter 3). There a Ms. Burke and a Ms. Wells, "attired in unmentionables made of silk," staged a six-round gloved bout that ended in a draw. The following year Mollie Berdan traveled all the way from England to fight Jessie Lewis in San Francisco, another hotbed of the pugilists. They too fought with gloves for a prize of $250.[20]

Throughout the latter decades of the nineteenth century New York provided a hub for female boxers. Nell Saunders beat Rose Harland at Hill's Theater in 1876 and was awarded with a silver butter dish. Harry Hill maintained a stable of fighters for his programs, including Libby Kelly, Nettie Burke, Jennie Meade, and Hattie Edwards, with Irish women seemingly as attracted to the sport as their male counterparts. Kelly traveled all the way from Jacksonville, Florida, to make her name in the pugilistic field. Alice Jennings, managed by Jimmy Kelly, who also boxed on his own behalf, adopted the London Prize Ring rules. She had issued a challenge to any woman in America. Her 1883 bout against Daisy Daly, reputedly the women's champion of California, held at Hill's establishment, utilized the Queensberry rules, and resulted in a victory for the Californian. Such "championship" bouts were often manufactured by Richard Kyle Fox (see chapter 3), an Irish immigrant who prospered in America as the editor of the *National Police Gazette*, headquartered in New York. Fox offered cash prizes to both male and female boxers, whose exploits, including lurid illustrations, drew throngs of readers to his publication.[21]

Bouts between black female boxers were recorded as early as 1866. By the 1880s the women emulated their male counterparts by issuing public challenges through the newspapers. A black female fighter transcended both social and racial boundaries when she challenged heavyweight champion John L. Sullivan in 1887. The heavily muscled challenger had already tested herself against a number of men; but the white champion shunned her appeal, as he did with black male fighters. The *National Police Gazette* continued to extol the martial skills of black women throughout the following decade, yet men disparaged women's boxing skills as inferior. When Marry McNamara confronted Julia Perry in 1888, the two fought under the Queensberry rules. The bout soon degenerated: "Vicious blows were interchanged, and when time was called both were badly disfigured. Time for the second round was called and the two women advanced with sleeves rolled up and with angry eyes rolling in every direction. A few passes were made and the code was thrown aside and both began a rough and tumble fight, in which scratching and hair-pulling predominated. The Perry woman was knocked down and dragged around by the hair."[22]

Only a few weeks later two actresses, Hattie Leslie and Alice Leary, fought on an island in the Niagara River dressed in their tights. Both had previous experience in the ring, with Leslie claiming a record of 34-0 with twenty-nine knockouts and Leary boasting fifty-two wins, no losses and forty-seven knockouts. Though they used gloves, it proved a brutal affair. Leslie was knocked down twice and suffered a broken nose, while Leary also kissed the canvas two times. Leslie recovered to win by a knockout in the seventh round, but their slugging was judged to be inept by male standards. At least one reporter concentrated on the beauty of the competitors. They and their male seconds were arrested at the conclusion of the bout and the district attorney stated:

> They were to share the proceeds of this most brutal, most outrageous affair. The price was $5 to be entertained upon the Sabbath by women fighting. . . . I don't blame the women so much, though they are indicted. It is these men, these creatures who are at fault. It is a disgrace . . . to think that men are so brutal, so lost to every instinct of manhood should engage in such an enterprise. . . . Prize-fights between men have perhaps been tolerated, but prize-fights between women never. . . . These men shall be severely punished at the hand of the law, and that never again can it be said that men can get together and pollute the honor of womankind.

The district attorney drew a clear distinction between middle-class and working-class versions of manhood; true to his word, as the protector of women he released Leslie and punished only the males whom he felt instigated the bout.[23]

Hattie Stewart needed no instigation to fight: "As a girl in Philadelphia I was always fighting with boys . . . I defeated a big bruiser named Jones in Missouri once, and have fought several 'draws' with men." Stewart learned the rudiments of the sweet science from her husband, who accompanied her on a theatrical tour, sparring with him and another female opponent. She also provided boxing lessons for other women in her birthplace of Norfolk, Virginia. After an 1885 bout with Annie Lewis, Stewart was declared to be the "female John L. Sullivan."[24] She later challenged Hattie Leslie for the female world championship and a bet of $500 per side, a very sizable sum. The *National Police Gazette* ran stories on both fighters, describing Stewart as 5 feet 7 inches in height and "an excellent specimen of physical development, and stripped looked a perfect amazon." Leslie was "tall, powerful, and possessed of great quickness." Stewart died an early death, however, in 1892, and was notorious among the middle class for her abandonment of traditional domesticity and challenge to the gender order.[25]

In the American West, many women had to be as tough as men. A commentator at an 1892 match in Gallup, New Mexico, between Faye Wiggins and Amy Brock described it as a four-round bout "with much slugging, awkward blows and minus the customary hair-pulling."[26] The sparring exhibitions and outright battles among actresses, bargirls, and actual pugilists presented lascivious entertainment for their male spectators and reports of such matches, as indicated above, generally derided the participants as bawdy women, unacceptable as proper females. Such opinions however were rendered by middle-class males and reflected their own perceptions of proper social decorum of polite society. The women who chose to box in such settings did so for monetary remuneration or local celebrity, not unlike their male counterparts. Following Pierre Bourdieu's concept of habitus, their behavior was not discordant with the physicality of working-class life. Even those domestic women who labored within the house or factories required a level of physical performance. The farmer often sought a sturdy woman as a wife, one who might help plow a field, unlike the more refined mates of the upper classes.

By the 1890s the interest in boxing began to extend to women of better means, which also brought a great role reversal in gender relations. Whereas men had always ogled female fighters, reporters detailed their feminine charms, and the *National Police Gazette* blatantly depicted the women as sex objects, "the new women" of the 1890s upset the gender order. Known as "Gibson girls" after the illustrations of Charles Dana Gibson, which displayed them as mostly young, independent, educated, and active participants in a variety of sports, they sought greater freedom in their lives. They admired and viewed the male body in earnest; "In the 1860s the middle class had seen the ideal male body as lean and wiry. By the 1890s, however, an ideal male body required physical bulk and well-defined muscles."[27] The modern world brought an infusion of sedentary jobs for middle-class men who no longer used their bodies for physical labor, presumably resulting in a condition known as neurasthenia, characterized by weakness, fatigue, and even a nervous breakdown. The ideal body type was personified in Eugen Sandow, a circus strongman born in Germany, who became an international celebrity. "Sandow portrayed his physique as a work of art, carefully marketed as the new standard of health and vitality. His chiseled body had an erotic appeal, and he posed nearly nude, wearing only loincloths or simple fig leafs to cover his genitals. At the Chicago World's Fair of 1893, he became an American sensation, and one wealthy socialite paid $300 to feel his muscles in a private exhibition." His American counterpart, Bernarr Macfadden, exhorted men to see that "weakness is a crime," marking a new body culture that promised a remedy to modern ills. In Europe, particularly Germany, a back-to-nature movement spearheaded the practice of hiking and camping to counteract modern urban ills.[28]

Dudley Sargent, a medical doctor and Harvard professor, pioneered the new science of anthropometry to measure and categorize human bodies as ectomorphs (tall and thin), endomorphs (short and round), and the desired mesomorphs (stocky and muscular). He pronounced Sandow to be the perfect human specimen. Male boxers also came under scrutiny, particularly Gentleman Jim Corbett, who had wrested the heavyweight title from John L. Sullivan in 1892. Women were captivated by his good looks and wholesome background as a bank teller. In 1897 another physician examined Corbett's body and proclaimed him to be "the most perfect specimen of physical manhood." Another medical doctor performed his own measurements and agreed that Corbett was "without one single flaw in his anatomy."[29]

With the introduction of movie films in the 1890s, women became avid spectators. Boxers, some attired in thongs with their buttocks exposed, became sex objects and provided a form of pornography for women. The film of the heavyweight championship fight between Jim Corbett and Bob Fitzsimmons in 1897 ran for years in the theaters. "Afternoon presentations, conspicuously, were largely made up of ladies." Women composed an estimated 60 percent of viewers in Chicago, with hundreds in Dallas, and large numbers in Boston, and another 60 percent in San Francisco despite the remonstration of the WCTU and other moralists.[30]

Select women had already invaded the public sphere as spectators. John L. Sullivan traveled to France for a fight with Charley Mitchell, accompanied by his mistress, Ann Livingston, who managed to observe the battle by masquerading as a boy. Other women used a similar ruse, attired in male clothing to witness the Nonpareil Jack Dempsey–Bob Fitzsimmons match at the male Olympic Club in New Orleans in 1891; wives used the same strategy to accompany their husbands for the Jim Corbett–Peter Jackson match in San Francisco that same year. Women were granted greater access to outdoor sites, and promoters welcomed them as wholesome influences on rowdy male patrons, such as the case for the Corbett-Fitzsimmons heavyweight championship bout held at the Race Track Arena in Carson City, Nevada, in 1897. Fitzsimmons's wife accompanied him and sat ringside, but hardly complied with the expected behavior. She not only encouraged her husband, but yelled vile epithets at his opponent. Corbett complained that "she yelled things that were not at all flattering either to my skill as a fighter or manly conduct as a gentleman."[31]

Although women still faced restrictions in Eastern boxing clubs, they attended matches in the South and the West. Some of the attendees were prostitutes selling their wares among the bachelor subculture; others came from respectable social circles. A 1905 bout in Reno, Nevada, attracted the lieutenant governor and his wife, and the next year in Goldfield, Nevada, the contest between Joe Gans and Battling Nelson brought hundreds of women to the desert. For the historic racial showdown that matched Jack Johnson against the Great White Hope, Jim Jeffries, promoter Tex Rickard constructed special screened boxes above the fray for female fans.[32]

By the 1890s women even filled the role of sport reporters. In 1892 the Hearst papers assigned Annie Laurie (Winifred Black) to cover boxing. After the turn of the century women had even greater access to boxing through the nickleodeons that dotted urban landscapes. The small theaters could be improvised almost anywhere, and their relatively cheap price provided entertainment for even working-class viewers who had little expendable income. By that time Jimmy Britt, a lightweight contender, had replaced Corbett as the new heartthrob, and women flocked to his San Francisco training camp to watch him perform. The erotic black body of Jack Johnson and the rugged machismo of Jack Dempsey continued to attract women to boxing in later years. Women became so commonplace at bouts that Pope Pius XI issued a condemnation of female spectators in 1933, to no avail.[33]

In addition to the early female professional pugilists, some of the "new women" began to take boxing lessons and engage in sparring. They no longer deferred to the chivalry of male protectors. In 1890 one participant urged her colleagues, "If you are insulted in the street, knock your insulter down."[34] The *Atlanta Constitution* encouraged women to spar for health as early as 1895. An instructor claimed that women were more graceful in the ring, but lacked male aggressiveness and did not hit hard enough. Another had similar impressions: "They go at boxing like a boy who tries to swim dog fashion. To box well one must think and keep cool, and that is something women have to learn. . . . Then, too, they are timid. They are afraid of black eyes, and stiff jaws, and bruised bodies."[35] Women thus received conflicting messages in this transformative era of gender change. They were criticized both for their timidity in their pursuit of boxing by not adopting male characteristics in the ring, and they were chastised for not adhering to more traditional Victorian norms of feminine domesticity if they did assume male characteristics.

Boxing held transatlantic interest, as women in France also took up the French form of kickboxing known as savate. In 1902 a French woman, Mademoiselle Augagnier, met a Miss Pinkney from England in a mixed match. Pinckney boxed, while Augagnier used both her hands and feet: "Pinkney was better with her fists and looked like a winner after about one and a half hours of bloody fighting, but Mlle. A. cleverly managed to kick Pinkney in the face. This blow made a terrible scar and stunned the English girl, then the French girl shot a smashing kick to Pinkney's stomach and knocked her out. The French girl was carried by her admirers in triumph from the ring." French pride was resurrected in 1911 when Jeanne La Mar, a female pugilist, defeated Steffi Bernet, reputed to be the women's champion of Germany.[36]

Women also became the subject of boxing films, such as the Gordon sisters who were featured in Thomas Edison's works, but these were not serious efforts and their titillating appeal was more commercial than athletic. More serious female boxers continued to practice their craft in the World War I years. Helen Hildreth of Pittsburgh started boxing as a stage act, but progressed to actual bouts by 1916. That year she even took on a male opponent, but authorities intervened to stop the affair which might

Ruth Murphy and Vera Rerhue boxing at Winter Garden. Courtesy of H. J. Lutcher Stark Center for Physical Culture and Sports, University of Texas at Austin.

have further toppled notions of male superiority, for Hildreth sported an undefeated record in ten fights between 1915 and 1917. She fought along the East Coast and in Canada, Pittsburgh, and Detroit, indicating that female professional boxers continued to challenge gender norms across a

Belle Gordon, an early subject of boxing films. Courtesy of H. J. Lutcher Stark Center for Physical Culture and Sports, University of Texas at Austin.

wide area. Despite her own success, on her retirement in 1917 she suggested a return to more acceptable feminine behavior: "Women can learn to box as cleverly as men, but I must admit that it is not a woman's sport and they are liable to be seriously hurt by constant tapping on the breasts, unless protected with strong steel corsets. I love to box myself, but would not advise women to take it up as exercise. For men it is the greatest exercise in the world."[37]

Despite her admonition, boxing gained even greater prominence among women in the aftermath of World War I. Georges Carpentier, a handsome military hero, became a popular attraction on both sides of the Atlantic. An estimated 2,000 attended his 1921 championship bout with Jack Dempsey and, in a reversal of traditional voyeurism, male boxers became objects of the women's gaze. Avant garde women in both Europe and the United States not only endorsed but practiced the sport as a reaction to effete modernism in the wake of the war. Walter Rothenburg, a German boxing promoter, warned in 1921 that "no man, even if he had been the biggest Don Juan, still risks it in this day and age to approach a lady on the street. The reason: the woman is beginning to box!" Steffi Bernet, who had been boxing since before the war, established the Berlin Women's Boxing Club in 1928.[38]

For some women, boxing became an antidote to weight gain, promoted as fitness and exercise during the 1920s. In a Philadelphia gym of a former boxer, the clientele quickly changed from all male to almost exclusively female by the end of the decade. Other women had more pragmatic reasons for boxing. Annie Newton, an English woman who had lost two husbands in the war, fought professionally as a means to support her daughter. She answered physicians' and moralists' concerns about female boxing by stating, "And really! All this talk about boxing for women being 'degrading' and 'risky' and 'too hard work' strikes me as very comic. Is it any more degrading, or half as hard work, as scrubbing floors?" Newton only expressed the working-class habitus, a perception of life through a physical lens. Less than an hour in the ring might earn her more than a full day of scrubbing on her knees, which seemed like a bargain, for the working class had little social status to lose.[39]

Sociologist Jennifer Hargreaves asserted that "in its [boxing] most pure form, it was a celebration of female muscularity, physical strength and aggression. Power was literally inscribed in the boxers' bodies—in their actual working muscles—an expression of physical capital usually ascribed to men."[40] One can only imagine the exhilaration felt by women previously confined to sedentary lives. In Germany the movement attracted artists, writers, and actresses, including the famed Marlene Dietrich. The merger of art and sport produced a number of specialized journals including *Die Arena* and *Der Querschnitt*, the latter published from 1921 to 1936 when the Nazis forced its abandonment. Boxing was thus "elevated from brute, low-class entertainment to a meaningful and artful ritual whose objective it was to promote images of fitness and health and to transform humanity itself."[41]

Similar developments occurred in the United States. Hollywood actresses also adopted boxing as a metaphor for life. Clara Bow, who personified the 1920s flapper, used her body to make a living and found that she was exploited like most boxers. Her photographic poses as a boxer only antagonized Mae West, the famed comedic actress whose father, Battling Jack West, had been an actual boxer. This allegedly led to a challenge between the two. West also claimed that she had boxed several matches as a young waitress, a vaudevillian, and an aspiring actress, including a clandestine bout with actress Eleanor Boardman about 1922. West clearly had an attraction to the sport and to boxers, several of whom became her lovers. Victor McLaglen, a former boxer turned actor, trained her for the Boardman battle and in the 1930s she would employ William "Gorilla" Jones (middleweight champ), Albert "Chalky" Wright (featherweight champ), and Speedy Dado (bantamweight contender) as bodyguards and chauffeurs, and sponsor their ring careers to various extents.[42]

Throughout their lives Clara Bow and Mae West challenged gender norms in their movie roles and even more so in their lifestyles. Both grew up in tough sections of Brooklyn and West's boxer father taught her to fight at an early age. Conflict, aggression, and self-defense came with the territory and physical altercations accompanied the working-class habitus. Bow claimed, "I was part of a secret sorority who loved to box each other privately or at by-invitation-only smokers around Hollywood. My boss at Paramount, Budd Schulberg, once said that I was a disgrace to the community, and I am sure he was referring to my secret boxing career."[43]

Such activities took place secretly because of conflicting opinions about the value of sport for women. In the United States, middle-class female physical educators at many American colleges and prominent members of the American Physical Education Association decried competitive sports that followed the male model. They felt that overly competitive, commercialized, and aggressive sports were harmful to women physically, psychologically, and morally. Instead they organized "play days" for female students, which consisted of invitations to other college teams that traveled to the invitee's campus for a friendly game with mixed teams and a social event afterward. In contrast, Alice Milliat, president of the French Association of Women's Sport founded in 1917, promoted full competition for female athletes. She organized a female Olympic Games in 1922, which continued until the International Olympic Committee reluctantly agreed to incorporate women's track and field activities into the Olympic Games in 1928. Working-class women continued to compete on industrial teams of their employers throughout the controversy. Both Clara Bow and Mae West emanated from working-class roots and physicality remained an essential part of their persona.[44]

Bow preceded West as a silent film star, and the latter made the boxing challenge as part of a publicity ploy to gain greater recognition in Hollywood. Regardless of the outcome, both actresses expressed their physicality in ways that countered the dominant male hegemony. Bow's silent films required physical expressiveness, and her roles as vamp and flapper transgressed on the framework of male power. In her not-so-private life she conscripted multiple lovers for her own needs. West continually played with and overturned assigned gender roles as an actress, playwright, and comedienne. She played a tomboy, a flapper, a prostitute, and a homosexual, flaunting social mores on her path to becoming a sex symbol. A master of the double entendre and sexual innuendo, West's works outraged moralists and censors who limited her creativity as she pushed the boundaries of sexual discourse within American culture. With more independence in her own life she reversed traditional gender roles in her liaisons with men of color, possibly including the black heavyweight pariah Jack Johnson. She assumed the dominant role in her relationships as manager, employer, financier, and protector of her male entourage. She explained, "I've always liked athletes because they don't smoke, don't drink, and understand the importance of keeping their bodies in top working order. . . . A hard man is good to find." In her later move to performances in Las Vegas, she once again reversed the typical use of a female supporting cast by utilizing a beefcake revue of topless men.[45]

As West pushed the boundaries of public discourse about gender and sexuality, women in other parts of the world took up the crusade. Two women engaged in a public match as early as 1926 in Nicaragua, and Mexico recorded its first female boxer in 1930, but women's boxing in Latin America would not reach significant proportions until the end of the century. World War II curtailed the female boxing scene; a British-born (1930) fighter from Yorkshire, Barbara Buttrick, achieved a measure of recognition thereafter. Standing only 5 feet tall and weighing only 100 pounds, Buttrick started boxing in fairground booths in England and France against both women and men. She progressed to more regulated competitions and was acknowledged as the female champion of England. In 1954 she became the first woman to obtain a boxing license in the United States, and defeated Phyllis Kugler three years later in a bout that decided the women's world championship. Buttrick boxed numerous exhibitions with male opponents, and a 1959 bout was the first female match to be broadcast on the radio. She retired with a record of 30-1, her only loss to American Jo Ann Hagen, a woman who held a twenty-pound weight advantage and towered over her at 5 feet 7 inches. Buttrick later founded the Women's International Boxing Association, for which she served as the first president in 1995.[46]

Women took one more step into the male world of boxing in the person of Aileen Eaton, who managed to secure her position as a promoter in Los Angeles. Known as "the Queen of the Jungle" and "the Dragon Lady," she proved to be not only tough and powerful, but honest, standing up to the IBC syndicate and mobsters such as Frankie Carbo, who controlled much of boxing in the post–World War II era. Eaton staged at least 100 championship bouts, outmaneuvering her male competitors, and her weekly programs grossed more than a million dollars a year in the 1960s. A *Sports Illustrated* article in 1967 described her as "a woman in a man's game-fight promotion that abounds in stealth and triple trickery. Dictatorial yet feminine, she is loved by some, hated by others and feared by all." Despite poor health she continued to run boxing in Los Angeles until 1980, and was elected to the International Boxing Hall of Fame.[47]

Other women followed Eaton into the previously male domain. Jackie Kallen (Kaplan) began her career as a writer and assumed the role of publicist for Thomas Hearns in 1977. Hearns became one of the premier fighters of the 1980s, amassing multiple championships. Kallen progressed to become a boxing manager, guiding James Toney to championships in three weight divisions. Kallen is considered to be the top female manager in the sport, and her life became the subject of a biopic in 2004. She also reigned as a commissioner of the International Female Boxing Association.[48]

During the 1970s other women resurrected the long history of female boxers by testing their skills in the ring. Two women, Pat Pineda and Caroline Svendsen, were granted boxing licenses in 1975. The next year the state of New York licensed three more women who sued for the right to fight. In 1979 Gladys "Bam Bam" Smith outpointed Toni "Leatherneck" Tucker in the first recognized licensed women's pro bout, which proved to be the only one for both participants. By the end of the decade there were enough female boxers to offer a program of eight pro bouts in Los Angeles, but the serious fighters had to contend with the "foxy boxing" spectacles offered by the porn industry, which only parodied and mocked their quest for respect and affirmation. Early pro bouts were also marred by few competitors and gross mismatches arranged by promoters only interested in quick profits rather than the gradual development of their parvenus.[49]

Women overcame yet another obstacle in the patriarchal wall in 1985 when Gleason's, the famed boxing gym in New York, became the first such male bastion to accept women as members. This apparently insignificant gesture actually "destabilized the sport's seemingly fixed social organization." Women had crossed yet another boundary, but admittance did not assure acceptance, as "boxing remains overwhelmingly a male environment, informed by a particular strain of masculine culture, one of the ramifications of which is that female boxers are constantly reminded (by the round-card girls in bikinis and stilettos, by the lyrics that blast from virtually all gym boom boxes, by the heckling taunts of spectators at matches, and by the inevitable advances from male trainers and boxers) that they are more easily regarded as sex objects than athletes."[50]

Boxing gyms have often been dirty, sweaty, gendered spaces where women were seen as unwanted distractions from the male regimen of enforcing discipline on one's body, a public display of stoic punishment to effect domination over not only an opponent, but oneself in the presence of other men. Even male newcomers must prove themselves worthy of acknowledgement, acceptance, and eventual camaraderie within the hierarchical space of the boxing gym. Newcomers must show themselves to be true boxers, rather than fitness dilettantes: "Whereas bodily prowess is the single most important marker of empowerment within the everyday context of the gym, outside the sport, women's very physicality is often considered suspect, subversive, or dangerous in light of conventional notions of masculinity or femininity."[51] Women who enter a true boxing gym, rather than a fitness club, are faced with a considerable dilemma in identity. They may be perceived as a sex object or a lesbian; "Any girl who boxes challenges . . . the idea of what it means to be a girl in our culture." That perception has gained greater latitude with the increase in professional women prizefighters over the past few decades.[52]

Even as the number of female professional boxers increases, they continue to face discrimination based on their sex. Coaches and trainers are reluctant to invest their time in women whose family responsibilities or a future pregnancy might interrupt or preclude their training. A Canadian study conducted in 2005–2006 found that it took two to three years for female boxers to gain the confidence of their trainers. Pregnant boxers are not allowed to fight, so women are forced to make family planning decisions that do not affect male fighters in the same way.[53] "Women boxers do not just fight each other; they fight against the belief that it is unnatural for a woman to be athletic, strong, aggressive, and confident in a sport historically dominated by males. Yet, many female boxers are mothers. Some are single parents with extended families to support." Such dilemmas put women in a liminal position, not fully accepted in one role as they deviate from traditional female roles.[54]

With the passage of Title IX, a part of the Educational Amendments Act of 1972 guaranteeing all Americans equal access to opportunities regardless of gender, women have increasingly used the legal system to achieve their goals. Female students at the University of Minnesota started a boxing club and endeavored to conduct state championship matches in 1978. The Amateur Athletic Union initially blocked their tournament, but negotiations resulted in its occurrence in May of that year. Claire Buckner, a twenty-four-year-old mother of three, became the first state champion. Gail Grandchamp, who had already been fighting on her own for seven years, challenged a Massachusetts ban on female boxers in 1992, but on reaching the age of thirty-five she became ineligible for amateur competition, which made her case moot. In 1993 sixteen-year-old Dallas Malloy sued U.S. Boxing in order to let her compete in the Golden Gloves competition. Backed by the American Civil Liberties Union (ACLU), she won an injunction that allowed her to fight. Having won in the court and in the ring, Malloy retired from boxing after that one bout. Both amateur and professional bouts for women were permitted in Texas that same year.[55]

The International Women's Boxing Federation (IWBF), founded in 1992, established uniform rules for women's competitions. They would fight ten rounds rather than twelve in championship bouts, and rounds would last for two minutes instead of the three-minute rounds in male bouts. Women who weighed less than 140 pounds wore eight-ounce gloves; those over that weight limit donned ten-ounce gloves. All women were required to have a medical exam that included a pregnancy test and had to provide a legitimate boxing license in order to fight. Five more governing bodies for women's boxing soon followed in subsequent years.[56]

In 1996 a women's professional bout was televised for the first time as Christy Martin defeated Deidre Gogarty of Ireland in a six-round unanimous decision for the world's super lightweight title. Although female fighters were limited to two-minute rounds (as opposed to three minutes for males), the bout drew 30 million pay-per-view subscribers as the preliminary to the Mike Tyson–Frank Bruno heavyweight battle. The two female competitors seemed an odd match. Martin, born Christy Salters, married her trainer Jim Martin, and would become the first major star in women's boxing but eschewed the role of a feminist heroine. She billed herself "the coal miner's daughter," a fighter, not a feminist, and dressed in pink for her bouts, choosing to emphasize her social class and femininity. Gogarty's father was a surgeon, her mother a dentist, and her siblings were a doctor and an orchestra director. She left Ireland because its boxing governing body would not sanction her bouts to pursue her craft in the United Kingdom and the United States. Despite a nearly twenty-pound advantage for Martin, the fight proved to be a competitive and bloody affair that showcased women's boxing talents. Gogarty would claim the women's featherweight title in 1997.[57]

United States Boxing authorized national championships for women in 1997, and women's competition expanded in Europe, Africa, and Asia. Women's amateur boxing attracted a different social class than the often poor and poorly educated practitioners of the past. The new breed of women still fulfilled the heroic roles of male ethnic and class champions of the past that evoked community pride. Erie, Pennsylvania, had been a hotbed of boxing since the 1930s, but it represented a rustbelt community hit hard by the demise of the industrial economy by the end of the century. Liz McGonigal emerged as a local heroine. After earning her black belt in karate, she sought other challenges. A college student, she garnered the state Golden Gloves championships in both 1996 and 1997, bringing a measure of local pride to the otherwise forlorn residents. When her triumphs provided the opportunity to contend for the 1997 national title in Augusta, Georgia, the workers of Erie contributed the $2,500 necessary for her trip. Despite their class differences, the workers felt an affinity for the female boxer, for both of them "worked with their hands." She rewarded them with a national title. McGonigal, however, declined offers for a professional ring career in favor of her studies, eventually earning a master's degree and a position as a psychologist. The women she defeated in Georgia were also college graduates, and Joy Liu, the 2001 Golden Gloves national champ in the junior welterweight division, graduated from Harvard and had a law degree from Columbia University, which she put to use as a corporate attorney. Such boxers represented a distinct departure from the male participants of the past.[58]

By 2001 women's world championship bouts for professional female boxers appeared in the United States, France, Egypt, and Thailand. The early champions included Ann Wolfe, who endured homelessness and unemployment before taking up boxing, where she found great success, ruling over four weight classes (IFBA, WIBA light middleweight, 2001; IFBA, WIBC super middleweight, 2002; NABA super middleweight, 2004; IBA, WIBA light heavyweight, 2004; IBA light heavyweight, 2005) during her career from 1998 to 2006. Upon her retirement she became a trainer at her own gym, where she offers the same opportunities for street kids: "Many of them have been homeless or been in trouble. They are looking for something, and this gym is where they can find peace. They help me by wanting to do something with their life, and I help them by giving them the opportunity they would have never had without the gym."[59]

The burgeoning women's pro circuit also created a number of international stars. Laura Serrano of Mexico claimed the WIBA lightweight title in 1995; Ada Velez from Puerto Rico won the bantamweight (2001, 2002–2003) and super bantamweight (2001–2002) championships. Regina Halmich, a German flyweight, began her career in 1994, compiling a record of 54-1-1, and held the WIBF title from 1995 until her retirement in 2007. Lucia Rijker, a Dutch light welterweight, fought from 1996 to 2004, winning the IBO title in 1998 and retiring undefeated in 2004. Some of the women already had name recognition due to their famous fathers. Laila Ali, the daughter of Muhammad Ali; J'Marie Moore, the daughter of Archie Moore; Jacqueline Frazier-Lyde, the daughter of Joe Frazier, Irichelle Duran, the daughter of Roberto Duran, as well as Freeda Foreman, the daughter of George Foremen, all followed a parent into the ring.[60]

Only Laila Ali and Jacqui Frazier-Lyde enjoyed substantial success. Frazier-Lyde fought for four years (2000–2004), garnering titles across three weight classes. She finished with a record of thirteen wins and only one loss, but that setback occurred in her most significant bout against Ali in 2001. Her father offered her $15,000 not to fight Ali, which she declined. The promoters staged it at a New York casino and billed it as Ali-Frazier IV, a reference to the three prodigious battles between their iconic fathers. Thousands attended to witness Ali take a majority decision. She would continue to fight until 2007 (1999–2007), finishing her career as an undefeated champion of the super welterweight class (WIBA, 2002–2007; WBC, 2005–2007).[61]

Inevitably, despite the rules intended to prohibit injury, female boxers have suffered serious injury and death. In 1996 Katie Dallam, fighting in her first pro bout, suffered a serious and permanent brain injury in a gross mismatch that left her a permanent invalid. Another fighter indicated the devious nature of one manager, whom she likened to a pimp: "pimping me out for all these fights. At the time (of the contract) I really trusted this man. I was his new fighter and I was treated like a princess." The first fatality in a women's match occurred in a Colorado Golden Gloves bout in 2005 when Becky Zerlentes, a thirty-four-year-old teacher, succumbed to injuries sustained in the ring. Although not occurring in the ring, the country of Trinidad and Tobago endured a national agony when it lost twenty-one-year-old Jisselle Salandy in a car accident in 2009. Orphaned at age eleven, she took up boxing. She won the first of her eight world championships at the tender age of fourteen. She fought wearing the national colors, stating, "I love boxing and I love my country so I try to accomplish my personal goals as well as fly my national flag with each fight." Her funeral was a national media event. The state awarded her its highest honor and established boxing gyms and classes to accommodate all the young girls that she had inspired. In her short life she had transcended traditional male spheres in both the sport and as a national hero.[62]

Such role models can be particularly influential in developing countries, where sport for women is still locked in patriarchal bondage. Esther Phiri of Zambia presents one such example. Her father died when she was young, leaving her in poverty and forced to fend for herself as a street peddler. She gave birth to her first child at sixteen, but persisted as a lone female in a community boxing program. By the age of twenty in 2007 she had succeeded in winning the WIBF super featherweight world title, and capturing both the WIBA and IBO light welterweight championships in subsequent years. The Zambian president declared, "Indeed Esther has made us proud again and continues to lift the Zambian flag higher. It is my sincere hope that she will continue with this spirit and commitment to bringing honour not only to herself but to the country as a whole." She was invited to lunch in the presidential palace and awarded a sum of more than $60,000, and a three-bedroom house furnished by local merchants. She received an endorsement contract worth $100,000, and her fights have made her wealthy and brought national celebrity. In short, Phiri has achieved both social and economic capital by invading previously male turf, and her success is indicative of the possibilities of individual initiative. While women's soccer programs in Zambia are still mired in masculine priorities, boxing has offered and inspired more girls and women to follow Phiri's path.[63]

Communist countries have long recognized the value of women's sports in promoting nationalism and global recognition in international sports events. Unlike Western nations who market female athletes as sex objects, Communist theory purports sexual equality. In North Korea female boxers are quite popular, drawing numerous fans to their bouts and producing a number of international champions. Pyongyang, the capital of North Korea, hosted the WBCF championships in 2005 in which three North Korean women won titles. The North Korean media portray female fighters as having the same characteristics as males, such as aggressiveness, speed, strength, and courage. Kwang-ok Kim was praised as "the proud daughter of the nation, whose fists attracted the world's attention." The female boxers represent the martial spirit of the nation. Another magazine likened Kim's punch to a mace that struck an opponent: "From the past, wisdom and courage constitute the essential character of our nation, and on many occasions, this character is expressed through the fists."[64]

The matches also served as surrogate warfare for the North Koreans, especially in Kwang-ok Kim's match against a Japanese boxer. Japan had colonized Korea and occupied it for much of the twentieth century, and North Koreans perceived Kim's knockout victory as retribution. "The excitement in the arena was so great that all the fans behaved as if they were in the ring, and beating the Japanese as one." The female boxers from North Korea have been more successful than their male counterparts in exacting such national revenge and thus contribute more to the sense of national identity and national character.[65]

International competitions assumed even greater prestige for women when the International Olympic Committee decided to include women's boxing on the 2012 program. The concession hardly promised equality, however. Whereas men still had ten weight classifications, women were allotted only three. Women boxers' attire had already become an issue when they were asked to wear skirts instead of boxing trunks at the 2010 world championships in Barbados, and again at the 2011 European championships. The president of the Amateur International Boxing Association stated that skirts were necessary to distinguish women from men as they both wore the same uniforms and headgear. Poland and Romania made the skirts a requirement for their competitors, with the Polish coach stating that "by wearing skirts, in my opinion, it gives a good impression, a womanly impression. Wearing shorts is not a good way for women boxers to dress."[66]

Irish champion Katie Taylor and most of the other women refused to comply with the request. Sportswriter Kathryn Bertine wrote, "The message boxing is sending to the world is this: women's sports are all about looks, not athleticism." An Australian commentator agreed, stating, "They're punching the crap out of each other and they're trying to make them look sexy. . . . Let's be honest, it's all about television and selling females. It's all about marketing." Despite the aggressive nature of women's boxing, male administrators continued to inscribe it with a particular feminine appearance rather than the gender-neutral status attained by the women.[67]

Given the obstacles facing female boxers, one might wonder about their motivations for pursuing the activity. Christine Mennesson examined how twelve French female boxers ranging in age from eighteen to thirty-eight constructed their identities over a two-year period. All but one of the women came from working-class families. Many had participated in other sports previously and had received paternal encouragement to do so. Eight described themselves as tomboys and most identified with masculine role models, but all stressed their feminine identity, displaying long hair and "feminine" clothing, expressing traditional gender outside the ring. All hoped to become mothers, and three already had children. In the ring, however, they adopted "male" psychological characteristics, such as aggressiveness and the ability to give and receive pain. The women considered themselves to be liberated females, living a dualistic identity.[68]

Yvonne Lafferty used an ethnographic approach in a study of Australian female boxers who were members of a middle-class club. All joined for fitness purposes, but the facilities and programs were geared toward male priorities. Although a state champion, one of the female members felt disrespected by the fact that she got less sparring time than a fourteen-year-old boy at the club. Nevertheless, the women experienced empowerment. A sixteen-year-old girl attributed the regimen as instilling discipline and self-confidence: "It has provided me with a focus for my energy and allowed me to develop not only physical fitness but also helped in giving my life purpose and direction." Another found a positive outlet for her aggression. A thirty-two-year-old who began boxing competitively marveled at her strength and the public demonstration of her knockout punch.[69]

A boxer in another study stated that "women are taught *not* to be physical" and "it feels good to be in a context where it is *acceptable* to be physical and to discover a side of ourselves we never knew we had. Getting rid of aggression in a physical way is really liberating and attractive."[70] Cathy van Ingen, a Canadian scholar, conducts a women's boxing program with that intent in mind. The participants are 120 abused women who have been victims of violence. Their anger is redirected through boxing, which offers a release of built-up tension. They find in their bodies a "source of strength and power."[71] Lynn Snowden Picket, a journalist, took up boxing after a failed marriage in which her husband engaged in an affair. Boxing allowed her to express and release her anger. "I'm full of rage and I want to beat someone up. I want to know what it is like to have physical power over men. I want to inspire fear. I want to matter." For women, boxing offers a catharsis. Strength, aggression, and toughness are no longer relegated to men alone.[72]

My own survey of more than fifty female boxers in the Chicago area included girls and women from ages twelve to fifty-five. Their reasons for participating in boxing varied, but more than two-thirds of the respondents indicated personal fitness as their primary objective. Mostly middle class, they had the leisure and expendable capital to join fitness clubs in which boxing, without sparring, provided a "tough," "intense," "challenging," "invigorating," and "exhilarating" workout that promoted their self-confidence.

Both middle-class and working-class participants also took up boxing as a means to learn self-defense. While girls in working-class communities, especially in the inner cities, engage in fistfights, Chicago is a city especially prone to violence. Almost daily the media tally and report murder and assault figures in even the wealthiest areas of the city. Although women in suburban areas may not experience violence to the same extent as city dwellers, they want to be prepared. One suburbanite stated that 'if someone were to attack me, I'd be prepared and feel confident to defend myself."[73] An inner-city resident wrote, "You never know if you may ever need the skills you learn here." A member of the same club claimed "I was intimidated due to the fact that I am a small female who couldn't win a fight against a fly. After taking a couple weeks of classes I am really comfortable and confident to say I could take the fly."[74]

Several girls and young working-class women engaged in boxing for competitive reasons. Tatyana McCool, a fourteen-year-old student, stated that "I fell in love with boxing in 2010 and now I hope to compete in the U.S. Olympics." She captured the national Police Athletic League championships in 2011 and 2012 and the Silver Gloves regional title in the latter year. She related her sense of empowerment when she stated, "When I began boxing there were two girls already in boxing and they were so mean to me. . . . And it got to the point where these girls no longer come to the gym because they said I hit so hard and they don't want to spar with me any longer. The boys at the gym actually respected me after they got in the ring with me to spar. They all say I have heart and I have more heart than they do."[75]

Tiffany Perez, a twenty-three-year-old, is a member of the same club and has achieved similar success, but like other women she had to earn respect. She stated that "you always have to prove yourself . . . as a female you get tested a little bit more . . . females are always looked down on until they showcase their skills in the ring." Perez won the Junior Olympic title in 2005 and Chicago Golden Gloves championships for four consecutive years (2007–2010). She qualified for the Puerto Rican national team, but lost in the Olympic trials.[76]

Laura Zamora, a seventeen-year-old student from a Hispanic neighborhood, captained her high school wrestling team and is also a flamenco dancer, but her sights are set on the Marine Corps and a future as a professional boxer. She enjoys imparting fear and dominating her opponents, looking for a knockout. For her the ring is a place to expend her aggressions.[77] Ann-Marie Saccurato, professional fighter and former WBC lightweight champ in 2006, feels the same sense of empowerment when she steps into the ring: "I feel more confident, focused, intense. . . . Inside of me, I feel my passion and my determination."[78]

An aspect of women's participation that differed from other studies was the sense of community or family that they found at the club and the personal relationships that they developed with their trainers. A member of a suburban club stated that "Coach Will does an amazing job of simultaneously motivating me, but never in a demeaning way (some other coaches . . . including other men at this very gym, insult the people working out, which I think is unnecessary and wrong)."[79] Ittzel Perez, from an inner-city club, claimed, "My coaches, peers, my friends, and what I now call my family has [sic] showed me a new way of life, it's made me stronger."[80] Lisa Hong, another suburbanite, liked the community atmosphere at her club, where "people here are friendly and positive and training is enjoyable." Nancy Luna, a member at the same club, agreed that Joe, a personal trainer, "always brings you up in spirit. . . . He's everybody's mentor and friend."[81]

Still others sought personal development, such as the instilling of discipline and challenge. Shelly Pratt, another inner-city participant who engaged in sparring matches, stated that boxing "allows me to push myself further than I knew was possible." Motivations differed somewhat by class, but all sought some positive benefit. Despite the obstacles, it is apparent that women's boxing has entered the mainstream, disrupting traditional notions of gender and identity.[82]

CHAPTER EIGHT

CONCLUSIONS

W hile boxing has had considerable cultural significance across time periods and many societies, this book has not been an attempt to glorify the sport. It has produced some heroic characters, but also many brutal tragedies. That should raise some questions.

Why has boxing lasted so long despite medical and ethical issues and governmental attempts to ban it? Why does it continue to draw practitioners despite the dangers and exploitation? Well-known boxing author Thomas Hauser stated, "The business of boxing . . . is the red-light district of professional sports, an arena marked by greed and corruption, rife with shifting alliances and private wars; a world where promises take funny bounces, and one is best to heed the referee's warning—'protect yourself at all times.'"[1]

Boxers have no labor union, no health insurance, and no pension plan. Due to the myriad governing bodies, each bestowing their own version of a championship, a contender must pay exorbitant licensing fees just to get a chance to wear a signifying belt, which may require an additional purchase price. Commentators have termed such deliberations a "culture of lawlessness," a "half monopoly, half piracy," and "more like bandits than regulators."[2] Teddy Atlas, a well-known commentator for televised bouts, explained the cooperative skullduggery among the boxing commission, the promoters, and the judges. In a fight in which the local boxer was clearly defeated by a foreigner, the judges ruled unanimously for the local fighter. The local promoters lobby the state commission for particular judges to be assigned to their bouts. If the judges don't choose the "right" boxer, their future employment will be quite limited. If the state boxing commission does not acquiesce to the promoters' demands and the promoters lose money and go out of business, there will no longer be a need for their services, either.[3]

Boxers suffer increased rates of Parkinson's disease, multiple sclerosis, Alzheimer's disease, and various forms of dementia. Even among amateur boxers who wear protective headgear, nearly half have abnormal brain scans. They suffer eye injuries such as detached retinas and blindness. Many find an early death. Jerry Quarry, a top heavyweight contender, had a relatively long career. He won the Junior Golden Gloves at the age of eight and fought sixty-six bouts as a professional, but he required full-time care by the age of fifty due to dementia and died three years later.[4] Many others did not have the resources for attention and died lonely deaths.

Hauser noted, "In a perfect world boxing might not exist. But the world is not perfect, and in the eyes of many, thousands of young men are better off because of boxing." For both male and female boxers in the inner cities, the gym is a safe haven from the violence of the streets. Every day the poor must fight for survival in and out of the ring. Boxing offers a more legitimate means than crime to acquire cash in a culture that values wealth. While the overwhelming majority of boxers will never acquire wealth, even a journeyman can garner ready cash.[5]

Journeymen "are the boxers who travel, often without cornermen, to take, and most likely lose, fights on short notice." Michael Murray, an English journeyman heavyweight, admitted that "we are men willing to fight anyone, anywhere, and all we need is money and enough time to put on our shorts and glove-up."[6] Journeymen are good losers, who may fight well enough to make a plausible showing in order to pad the winning record of an up-and-coming prospect.

Joe Grim, one of the earliest journeymen, was born in Italy as Saverio Giannone in 1881, and realized that he could earn a considerable sum in his adopted land simply by absorbing punishment. Known as the "human punching bag," he fought forty-five recorded bouts with an official record of 10-30-5 from 1899 to 1913; it is estimated that he actually participated in as many as 300. He battled with many of the top fighters of the era, usually going the distance, to the continual amazement of spectators, which earned him subsequent bouts. Fans always got their money's worth.

He finished a 1905 bout with Jack Johnson despite being knocked down a dozen times. When he died his obituary stated, "There is no doubt that Joe Grim was the toughest man who ever entered the squared circle."[7]

More recently, other journeymen have been able to manipulate the system by assuming aliases to circumvent the regulations that limit how often they can fight or that establish recovery time after a knockout. Reggie Strickland, who also fought as Reggie Buse and Reggie Raglin between 1987 and 2005, amassed a record of 67-263-17. Bruce "the Mouse" Strauss also employed numerous aliases starting in 1976 with an official record of 77-53-6; he estimated that he had 260 losses fighting in weight classes from lightweight to light heavyweight from 1976 to 1989. Simmie Black, who also had several aliases including Spider Black and Fred Johnson, and allegedly used the names of amateur and deceased boxers, had thirty consecutive losses from 1979 to 1981, and an official record of 35-165-4 from 1971 to 1996; but always put on a good show. He even did a cartwheel in the ring after supposedly being knocked out.[8]

Other journeymen are not so entertaining in their approach. Obie Garnett, a super middleweight, fought only a dozen times from 1978 to 1986 to make some extra money to augment his job as a mill worker. Each fight ended in a first-round knockout. In one Chicago bout he fell to the canvas with the first jab delivered by his opponent. He "earned" $175 for such a fiasco. Sylvester Wilder had greater longevity as a heavyweight from 1973 to 1981 but little more success, going 4-47 with thirty-nine straight losses during that time. In another Memphis bout, the journeyman landed a big punch that apparently knocked out the local favorite. Before the referee finished his count the arena lights blacked out and remained off for twenty minutes. By that time the local hero had recovered and the fight resumed. The hometown boxer was awarded the decision.[9]

Italian philosopher Antonio Gramsci proposed the hegemony theory, which may account for the continued participation in boxing. Simply stated, the theory posits that in any society there is a dominant group that sets the norms, standards, and values of the society and is engaged in a continuous power struggle with one or more subordinate groups. Upper-class males generally compose the dominant group. In Western societies, one can be even more specific by asserting that the dominant group is composed of white, Anglo-Saxon, Protestant males (WASPS). Subordinate groups can accept the dictates of the dominant group and aspire to become part of it, or they can reject such directives, and resist or revolt. Another option is to adapt dominant group values to the subordinates' own cultures and lifestyles. This book favors the latter option (see chapter 3), as the working class has adapted the capitalist concepts of competition, individualism, work ethic, and discipline and merged them with their own concepts (habitus) of honor, esteem, and communal pride achieved through physical prowess rather than education or entrepreneurship. The working class often has an incomplete understanding of the capitalist system. In Gramsci's words, "they feel, but they don't understand." They are relegated to the lowest wages and perform the most physically demanding tasks, with fewer opportunities for social mobility and social status. Yet when such minority entrepreneurs as Don King or Oscar De La Hoya gain immense wealth and power via sport, it reinforces the perception of a meritocracy. Popular culture, too, such as the series of *Rocky* movies or the ascendance of basketball stars Michael Jordan or LeBron James, promotes the rags-to-riches ideology that continues to fuel the hopes of a multitude of American youth. If they maintain a belief in the system, they will not revolt and attempt to overthrow it.[10]

Such an incomplete understanding of the exploitative features of boxing allows for a steady supply of fighters in pursuit of their dreams. Yet the demise of boxing has been predicted for many years. Collegiate boxing was banned after the death of Charlie Mohr in an NCAA championship bout in 1960. Numerous state and even federal inquiries into boxing following the deaths of Benny Paret and Davey Moore in 1962 and 1963 respectively, and consequent condemnation by the pope, failed to prevent the continuation of the sport. The British, Canadian, and American Medical Associations have called for its abolition since 1984 without success. Current prognosticators point to the decline of amateur boxing; the loss of patrons due to the increasing use of cable and pay-per-view broadcasts of the top fights, which excludes many working-class wage earners; the chaotic (mis)administration of the sport by a multitude of governing bodies, each with their own conflicting champions in a growing number of weight classes; the lack of any federal oversight of such regulation; and the preponderance of foreign champions, especially in the symbolic heavyweight division, with little interest to American fans. In contrast, the mixed martial arts (MMA) form of fighting with its one world champion has seemingly captured the younger fan base.[11]

Still, boxing enjoys considerable interest in Hispanic countries and throughout Asia, the biggest markets in an increasingly global economy. The growth of women's boxing could provide a substantial increase in the fan base, but the sexual objectification of women remains an issue and only reinforces the traditional male hegemony. Mia St. John fought professionally from 1997–2013, winning the IFBA lightweight and WBC super welterweight championships, the latter at age forty-five. She is a college graduate with a black belt, and her accomplishments include work as an actress, model, entrepreneur, and community speaker, but she is best known for her 1999 feature in *Playboy* magazine. Very few women's bouts are televised. Despite winning a gold medal as a seventeen-year-old at the 2012 Olympic Games, Claressa Shields got little publicity and no endorsement deals. Such a lack of attention does not bode well for the future of women's boxing.[12]

The fact that boxing persists, despite studies by historians and sociologists indicating that such a decidedly primitive, savage, and barbaric activity should have been abolished as part of the civilizing process, raises another question. It is a residual sport that has defied modernization. It is an activity with the intention of causing harm to others (even though both parties consent to that perpetration). What does that tell us about ourselves and our primal instincts? Both the United States and the United Kingdom are martial cultures. The British gained a global empire by force of arms. Since the United States achieved its independence from Great Britain, every generation of Americans has been engaged in warfare. Sociologists consider this a cultural pattern, and martial values are transmitted across eras by the glorification of military heroes. Violence and aggression are typical characteristics of American movies. A British study found that unlicensed boxers in the United Kingdom fought not only for money, but to gain a perception of self-worth and masculinity through physical expression. They follow no rules as in regulated bouts, and value toughness above all else. For them it represents a "peak experience," a phenomenological quest for identity and fulfillment. Banning boxing would only drive such clandestine bouts further underground without any regulation. Similar fight clubs have appeared in the United States, and the European phenomenon of soccer hooligans revolves around the same principle of physical confrontation with opposing fans.[13]

CONCLUSIONS

The working class across cultures expresses itself through physicality, for it lacks the education and values of the upper classes that seek more aesthetic forms of expression in music, dance, or art. Yet boxing provides its own form of aesthetic expression. For the laboring classes, it can be the ultimate form of craftsmanship without tools. As author Carlo Rotello explains, both workers and boxers are "good with their hands." The agile footwork of Sugar Ray Robinson or Muhammad Ali was akin to that of great dancers, and the precision of Joe Louis might win the respect of architects or engineers. Military generals can admire the strategies of the surrogate warriors within the ring. Artists have found inspiration in boxers as well as ballerinas.[14]

Given such balancing factors, it does not seem that boxing will suffer any demise in the near future. If authorities moved to ban a sport, no matter how dangerous, whose practitioners freely engage in the activity by mutual consent, they would have to consider a multitude of even more dangerous activities such as rugby, football, motorcycle riding, and all combat sports that fall under the umbrella of martial arts. If history is our guide, past efforts to do so have only encouraged new and more creative efforts at circumvention.[15]

BOXING SANCTIONING BODIES

1946 International Amateur Boxing Association (AIBA)
1962 World Boxing Association (WBA), replaced the National
   Boxing Association of 1921
1963 World Boxing Council (WBC)
1983 International Boxing Federation (IBF)
1988 World Boxing Organization (WBO)
1988 World Boxing Federation (WBF)
1995 World Boxing Union (WBU)

WEIGHT CLASSES

Following are boxing's traditional weight classes, which have since been modified by various sanctioning bodies to include light, super, and junior categories, i.e., light or junior flyweight, and super bantamweight, to maximize their marketing opportunities. Note: data from BoxRec, http://boxrec.com/media/index.php/Weight_divisions (accessed May 18, 2013).

Professional Men's Weight Classes

Flyweight: maximum 112 pounds
Bantamweight: 113–117 pounds
Featherweight: 118–126 pounds
Lightweight: 127–135 pounds
Welterweight: 136–147 pounds
Middleweight: 148–160 pounds
Light heavyweight: 161–175 pounds
Cruiserweight (since 1979): 175–200 pounds
Heavyweight: more than 175 pounds until 1979, then more than 200 pounds

Professional Women's Weight Classes

Pinweight/Atomweight: less than 102 pounds
Light flyweight/Strawweight: 102–106 pounds

Flyweight: 107–110 pounds
Light bantamweight: 111–114 pounds
Bantamweight: 115–119 pounds
Featherweight: 120–125 pounds
Lightweight: 126–132 pounds
Light welterweight: 133–138 pounds
Welterweight: 139–145 pounds
Light middleweight: 146–154 pounds
Middleweight: 155–160 pounds
Super middleweight: 161–168 pounds
Light heavyweight: 169–175 pounds
Heavyweight: more than 175 pounds

Amateur Weight Classes

Light flyweight: less than 107 pounds
Flyweight: 107–112 pounds
Bantamweight: 113–119 pounds
Featherweight: 120–125 pounds
Lightweight: 126–132 pounds
Light welterweight: 133–141 pounds
Welterweight: 142–152 pounds
Middleweight: 153–165 pounds
Light heavyweight: 166–178 pounds
Heavyweight: 179–201 pounds
Super heavyweight: more than 201 pounds

Men's Olympic Weight Classes

Light flyweight: less than 107 pounds
Flyweight: 107–112 pounds
Bantamweight: 113–119 pounds
Featherweight: 120–125 pounds
Lightweight: 126–132 pounds
Light welterweight: 133–139 pounds
Welterweight: 140–147 pounds
Light middleweight: 148–156 pounds

Middleweight: 157–165 pounds
Light heavyweight: 166–178 pounds
Heavyweight: 179–201 pounds
Super heavyweight: more than 201 pounds

Women's Olympic Weight Classes

Note: data from "London 2012 Olympics Boxing Guide," the *Telegraph*, n.d., http://www.telegraph.co.uk/sport/olympics/7904164/London-2012-Olympics-boxing-guide.html (accessed May 18, 2013).

Flyweight: less than 112 pounds
Lightweight: less than 132 pounds
Middleweight: less than 165 pounds

APPENDIX 3

BOXING RULES

In amateur bouts men fight three rounds of three minutes each, while women fight rounds of two minutes each. Both males and females are required to wear a protective headgear, a mouth shield, and a groin protector. Women must also don a breast protector. As of June 1, 2013, elite amateur male boxers will no longer wear the headgear in an attempt to reduce head injuries. The removal of the headgear is intended to allow greater vision for combatants and reduce the amount of force applied to the head. Women will continue to wear the headgear. Hair cannot be longer than five inches below the headgear, and no facial hair is allowed. The upper body must be covered by a jersey in a color that contrasts with the waistband of the trunks so that the referee can distinguish illegal low blows. Boxers must wear gloves with a white forefront, and points are scored only if that portion of the glove contacts the opponent's body. No blows can be struck below the belt or behind the neck. An opponent cannot be struck when down, nor can he/she be butted with the head, hit with a forearm, kneed, or kicked. Wrestling is not allowed.[1]

Olympic scoring will change as of the 2016 Games. The computer punch count scoring introduced in 1988 did not recognize body blows, consequently favoring head blows, and will be eliminated in favor of a panel of five judges who will award ten points for the winner of the round and nine or fewer points to the loser of each round in imitation of the professional scoring method. Men fight three rounds of three minutes each, and women fight for four rounds of two minutes each. A one-minute rest interval between rounds is required.[2]

Rules for professional bouts are similar to amateur matches, except in their longevity. Professional competitions can be arranged for any length up to ten rounds, and up to twelve rounds for male championships. Women's bouts are limited to a maximum of ten rounds. Rounds last for three-minute intervals with a one-minute rest in between. Colored gloves have no bearing on the scoring system, in which three judges award ten points to the winner of the round and nine or less to the loser depending upon their judgment. Male boxers do not wear jerseys. Otherwise, the same amateur rules apply for professional matches.[3]

NOTES

Introduction

1. English poet and boxer Vernon Scannell, quoted in David Scott, *The Art and Aesthetics of Boxing* (Lincoln: University of Nebraska Press, 2008), xix. See Robert Hedin and Michael Waters, eds., *Perfect in Their Art: Poems on Boxing from Homer to Ali* (Carbondale: Southern Illinois University Press, 2003).

2. Maeterlinck, cited in Scott, *Art and Aesthetics of Boxing*, 17.

3. Scannell, quoted in Scott, *Art and Aesthetics of Boxing*, xix.

4. Daniel Okrent, "Introduction," xi; see also Ted Hoaglund, "Violence, Violence," 61–63; Michael Stephens, "The Poetics of Boxing," 259–66; Joyce Carol Oates, "On Boxing," 286–305—all in Joyce Carol Oates and Daniel Halpern, eds., *Reading the Fights: The Best Writing about the Most Controversial Sport* (New York: Prentice Hall, 1988).

5. Scott, *Art and Aesthetics of Boxing*, xviii.

6. Scott, *Art and Aesthetics of Boxing*, 134.

7. George Gordon, Lord Byron, "From Letters and Journals," quoted in Hedin and Waters, eds., *Perfect in Their Art*, 39, 40 respectively.

8. George Plimpton, *Shadow Box* (New York: Berkley Books, 1977), 40, 47–48; Daniel Halpern, "Distance and Embrace," 276, and George Plimpton, "Three with Moore," both in Oates and Halpern, eds., *Reading the Fights*; Murry R. Nelson, ed., *Encyclopedia of Sports in North America* (Westport, CT: Greenwood, 2009), 222.

9. A. J. Liebling, *The Sweet Science* (New York: North Point Press, 2004 [1951]).

10. Gerald Early, "I Only Like It Better When the Pain Comes: More Notes toward a Cultural Definition of Prizefighting," in Oates and Halpern, eds., *Reading the Fights*, 53.

11. See Norbert Elias, *The Civilizing Process* (New York: Urizen Books, 1978) on the evolution of a class-based development of acceptable behavior.

Chapter 1: Ancient Boxing

1. Robert G. Rodriguez, *The Regulation of Boxing: A History and Comparative Analysis of Policies among American States* (Jefferson, NC: McFarland & Co., 2009), 23; Michael B. Poliakoff, *Combat Sports in the Ancient World: Competition, Violence, and Culture* (New Haven, CT: Yale University Press, 1987), 65, 68–69; Stephen G. Miller, *Ancient Greek Athletics* (New Haven, CT: Yale University Press, 2004), 24–25; David Potter, *The Victor's Crown: A History of Ancient Sport from Homer to Byzantium* (New York: Oxford University Press, 2012), 18–19; Steven Ross Murray, "Boxing Gloves of the Ancient World," *Journal of Combative Sport* (July 2010), http://ejmas.com/jcs/jcsframe.htm (accessed 12 June 2012).

2. Bryce Lyon, Herbert H. Rowen, and Theodore S. Hamerow, *A History of the Western World* (Chicago: Rand McNally, 1974), 28; Rodriguez, *Regulation of Boxing*, 23; Potter, *Victor's Crown*, 13, 27; Joseph Ward Swain and William H. Armstrong, *The Peoples of the Ancient World* (New York: Harper & Brothers, 1959), 168–70; Homer, "From *The Iliad: Boxing at the Funeral Games of Patroklas*," in Robert Hedin and Michael Waters, eds., *Perfect in Their Art: Poems on Boxing from Homer to Ali* (Carbondale: Southern Illinois University Press, 2003), 99–100.

3. Potter, *Victor's Crown*, 41–84; Poliakoff, *Combat Sports in the Ancient World*, 8–11, 18–19, 79–80, 85, 87; Miller, *Ancient Greek Athletics*, 51–56, Murray, "Boxing Gloves of the Ancient World," 9, 11; Nigel Spivey, *Ancient Olympics* (New York: Oxford University Press, 2012), 106–9.

4. Spivey, *Ancient Olympics*, 157–58; Potter, *Victor's Crown*, 41, 50–55, 86; Miller, *Ancient Greek Athletics*, 57.

5. Murray, "Boxing Gloves of the Ancient World," 12–13; Potter, *Victor's Crown*, 85, 87; Miller, *Ancient Greek Athletics*, 56–57.

6. Miller, *Ancient Greek Athletics*, 52–53; Poliakoff, *Combat Sports in the Ancient World*, 12, 15–16; Potter, *Victor's Crown*, 56–57, 59, 148; Murray, "Boxing Gloves of the Ancient World," 14–17.

7. Lucilius, "Epigrams" (Hubert Wolfe translation), in Hedin and Waters, eds., *Perfect in Their Art*, 130.

8. Potter, *Victor's Crown*, 50, 80, 86, Miller, *Ancient Greek Athletics*, 57.

9. Spartans practiced a strict stoicism in the face of pain, and boys who cried upon injury might be whipped. Three hundred Spartans fought to the death, but succeeded in holding off an invading Persian army at Thermopylae in 480 BCE. Potter, *Victor's Crown*, 58, 80; Miller, *Ancient Greek Athletics*, 147; Poliakoff, *Combat Sports in the Ancient World*, 14; John B. Harrison and Richard B. Sullivan, *A Short History of Western Civilization* (New York: Alfred A. Knopf, 1980), 68.

10. Allen Guttmann, *Sports: The First Five Millennia* (Amherst: University of Massachusetts Press, 2004), 26; Rodriguez, *Regulation of Boxing*, 23.

11. Murray, "Boxing Gloves of the Ancient World," 18, quotes T. F. Scanlon. See Poliakoff, *Combat Sports of the Ancient World*, 75–79, for an extended discussion of the Roman caestus.

12. Virgil, *Aeniad*, vol. 413, quoted in Murray, "Boxing Gloves of the Ancient World," 20, 21.

13. Konstantin Nossov, *Gladiator: Rome's Bloody Spectacle* (Oxford: Osprey, 2009), 11, 118; Poliakoff, *Combat Sports in the Ancient World*, 11; Seutonius, *The Twelve Caesars* (New York: Penguin Books, 1978), 76–77; Charles FitzRoy, *Renaissance Florence on 5 Florins a Day* (London: Thames & Hudson, 2010), 25; Robert C. Davis, *The War of the Fists: Popular Culture and Public Violence in Late Renaissance Venice* (New York: Oxford University Press, 1994).

14. Murray, "Boxing Gloves of the Ancient World," 22.

15. "A Rumble in the Sahel," *The Economist*, November 18, 2010, http://www.economist.com/node/17528098?story_id=17528098 (accessed June 12, 2012).

16. T. J. Desch Obi, "Black Terror: Bill Richmond's Revolutionary Boxing," *Journal of Sport History* 36, no. 1 (Spring 2009): 99–114.

17. Hamilton Wende, "South African Boxing That Makes the Heart Strong,'" *BBC News*, February 5, 2011, http://news.bbc.co.uk/2/hi/programmes/from_our_own_correspondent/9387520.stm (accessed June 12, 2012).

18. Zhang Pengfei, ed., "Rise of Boxing in China Episode I: The Evolution," China Network Television, August 9, 2012, http://english.cntv.cn/special/2012london_olympics/20120809/112640.shtml (accessed November 24, 2012).

19. "The History of Muay Thai," Muay Thai Fighting, n.d., http://www.muaythai-fighting.com/the-history-of-muay-thai.html (accessed June 16, 2012); Charles Little, "Muay Thai," in John Nauright and Charles Parrish, eds., *Sports Around the World: History, Culture, and Practice* (Santa Barbara: ABC-CLIO, 2012), http://ebooks.abc-clio.com/print.aspx?isbn=9781598843019&id=A18 84C V1-4262 (accessed August 4, 2012); "Muay Thai History," Extreme Sports Café, n.d., http://www.extremesportscafe.com/brochure/content/muay-thai-history (accessed September 24, 2102); Pauline Go, "The Tiger King of Ayutthaya

in Thailand," n.d., http://ezinearticles.com/?The-Tiger-King-Of-Ayutthaya-In-Thailand&id=581043 (accessed September 24, 2012).

20. "The History of Muay Thai"; Little, "Muay Thai."

21. "Category: Filipino World Champions," BoxRec.com, n.d., http://boxrec.com/media/index.php/Category:Filipino_World_Champions (accessed June 3, 2013).

Chapter 2: The Evolution of Boxing

1. Allen Guttmann, *From Ritual to Record: The Nature of Modern Sports* (New York: Columbia University Press, 1978); Melvin L. Adelman, *A Sporting Time: New York City and the Rise of Modern Athletics, 1820–1870* (Urbana: University of Illinois Press, 1986).

2. Henry Downs Miles, *Pugilistica: The History of British Boxing* (Edinburgh: John Grant, 1906), 12 (ebook); Pierce Egan, *Boxiana, Vol. 1* (Scott Noble, ed., London: G. Smeeton, 1812, Nicol Island Pub., 1997), 255–58.

3. Egan, *Boxiana*, 258–59; Roberta J. Park, "Contesting the Norm: Women and Professional Sports in Late Nineteenth-Century America," *International Journal of the History of Sport* 29, no. 5 (April, 2012): 734; Allen Guttmann, *Sports: The First Five Millennia* (Amherst: University of Massachusetts Press, 2004), 73.

4. Egan, *Boxiana*, 18–21 (quotes, 18).

5. Egan, *Boxiana*, 21.

6. Quotes from Egan, *Boxiana*, 16 and 13 respectively; see also 23, 41, 43–44; Robert G. Rodriguez, *The Regulation of Boxing: A History and Comparative Analysis of Policies among American States* (Jefferson, NC: McFarland & Co., 2009), 24–25; Miles, *Pugilistica*, 61, 66–67; Dennis Brailsford, "Morals and Maulers: The Ethics of Early Pugilism," *Journal of Sport History* 12, no. 2 (Summer 1985), 126–42; Guttmann, *First Five Millennia*, 72–73. Egan, *Boxiana*, quotes liberally from Captain Barclay, *Treatise upon the Useful Science of Defence*, published in 1747 and dedicated to the Duke of Cumberland, that quickly went through two editions.

7. Brailsford, "Morals and Maulers," 134–5.

8. Joe McCarthy, *Ireland* (New York: Time, 1964), 43–49.

9. Miles, *Pugilistica*, 79; Egan, *Boxiana*, 69–75.

10. Egan, *Boxiana*, 193–95, 292.

11. Egan, *Boxiana*, 99, 104–5, 107–9, 205–8, 264–66, 273–74.

12. Brailsford, "Morals and Maulers," 130–31. Egan, *Boxiana*, 112–15, provides a more detailed account of the feud and a round by round account of the Hyde Park match.

13. Egan, *Boxiana*, 86, 264–66, 273–66; Miles, *Pugilistica*, 9–61, 120, 140, 214, 313; Ron Jackson, "The origins of boxing in SA," SuperSport, February 7, 2006, http://www.supersport.com/boxing/blogs/ron-jackson/The origins of boxing in SA (accessed July 8, 2011).

14. David K. Wiggins, " Good Times on the Old Plantation: Popular Recreations of the Black Slave in the Antebellum South, 1810–1860," *Journal of Sport History* 4 (1977), 260–84; Sergio Lussana, "To See Who Was the Best on the Plantation: Enslaved Fighting Contests and Masculinity in the Antebellum Plantation South," *Journal of Southern History* 76, no. 4, 901–22; Jeffrey T. Sammons, *Beyond the Ring: The Role of Boxing in American Society* (Urbana: University of Illinois Press, 1988), 31; Kevin Smith, *Black Genesis: The History of the Black Prizefighter, 1760–1870* (Lincoln, NE: iUniverse, 2003), 7–10. See Rodriguez, *Regulation of Boxing*, 28, on slave bouts in the diary of William Black.

15. T. J. Desch Obi lists Sam Robinson, Henry Sutton, George Head, and Tom Molyneaux as other American ex-slaves who followed Richmond to England in "Black Terror: Bill Richmond's Revolutionary Boxing," *Journal of Sport History* 36, no. 1 (Spring 2009), 99–114; Andrew M. Kaye, *The Pussycat of Prizefighting: Tiger Flowers and the Politics of Black Celebrity* (Athens: University of Georgia Press, 2004), lists Bob Travers and Bob Smith as English sojourners as well. Miles, *Pugilistica*, 319, 372–388; Egan, *Boxiana*, 176, 180–83, 392–402, details Richmond's bouts in England.

16. Egan, *Boxiana*, 317–19 (quote, 317); Kaye, *Pussycat of Prizefighting*, 22; Bill Calogero, "Tom Molineaux: From Slave to American Heavyweight Champion," in Colleen Aycock and Mark Scott, eds., *The First Black Boxing Champions: Essays on Fighters of the 1800s to the 1920s* (Jefferson, NC: McFarland, 2011), 9–21; Miles, *Pugilistica*, 329–72.

17. Egan, *Boxiana*, 354–362, 440.

18. Egan, *Boxiana*, 320–23; quote from Miles, *Pugilistica*, 363.

19. Egan, *Boxiana*, 362–69 (quote, 363); Miles, *Pugilistica*, 365–71; Rodriguez, *Regulation of Boxing*, 25; David Levinson, Stan Shipley, and Edward R. Beauchamp, "Boxing," in David Levinson and Karen Christensen, eds., *Berkshire Encyclopedia of World Sport, Vol. 1* (Great Barrington, MA: Berkshire Publishing, 2005), 241–48; "Australian Boxing History," AussieBox.com, n.d., www.aussiebox.com/australian-boxing-history-php (accessed July 8, 2011).

20. Egan, *Boxiana*, 86, 92, 189, 250; George Plimpton, *Shadow Box* (New York: Berkley Books, 1977), 40–42; Lionel Fanthorpe and Patricia Fanthorpe, *The World's Most Mysterious People* (Ontario: Hounslow Press, 1998), 101.

21. Peter Benson, *Battling Siki: A Tale of Ring Fixes, Race, and Murder in the 1920s* (Fayetteville: University of Arkansas Press, 2006), 3.

22. Rodriguez, *Regulation of Boxing*, 25–28; David Scott, *The Art and Aesthetics of Boxing* (Lincoln: University of Nebraska Press, 2008), 6; Brailsford, "Morals and Maulers," 142.

23. Horace Greeley, "The Horrible Death of McCoy," *New York Daily Tribune*, September 19, 1842, in George B. Kirsch, *Sports in North America: A Documentary History, Vol. 3: The Rise of Modern Sports, 1840–1860* (Gulf Breeze, FL: Academic International Press, 1992), 117–19 (quote, 118–19).

24. Chuck Wills, *Destination America: The People and Cultures That Created a Nation* (New York: DK Publishing, 2005), 140–45; Steven A. Riess, *Sport in Industrial America, 1850–1920* (Wheeling, IL: Harlan Davidson, 1995), 87; Karen F. McCarthy, *The Other Irish: The Scots-Irish Rascals Who Made America* (New York: Sterling, 2011). See John M. Blum, Edmund S. Morgan, Willie Lee Rose, Arthur M. Schlesinger, Jr., Kenneth M. Stampp, and C. Vann Woodward, *The National Experience: A History of the United States* (New York: Harcourt Brace Jovanovich, 1981), 312–15 on nativism and the Know-Nothing movement. The Scots-Irish had migrated from Scotland to Ulster in Northern Ireland as colonial settlers after the English subjugation of Ireland as a counter to Irish Catholicism. Annexation of Scotland to form Great Britain in 1707 resulted in further migration.

25. Riess, *Sport in Industrial America*, 84, 87.

26. *Spirit of the Times*, February 17, 1849, 618–19, in Kirsch, *Sports in North America*, 121–29.

27. Cited in Elliott J. Gorn and Warren Goldstein, *A Brief History of American Sports* (New York: Hill & Wang, 1993), 71–73 (quote, 73); George B. Kirsch, Othello Harris, and Claire Nolte, eds., *Encyclopedia of Ethnicity and Sports in the United States* (Westport, CT: Greenwood, 2000), 320–21.

28. *New York Clipper*, May 30, 1857, 45, in Kirsch, *Sports in North America*, 130–32.

29. My reconstruction of the fight is gleaned from excerpts from the *New York Clipper*, May 5, 1860, 20; May 19, 1860, 33; and June 9, 1860, 64; as well as *Bell's Life in London*, April 27, 1860; April 29, 1860; and May 20, 1860; all in Kirsch, *Sports in North America*, 142–50.

30. Melvin L. Adelman, "Pedestrianism, Boxing, Billiards and Animal Sports," in David K. Wiggins, ed., *Sport in America: From Colonial Leisure to Celebrity Figures and Globalization* (Champaign, IL: Human Kinetics, 2010), 45–83. See *Winnipeg Free Press*, June 6, 1879, 1; March 18, 1881, 4; and March 22, 1882, 8, on early boxing in Canada.

31. Rodriguez, *Regulation of Boxing*, 28–30.

32. Sammons, *Beyond the Ring*, 6.

33. Rodriguez, *Regulation of Boxing*, 29; Sammons, *Beyond the Ring*, 6–7; Gorn and Goldstein, *Brief History of American Sports*, 122 (quote).

34. Gorn and Goldstein, *Brief History of American Sports*, 115: Guy Reel, *The National Police Gazette and the Making of the Modern American Man, 1879–1906* (New York: Palgrave Macmillan, 2006).

35. Reel, *National Police Gazettennn*, 139, 185. The belt offered for the 1889 championship bout contained diamond, ruby, emerald, and sapphire stones valued at $4,000.

36. Rodriguez, *Regulation of Boxing*, 29–30; Sammons, *Beyond the Ring*, 259–60.

37. See *North China Herald* (Shanghai), January 16, 1891, 15 and March 18, 1892, 3, for early matches in China and Singapore. "Australian Boxing History," AussieBox.com; David K. Wiggins, "Peter Jackson and the Elusive Heavyweight Championship: A Black Athlete's Struggle against the Late Nineteenth-Century Color Line," *Journal of Sport History* 12 (Summer 1985): 143–68; Bob Peterson, "Peter Jackson: Heavyweight Champion of Australia," in Aycock and Scott, eds., *First Black Boxing Champions*, 32–47; David A. Jack, "Bob Fitzsimmons: 1863–1917," http://www.fitzsimmons.co.nz/main.html (accessed October 18, 2011). See Gerald R. Gems, *The Athletic Crusade: Sport and American Cultural Imperialism* (Lincoln: University of Nebraska Press, 2006), 56; Joseph R. Svinth, "The Origins of Philippine Boxing, 1899–1926," *Journal of Combative Sport*, July 2001, http://ejmas.com/jcs/jcsart_svinth_0701.htm (accessed July 8, 2011); and Don Stradley, "A Look at the History of Boxing in the Philippines," ESPN, June 25, 2008, http://sports.espn.go.com/sports/boxing/news/story?id=3458707 (accessed July 8, 2011). See also Richard V. McGehee, "Boxing in Latin America from the Bull of the Pampas to Julius Caesar," presentation delivered at the North American Society for Sport History Conference, Austin, Texas, May 30, 2011.

38. "Young Griffo," The Cyber Boxing Zone, n.d., http://cyberboxingzone.com/boxing/griffo-young.htm (accessed October 18, 2011); "Solly Smith," The Cyber Boxing Zone, n.d., http://cyberboxingzone.com/boxing/smith-s.htm (accessed October 18, 2011); Mike Glenn, "George Dixon: World Bantamweight and Featherweight Champion," in Aycock and Scott, eds., *First Black Boxing Champions*, 48–59.

39. "Stanley Ketchel," International Boxing Hall of Fame, n.d., http://www.ibhof.com/pages/about/inductees/oldtimer/ketchel.html (accessed October 18, 2012); "Battling Nelson," International Boxing Hall of Fame, n.d., http://www.ibhof.com/pages/about/inductees/oldtimer/nelsonbattling.html (accessed October 18, 2012); "Jack Root," International Boxing Hall of Fame, n.d., http://www.ibhof.com/pages/about/inductees/oldtimer/root.html (accessed October 18, 2012).

40. *The Day*, March 10, 1914, 2; "Kid McCoy, Once Greatest Scrapper, Tells How He Used to Get the Coin in the Olden Days," *Milwaukee Sentinel*,

August 1, 1915, 10; Cathy van Ingen, "'Dixie Kid' Aaron Brown: World Welterweight Champ," in Aycock and Scott, eds., *First Black Boxing Champions*, 129–143; "Andrew Jeptha," BoxRec, n.d., http://boxrec.com/list_bouts. php?human_id=45977&cat=boxer. See Kelly Nicholson, "The Curious Case of Norman Selby," International Boxing Research Organization, n.d., http://www.ibroresearch,com/?p=5303 (accessed October 18, 2012) on Selby's wild life that included ten marriages, movie roles, and eventual incarceration for manslaughter.

41. Homer Plessy, an octoroon who was seven-eighths white and one-eighth black, but considered black by Louisiana law, was arrested for riding in a whites-only railroad car in 1892. In conjunction with a New Orleans civil rights organization he sued and his case reached the U.S. Supreme Court in 1896, which ruled against him and established the separate but equal doctrine that allowed for the legal separation and segregation of blacks.

42. Colleen Aycock and Mark Scott, *Joe Gans: A Biography of the First African American World Boxing Champ* (Jefferson, NC: McFarland & Co., 2008), 46, 53–54, 66, 96, 131, 133; Aycock and Scott, eds., *First Black Boxing Champions*, 60–78, 105, 116–17; T. S. Andrews, ed., *Ring Battles of Centuries and Sporting Almanac* (Tom Andrews Record Book Co., 1924), 28–29; Knud Kohr and Martin Krauss, *Kampftage: Die Geschichte des deutschen Berufsboxens* (Gottingen: erlad Die Werkstatt, 2002), 3–40; *Politiken*, July 11, 1910; Jim Riordan, "Sidney Jackson: An American in Russia's Boxing Hall of Fame," *Journal of Sport History* 20, no. 1 (Spring 1993), 49–56.

43. Jean-Francois Loudcher, "The Origins of French Boxing: Bare-Knuckle Duelling, Savate and Chausson, 1820–45," *International Journal of the History of Sport* 18, no. 2 (June 2001), 168–78; Andrews, *Ring Battles of Centuries*, 27–29.

44. Clay Moyle, "Sam Langford: Heavyweight Champion of Australia, Canada, England, and Mexico," in Aycock and Scott, eds., *First Black Boxing Champions*, 158–70; "Sam Langford," BoxRec, n.d., boxrec.com/list_bouts. php?human_id=011023&cat=boxer&pageID=3 (accessed November 26, 2011); Alexander Pierpaoli, "Joe Jennette and Sam McVey: Colored Heavyweight Champions," in Aycock and Scott, eds., *First Black Boxing Champions*, 171–99; "Joe Jeannette," BoxRec, n.d., http://boxrec.com/list_bouts.php?human_id=011631&cat=boxer&pageID=3. Josephine Baker, an African American dancer and singer, also achieved great fame in France during the 1920s.

45. Carpentier, My Fighting Life, cited in Pierpaoli, "Joe Jennette and Sam McVey," 180.

46. Theresa Runstedtler, "African American Boxers, the New Negro, and the Global Color Line," *Radical History Review* 103 (Winter 2009): 59–81 (quotes from 61 and 66 respectively).

47. Kevin Smith, "Bobby Dobbs: Lightweight Challenger and Father of Boxing in Germany," in Aycock and Scott, eds., *First Black Boxing Champions*, 72–75.

48. Chris Cozzone and Jim Boggio, *Boxing in New Mexico, 1868–1940* (Jefferson, NC: McFarland, 2013), 7; Sammons, *Beyond the Ring*, 22–24, 28, 62; Rodriguez, *Regulation of Boxing*, 31–36. The Burke-Bowen bout was detailed in the *Chicago Tribune*, April 8, 1892, 6, in Gerald R. Gems, *Sports in North America: A Documentary History, Vol. 5: Sports Organized, 1880–1900* (Gulf Breeze, FL: Academic International Press, 1996), 214–15; Andrews, ed., *Ring Battles of Centuries*, 39. Bowen won an eighty-five-round bout that took five hours and thirty-eight minutes only three months earlier, but died after a bout with Kid Lavigne two years later.

49. Rodriguez, *Regulation of Boxing*, 30.

50. "International Boxing Union," BoxRec, n.d., http://boxrec.com/media/index.php/International_Boxing_Union (accessed Nov. 29, 2011); see the *Perry* (Iowa) *Daily Chief*, Dec. 28, 1920, 7; the *Sandusky* (Ohio) *Register*, Jan. 13, 1921, 8; and the *Joplin* (Missouri) *Globe*, Jan. 13, 1921, 5, on failed attempts to form regulating bodies. Randy Roberts, *Papa Jack: Jack Johnson and the Era of White Hopes* (New York: Free Press, 1983); "Battling Siki," BoxRec, n.d., http://boxrec.com/media/index.php/Battling_Siki (Nov. 29, 2011); "Frank Klaus Sees Firpo in Action," *New York Times*, September 2, 1923, 18. See Uniontown (Pennsylvania) *Morning Herald*, July 16, 1923, 6; *Oakland Tribune*, September 14, 1923, 34; "Firpo Had the Title within His Grasp," *New York Times*, September 15, 1923, 1; Sid Sutherland, "Latin Lacks Ring Wit to Cope with Yank, the Experienced," *Chicago Tribune*, September 15, 1923, 11; and Gerald Early, "Battling Siki as 'Other': the Boxer as Natural Man," *Massachusetts Review* 29, no. 3 (Fall 1988), 451–72. The IBU continued to designate weight class champions until 1944. See Katharine Moore and Murray G. Phillips, "From Adulation to Persecution and Back: Australian Boxer Les Darcy in America, 1916–1917," *Journal of Sport History* 23, no. 2 (Summer 1996); 140–56, on the tragic interplay of sport, politics, and war during the era.

51. Bruce J. Evensen, "Rickard, George Lewis ('Tex')," in Arnold Markoe, ed., *The Scribner Encyclopedia of American Lives* (New York: Charles Scribner's Sons, 2002), 268–70; Lucy Moore, *Anything Goes: A Biography of the Roaring Twenties* (New York: Overlook Press, 2010), 297–98 (quote).

52. "The Ring Magazine," BoxRec, n.d., http://boxrec.com/media/index.php/The_Ring_Magazine (accessed October 21, 2012); "About the International Boxing Hall of Fame," n.d., http://www.ibhof.com/pages/about/about.html/ (accessed October 21, 2012).

53. Linda N. Espana-Maram, "Colonial Boundaries: Filipinos in the U.S. Before 1946," paper delivered at the Organization of American Historians

Conference (Indianapolis, April 1998); Bob Peterson, "Boxing, Australia," in John Nauright and Charles Parrish, eds., *Sports around the World: History, Culture, and Practice*, http://ebooks.abc-clio.com/print.aspx?isbn=978159884301 9&id=A1884C_V3-1205 (accessed August 4, 2012); "History," Oriental and Pacific Boxing Federation, n.d., www.opbf.jp/info/history.html (accessed July 8, 2011); Gems, *Athletic Crusade*, 60–61, 77; Svinth, "Origins of Filipino Boxing," 6 (quote).

54. Richard V. McGehee, "Boxing, Latin America," in Nauright and Parrish, eds., *Sports around the World*; Richard V. McGehee, "The Dandy and the Mauler in Mexico: Johnson, Dempsey, et al., and the Mexico City Press, 1919–1927," *Journal of Sport History* 23, no. 1 (Spring 1996): 20–33.

55. Floris van der Merwe, "Boxing, South Africa," in Nauright and Parrish, eds., *Sports around the World*; Tyler Fleming, "'Now the African Reigns Supreme': The Rise of African Boxing on the Witwatersrand, 1924–1959," *International Journal of the History of Sport* 28, no. 1 (January 2011): 47–62 (quote, 47).

56. Terence Ranger, "Pugilism and Pathology: African Boxing and the Black Urban Experience in Southern Rhodesia," in William J. Baker and James A. Mangan, eds., *Sport in Africa: Essays in Social History* (New York: Africana, 1987), 196–213 (quote, 199).

57. Jan Dunzendorfeer, "The Early Days of Boxing in Accra: A Sport Is Taking Root," *International Journal of the History of Sport* 28, no. 15 (October 2011): 2142–58.

58. Rodriguez, *Regulation of Boxing*, 166–67.

59. Joseph S. Page, *Primo Carnera: The Life and Career of the Heavyweight Boxing Champion* (Jefferson, NC: McFarland, 2011); "Men of Iron: Paulino Uzcudun," Boxing Insider, April 15, 2008, http://www.boxinginsider.com/history/men-of-iron-paulino-uzcudun/ (accessed November 29, 2011); David Margolick, *Beyond Glory: Joe Louis, Max Schmeling, and the World on the Brink* (New York: Alfred A. Knopf, 2005).

60. "Panama Al Brown," BoxRec, n.d., http://boxrec.com/media/index.php/Panama-Al_Brown (accessed July 8, 2011); "Kid Chocolate," The Cyber Boxing Zone, n.d., http://cyberboxingzone.com/boxing/kidchoc.htm (accessed November 29, 2011); "Sixto Escobar," BoxRec, n.d., http://boxrec.com/media/index.php/Sixto_Escobar (accessed November 29, 2011); "Sixto Escobar vs. Rodolfo (Baby) Casanova," BoxRec, n.d., boxrec.com/media/index.php/Sixto_Escobar_vs._Rodolfo_(Baby)_Casanova (accessed November 29, 2011); Jon J. Mac Aloon, "La Pitada Olimpica," 326, cited in Gems, *Athletic Crusade*, 105; Sixto Escobar file, International Boxing Hall of Fame archives. See Jorge Iber, Samuel O. Regalado, Jose M. Alamillo, and Arnaldo De Leon, *Latinos in U.S. Sport: A History*

of Isolation, Cultural Identity, and Acceptance (Champaign, IL: Human Kinetics, 2011), 101–42, on the rise of Mexican and Caribbean boxers.

61. Gerald R. Gems, "Sport, Religion and Americanization: Bishop Sheil and the Catholic Youth Organization," *International Journal of the History of Sport* 10, no. 2 (August 1993): 233–41; Gerald R. Gems, "The Politics of Boxing: Resistance, Religion, and Working-Class Assimilation," *International Sports Journal* 8, no. 1 (Winter 2004): 89–103.

62. Sammons, *Beyond the Ring*, 130–80.

63. Rodriguez, *Regulation of Boxing*, 35–43; "World Boxing Council," BoxRec, n.d., http://boxrec.com/media/index.php/wbc (accessed June 20, 2012); "World Boxing Organisations," East Rand Veterans Boxing Association, n.d., http://www.ervba.co.za/world-boxing-organisations.html (accessed June 20, 2012).

64. Andrew Eisele, "What is Olympic Boxing?" About.com Boxing, n.d., http://boxing.about.com/od/amateurs/a/whatisolyboxing.htm (accessed October 23, 2012).

Chapter Three: The Relationship between Boxing and Social Class

1. Pierce Egan, *Boxiana, Vol. 1*(Scott Noble, ed., London: G. Smeeton, 1812 [Nicol Island Pub., 1997]), passim.

2. Barbara Holland, *Gentlemen's Blood: A History of Dueling from Swords at Dawn to Pistols at Dusk* (New York: Bloomsbury, 2003).

3. See Elliot J. Gorn, "'Gouge and Bite, Pull Hair and Scratch': The Social Significance of Gouging in the Southern Backcountry," *American Historical Review* 90, no. 1 (February 1985), 18–43, for insights into masculinity, honor, and rough-and-tumble fighting of the era. Initial quote from Thomas L. Altherr, *Sports in North America: A Documentary History, Vol. 1, Part 1: Sports in the Colonial Era, 1618–1673* (Gulf Breeze, FL: Academic International Press, 1997), 127, citing Whitman Mead, *Travels in North America* (New York: C. S. Van Winkle, 1820), 16–18. See also John Palmer, *Journal of Travels in the United States of America and in Lower Canada, Performed in the Year 1817* (London: Sherwood, Nealy and Jones, 1818), 131–32, in Altherr, 127, on the rules. Second quote also from Altherr, 136–37, citing Isaac Weld, Jr., *Travels through the States of North America and the Provinces of Upper and Lower Canada during the Years 1795, 1796, and 1797, Vol. 1* (New York: Augustus M. Kelley, 1807), 192–93.

4. Altherr, *Sports in North America, Vol. 1*, 138, quotes William Stuart, *Sketches of the Life of William Stuart, the First and Most Celebrated Counterfeiter of Connecticut* (Bridgeport, CT: privately printed, 1854), 27–28.

5. Altherr, *Sports in North America, Vol. 1*, 130, 132 on boxing lessons; 131–32, on the Connecticut trial by combat; and 134–36, 141–42 on widespread gouging matches in North and South Carolina, Georgia, Virginia, and Kentucky from 1787–1819; and 142 (quote), citing the melee described in Fortescue Cuming, *Sketches of a Tour to the Western Country, through the States of Ohio and Kentucky. A Voyage down the Ohio and Mississippi Rivers, and a Trip through the Mississippi Territory, and Part of West Florida* (Pittsburgh: Cramer, Spear, and Eichbaum, 1810), 156–57.

6. Altherr, *Sports in North America, Vol. 1* 96, cites Thomas Anburey, *Travels through the Interior Parts of America, Vol. 2* (London: William Lane, 1791), 309–311, 333–34, 350, on rules and preparations; and page 97 cites *Laws of the State of Delaware, From the Fourteenth Day of October, One Thousand Seven Hundred, to the Eighteenth Day of August, One Thousand Seven Hundred and Ninety-Seven, Vol. 1* (New Castle, DE: Samuel and John Adams, 1797), 64.

7. Elliot J. Gorn, *The Manly Art: Bare-Knuckle Prize Fighting in America* (Ithaca, NY: Cornell University Press, 1986), 147.

8. Pierre Bourdieu, *Outline of a Theory of Practice* (Cambridge: Cambridge University Press, 1972), 72–87.

9. Quotes from Dan Streible, *Fight Pictures: A History of Boxing and Early Cinema* (Berkeley: University of California Press, 2008), 192 and 193 respectively.

10. Andrew O'Toole, *Sweet William: The Life of Billy Conn* (Champaign: University of Illinois Press, 2008), 109.

11. Both LaMotta and Graziano are quoted in James W. Pipkin, *Sporting Lives: Metaphor and Myth in American Sports Autobiographies* (Columbia: University of Missouri Press, 2008), 114 and 115 respectively.

12. Carlo Rotella, *Good with Their Hands: Boxers, Bluesmen, and Other Characters from the Rust Belt* (Berkeley: University of California Press, 2002), 2.

13. Quintin Hoare and Geoffrey N. Smith, eds., *Selections form the Prison Notebooks of Antonio Gramsci* (New York: International Publishers, 1971).

14. Frank Graham, "Tony Canzoneri: One for the Book," in Thomas Hauser and Stephen Brunt, eds., *The Italian Stallions: Heroes of Boxing's Glory Days* (Toronto: Sport Media Publishing, 2003), 44–47; A. J. Liebling, *The Sweet Science* (New York: North Point Press, 2004 [1951]), 4.

15. Rotella, *Good with Their Hands*, 180.

16. Benita Heiskanen, *The Urban Geography of Boxing: Race, Class, and Gender in the Ring* (New York: Routledge, 2012), 3.

17. Heiskanen, *Urban Geography of Boxing*, 5, 19–20, 24, 85 (quote).

18. Joyce Carol Oates, *On Boxing* (New York: Harper Collins, 2002), 8.

19. Loic J. D. Wacquant, "The Pugilistic Point of View: How Boxers Think and Feel about Their Trade," *Theory and Society* 24, no. 4 (August 1995), 489–535 (quote, 501).

20. Heiskanen, *Urban Geography of Boxing*, 36. Among the numerous treatises on body culture and sport, see Henning Eichberg, *Body Cultures: Essays on Sport, Space and Identity* (London: Routledge, 1998), and Allen Guttmann, *The Erotic in Sport* (New York: Columbia University Press, 1996).

21. Wacquant, "Pugilistic Point of View," 511.

22. Dave Tiberi, quoted in Heiskanen, *Urban Geography of Boxing*, 55.

23. Wacquant, "Pugilistic Point of View," 529 indicates that boxers of the era earned $150–$500 for preliminary bouts and $500–$1000 for main events in the Midwest. Quotes from Wacquant, 502 and 518 respectivly.

24. Wacquant, "The Pugilistic Point of View," 504. Quotes from Wacquant, 515 and 505 respectively.

25. Carlo Rotella, *Cut Time: An Education at the Fights* (Boston: Houghton Mifflin, 2003), 84.

26. Rotello, *Good with Their Hands*, 178–79 (179, quote).

27. Timothy J. Gilfoyle, *City of Eros: New York City, Prostitution, and the Commercialization of Sex, 1790–1920* (New York: W. W. Norton, 1992), 102–16, 236–39. According to Brett and Kate McKay in "A History of the American Bachelor, Part 2: Post–Civil War America (Art of Manliness, April 12, 2012, http://artofmanliness.com/2012/04/12/history-of-the-american-bachelor-post-civil-war-america/, accessed November 13, 2012), the U.S. Census Bureau estimated that 67 percent of males aged 15–34 were bachelors in 1890.

28. Timothy J. Gilfoyle, *A Pickpocket's Tale: The Underworld of Nineteenth-Century New York* (New York: W.W. Norton, 2006), 189–90, 319; Gorn, *The Manly Art*; Howard P. Chudacoff, *The Age of the Bachelor: Creating an American Subculture* (Princeton, NJ: Princeton University Press, 1999); Wacquant, "Pugilistic Point of View," 496 (quote). See Jon M. Kingsdale, "The Poor Man's Club: Social Functions of the Urban Working-Class Saloon," *American Quarterly* 25, no. 4 (October 1973), 472–89; Royal L. Melendy, "The Saloon in Chicago (Part 1)," *American Journal of Sociology* 6 (November 1900), 289–306; Melendy, "The Saloon in Chicago (Part 2)," *American Journal of Sociology* 6 (January 1901), 433–64; and Perry R. Duis, *The Saloon: Public Drinking in Chicago and Boston, 1880–1920* (Urbana: University of Illinois Press, 1983) on the importance of saloons in the bachelor subculture.

29. Madelon Powers, *Faces along the Bar: Lore and Order in the Workingman's Saloon, 1870–1920* (Chicago: University of Chicago Press, 1998), 156. See Kevin B. Wamsley and Robert S. Kossuth, "Fighting It Out in Nineteenth-Century Upper Canada/Canada West: Masculinities and Physical Challenges in the

Tavern," *Journal of Sport History* 27, no. 3 (Fall 2000): 405–30, for similar developments in that country.

30. Elliott J. Gorn, "'Good-Bye Boys, I Die a True American': Homicide, Nativism, and Working-Class Culture in Antebellum New York City," *Journal of American History* 74, no. 2 (September 1987), 388–410.

31. Elliott J. Gorn and Warren Goldstein, *A Brief History of American Sports* (New York: Hill & Wang, 1993), 71–73, 119.

32. Gerald R. Gems, *Windy City Wars: Labor, Leisure, and Sport in the Making of Chicago* (Lanham, MD: Scarecrow Press, 1997), 14; Stephen Longstreet, *Chicago, 1860–1919* (New York: David McKay Co., 1973), 30; Gorn, *The Manly Art*, 105.

33. Charles H. Hermann, *Recollections of Life and Doings in Chicago* (Chicago: Normandie House, 1945), 30–31; *Sporting and Theatrical Journal*, May 24, 1884, 4:2, 17–18 (quote), 25; July 5, 1884, 4:8, 121.

34. Quoted in Gorn and Goldstein, *A Brief History of American Sports*, 71.

35. Gilfoyle, *City of Eros*, 225–27; Powers, *Faces along the Bar*, 157; Gorn and Goldstein, *Brief History of American Sports*, 100. Quote in McKay, "A History of the American Bachelor, Part 2," n.p.

36. Guy Reel, *The National Police Gazette and the Making of the Modern American Man, 1879–1906* (New York: Palgrave Macmillan, 2006).

37. Michael T. Isenberg, *John L. Sullivan and His America* (Urbana: University of Illinois Press, 1988), 85–111; Elliott J. Gorn, "John L. Sullivan: The Champion of All Champions," in Stephen Wagg, ed., *Myths and Milestones in the History of Sport* (New York: Palgrave Macmillan, 2011), 224–38; David L. Hudson, Jr., *Boxing in America: An Autopsy* (Santa Barbara, CA: Praeger, 2012), 6; Gorn and Goldstein, *Brief History of American Sports*, 115, 122; Duis, *The Saloon*, 69; *Sporting and Theatrical Journal*, March 1, 1884, 3, no. 16, 260; Powers, *Faces along the Bar*, 102.

38. Anonymous, "You Valiant Sons of Erin's Isle," in Robert Hedin and Michael Waters, eds., *Perfect in Their Art: Poems on Boxing from Homer to Ali* (Carbondale: Southern Illinois University Press, 2003), 28.

39. "The Tug of War," *Rocky Mountain News* (Denver, Colorado), July 24, 1882, cited in Jeonguk Kim, "Fighting Men and Fighting Women: American Prizefighting and the Contested Gender Order in the Late Nineteenth and Early Twentieth Centuries," *Sport History Review* 43 (2012): 103–27 (quote, 106–7).

40. Michael S. Kimmel, *The History of Men: Essays in the History of American and British Masculinities* (Albany: State University of New York Press, 2005), 45–46 (quote), 48; Chudacoff, *The Age of the Bachelor*, 229.

41. William Wood, *Manual of Physical Exercises, Comprising Gymnastics, Calisthenics, Rowing, Sailing, Skating, Swimming, Fencing, Sparring, Cricket, Base Ball,*

Together with Rules for Training and Sanitary Suggestions (New York: Harper & Bros., 1867), 238.

42. Kim, "Fighting Men and Fighting Women," 107–10.

43. Isenberg, *John L. Sullivan and His America*, 83; see Warren Zimmerman, *First Great Triumph: How Five Americans Made Their Country a World Power* (New York: Farrar, Straus, Giroux, 2002), 190–209, on Roosevelt's early life, upbringing, and Western adventures.

44. Hermann, *Recollections of Life and Doings in Chicago*, 33.

45. The Queensbury rules added a third rope to the ring. David Scott, *The Art and Aesthetics of Boxing* (Lincoln: University of Nebraska Press, 2008), 6, 20; *Sporting and Theatrical Journal*, May 17, 1884, 4, no. 1, 18; May 24, 1884, 4, no. 2, 18; *Chicago Tribune*, February 18, 1866, 6 (quote).

46. R. C. MacDonald, "Scientific Boxing under the Boston A. A. Rules," *Outing* 21, no. 1 (October 1892), 23–24.

47. Charles E. Clay, "A Bout with the Gloves," *Outing* (April 1887), 26–31 (quotes, 30–31).

48. "New Subterfuge Must Be Invented To Revive Pugilism," *Chicago Tribune*, January 29, 1894, 11, cited in Gerald R. Gems, *Sports in North America: A Documentary History, Vol. 5: Sports Organized, 1880–1900* (Gulf Breeze, FL: Academic International Press, 1996), 201–2.

49. Gorn, "John L. Sullivan," 224–38; Gorn and Goldstein, *Brief History of American Sports*, 123.

50. Barry Alfonso, "Corbett, James John," in Arnold Markoe, ed., *The Scribner Encyclopedia of American Lives: Sports Figures* (New York: Charles Scribner's Sons, 2002), 193–95.

51. "Olympic Club's New Articles," *Chicago Tribune*, March 20, 1892, 6; Gorn, "John L. Sullivan."

52. Dan Streible, *Fight Pictures: A History of Boxing and Early Cinema* (Berkeley: University of California Press, 2008), xiv, 4, 7,9,18, 23, 30–31, 53–55, 60, 83–95, 111, 173 (quote, 81). See Leger Grindon, *Knockout: The Boxer and Boxing in American Cinema* (Jackson: University of Mississippi Press, 2011) on the influence and composition of boxing films in American culture.

53. Steven A. Riess, "Closing Down the Open-City: The Demise of Horse Racing and Boxing in Chicago in 1905," manuscript in author's possession, of a presentation delivered at the North American Society for Sport History Conference, Banff, Canada, May 27, 2000 (quotes, 3 and 6 respectively).

54. "Ad Wolgast," International Boxing Hall of Fame, n.d., http://www.ibhof.com/pages/about/inductees/oldtimer/wolgastad.html (accessed November 18, 2012); "Fight," BoxRec, n.d., http://boxrec.com/media/index.php?title=Fight (accessed November 20, 2012).

55. For short biographies of Attel, Dundee, Britton, and McFarland, see International Boxing Hall of Fame Inductees, n.d., http://www.ibhof.com/pages/about/inductees/oldtimer.html (accessed November 18, 2012).

56. See *Chicago Tribune*, July 5, 1918, 5, 8; and August 1, 1918, 12, on boxing as training. "Eugene Criqui," BoxRec, n.d., http://boxrec/media/index.php/Eugene_Criqui (accessed November 20, 2012); "Georges Carpentier," BoxRec, n.d., http://boxrec.com/media/index.php/Georges_Carpentier (accessed November 20, 2012); Jim Waltzer, *The Battle of the Century: Dempsey, Carpentier, and the Birth of Modern Promotion* (Santa Barbara, CA: Praeger, 2011), 43–50.

57. "Steven T. McDonald, BoxRec, n.d., http://boxrec.com/media/index.php/Stephen_T._McDonald (accessed November 20, 2012); Steven A. Riess, *Sport in Industrial America, 1850–1920* (Wheeling, IL: Harlan Davidson, 1995),148–49.

58. Lucy Moore, *Anything Goes: A Biography of the Roaring Twenties* (New York: The Overlook Press, 2010), 294.

59. Waltzer, *Battle of the Century*, 185–197; Gerald R. Gems, Linda Borish, and Gertrud Pfister, *Sports in American History: From Colonization to Globalization* (Champaign, IL: Human Kinetics, 2008), 258.

60. Charles Fountain, *Sportswriter: The Life and Times of Grantland Rice* (New York: Oxford University Press, 1993), 199–200; Waltzer, *Battle of the Century*, 192–95; Gems, Borish, and Pfister, *Sports in American History*, 258; "Firpo Had the Title within His Grasp," *New York Times*, September 15, 1923, 1; also see Sid Sutherland, "Latin Lacks Ring Wit to Cope with Yank, the Experienced," *Chicago Tribune*, September 15, 1923, 11. For a firsthand account of one of the original perpetrators of the Shelby event, see James W. (Body) Johnson, "The Fight That Won't Stay Dead," SI Vault, July 4, 1966, http://sportsillustrated.cnn.com/vault/article/magazine/MAG1078731/1/index.htm (accessed November 20, 2012).

61. Kirk H. Beetz, "Tunney, James Joseph," in Markoe, ed., *The Scribner Encyclopedia of American Lives*, 441–43; quotes from Moore, *Anything Goes*, 306 and 309 respectively; Gems, Borish, and Pfister, *Sports in American History*, 258–59; Gorn and Goldstein, *Brief History of American Sports*, 195; and Bruce J. Evenson, *When Dempsey Fought Tunney: Heroes, Hokum, and Storytelling in the Jazz Age* (Knoxville: University of Tennessee Press, 1996). While other sources give lower figures for fight attendance, the figure of 122,000 spectators at Soldier Field comes from Arthur J. Todd, ed., *Chicago Recreation Survey, 1937* (Chicago: Chicago Recreation Commission, 1937), vol.1: 213. The best analysis of the social class ramifications of the bout is by Elliott J. Gorn in "The Manassa Mauler and the Fighting Marine: An Interpretation of the Dempsey-Tunney Fights," *Journal of American Studies* 19 (1985), 27–47.

62. Intercity Boxing, Third Annual Meeting of Golden Gloves Champions and Runners-Up program, March 19, 1930, Chicago; Thomas B. Littlewood, *Arch: A Promoter, Not a Poet: The Story of Arch Ward* (Ames: Iowa State University Press, 1990), 79. As sports editor of the *Chicago Tribune*, Ward initiated the first Major League Baseball All-Star Game in 1933, the College All-Star Football Game in 1934, and the professional All-American Football Conference in 1946 that eventually merged with the National Football League.

63. Eighth Annual Golden Gloves Tournament program, March 8, 1935; George Winn, ed., *Boxing News Record* (New York: George Winn, 1939), 60–76, 86; "History," National Golden Gloves Official Website, n.d., http://www.gold-engloves.com/history/?id=4 (accessed November 20, 2012); Littlewood, *Arch*, 79–86; quotes from Todd, *Chicago Recreation Survey*, 79 and 77 respectively. By 1942 Chicago had won nine, lost four, and had two draws in the head-to-head competition with New York.

64. Littlewood, *Arch*, 81–84; Intercity Boxing, Third Annual Meeting of Golden Gloves Champions and Runners-Up program, March 19, 1930, Chicago; *Chicago Tribune*, Seventh International Golden Gloves: Champions of Europe vs. Champions of Chicagoland, 1938 program.

65. Littlewood, *Arch*, 81–82.

66. Jeffrey T. Sammons, *Beyond the Ring: The Role of Boxing in American Society* (Urbana: University of Illinois Press, 1988), 236–43; Richard Goldstein, "Beau Jack, 78, Lightweight Boxing Champion in the 1940s," *New York Times*, February 12, 2000, http://www.nytimes.com/2000/02/12/sports/beau-jack-78-lightweight-boxing-champion-in-the-1940-s.html (accessed November 22, 2012). See Maurice Golesworthy, *The Encyclopedia of Boxing* (London: Robert Hale, Ltd., 1960), 20, for a list of Golden Gloves boxers who later won world championships as professionals.

67. S. Kirson Weinberg and Henry Arond, "The Occupational Culture of the Boxer," *American Journal of Sociology* 57, no. 5 (March 1952), 460–69.

68. "College Boxing Explained," iSport Boxing, n.d., http://boxing.isport.com/boxing-guides/college-boxing-explained (accessed November 22, 2012); Robert S. Griffin, "On Chuck Davey," www.robertsgriffin.com, October 2007 (accessed November 17, 2012); Lewis Burton, "A Heavyweight Named Roland," in Thomas Hauser and Stephen Brunt, eds., *The Italian Stallions: Heroes of Boxing's Glory Days* (Toronto: Sport Media Publishing, 2003), 195–99, (quotes from 195 and 199 respectively).

69. Loic J. D. Wacquant, "The Social Logic of Boxing in Black Chicago: Toward a Sociology of Pugilism," *Sociology of Sport Journal* 9 (1992): 221–54; Gorn, *The Manly Art*, 147.

70. Stillwell quoted in Kate Sekules, *The Boxer's Heart: How I Fell in Love with the Ring* (New York: Villard, 2000), 53.

71. Leah Hager Cohen, *Without Apology: Girls, Women, and the Desire to Fight* (New York: Random House, 2005), 25.

72. Loic Wacquant, "Whores, Slaves and Stallions: Languages of Exploitation and Accommodation among Boxers," *Body & Society* 7, nos. 2–3 (2001), 181–94, (quote,188), citing Erving Goffman, *The Presentation of Self in Everyday Life* (Harmondsworth: Penguin, 1959), 151–52).

73. Tim Struby, "Fighting Chance," *ESPN Magazine*, April 30, 2001, 104–11 (quotes, 108, 106, 108, and 110 respectively).

74. Struby, "Fighting Chance," quotes from 106, 110, and 108 respectively).

Chapter Four: The Social Construction of Race

1. Richard Restak, Stefan Bechtel, Patricia Daniels, Susan Tyler Hitchcock, Trisha Gura, Lisa Stein, and John Thompson, *Body: The Complete Human* (Washington, D.C; National Geographic Society, 2007), 25.

2. Jeonguk Kim, "Fighting Men and Fighting Women: American Prizefighting and the Contested Gender Order in the Late Nineteenth and Early Twentieth Centuries," *Sport History Review* 43 (2012): 110. Quote from John M. Blum, Edmund S. Morgan, Willie Lee Rose, Arthur M. Schlesinger, Jr., Kenneth M. Stampp, and C. Vann Woodward, *The National Experience: A History of the United States* (New York: Harcourt Brace Jovanovich, 1981), 334. Among the voluminous literature on scientific racialization, see Theodore W. Allen, *The Invention of the White Race: Racial Oppression and Social Control* (London: Verso, 1998); Lee D. Baker, *From Savage to Negro: Anthropology and the Construction of Race, 1896–1954* (Berkeley: University of California Press, 1998); Jack D. Forbes, "The Manipulation of Race, Caste, and Identity: Classifying Afroamericans, Native Americans, and Red-Black People," *Journal of Ethnic Studies* 17, no. 4 (Winter 1990), 1–51; Matthew Pratt Guterl, *The Color of Race in America, 1900–1940* (Cambridge, MA: Harvard University Press, 2001); Stephen Jay Gould, *The Mismeasure of Man* (New York: Norton, 1996, 1981); Otto Klineberg, *Race Differences* (New York: Harper & Bros., 1935); and William H. Tucker, *The Science and Politics of Racial Research* (Urbana: University of Illinois Press, 1994).

3. William Wells Brown, "On Race and Change," in David R. Roediger, ed., *In Black on White: Black Writers on What It Means to Be White* (New York: Schocken Books, 1998), 56–57.

4. Henry Childs Merwin, "The Irish in American Life," *Atlantic Monthly* (March 1896), cited in Matthew Frye Jacobson, *Whiteness of a Different Color*

European Immigrants and the Alchemy of Race (Cambridge, MA: Harvard University Press, 1998), 49.

5. Quoted in Karen Brodkin, *How Jews Became White Folks and What That Says about Race in America* (New Brunswick, NJ: Rutgers University Press, 1998), 29.

6. Pierce Egan, *Boxiana Vol. 1* (Scott Noble, ed., London: G. Smeeton, 1812 (Nicol Island Pub., 1997), 320–25; David K. Wiggins, "Good Times on the Old Plantation: Popular Recreations of the Black Slave in the Antebellum South, 1810–1860," *Journal of Sport History* 4 (1977): 260–84; Sergio Lussana, "To See Who Was the Best on the Plantation: Enslaved Fighting Contests and Masculinity in the Antebellum Plantation South," *Journal of Southern History* 76, no. 4 (November 2010): 901–22; Jeffrey T. Sammons, *Beyond the Ring: The Role of Boxing in American Society* (Urbana: University of Illinois Press, 1988), 31–32; Andrew M. Kaye, *The Pussycat of Prizefighting: Tiger Flowers and the Politics of Black Celebrity* (Athens: University of Georgia Press, 2004), 22.

7. Gerald R. Gems, Linda Borish, and Gertrud Pfister, *Sports in American History: From Colonization to Globalization* (Champaign, IL: Human Kinetics, 2008), 117; Tony Triem, "George Godfrey: First Colored Heavyweight Champion," in Colleen Aycock and Mark Scott, eds., *The First Black Boxing Champions: Essays on Fighters of the 1800s to the 1920s* (Jefferson, NC: McFarland, 2011), 22–31.

8. *Sporting and Theatrical Journal* 4:13 (August 9, 1884), 194.

9. David K. Wiggins, "Peter Jackson and the Elusive Heavyweight Championship: A Black Athlete's Struggle Against the Late Nineteenth-Century Colorline," *Journal of Sport History*, 12, no. 2 (Summer 1985), 143–68; Peterson, Bob, "Peter Jackson: Heavyweight Champion of Australia," in Aycock and Scott, *First Black Boxing Champions*, 32–47. Peterson lists the date of the Jackson-Jeffries fight as 1899; but BoxRec (accessed January 4, 2013) states the date as March 22, 1898.

10. Mike Glenn, "George Dixon: World Bantamweight and Featherweight Champion," in Aycock and Scott, eds., *First Black Boxing Champions*, 52.

11. Glenn, "George Dixon," 54; "The Negro Wins," New Orleans *Times-Democrat*, September 7, 1892, 1 (quote).

12. *Chicago Tribune*, cited in Glenn, "George Dixon," 54.

13. "The Olympic Contests," *New Orleans Times-Democrat*, September 8, 1892, 4.

14. Glenn, "George Dixon," 56–58. Professional black baseball players had been banned from the National League in the 1880s, and top black jockeys who had won laurels on the track were ostracized and excluded by jealous whites in the following decade. The same fate befell Major Taylor, the world champion

black cyclist, who sought his fortune abroad after the turn of the century, leaving boxing as one of the few professional sports still available to blacks.

15. "New Story Told of Bowen's Death," *Chicago Tribune*, December 24, 1894, 11; Sammons, *Beyond the Ring*, 18–19.

16. Colleen Aycock and Mark Scott, *Joe Gans: A Biography of the First African American World Boxing Champ* (Jefferson, NC: McFarland & Co., 2008), 1–62.

17. Aycock and Scott, *Joe Gans*, 62–81 (quote, 75).

18. Aycock and Scott, *Joe Gans*, 82–124. Some boxing records do not recognize Gans as a champion from 1904 to 1906 because he also fought for the welterweight title during those years.

19. Tracy Callis, cited in Aycock and Scott, *Joe Gans*, 156.

20. Aycock and Scott, *Joe Gans*, 152–79; "Time Line of African American History, 1901–1925," African American Perspectives, Library of Congress, http://memory.loc.gov/ammem/aap/timelin3.html (accessed January 10, 2013); http://www.npr.org/wnet/jimcrow/stories_events_atlanta.html (accessed January 10, 2013).

21. Aycock and Scott, *Joe Gans*, 212–26 (quote, 6–7).

22. John A. Garaty, *The American Nation: A History of the United States* (New York: Harper & Row, 1983), 427.

23. W. E. B. Du Bois, *The Souls of Black Folk* (1903; New York: Penguin Books, 1989), xvii.

24. Du Bois, *The Souls of Black Folk*, xx.

25. There are numerous biographies of Jack Johnson. His autobiography, *Jack Johnson Is a Dandy* (Chelsea House, 1969), is unreliable and often contrived. Al-Tony Gilmore, *Bad Nigger! The National Impact of Jack Johnson* (Port Washington, NY: Kennikat Press, 1975) is a worthwhile study, but the best is Randy Roberts's *Papa Jack: Jack Johnson and the Era of White Hopes* (New York: Free Press, 1983). Theresa Runstedtler, *Jack Johnson, Rebel Sojourner: Boxing in the Shadow of the Global Color Line* (Berkeley: University of California Press, 2012) provides a detailed analysis of Johnson's international travels and impact, and a documentary film by Ken Burns, *Unforgivable Blackness: The Rise and Fall of Jack Johnson* (PBS, 2005), presents Johnson's fascinating story in a visual medium. But I rely mainly on my own account in Gerald R. Gems, "Jack Johnson and the Quest for Racial Respect," in David K. Wiggins, ed., *Out of the Shadows: A Biographical History of African American Athletes* (Fayetteville: University of Arkansas Press, 2006), 59–77.

26. Gems, "Jack Johnson and the Quest for Racial Respect;" Roberts, *Papa Jack*, 11–21; A. S. "Doc" Young, "Was Jack Johnson Boxing's Greatest Champ?" *Ebony*, 18, no. 3 (January 1963): 67–74.

27. Roberts, *Papa Jack*, 42–3, 51–67; Runstedtler, *Jack Johnson*, 31–67.

28. Runstedtler, *Jack Johnson*, 63–64.

29. Gems, "Jack Johnson and the Quest for Racial Respect," 62; Runstedtler, *Jack Johnson*, 68–70.

30. Gems, "Jack Johnson and the Quest for Racial Respect," 62 (quote, 63); Roberts, *Papa Jack*, 81–84; Burns, *Unforgivable Blackness;* Sammons, *Beyond the Ring*, 266–67. See Kevin B. Wamsley and David Whitson, "Celebrating Violent Masculinities: The Boxing Death of Luther McCarty," *Journal of Sport History* 25, no. 3 (Fall 1998): 419–31, which resulted in the death of one white hope and the indictment of his opponent for manslaughter in 1913.

31. Roberts, *Papa Jack*, 103–4.

32. *Chicago Tribune*, July 5, 1910, 1 (quote); Roberts, *Papa Jack*, 105–7.

33. *Chicago Tribune*, July 5, 1910, 5; Gems, "Jack Johnson and the Quest for Racial Respect;" Roberts, *Papa Jack*, 71–73; Finis Farr, "Jeff, It's Up to You!" *American Heritage* (February 1964): 64–77.

34. Sammons, *Beyond the Ring*, 41–5; Steven A. Riess, *Sport in Industrial America, 1850–1920* (Wheeling, IL: Harlan Davidson, 1995), 112; William H. Wiggins, "Boxing's Sambo Twins: Racial Stereotypes in Jack Johnson and Joe Louis Newspaper Cartoons, 1908 to 1938," *Journal of Sport History* 15, no. 3 (Winter 1988): 242–54; see *Illustr. Osterr Sportblatt* 7:2 (January 7, 1911)—7:50 (December 9, 1911) for year-long coverage in Austria and Germany. My thanks to Gertrud Pfister for calling my attention to the European coverage and providing translations.

35. Chad Heap, *Slumming: Sexual and Racial Encounters in American Nightlife, 1885–1940* (Chicago: University of Chicago Press, 2009); *Chicago Defender*, October 26, 1912, 1 (quote).

36. "Statistics on Lynching," University of Missouri–Kansas City School of Law, n.d., http://law2.umkc.edu/faculty/projects/ftrials/shipp/lynchingyear.html (accessed January 14, 2013).

37. Roberts, *Papa Jack*, 138–84, details the charges, intrigues, and likely bribes that allowed Johnson's flight.

38. *Chicago Tribune*, April 6, 1915, 13.

39. *Chicago Tribune*, April 6, 1915, 12.

40. Quotes are compiled from newspaper clippings in the Boxing Scrapbooks, Vol. 24, at the Chicago History Museum, including "Cowboy Wins Battle When Jack Weakens."

41. *Chicago Tribune*, April 6, 1915, 12.

42. "Chicagoans in Joy Carnival Over Big Fight"; "Riot Calls in Black Belt"; and Walter Eckersall, "Players Call Big Fight Fake," all in Boxing Scrapbooks, Vol. 24, Chicago History Museum; Roberts, *Papa Jack*, 204–10; Johnson, *Jack Johnson Is a Dandy*, 24, 103–10. See Richard V. McGehee, "The Dandy and

the Mauler in Mexico: Johnson, Dempsey, et al., and the Mexico City Press, 1919–1927," *Journal of Sport History* 23, no. 1 (Spring 1996): 20–33, on media representations and the growing interest in boxing in that country.

43. William M. Tuttle, Jr., *Race Riot: Chicago in the Red Summer of 1919* (New York: Atheneum, 1970).

44. Brian D. Bunk, "Harry Wills and the Image of the Black Boxer from Jack Johnson to Joe Louis," *Journal of Sport History* 39, no.1 (Spring 2012), 63–80.

45. Gems, "Jack Johnson and the Quest for Racial Respect," 70–71; Sammons, *Beyond the Ring*, 46, 49; Runstedtler, *Jack Johnson*, 236 (quote). See Nathan Irvin Huggins, ed., *Voices from the Harlem Renaissance* (New York: Oxford, 1995) on the relationship between music and boxing and the sojourns of both practitioners to France during the era.

46. Susan Brownell, ed., *The 1904 Anthropology Days and Olympic Games: Sport, Race, and American Imperialism* (Lincoln: University of Nebraska Press, 2008).

47. Robert G. Rodriguez, *The Regulation of Boxing: A History and Comparative Analysis of Policies among American States* (Jefferson, NC: McFarland & Co., 2009), 166–67; "Luis Angel Firpo," BoxRec, n.d., http://boxrec.com/media/index.php?title=Human:10607 (accessed January 19, 2013).

48. Dr. Juan Reilly quoted in "Frank Klaus Sees Firpo in Action," *New York Times*, September 2, 1923, 18. See *Uniontown* (Pennsylvania) *Morning Herald*, July 16, 1923, 6, and *Oakland Tribune*, September 14, 1923, 34, for examples of other denigratory characterizations of Firpo.

49. Jim Waltzer, *The Battle of the Century: Dempsey, Carpentier, and the Birth of Modern Promotion* (Santa Barbara, CA: Praeger, 2011), 203–4.

50. "Firpo Had the Title Within His Grasp," *New York Times*, September 15, 1923, 1; also see Sid Sutherland, "Latin Lacks Ring Wit to Cope with Yank, the Experienced," *Chicago Tribune*, September 15, 1923, 11.

51. "Luis Angel Firpo," BoxRec, n.d., http://boxrec.com/media/index.php?title=Human:10607 (accessed January 19, 2013).

52. Rudolph Fisher, "The Caucasian Storms Harlem," in Huggins, ed., *Voices from the Harlem Renaissance*, 80. See Gwendolyn Bennett, "Wedding Day," 191–97, in the same anthology for the story of Paul Watson, an African American musician and boxer who joined the French air corps during the war. See Peter Benson, *Battling Siki: A Tale of Ring Fixes, Race, and Murder in the 1920s* (Fayetteville: University of Arkansas Press, 2006), 111, on the war service of Africans.

53. Gerald Early, *The Culture of Bruising: Essays on Prizefighting, Literature, and Modern American Culture* (Hopewell, NJ: Ecco Press, 1994), 68, reports facility in as many as ten languages. Benson, *Battling Siki*, 88–100, 112–13, 123–30;

quote from Harry Furniss, *By Ways and Queer Ways of Boxing* (London: Harrison & Sons, 1919), 183.

54. Early, *Culture of Bruising*, 72–73; Ho Chi Minh, "About Siki," *Le Paria*, December 1, 1922, cited in Runstedtler, *Jack Johnson*, 231, 249.

55. Benson, *Battling Siki*, 3 (quotes, 70 and 89 respectively).

56. Early, *Culture of Bruising*, 75–76; Benson, *Battling Siki*, 23–32; Robert Cantwell, "The Great Dublin Robbery," SI Vault, March 19, 1979, http://sportsillustrated.cnn.com/vault/article/magazine/MAG1094742/1/index.htm (accessed January 22, 2013).

57. Early, *Culture of Bruising*, 76.

58. Early, *Culture of Bruising*, 70.

59. Benson, *Battling Siki*, 69.

60. Benson, *Battling Siki*, 154–55, 165–67, 183–84, 205, 221–23, 263–69, 277–78; quotes from Early, *Culture of Bruising*, 68.

61. *Catholic Citizen*, September 10, 1898, 4, cited in Matthew Frye Jacobson, *Whiteness of a Different Color*, 211.

62. Gerald R. Gems, *The Athletic Crusade: Sport and American Cultural Imperialism* (Lincoln: University of Nebraska Press, 2006), 45–66. Among numerous works on the war , see Eric T. L. Love, *Race over Empire: Racism and U.S. Imperialism, 1865–1900* (Chapel Hill: University of North Carolina Press, 2004), 159–95; Leon Wolff, *Little Brown Brother: How the United States Purchased and Pacified the Philippine Islands at the Century's Turn* (New York: Bookspan, 2006); David J. Silbey, *A War of Frontier and Empire: The Philippine-American War, 1899–1902* (New York: Hill & Wang, 2007); and James R. Arnold, *The Moro War: How America Battled a Muslim Insurgency in the Philippine Jungle, 1902–1913* (New York: Bloomsbury Press, 2011).

63. Hal Hennesey, "Pancho Villa: The Tiniest Giant," magazine clipping, 40; Bill Miller, "Boxing's Mosquito Fleet," magazine clipping; and Stanley Weston, "Pancho Villa: The Gigantic Runt," magazine clipping, all in the Villa file, International Boxing Hall of Fame. Villa's record against Ballerino was 12-0-1. See "Pancho Villa," BoxRec, n.d., http://boxrec.com/media/index.php?title=Human:9433; "Mike Ballerino," BoxRec, n.d., http://boxrec.com/list_bouts.php?human_id=41487&cat=boxer (both accessed January 24, 2013). Ballerino would later be recognized as the U.S. super featherweight champion (some sources indicate junior lightweight champion).

64. J. H. Pardee to Major General Frank McIntyre, August 12, 1919, in Christina Evangelista Torres, *The Americanization of Manila, 1898 1921* (Diliman, Quezon City, Philippines, 2010), 96–97. See Paul G. Cressey, *The Taxi-Dance Hall* (Chicago: University of Chicago Press, 1932), 43, 218–19, on Filipino exploitation, violence, and segregation.

65. Weston, "Pancho Villa," 64 (quote), 66.

66. Weston, "Pancho Villa," 66; quote from Torres, *Americanization of Manila*, 176. Villa's wife claimed that he had been purposely poisoned after gamblers lost large sums when he lost a fight to Jimmy McLarnin while suffering from the infection.

67. Andrew M. Kaye, *The Pussycat of Prizefighting: Tiger Flowers and the Politics of Black Celebrity* (Athens: University of Georgia Press, 2004), 60, 73–74, 83–85, 88, 90, 112 (quote). The entry "Flowers, Theodore 'Tiger,' 1895–1927," Blackpast.org, n.d., http://www.blackpast.org/?q=aaw/flowers-theodore-tiger-1895-1927 (accessed January 24, 2013) claims as many as 290 bouts.

68. Kaye, *Pussycat of Prizefighting*, 105, 107–16, 112 (quote).

69. "Tiger Flowers," International Boxing Hall of Fame, n.d., http://www.ibhof.com/pages/about/inductees/oldtimer/flowers.html (accessed January 26, 2013); Kaye, *Pussycat of Prizefighting*, 147–51.

70. Joseph S. Page, *Primo Carnera: The Life and Career of the Heavyweight Boxing Champion* (Jefferson, NC: McFarland & Co., 2011), 1–109, 194; Arne K. Lang, *Prizefighting: An American History* (Jefferson, NC: McFarland & Co., 2008), 90–92. Gaze theory (objectification of the body) was popularized by French scholars Jacques Lacan and Michel Foucault. For applications to sport, see the Forum articles in *Journal of Sport History* 29, no. 3 (Fall 2002); and Mike Huggins, "The Sporting Gaze: Towards a Visual Turn in Sport History—Documenting Art and Sport," *Journal of Sport History* 35, no. 2 (Summer 2008): 311–29.

71. See *Bulletin Italo-American National Union*, July, 1934, for an account of Balbo at the World's Fair. See Scott Ackman and Christopher Schwarz, "Dubious Legacy," *Chicago Magazine*, August 2008, 60–64, and heated retorts to the piece in *Chicago Magazine*, October 2008, 14, on the enduring legacy of the Balbo trip in Chicago. The quote refers to quotas instituted by the federal government in the 1920s that limited the number of immigrants, including Italians, who could gain admission to the United States.

72. Jennifer Guglielmo, *Living the Revolution: Italian Women's Resistance and Radicalism in New York City, 1880–1945* (Chapel Hill: University of North Carolina Press, 2010), 218.

73. Page, *Primo Carnera*, 135–65; 192–208.

74. David Bathrick, "Max Schmeling on the Canvas: Boxing as an Icon of Weimar Culture," *New German Critique* 51 (1990): 113–36 (quote, 134).

75. "Max Schmelling," BoxRec, n.d., http://boxrec.com/media/index.php?title=Human:9041 (accessed January 26, 2013).

76. Anthony O. Edmonds, "Joe Louis, Boxing, and American Culture," in David K. Wiggins, ed. *Out of the Shadows: A Biographical History of African Ameri-*

can Athletes (Fayetteville: University of Arkansas Press, 2006), 133–45; Randy Roberts, *Joe Louis: Hard Times Man* (New Haven, CT: Yale University Press, 2010), 14–16, 23 (quote).

77. Edmonds, "Joe Louis," 139–42; Theresa E. Runstedtler, "In Sport the Best Man Wins: How Joe Louis Whupped Jim Crow," in Amy Bass, ed., *In the Game: Race, Identity, and Sports in the Twentieth Century* (New York: Palgrave Macmillan, 2005), 47–91; George Samuel Schuyler, *Ethiopian Stories* (Boston: Northeastern University Press, 1994), 14; Jay Maeder, "Smashup Ethiopia, 1935," *New York Daily News*, June 15, 2000, http://articles.nydailynews.com/2000-06-15/news/18131296_1_addis-ababa-emperor-haile... (accessed October 2, 2011).

78. Roberts, *Joe Louis*, 80–81.

79. Roberts, *Joe Louis*, 72–3, 79, 97; see Wiggins, "Boxing's Sambo Twins," for other racist depictions of Louis.

80. David Margolick, *Beyond Glory: Joe Louis, Max Schmeling, and the World on the Brink* (New York: Alfred A. Knopf, 2005), 97–122; Sammons, *Beyond the Ring*, 103; Roberts, *Joe Louis*, 95–97 (quote, 95).

81. Roberts, *Joe Louis*, quotes 98 and 101 respectively.

82. Peter Heller, *"In This Corner . . . !": 42 World Champions Tell Their Stories* (New York: Da Capo Press, 1994), 185; Margolick, *Beyond Glory*, 137–45, 150 (quote, 141).

83. Lane Demas, "The Brown Bomber's Dark Day: Louis-Schmeling I and America's Black Hero," *Journal of Sport History* 31, no. 3 (Fall 2004): 252–71 (quotes, 263).

84. Margolick, *Beyond Glory*, 143–61, 171; "Summary: I know Why the Caged Bird Sings," SparkNotes, n.d., http://www.sparknotes.com/lit/cagedbird/section8.rhtml (accessed January 26, 2013, quote).

85. Margolick, *Beyond Glory*, 161–62, 170–82 (quotes, 162 and 173 respectively).

86. Margolick, *Beyond Glory*, 289–310; Roberts, *Joe Louis*, xii, claims a worldwide audience of "close to one hundred million."

87. Roberts, *Joe Louis*, 170.

88. Langston Hughes, "Joe Louis," in Robert Hedin and Michael Waters, eds., *Perfect in Their Art: Poems on Boxing from Homer to Ali* (Carbondale: Southern Illinois University Press, 2003), 101.

89. Roberts, *Joe Louis*, 223–24, 230–31, 251; Heller, *"In This Corner . . ."*; Sammons, *Beyond the Ring*, 130. Schmeling was drafted into the German army as a paratrooper, but saved a number of Jewish lives during the war. He owned the Coca-Cola franchise in Germany and became a millionaire.

90. Sammons, *Beyond the Ring*, 185–86; Heller, *"In This Corner . . . ,"* 191–219; quote from Roberts, *Joe Louis*, 121. Tony Canzoneri and Barney Ross also acquired three titles each, but did not hold them concurrently.

91. Graham Russell Hodges, "Robinson, Walker Smith, Jr. ('Sugar Ray')," in Arnold Markoe, ed., *Scribner Encyclopedia of American Lives, Vol. 2* (New York: Charles Scribner's Sons, 2002: 292–94. See Kenneth Shropshire, *Being Sugar Ray: The Life of Sugar Ray Robinson, America's Greatest Boxer and the First Celebrity Athlete* (New York: Basic Civitas, 2007), 54, 61–65, 78, on military service.

92. Heller, *"In This Corner . . . ,"* 278–79; Franklin Lewis, "Whose Fault?" Cleveland Press, June 25, 1947, in Irving T. Marsh and Edward Ehre, eds., *Best Sports Stories: 1948 Edition* (New York: E. P. Dutton, 1948), 167–69 (quote, 168–69); Hodges, "Robinson," 293, and Mark J. Price, "Local History: Sugar Ray Robinson Reigns over Akron in 1947," *Akron Beacon Journal*, August 12, 2012, http://www.ohio.com/lifestyle/history/local-history-sugar-ray-robinson-reigns-over-akron-in-1947-1.326708 (accessed February 2, 2013) on the trust fund.

93. Wacquant, "The Pugilistic Point of View: How Boxers Think and Feel about Their Trade," *Theory and Society* 24, no. 4 (August 1995): 495 (quote).

94. Heller, *"In This Corner . . . ,"* 278.

95. Harry Carpenter, *Boxing: An Illustrated History* (New York: Crescent Books, 1982), 105, 110; Daniel A. Nathan, "Sugar Ray Robinson, the Sweet Science, and the Politics of Meaning," *Journal of Sport History* 26, no. 1 (Spring 1999): 163–74 (quotes, 166); Shropshire, *Being Sugar Ray*, xix–xx, 83–105.

96. "Sugar Ray Robinson," BoxRec, n.d., http://boxrec.com/list_bouts.php?human_id=9625&cat=boxer (February 2, 2013).

97. Shropshire, *Being Sugar Ray*, 164.

98. Quote from Richard Lacayo, "Pound for Pound, the Best Ever," *Time*, April 24, 1989, 89, cited in Daniel A. Nathan, "Sugar Ray Robinson," in David K. Wiggins, ed., *African Americans in Sports* (Armonk, NY: M. E. Sharpe, 2004), 312.

99. Kevern Verney, *African Americans and U.S. Popular Culture* (New York: Routledge, 2003), 49–86; quote from Gems, Borish, and Pfister, *Sports in American History*, 291. Black athletes had played in the early NFL of the 1920s, but were not offered contracts after 1933. The All-American Football Conference began hiring black players in 1946. Black basketball teams won the first two professional basketball tournaments in 1939 and 1940. The NBA was officially formed in 1949 and began drafting black players the following year.

100. Amir Saeed, "What's in a Name? Muhammad Ali and the Politics of Cultural Identity," *Culture, Sport, Society* 5, no. 3 (2002): 51–72, 58 (quote).

101. Saeed, "What's in a Name?" 66, 60, 64 (quotes, respectively.)

102. Patrick B. Miller and David K. Wiggins, eds., *Sport and the Color Line: Black Athletes and Race Relations in Twentieth-Century America* (New York: Routledge, 2004), 293; quotes from Gems, Borish, and Pfister, *Sports in American History*, 292.

103. Quoted in Christian G. Appy, *Working-Class War: American Combat Soldiers and Vietnam* (Chapel Hill: University of North Carolina Press, 1993), 20. The ratio of black deaths in the war eventually reached numbers proportionate to their figures in the general population, but only after the assassination of Martin Luther King.

104. Gems, Borish, and Pfister, *Sports in American History*, 293–94; David W. Zang, "The Greatest: Muhammad Ali's Confounding Character," in Miller and Wiggins, eds., *Sport and the Color Line*, 300. Flood lost his case at the Supreme Court level, but his strategy ultimately resulted in the adoption of the free agency system that allowed players to seek their market value.

105. Michael Ezra, "Main Bout, Inc., Black Economic Power and Professional Boxing: The Cancelled Muhammad Ali/Ernie Terrell Fight," *Journal of Sport History* 29, no. 3 (Fall 2002): 413–37; David Zirin, "The Hidden History of Muhammad Ali," *International Socialist Review* 33 (January–February, 2004), http://www.isreview.org/issues/33/muhammadali.shtml (accessed February 9, 2013).

106. Gerald Early, "Muhammad Ali: Flawed Rebel with a Cause," in Wiggins, ed., *Out of the Shadows*, 272; Elliott J. Gorn, ed., *Muhammad Ali, the People's Champ* (Urbana: Univesity of Illinois Press, 1995).

107. Lewis A. Erenberg, "'Rumble in the Jungle': Muhammad Ali vs. George Foreman in the Age of Global Spectacle," *Journal of Sport History* 39, no. 1 (Spring 2012): 81–97.

108. ESPN, *Ali's 65: Not All Battles Are Fought in the Ring* (CD: 2007); Early, "Muhammad Ali," 273–74.

109. Early, "Muhammad Ali," 274–75.

110. Saeed, "What's in a Name?" 63. See Gorn, *Muhammad Ali: The People's Champ*, for various interpretations of Ali's meaning and legacy.

111. Angelou quoted in David L. Hudson Jr., *Boxing in America: An Autopsy* (Santa Barbara, CA: Praeger, 2012), 75.

112. Oates quoted in Daniel O'Connor, *Iron Mike: A Mike Tyson Reader* (New York: Thunder's Mouth Press, 2002), xiii–xiv, xxiii.

113. Joyce Carol Oates, "Rape and the Boxing Ring," *Newsweek*, February 24, 1992, in O'Connor, *Iron Mike*, 153–58 (quote, 157).

114. Jack Newfield, "Dr. K.O.," *Village Voice*, December 10, 1985, in O'Connor, *Iron Mike*, 9–22; Gerald Early, "Mike's Brilliant Career," *Transition* 71 (Fall 1996), in O'Connor, *Iron Mike*, 197–208 (quote, 200).

115. Newfield, "Dr. K.O.;" William Plummer, "Cus D'Amato," *People*, July 15, 1985, in O'Connor, *Iron Mike*, 1–8. See Early, "Mike's Brilliant Career," for an alternative description that demythologizes the D'Amato-Tyson relationship.

116. Early, "Mike's Brilliant Career," 202.

117. Newfield, "Dr. K.O;" Joyce Carol Oates, "Mike Tyson," *Life*, March 1987, in O'Connor, *Iron Mike*, 49–72.

118. Rudy Gonzalez with Martin Feigenbaum, *The Inner Ring*, 1995, in O'Connor, *Iron Mike*, 105–132; Phil Berger, "Mike Tyson: Tales from the Dark Side," *M Magazine*, January 1992, in O'Connor, *Iron Mike*, 139–51; Peter Heller, *Bad Intentions*, 1989, in O'Connor, *Iron Mike*, 83–97.

119. Hugh McIlvanney, "When an Ogre Looks Forlorn," *McIlvanney on Boxing*, February 18, 1990, in O'Connor, *Iron Mike*, 103.

120. Berger, "Mike Tyson: Tales from the Dark Side"; Early, "Mike's Brilliant Career," 203.

121. Joyce Carol Oates, "Mike Tyson," 70.

122. Berger, "Mike Tyson: Tales from the Dark Side," 147.

123. Dave Anderson, "Sports of the Times: Referee's Count Is What Counts," *New York Times*, February 12, 1990; Bernard Gavzer, "Is It Time to Investigate Boxing?" *Parade Magazine*, October 21, 1990, 4–6; Gonzalez and Feigenbaum, *Inner Ring*, 127–32.

124. Pete Hamill, "The Education of Mike Tyson," *Esquire*, March 1994; Hugh McIlvanney, "Tyson Tests His Drawing Power," *The Sunday Times*, August 13, 1995; and Early, "Mike's Brilliant Career," all in O'Connor, *Iron Mike*, 169–86, 191–96, and 197–208, respectively.

125. John Lombardi, "The Mike Myth," *New York*, June 23–30, 1997; and Katherine Dunn, "Defending Tyson," *PDXS* (July 9, 1997), both in O'Connor, *Iron Mike*, 241–45 and 247–55, respectively (quotes, 243 and 247 respectively). See Neil A. Wynn, "Deconstructing Tyson: The Black Boxer as American Icon," *International Journal of the History of Sport* 20, no. 3 (September 2003): 99–114, for similar British condemnations of Tyson.

126. Review quote from Hedy Weiss, "Tyson Scores a Knockout," *Chicago Sun-Times*, February 17, 2013, 20A. See Mary Elizabeth Williams, "Mike Tyson's Gross Return," *Chicago Sun-Times*, July 1, 2012, 23A for a decidedly more negative review of Tyson's Broadway show. Mike Tyson interview, February 23, 2013, *Windy City Live* (ABC, Chicago). Barry Meier and Timothy W. Smith, "Big Money, Big Fallout for Tyson," *New York Times*, May 24, 1998, in O'Connor, *Iron Mike*, 257–64, claim that Tyson sued King and former managers Horne and Holloway for bilking him of more than $100 million. Former chauffeur Rudy Gonzalez, "No Happy Ending" (March 21, 2002 interview) in O'Connor, *Iron Mike*, 301–9, states that Tyson had accumulated 250 cars, three mansions, and a private jet by that time. Wynn, "Deconstructing Tyson," 110, quotes James Lawson, "Boxing: Tyson's Freak Show on the Road to Oblivion," *The Independent*, January 31, 2002.

127. "Panama Al Brown," BoxRec, n.d., http://boxrec.com/list_bouts. php?human_id=8994&cat=boxer&pageID=; (Panama) Al Brown file, International Boxing Hall of Fame.

128. Enver M. Casimir, "Contours of Transnational Contact: Kid Chocolate, Cuba, and the United States in the 1920s and 1930s," *Journal of Sport History* 39, no. 3 (Fall 2012): 487–506; "Kid Chocolate," BoxRec, n.d., http://boxrec.com/list_bouts.php?human_id=9006&cat=boxer&pageID=2 (accessed February 25, 2013).

129. Casimir, "Contours of Transnational Contact," 488, 490, 494 (quote), 496; Kid Chocolate file, International Boxing Hall of Fame.

130. Casimir, "Contours of Transnational Contact," 496–501; Gems, *Athletic Crusade*, 95 (quote).

131. Jorge Duany, *The Puerto Rican Nation on the Move: Identities on the Island and in the United States* (Chapel Hill: University of North Carolina Press, 2002), 70.

132. Gems, *Athletic Crusade*, 102. See Laura Briggs, *Reproducing Empire: Race, Sex, Science and U.S. Imperialism in Puerto Rico* (Berkeley: University of California Press, 2002), on colonial relationships.

133. Gems, *Athletic Crusade*, 105 (quote); Sixto Escobar file, International Boxing Hall of Fame; "Sixto Escobar," http://boxrec.com/list_bouts.php?human_id=41270&cat=boxer (February 26, 2013).

134. Gems, *Athletic Crusade*, 105; quote from Jose Torres, "Last Round: The First Puerto Rican Champion Remembered by Another," clipping, Sixto Escobar file, International Boxing Hall of Fame.

135. "Carlos Ortiz," BoxRec, n.d., http://boxrec.com/media/index.php/Carlos_Ortiz; "Jose Torres," BoxRec, n.d., http://boxrec.com/media/index.php?title=Human:23151 (both accessed February 26, 2013).

136. "Baby Arizmendi," BoxRec, n.d., http://boxrec.com/list_bouts.php?human_id=009459&cat=boxer&pageID=2 (accessed February 26, 2013).

137. "Kid Gavilan," BoxRec, n.d., http://boxrec.com/media/index.php/File:KidGavilan.jpg (accessed February 26, 2013).

138. "Emile Griffith," BoxRec, n.d., http://boxrec.com/media/index.php?title=Human:9017 (accessed February 26, 2013).

139. "Speedy Dado," BoxRec, n.d., http://boxrec.com/media/index.php?title=Human:9907 (accessed February 24, 2013).

140. "Ceferino Garcia," BoxRec, n.d., http://boxrec.com/media/index.php?title=Human:9601 (accessed February 24, 2013); Gems, *Athletic Crusade*, 62, 77; Roger Mooney, "Going Home a Hero: How Ceferino Garcia Finally Realized His Dream," *Ring* (April 1994), 26–28, 60, in Garcia file, International Boxing Hall of Fame.

141. "Flash Elorde," BoxRec, n.d., http://boxrec.com/media/index. php?title=Human:12678(February 26, 2013); Elorde file, International Boxing Hall of Fame.

142. *Manila Cablenews*, August 8, 1907, cited in Peter W. Stanley, *A Nation in the Making: The Philippines and the United States, 1899–1921* (Cambridge, MA: Harvard University Press, 1974), 107.

143. Leonard Wood to Dear Bishop Brent, March 24, 1910, Bishop Charles H. Brent Papers, Box 9, Library of Congress. Similar and earlier concerns are expressed in M. W. Hoeger to Wood, November 7, 1904, Leonard Wood Papers, Philippines Box, Library of Congress.

144. Gems, *Athletic Crusade*, 59–61; Richard Schaap, *An Illustrated History of the Olympics* (New York: Alfred A. Knopf, 1963), 204. Kinue Hitomi, a remarkable female athlete and national heroine, won a silver medal in the 800-meter run in 1928. Two Koreans medaled for Japan in the 1936 marathon, including gold medalist Kitei Son (Sohn Kee-Chung). Korea was a colony of Japan and Koreans were required to run under the Japanese flag.

145. "Emile Pladner," BoxRec, n.d., http://boxrec.com/list_bouts. php?human_id=009914&cat=boxer&pageID=1 (accessed February 28, 2013); Sayuri Guthrie-Shimizu, *Transpacific Field of Dreams: How Baseball Linked the United States and Japan in Peace and War* (Chapel Hill: University of North Carolina Press, 2012), 148.

146. Yoshio Shirai file; Fighting Harada file, both in International Boxing Hall of Fame; Yoshio Shirai," BoxRec, n.d., http://boxrec.com/list_bouts. php?human_id=012925&cat=boxer; "Fighting Harada," BoxRec, n.d., http:// boxrec.com/media/index.php?title=Human:11494 (both accessed February 28, 2013).

147. See Gerald R. Gems, *Sport and the Shaping of Italian American Identity* (Syracuse, NY: Syracuse University Press, 2013) on the Italian quest for whiteness and acceptance within American society.

Chapter 5: The Concept of Ethnicity

1. "Ethnicity and Race in Anthropology," Science Encyclopedia, n.d., http:// science.jrank.org/pages/7673/Ethnicity-Race-in-Anthropology.html (accessed March 2, 2013); Stowe Persons, *Ethnic Studies at Chicago, 1905–1945* (Urbana: University of Illinois Press, 1987): Matthew Pratt Guterl, *The Color of Race in America, 1900–1940* (Cambridge, MA: Harvard University Press, 2001); Richard W. Rees, *Shadows of Difference: History of Ethnicity in America* (Lanham, MD: Rowman & Littlefield, 2007).

2. Jeffrey E. Mirel, *Patriotic Pluralism: Americanization, Education, and European Immigrants* (Cambridge, MA: Harvard University Press, 2010). T. S. Andrews, *World Sporting Annual Record Book, 1926* (Milwaukee: n.p., 1926), 101–302, provides an extensive list of ethnic boxers who tested each other in the ring, including Jews, Italians, blacks, Mexicans, Croatians, Scots, Swedes, Danes, French Canadians, Irish, English, Spanish Indians, Filipinos, Poles, Lithuanians, Portuguese, Slavs, Panamanians, Germans, French, Armenians, Spanish Americans, Bohemians, Dutch, Greeks, and Finns.

3. Victor W. Turner, *The Ritual Process: Structure and Anti-Structure* (Chicago: Aldine Publishing, 1969). Irvin L. Child, *Italian or American? The Second Generation in Conflict* (New Haven, CT: Yale University Press, 1943) is representative of the multitude of studies on a variety of ethnic immigrant groups.

4. "The Ring Magazine," BoxRec, n.d., http:boxrec.com/media/index.php/Ring_Magazine (accessed October 21, 2012); see Gerald R. Gems, "The Politics of Boxing: Resistance, Religion, and Working-Class Assimilation," *International Sports Journal* 8, no. 1 (Winter 2004): 89–103 for a more complete analysis. Gerald R. Gems, *Windy City Wars: Labor, Leisure, and Sport in the Making of Chicago* (Lanham, MD; Scarecrow Press, 1997), 102–11, indicates suspensions from play and discontinuation of games when boys did not meet middle-class standards of play.

5. Gems, *Windy City Wars*, 10, 14; Steven A. Riess, *Sport in Industrial America, 1850–1920* (Wheeling, IL: Haran Davidson, 1995), 87–88; Elliot J. Gorn, *The Manly Art: Bare-Knuckle Prize Fighting in America* (Ithaca, NY: Cornell University Press, 1986), 105.

6. Steven A. Riess, "Professional Sports as an Avenue of Social Mobility in America: Some Myths and Realities," in Donald G. Kyle and Gary D. Stark, eds., *Essays on Sport History and Sport Mythology* (College Station: Texas A&M Press, 1990), 83–117. See S. Kirson Weinberg and Henry Arond, "The Occupational Culture of the Boxer," *American Journal of Sociology* 57, no. 5 (March 1952): 460–69, for similar figures and results in a 1952 study.

7. "James J. Corbett," International Boxing Hall of Fame website, n.d., http://www.ibhof.com/pages/about/inductees/oldtimer/corbettjamesj.html (accessed March 4, 2013); George Rugg, "Corbett, James John," in George B. Kirsch, Othello Harris, and Claire E. Nolte, *Encyclopedia of Ethnicity and Sports in the United States* (Westport, CT: Greenwood, 2000), 110–11; Dan Streible, *Fight Pictures: A History of Boxing and Early Cinema* (Berkeley: University of California Press, 2008), 81–90.

8. J. J. Johnston and Sean Curtin, *Chicago Boxing* (Chicago: Arcadia, 2005), 12; "Mike Donovan," International Boxing Hall of Fame website, n.d., http://www.ibhof.com/pages/about/inductees/pioneer/donovanmike.html; "Mike Donovan,"

BoxRec, n.d., http://boxrec.com/list_bouts.php?human_id=088547&cat=boxer (both accessed March 4, 2013).

9. "Bob Fitzsimmons," BoxRec, n.d., http://boxrec.com/media/index.php?title=Human:10552 (accessed March 6, 2013).

10. "Nonpareil Jack Dempsey," BoxRec, n.d., http://boxrec.com/media/index.php?title=Human:17958; "(Nonpareil) Jack Dempsey,"International Boxing Hall of Fame website, n.d., http://www.ibhof.com/pages/about/inductees/oldtimer/dempseynonpareil.html (both accessed March 7, 2013).

11. "Irish and Irish-American Boxers," Ancient Order of Hibernians Division 61, n.d., http://www.aoh61.com/history/boxing.htm (accessed March 10, 2013); "Jack McAuliffe," The MacAuliffe Site, n.d., http://www.clanmcauliffe.com/famous/jack.html (accessed March 10, 2013).

12. Tracy Callis, "Jimmy Barry," The Cyber Boxing Zone, n.d., http://www.cyberboxingzone.com/boxing/article-jimmybarry.htm#TOP; Robbie Smith, "Fighters Revisited: The Little Tiger Jimmy Barry," Irish-Boxing.com, n.d., http://www.irish-boxing.com/2012/10/the-little-tiger-jimmy-barry/; "Jimmy Barry," BoxRec, n.d., http://boxrec.com/list_bouts.php?human_id=46200&cat=boxer (all accessed March 10, 2013).

13. "Philadelphia Jack O'Brien," BoxRec, n.d., http://boxrec.com/media/index.php?title=Human:10817(accessed March 11, 2013); Randy Roberts, *Papa Jack: Jack Johnson and the Era of White Hopes* (New York: Free Press, 1983), 76, 81 respectively on the quotes, 77 on O'Brien's loss to Johnson.

14. "Terry McGovern," International Boxing Hall of Fame website, n.d., http://www.ibhof.com/pages/about/inductees/oldtimer/mcgovern.html; "Terry McGovern," BoxRec, n.d., http://boxrec.com/media/index.php?title=Human:9044 (both accessed March 12, 2013).

15. "Johnny Kilbane," International Boxing Hall of Fame website, n.d., http://www.ibhof.com/pages/about/inductees/oldtimer/kilbane.html; "Johnny Kilbane," BoxRec, n.d., http://boxrec.com/media/index.php?title=Human:11865 (both accessed March 12, 2013).

16. Johnston and Curtin, *Chicago Boxing*, 31, indicates two initial losses in 1904; other boxing records indicate a 1904 loss, but there is confusion over names, as a number of McFarlands fought during that era. The Boxing Hall of Fame gives his record as 64-1-5 with forty-seven knockouts. "Packey McFarland," International Boxing Hall of Fame website, n.d., http://www.ibhof.com/pages/about/inductees/oldtimer/mcfarland.html; "Packey McFarland," BoxRec, n.d., http://boxrec.com/list_bouts.php?human_id=036384&cat=boxer&pageID=2 (both accessed March 12, 2013).

17. Johnston and Curtin, *Chicago Boxing*, 30; "Jack Britton," International Boxing Hall of Fame website, n.d., http://www.ibhof.com/pages/about/inductees/oldtimer/britton.html (accessed March 12, 2013).

18. "Mickey Walker," BoxRec, n.d., http://boxrec.com/media/index. php?title=Human:9035 (accessed March 12, 2013); Ronnie D. Lankford, Jr., "Walker, Edward Patrick (Mickey)" in Arnold Markoe, ed., *The Scribner Encyclopedia of American Lives* (New York: Charles Scribner's Sons, 2002), 471–72.

19. "Mickey Walker," BoxRec.com; Lankford, "Walker, Edward Patrick (Mickey") in Markoe, ed., *Scribner Encyclopedia of American Lives*, 471–72.

20. "Tommy Loughran," International Boxing Hall of Fame website, n.d., http://www.ibhof.com/pages/about/inductees/oldtimer/loughran.html; "Victoria aut Mors: Tommy Loughran," Beloved Onslaught, September 28, 2011,http://www.belovedonslaught.com/2011/09/victoria-aut-mors-tommy-loughran.html; "Tommy Loughran," BoxRec, n.d., http://boxrec.com/media/index.php?title=Human:11326 (all accessed March 13, 2013).

21. Richard O. Davies, *Sports in American Life: A History* (Malden, MA: Blackwell, 2007), 232–33 (quote, 233); Elliott J. Gorn and Warren Goldstein, *A Brief History of American Sports* (New York: Hill & Wang, 1993), 238–39.

22. "Cinderella Man: James Braddock, Max Baer, and the Greatest Upset in Boxing History," BoxRec, n.d., http://boxrec.com/media/index.php/Cinderella_Man:_James_Braddock,_Max_Baer,_and_the_Greatest_Upset_in_Boxing_History (accessed March 13, 2013).

23. "Billy Conn," International Boxing Hall of Fame website, n.d., http://www.ibhof.com/pages/about/inductees/modern/conn.html (accessed March 14, 2013); "Billy Conn," BoxRec, n.d., http://boxrec.com/media/index.php?title=Human:9007 (accessed March 14, 2013); Edward Gruver, "Conn, William David, Jr. 'Billy,'" in Markoe, ed., *Scribner Encyclopedia of American Lives, Vol. 1,* 181–83 (quote, 182). "'Sweet William: The Life of Billy Conn' by Andrew O'Toole," *Pittsburgh Post-Gazette*, January 6, 2008, http://www. post-gazette.com/stories/ae/book-reviews/sweet-william-the-life-of-billy-conn-by-andrew-otoole-374759/ (accessed March 14, 2013). There is some dispute over the date of Conn's first bout in 1934; a June 28 loss to Dick Woodward is not yet recognized as official in the boxing record.

24. Gruver, "Conn, William David, Jr. 'Billy,'" 183. The quote is from "'Sweet William: The Life of Billy Conn,'" *Pittsburgh Post-Gazette*.

25. "Sean O'Grady Biography," Biography Base, n.d., http://www.biography-base.com/biography/O_Grady_Sean.html (accessed March 14, 2013).

26. "Rinty Monaghan," BoxRec, n.d., http://boxrec.com/list_bouts. php?human_id=24317&cat=boxer; "David McAuley," BoxRec, n.d., http://boxrec.com/list_bouts.php?human_id=12246&cat=boxer; "Wayne McCullough," BoxRec, n.d., http://boxrec.com/list_bouts.php?human_id=4985&cat=boxer; "Barry McGuigan," BoxRec, n.d., http://boxrec.com/list_bouts.php?human_id=12746&cat=boxer (all accessed March 14, 2013); Joyce Carol Oates, "On

Boxing," in Joyce Carol Oates and Daniel Halpern, eds., *Reading the Fights: The Best Writing about the Most Controversial Sport* (New York: Prentice Hall, 1988), 286–305 (quote, 288).

27. Ken Blady, *The Jewish Boxers' Hall of Fame* (New York: Shapolsky Pub., 1988), 25–36; Tracy Callis, "Joe Choynski . . . 'Clever, Shifty, and Explosive,'" n.d., http://www.oocities.org/colosseum/lodge/6525/Article-JoeChoynski.htm (accessed April 20, 2013); "Joe Choynski," International Boxing Hall of Fame website, n.d., http://www.ibhof.com/pages/about/inductees/oldtimer/choynski. html (accessed March 21, 2013); Roberts, *Papa Jack*, 13–16.

28. "Harry Harris," International Boxing Hall of Fame website, n.d., http:// www.ibhof.com/pages/about/inductees/oldtimer/harris.html (accessed March 21, 2013); Johnston and Curtin, *Chicago Boxing*, 16–17; Blady, *Jewish Boxers' Hall of Fame*, 57–58.

29. "Abe Atell," International Boxing Hall of Fame website, n.d., http:// www.ibhof.com/pages/about/inductees/oldtimer/attell.html (accessed March 21, 2013); Blady, *Jewish Boxers' Hall of Fame*, 39–40, 65–66; David Pietrusza, *Rothstein: The Life, Times, and Murder of the Criminal Genius Who Fixed the 1919 World Series* (New York: Carroll & Graf Publishers, 2003), 149–73.

30. Blady, *Jewish Boxers' Hall of Fame*, 65–66; "Charley Goldman," BoxRec, n.d., http://boxrec.com/media/index.php?title=Human:52597 (accessed March 24, 2013), gives a birthdate in 1887.

31. "Ted 'Kid' Lewis," International Boxing Hall of Fame website, n.d., http://www.ibhof.com/pages/about/inductees/oldtimer/lewisted.html (accessed March 21, 2013); David Dee, "'The Hefty Hebrew': Boxing and British-Jewish Identity, 1890–1960," *Sport in History* 32, no. 3 (September 2012): 370–72.

32. "Battling Levinsky," International Boxing Hall of Fame website, n.d., http://www.ibhof.com/pages/about/inductees/oldtimer/levinsky.html (accessed March 21, 2013); Blady, *Jewish Boxers' Hall of Fame*, 98–100.

33. Peter Heller, *"In This Corner . . . !": 42 World Champions Tell Their Stories* (New York: Da Capo Press, 1994), 108–115; "Jackie (Kid) Berg," International Boxing Hall of Fame website, n.d., http://www .ibhof.com/pages/about/inductees/modern/berg.html (accessed March 21, 2013); Dee, "The Hefty Hebrew," 370–72.

34. Ira Berkow, *Maxwell Street* (Garden City, NY: Doubleday, 1977), 143–47; Peter Levine, *Ellis Island to Ebbets Field: Sport and the American Jewish Experience* (New York: Oxford University Press, 1992), 152, 155, 165; Blady, *Jewish Boxers' Hall of Fame*, 109, 111–25 (quote, 111); Marc Singer, "Leonard, Benny," in Kirsch, Harris, and Nolte, eds., *Encyclopedia of Ethnicity and Sports in the United States*, 284–85; "Benny Leonard," BoxRec, n.d., http://boxrec.com/list_bouts. php?human_id=009001&cat=boxer&pageID=3 (accessed March 24, 2013).

35. Blady, *Jewish Boxers' Hall of Fame*, 111,122 (*Jewish Daily Bulletin* of March 25, 1925 cited on 125); Singer, "Leonard, Benny," 285.

36. Heller, *"In This Corner . . . ,"* 128–39 (quote, 130); Blady, *Jewish Boxers' Hall of Fame*, 201; "Jackie Fields," BoxRec, n.d., http://boxrec.com/list_bouts. php?human_id=12314&cat=boxer (accessed March 25, 2013).

37. "Max Baer," BoxRec, n.d., http://boxrec.com/media/index. php?title=Human:12077 (accessed March 25, 2013); Marc Singer, "Baer, Max," in Kirsch, Harris, and Nolte, eds., *Encyclopedia of Ethnicity and Sports in the United States*, 40.

38. "Maxie Rosenbloom," International Boxing Hall of Fame website, n.d., http://www.ibhof.com/pages/about/inductees/oldtimer/rosenbloom.html (accessed March 25, 2013); Jeffrey T. Sammons, *Beyond the Ring: The Role of Boxing in American Society* (Urbana: University of Illinois Press, 1988), 91–94.

39. Peter Hopsicker, "'No Hebrews Allowed': How the 1932 Lake Placid Olympic Games Survived the 'Restricted' Adirondack Culture, 1877–1932," *Journal of Sport History* 36, no. 2 (2009): 205–22.

40. Barney Ross and Martin Abramson, *No Man Stands Alone: The True Story of Barney Ross* (New York: J. B. Lippincott, 1957), 1–91 (quote, 77); Douglas Century, *Barney Ross* (New York: Schocken Books, 2006), 12–28.

41. "Barney Ross," BoxRec, n.d., http://boxrec.com/list_bouts.php?human_ id=008996&cat=boxer&pageID=1 (accessed March 26, 2013); Ross and Abramson, *No Man Stands Alone*, 92–240; Levine, *Ellis Island to Ebbets Field*, 170–79; Marc Singer, "Ross, Barney," in Kirsch, Harris, and Nolte, eds., *Encyclopedia of Ethnicity and Sports in the United States*, 392–93; Century, *Barney Ross*, 149–58, 205.

42. Chuck Wills, *Destination America: The People and Cultures that Created a Nation* (New York: DK Publishing, 2005), 164; Richard Gambino, *Vendetta: The True Story of the Largest Lynching in U.S. History* (1977; Toronto: Guernica, 1998), 142–43; David R. Roediger, *Working Toward Whiteness: How America's Immigrants Became White: The Strange Journey from Ellis Island to the Suburbs* (New York: Basic Books, 2005), 47, 74–77; Gerald R. Gems, *Sport and the Shaping of Italian American Identity* (Syracuse, NY: Syracuse University Press, 2013).

43. "Casper Leon," BoxRec, n.d., http://boxrec.com/list_bouts.php?human_ id=12276&cat=boxer (accessed March 28, 2013).

44. Thomas Hauser and Stephen Brunt, *The Italian Stallions: Heroes of Boxing's Glory Days* (Toronto: Sports Media, 2003), 14; Dundee file, International Boxing Hall of Fame; Carmelo Bazzano, "The Italian-American Sporting Experience," in George Eisen and David K. Wiggins, eds., *Ethnicity and Sport in North American History and Culture* (Westport, CT: Praeger, 1994), 103–16; "Young Zulu Kid," BoxRec, n.d., http://boxrec.com/list_bouts.php?human_

id=53374&cat=boxer; "Little Jackie Sharkey," BoxRec, n.d., http://boxrec.com/media/index.php?title=Human:37689; "Bushy Graham," BoxRec, n.d., http://boxrec.com/list_bouts.php?human_id=010091&cat=boxer&pageID=2 (all accessed March 29, 2013).

45. Gambino, *Vendetta*; A. V. Margavio and Jerome J. Salomone, *Bread and Respect: The Italians of Louisiana* (Gretna, LA: Pelican Publishing, 2002), 200–12.

46. Herman file, International Boxing Hall of Fame; Joseph Maselli and Domenic Candeloro, *Italians in New Orleans* (Chicago: Arcadia Pub., 2004), 93–94, 96; Heller, *"In This Corner . . . ,"* 48–53; quote from John Billi, "U.S. Sports Firmament is Dotted with Many First Magnitude Stars of Italian Origin," *Il Progresso Italo-Americano*, November 9, 1930, 7.

47. Dr. Juan Reilly, quoted in "Frank Klaus Sees Firpo in Action," *New York Times*, September 2, 1923, 18.

48. Quote from "Firpo Had the Title within His Grasp," *New York Times*, September 15, 1923, 1. Among scholarly treatises, see Edward Alsworth Ross, *The Old World in the New: The Significance of Past and Present Immigration to the American People* (New York: The Century Co., 1914), and Madison Grant, *The Passing of the Great Race or the Racial Basis of European History* (New York: Charles Scribner's Sons, 1916).

49. Genaro, LaBarba, and Mandell files, International Boxing Hall of Fame; "Sammy Mandell," BoxRec, n.d., http://boxrec.com/list_bouts.php?human_id=10116&cat=boxer&pageID=3; "Fidel LaBarba," BoxRec, n.d., http://boxrec.com/list_bouts.php?human_id=12310&cat=boxer (both accessed March 29, 2013); Heller, *"In This Corner . . . ,"* 98–107; Gerald R. Gems, "Sport and the Italian American Quest for Whiteness," *Sport in History* 32, no. 4 (December 2012): 479–503.

50. "Midget Wolgast," International Boxing Hall of Fame website, n.d., http://www.ibhof.com/pages/about/inductees/oldtimer/wolgastmidget.html; "Battling Battalino," International Boxing Hall of Fame website, n.d., http://www.ibhof.com/pages/about/inductees/oldtimer/battalino.html (both accessed March 29, 2013); Heller, *"In This Corner . . . ,"* 140–48.

51. Canzoneri file, International Boxing Hall of Fame; Hauser and Brunt, *Italian Stallions*, 44–47; "Tony Canzoneri," BoxRec, n.d., http://boxrec.com/media/index.php?title=Human:9003 (accessed March 30, 2013).

52. "How I Will Take Another Title from Armstrong," magazine clipping in Ambers file, International Boxing Hall of Fame (quote); Heller, *"In This Corner . . . ,"* 178–83; "Lou Ambers," International Boxing Hall of Fame website, n.d., http://www.ibhof.com/pages/about/inductees/oldtimer/ambers.html (accessed March 30, 2013).

53. Angott file, International Boxing Hall of Fame; "Sammy Angott," International Boxing Hall of Fame website, n.d., http://www.ibhof.com/pages/about/inductees/modern/angott.html; "Harry Jeffra," BoxRec, n.d., http://boxrec.com/list_bouts.php?human_id=025529&cat=boxer&pageID=2; "Fred Apostoli," International Boxing Hall of Fame website, n.d., http://www.ibhof.com/pages/about/inductees/modern/apostoli.html; "Fred Apostoli," BoxRec, n.d., http://boxrec.com/media/index.php?title=Human:10525 (all accessed March 30, 2013).

54. Joseph S. Page, *Primo Carnera: The Life and Career of the Heavyweight Boxing Champion* (Jefferson, NC: McFarland, 2011), 226–28; *Chicago Tribune*, September 14, 1930, part 2, 5 (quote).

55. Page, *Carnera*, 100–20, 200–8; Heller, *"In This Corner . . . ,"* 328 (quote). See Sammons, Beyond the Ring, 86–91, for a critical assessment of Carnera's boxing career.

56. Page, *Carnera*, 135–57.

57. Willie Pep with Robert Sacchi, *Willie Pep Remembers . . . Friday's Heroes* (New York: Friday's Heroes, Inc., 1973), 4–8, 5 (quote).

58. Pep file, International Boxing Hall of Fame; Heller, *"In This Corner . . . ,"* 248–55; Hauser and Brunt, *Italian Stallions*, 49–73.

59. Gerald Early, The Romance of Toughness," *Antioch Review* 45, no. 4 (Autumn 1987): 385–408 (quotes, 387, including the citation for Daley, and 390 for Cannon).

60. Graziano file, International Boxing Hall of Fame; Phil Berger, "Rocky Graziano, Ex Ring Champion, Dead at 71" (obituary), *New York Times*, May 23, 1990, http://www.nytimes.com/1990/05/23/obituaries/rocky-graziano-ex-ring-champion-dead-at-71.html (accessed April 1, 2013).

61. Rex Lardner, "The Improbable Graziano," in Hauser and Brunt, *Italian Stallions*, 75–89 (quote, 79).

62. Lardner, "Improbable Graziano."

63. W. C. Heinz, "Goodbye, Graziano," in Al Silverman, *Best from Sport* (New York: Bartholomew House, 1961), 88–95.

64. Rocky Graziano with Ralph Corsel, *Somebody Down Here Likes Me Too* (New York: Stein & Day, 1981), 133.

65. Graziano file, International Boxing Hall of Fame; Graziano with Corsel, *Somebody Down Here*, xii, 206; Heinz, "Goodbye Graziano," 33–34.

66. LaMotta file, International Boxing Hall of Fame; Early, "Romance of Toughness," 393 (quotes); Barney Nagler, "The Story of a Champion," in Hauser and Brunt, *Italian Stallions*, 115–35; Chris Anderson and Sharon McGehee with Jake LaMotta, *Raging Bull II* (Secaucus, NJ: Lyle Stuart, Inc., 1986), 145, 172, 239.

67. Early, "Romance of Toughness," 392.

68. Joe Bruno, *Penthouse Magazine* clipping in LaMotta file, International Boxing Hall of Fame; Heller, *"In This Corner . . . ,"* 298.

69. Heller, *"In This Corner . . . ,"* 297 (quote), 300.

70. "Jake LaMotta," Bio.com, n.d., http://www.biography.com/people/jake-lamotta-259489?page=2 (accessed April 1, 2013).

71. "Joey Maxim," BoxRec, n.d., http://boxrec.com/list_bouts.php?human_id=010329&cat=boxer&pageID=1 (accessed April 2, 2013).

72. "Carmen Basilio," BoxRec, n.d., http://boxrec.com/list_bouts.php?human_id=8997&cat=boxer (accessed April 4, 2013); David Iamele, "Basilio," *Cigar Smoker Magazine*, n.d., 83–84 (quote), in Basilio file, International Boxing Hall of Fame; Gary B. Youmans, *The Onion Picker: Carmen Basilio and Boxing in the 1950s* (Syracuse, NY: Campbell Road Press, North, 2007).

73. Youmans, *Onion Picker*, book cover.

74. "Joey Giardello," BoxRec, n.d., http://boxrec.com/media/index.php?title=Human:10923 (accessed April 4, 2013); Mike Rathet, "I Said No to the Mafia," *Boxing Scene*, clipping, 30–34 (quote, 30), in Giardello file, International Boxing Hall of Fame; Heller, *"In This Corner . . . ,"* 400–7.

75. Stan Hochman, "The Joey Giardello Comeback," *Sport*, April 1964, in Hauser and Brunt, *Italian Stallions*, 207–13 (quote, 209).

76. Russell Sullivan, *Rocky Marciano: The Rock of His Times* (Urbana: University of Illinois Press, 2002), 12–16; Marciano file in International Boxing Hall of Fame; Ed Fitzgerald, "The Blockbuster from Brockton," in Hauser and Brunt, *Italian Stallions*, 137–55.

77. Sullivan, *Rocky Marciano*, 44–45; "Rocky Marciano," BoxRec, n.d., http://boxrec.com/list_bouts.php?human_id=9032&cat=boxer (accessed April 5, 2013).

78. Sullivan, *Rocky Marciano*, 68, 75–105; "Personality," *Time*, September 22, 1952, 50.

79. Sullivan, *Rocky Marciano*, 144–63, 21–26, 268–73, 288–300; "Rocky Marciano," BoxRec.com; Arch Ward, "In the Wake of the News," *Chicago Tribune*, September 25, 1953, part 4, 2 (quote).

80. Quotes from Sullivan, *Rocky Marciano*, 238 and 244 respectively. See Sullivan, *Rocky Marciano*, 52–59, 205–9, 249; Sammons, *Beyond the Ring*, 136–80; Youmans, *Onion Picker*, 31–35, 67–70, 93–98, 112, 117–19, 124–25, 166–71, and 207–8, on the machinations of the IBC.

81. "Willie Pastrano," International Boxing Hall of Fame website, n.d., http://www.ibhof.com/pages/about/inductees/modern/pastrano.html (accessed April 6, 2013); Heller, *"In This Corner . . . ,"* 388–99, in which Pastrano claims he boxed professionally as early as fifteen.

82. Hauser and Brunt, *Italian Stallions*, 216.

83. Mark Kriegel, *The Good Son: The Life of Ray "Boom Boom" Mancini* (New York: Free Press, 2012), 8–26.

84. Kriegel, *The Good Son*, 56–92; quote from "A Sketch of Ray "Boom Boom" Mancini," clipping in Mancini file, International Boxing Hall of Fame.

85. "Marcus Lee Hansen," Neenah Historical Society, n.d., http://www.focol. org/neenahhistorical/Historical%20Photos/Notables%20Images/Notable%20 Text/Hansen.html (accessed April 7, 2013); Kriegel, *The Good Son*, 94, 98, 105–18; Mancini file, International Boxing Hall of Fame.

86. Kriegel, *The Good Son*, 126–61; "Deuk-Koo Kim," BoxRec, n.d., http:// boxrec.com/media/index.php?title=Human:12186 (accessed April 7, 2013).

87. Kriegel, *The Good Son*, 185–233.

88. "Vinny Pazienza," BoxRec, n.d., http://boxrec.com/list_bouts.php?human_ id=601&cat=boxer; "Arturo Gatti," BoxRec, n.d., http://boxrec.com/media/ index.php?title=Human:3999; "Paul Malignaggi," BoxRec, n.d., http://boxrec. com/list_bouts.php?human_id=52984&cat=boxer (all accessed April 7, 2013).

89. "Hogan Kid Bassey," BoxRec, n.d., http://boxrec.com/list_bouts. php?human_id=22405&cat=boxer (accessed April 9, 2013).

90. "Dick Tiger," BoxRec, n.d., http://boxrec.com/list_bouts.php?human_ id=9010&cat=boxer (accessed April 9, 2013).

91. "Cornelius Boza-Edwards," BoxRec, n.d., http://boxrec.com/list_bouts. php?human_id=608&cat=boxer; "John Mugabi," BoxRec, n.d., http://boxrec. com/list_bouts.php?human_id=694&cat=boxer (both accessed April 9, 2013).

92. "Azumah Nelson," BoxRec, n.d., http://boxrec.com/media/index. php?title=Human:440; "Ike Quartey," BoxRec, n.d., http://boxrec.com/media/ index.php?title=Human:1491(both accessed April 9, 2013).

93. "Marvin Hagler," BoxRec, n.d., http://boxrec.com/media/index. php?title=Human:8684 (accessed April 11, 2013).

94. "Thomas Hearns," BoxRec, n.d., http://boxrec.com/media/index. php?title=Human:303 (accessed April 11, 2013).

95. "Sugar Ray Leonard," BoxRec, n.d., http://boxrec.com/list_bouts. php?human_id=269&cat=boxer (accessed April 14, 2013); Daniel A. Nathan, "Sugar Ray Leonard," in David K. Wiggins, ed., *African Americans in Sports* (Armonk, NY: M.E. Sharpe, 2004), 206–7.

96. "Sugar Ray Leonard," BoxRec.com; Don Amerman, "Leonard, Ray Charles ("Sugar Ray"), in Markoe, ed., *Scribner Encyclopedia of American Lives*, 34–36.

97. "Roy Jones Jr.," BoxRec, n.d., http://boxrec.com/media/index. php?title=Human:1758 (accessed April14, 2013).

98. "Floyd Mayweather Jr.," BoxRec, n.d., http://boxrec.com/media/index. php?title=Human:352 (accessed April 14, 2013).

99. "Bernard Hopkins," BoxRec, n.d., http://boxrec.com/list_bouts. php?human_id=1414&cat=boxer (accessed April 14, 2013).

100. Samuel O. Regalado, quoted in Gerald R. Gems, *The Athletic Crusade: Sport and American Cultural Imperialism* (Lincoln: University of Nebraska Press, 2006), 109.

101. "Wilfred Benitez," BoxRec, n.d., http://boxrec.com/media/index. php?title=Human:438 (accessed April 15, 2013); Jim Henry, "For Wilfred Benitez, Boxing's Brutal Toll Never Ends," AOL news, October 7, 2010, http:// www.aolnews.com/2010/10/07/for-wilfred-benitez-boxings-brutal-toll-never-ends/ (accessed April 15, 2013).

102. "Wilfredo Gomez," BoxRec, n.d., http://boxrec.com/list_bouts. php?human_id=002542&cat=boxer (accessed April 15, 2013).

103. "Edwin Rosario," BoxRec, n.d., http://boxrec.com/media/index. php?title=Human:610; "Felix Trinidad," BoxRec, n.d., http://boxrec.com/media/ index.php/Felix_Trinidad (both accessed April 15, 2013).

104. "Hector Camacho," BoxRec, n.d., http://boxrec.com/media/index. php?title=Human:607 (accessed April 15, 2013).

105. Joseph Moncure March, "The Setup," in Hedin and Waters, eds., *Perfect in Their Art*, 134.

106. Gems, *The Athletic Crusade*, 151.

107. Chris Cozzone and Jim Boggio, *Boxing in New Mexico, 1868–1940* (Jefferson, NC: McFarland, 2013); Jorge Iber, Samuel O. Regalado, Jose M. Alamillo, and Arnoldo De Leon, *Latinos in U.S. Sport: A History of Isolation, Cultural Identity, and Acceptance* (Champaign, IL: Human Kinetics, 2011), 101–40.

108. "Jose Napoles," BoxRec, n.d., http://boxrec.com/media/index. php?title=Human:9025 (accessed April 16, 2013); Benita Heiskanen, *The Urban Geography of Boxing: Race, Class, and Gender in the Ring* (New York: Routledge, 2012), 78.

109. "Ruben Olivares," BoxRec, n.d., http://boxrec.com/media/index. php?title=Human:9040; "Carlos Zarates," BoxRec, n.d., http://boxrec.com/media/index.php?title=Human:402 (both accessed April 16, 2013).

110. "Salvador Sanchez," BoxRec, n.d., http://boxrec.com/media/index. php?title=Human:2201 (accessed April 16, 2013).

111. "Julio Cesar Chavez," BoxRec, n.d., http://boxrec.com/media/index. php?title=Human:8119 (accessed April 16, 2013).

112. "Juan Manuel Marquez." BoxRec, n.d., http://boxrec.com/media/index. php?title=Human:12222 (accessed April 16, 2013).

113. All three quotations from Heiskanen, *Urban Geography of Boxing*, 86.

114. "John Ruiz." BoxRec, n.d., http://boxrec.com/media/index. php?title=Human:4655 (accessed April 16, 2013).

115. "Oscar De La Hoya," BoxRec, n.d., http://boxrec.com/media/index. php?title=Human:8253 (accessed April 16, 2013); "Oscar De La Hoya," Bio. com, n.d., www.biography.com/people/oscar-de-la-hoya-9542428? (accessed April 16, 2013).

116. "Carlos Monzon," BoxRec, n.d., http://boxrec.com/media/index. php?title=Human:9036 (accessed April 16, 2013).

117. John Cincotta, "Alexis Arguello: Portrait of a Killer with Class," *Boxing Today*, n.d., 11–15, in Arguello file, International Boxing Hall of Fame.

118. "Alexis Arguello," BoxRec, n.d., http://boxrec.com/list_bouts. php?human_id=002179&cat=boxer (accessed April 16, 2013).

119. Jeremy Greenwood, "Roberto Duran . . . Latin Ambassador of Macho," *World Wide Boxing Digest*, clipping, 4–5 (quote) in Duran file, International Boxing Hall of Fame; Fox Sports Network, "Beyond the Glory," Season 1, February 4, 2001.

120. William Nack, "Back, But Still a Long Way to Go," *Sports Illustrated* clipping, 16–17 (quotes), in Duran file, International Boxing Hall of Fame; "Roberto Duran," BoxRec, n.d., http://boxrec.com/media/index.php?title=Human:80 (accessed April 16, 2013).

121. Richard Goldstein, "Teofilo Stevenson, Cuban Boxing Great, Dies at 60," June 12, 2012, http://www.nytimes.com/2012/06/13/sports/teofilo-stevenson-cuban-boxing-great-dead-at-60.html?_r=0 (accessed April 16, 2013).

122. "Chartchai Chionoi," BoxRec, n.d., http://boxrec.com/media/index. php?title=Human:16406; "Saensak Muangsurin," BoxRec, n.d., http://boxrec. com/list_bouts.php?human_id=35832&cat=boxer (both accessed April 17, 2013).

123. "Khaosay Galaxy," BoxRec, n.d., http://boxrec.com/media/index. php?title=Human:4059 (accessed April 17, 2013).

124. "Sot Chitalada," BoxRec, n.d., http://boxrec.com/list_bouts.php?human_ id=3348&cat=boxer; "Saman Sorjaturong," BoxRec, n.d., http://boxrec.com/media/index.php?title=Human:2155; "Veeraphol Sahaprom," BoxRec, n.d., http:// boxrec.com/media/index.php?title=Human:6077; "Pongsaklek Wonjongkam," BoxRec, n.d., http://boxrec.com/media/index.php?title=Human:34051 (all accessed April 17, 2013).

125. "Ki-Soo Kim," BoxRec, n.d., http://boxrec.com/media/index. php?title=Human:9802 (accessed April 18, 2013).

126. "Chong-Pal Park," BoxRec, n.d., http://boxrec.com/media/index.php/ Chong-Pal_Park; "Jung-Koo Chang," BoxRec, n.d., http://boxrec.com/media/ index.php/Jung-Koo_Chang; "Myung-Woo Yuh," BoxRec, n.d., http://boxrec. com/list_bouts.php?human_id=003342&cat=boxer (all accessed April 18, 2013).

127. "Joo-Hee Kim," BoxRec, n.d., http://boxrec.com/media/index. php?title=Human:186543 (accessed April 18, 2013).

128. "N. Korean Champ Becomes S. Korean," *Korean Times*, March 18, 2007, Empas News (January 2, 2008); "Masamori Tokuyama," BoxRec, n.d., http://boxrec.com/list_bouts.php?human_id=7788&cat=boxer (accessed April 18, 2013).

129. "Hiroshi Kobayashi," BoxRec, n.d., http://boxrec.com/list_bouts. php?human_id=134&cat=boxer; "Shozo Saijo," BoxRec, n.d., http://boxrec. com/list_bouts.php?human_id=31083&cat=boxer; "Masao Ohba," BoxRec, n.d., http://boxrec.com/media/index.php?title=Human:33541 (all accessed April 18, 2013).

130. "Kuniaki Shibata," BoxRec, n.d., http://boxrec.com/list_bouts. php?human_id=17589&cat=boxer; "Yoko Gushiken," BoxRec, n.d., http:// boxrec.com/list_bouts.php?human_id=51302&cat=boxer; "Jiro Watanabe," BoxRec, n.d., http://boxrec.com/list_bouts.php?human_id=51111&cat=boxer (all accessed April 18, 2013).

131. "Yutaka Niida," BoxRec, n.d., http://boxrec.com/list_bouts.php?human_ id=15211&cat=boxer (accessed April 18, 2013).

132. "Erbito Salavarria," BoxRec, n.d., http://boxrec.com/media/index. php?title=Human:20555; "Dodie Boy Penalosa," BoxRec, n.d., http://boxrec. com/media/index.php?title=Human:5498; "Jon Penalosa," BoxRec, n.d., http:// boxrec.com/list_bouts.php?human_id=4748&cat=boxer; "Gerry Penalosa," BoxRec, n.d., http://boxrec.com/media/index.php?title=Human:1782 (all accessed April 19, 2013).

133. "Luisito Espinosa," BoxRec, n.d., http://boxrec.com/media/index. php?title=Human:460; "Nonito Donaire," BoxRec, n.d., http://boxrec.com/media/index.php?title=Human:48243 (both accessed April 19, 2013).

134. "Manny Pacquiao," BoxRec, n.d., http://boxrec.com/media/index. php?title=Human:6129#World_Titles; BoxRec, n.d., "Manny Pacquiao," http://boxrec.com/list_bouts.php?human_id=006129&cat=boxer; "Manny Pacquiao," Bio.com, n.d., http://www.biography.com/people/manny-pacquiao-20851009?page=2; quotes from "Manny Pacquiao," Internet Movie Database, n.d., http://www.imdb.com/name/nm1301525/bio (all accessed April 19, 2013).

Chapter 6: Religion

1. David Dee, "'The Hefty Hebrew': Boxing and British-Jewish Identity, 1890–1960," *Sport in History* 32, no. 3 (September 2012): 361–81.

2. Douglas Century, *Barney Ross* (New York: Schocken Books, 2006), 32.

3. Pierce Egan, *Boxiana, Vol. 1*(Scott Noble, ed., London: G. Smeeton, 1812, Nicol Island Pub., 1997), 87–92, 219–22, 224, 229–30, 241, quote, 226; Dennis Brailsford, "Morals and Maulers: the Ethics of Early Pugilism," *Journal of Sport History* 12, no. 2 (Summer 1985): 136; "Daniel Mendoza," Answers.com, n.d., http://www.answers.com/topic/daniel-mendoza (accessed March 20, 2013).

4. Brailsford, "Morals and Maulers," 139 (quote); Egan, *Boxiana*, 7, 241; "Daniel Mendoza," Answers.com.

5. Egan, *Boxiana*, 217–18 (quote), 236–40; "Daniel Mendoza," Answers.com.

6. Egan, *Boxiana*, 266–68, 277–90, 295; "Dutch Sam," International Boxing Hall of Fame, n.d., http://www.ibhof.com/pages/about/inductees/pioneer/samdutch.html; "Young Dutch Sam," International Boxing Hall of Fame, n.d., http://www.ibhof.com/pages/about/inductees/pioneer/samyoungdutch.html (both accessed March 20, 2013).

7. Rob Snell, "Belasco, Aby," Boxing Biographies, June 1, 2009, http://boxingbiographies.com/bio/index.php?option=com_content&task=view&id=322&Itemid=27 (accessed April 22, 2013).

8. Snell, "Belasco, Aby."

9. "Barney Aaron," International Boxing Hall of Fame, n.d., http://www.ibhof.com/pages/about/inductees/pioneer/aaronbarney.html; "Young Barney Aaron," International Boxing Hall of Fame, n.d., http://www.ibhof.com/pages/about/inductees/pioneer/aaronyoungbarney.html (both accessed March 20, 2013).

10. Gerald R. Gems, *Windy City Wars: Labor, Leisure, and Sport in the Making of Chicago* (Lanham, MD; Scarecrow Press, 1997), 34, 112–13; Ronald H. Bayor, *Neighbors in Conflict: The Irish, Germans, Jews, and Italians of New York City, 1929–1941* (Baltimore: Johns Hopkins Press, 1978).

11. Quotes from Dee, "'The Hefty Hebrew,'" 373 and 374 respectively.

12. Dee, "'The Hefty Hebrew,'" 375–77.

13. Doriane Gomet, "Survival Strategy or Bloody Violence? Boxing in Concentration and Extermination Camps," paper presented at the North American Society for Sport History Conference, Halifax, Canada, May 25, 2013.

14. Ken Blady, *Jewish Boxers' Hall of Fame* (New York: Shapolsky Pub., 1988), 54–62; Peter Levine, "'Oy Such a Fighter!': Boxing and the American Jewish Experience," in S. W. Pope, ed. *The New American Sport History: Recent Approaches and Perspectives* (Urbana: University of Illinois Press, 1997), 251–83; "Charley Goldman," BoxRec, n.d., http://boxrec.com/list_bouts.php?human_id=052597&cat=boxer&pageID=2 (accessed April 24, 2013).

15. Steve Mills, "Vending Violence in a '38-Caliber Circulation Drive,'" *Chicago Tribune*, June 8, 1997, http://articles.chicagotribune.com/1997-06-08/

news/9706300093_1_walter-h-annenberg-circulation-william-randolph-hearst (accessed April 25, 2013).

16. Louis Wirth, *The Ghetto* (Chicago: University of Chicago Press, 1956, 1928), 176.

17. *Chicago Hebrew Institute Observer* 1:3 (February 1913), 5–6 (quote); *Observer* 1:4 (March 1913).

18. Gerald R. Gems, "Sport and the Forging of a Jewish-American Culture: The Chicago Hebrew Institute," *Journal of American Jewish History* 83 (March 1995): 15–26; *Chicago Hebrew Institute Observer*,1:2 (December 1912), 23; 1:3 (February 1913), 4–6; , 1:6 (May 1913), 10; 1:7 (June 1913), 27; "Danny Goodman," BoxRec, n.d., http://boxrec.com/media/index.php?title=Human:52418 (accessed April 20, 2013); J. J. Johnston and Sean Curtin, *Chicago Boxing* (Chicago: Arcadia, 2005), 33.

19. Interview with Judge Abraham Lincoln Marovitz, December 10, 1990.

20. Levine, "Oy Such a Fighter!' 251–83, quote, 256.

21. Levine "Oy Such a Fighter!'" 257.

22. Frederic M. Thrasher, *The Gang: A Study of 1,313 Gangs in Chicago* (Chicago: University of Chicago Press, 1927), 45–48, 126, 150 (quote), 126; P. E. Burkholder, "The Gang Leader," in Ernest W. Burgess Papers, University of Chicago Special Collections, Box 128, folder 1; Steven Riess, "A Fighting Chance: The Jewish American Boxing Experience, 1890–1940," *American Jewish History* 74, no. 3 (March 1985): 223–54; Barney Ross and Martin Abramson, *No Man Stands Alone: The True Story of Barney Ross* (New York: J.B. Lippincott, 1957), 38–39, 57.

23. S. Kirson Weinberg, "Jewish Youth in the Lawndale Community: A Sociological Study," in Ernest W. Burgess Papers, University of Chicago, Box 139, folder 3; Ross and Abramson, *No Man Stands Alone*, 77, 87, 92, 96–97; Blady, *Jewish Boxers' Hall of Fame*, 90–96; Johnston and Curtin, *Chicago Boxing*, 70; "A Look Back: King Levinsky," The Jewish Boxing Blog, June 20, 2011, http://jewishboxing.blogspot.com/2011/06/look-back-king-levinsky.html (accessed April 24, 2013); "King Levinsky, BoxRec, n.d., http://boxrec.com/list_bouts.php?human_id=012076&cat=boxer (accessed April 24, 2013); Jeffrey T. Sammons, *Beyond the Ring: The Role of Boxing in American Society* (Urbana: University of Illinois Press, 1988), 92. See P. E. Burkholder, June 10, 1929, "The Gang Leader," in Burgess Papers, University of Chicago, Box 128, folder 1, on intimidation by gangs in Jewish neighborhoods.

24. "Dana Rosenblatt," BoxRec, n.d., http://boxrec.com/list_bouts.php?human_id=4465&cat=boxer (accessed April 25, 2013); "Biography," Dmitriy Salita Official Website, n.d., http://www.dsalita.com/?c=17 (June 3, 2013).

25. "Nat Fleischer," International Boxing Hall of Fame, n.d., http://www.ibhof.com/pages/about/inductees/nonparticipant/fleischer.html (accessed April 25, 2013).

26. Gems, "Sport and the Forging of a Jewish-American Culture," 26.

27. "Frawley Act," BoxRec, n.d., http://boxrec.com/media/index.php/Frawley_Act (accessed April 26, 2013); Tony Mason and Eliza Riedi, *Sport and the Military: The British Armed Forces, 1880–1960* (New York: Cambridge University Press, 2010), 108–109.

28. "Walker Law," BoxRec, n.d., http://boxrec.com/media/index.php/Walker_Law (accessed April 26, 2013); Thomas B. Littlewood, *Arch: A Promoter, Not a Poet: The Story of Arch Ward* (Ames: Iowa State University Press, 1990), 37–39.

29. Robert E. Park, Ernest Burgess, and Roderick D. McKenzie, *The City* (Chicago: University of Chicago Press, 1925), 112.

30. Gerald R. Gems, "The Politics of Boxing: Resistance, Religion, and Working Class Assimilation," *International Sports Journal* 8, no. 1 (Winter 2004): 89–103; Bayor, *Neighbors in Conflict*, 87–90; Charles Shanabruch, "The Catholic Church's Role in the Americanization of Ethnic Groups," PhD dissertation, University of Chicago, 1975; Edward R. Kantowicz, "Cardinal Mundelein of Chicago and the Shaping of Twentieth-Century American Catholicism," *Journal of American History* 68 (June 1981): 52–69; John T. McGreevy, *Parish Boundaries: The Catholic Encounter with Race in the Twentieth-Century Urban North* (Chicago: University of Chicago Press, 1996), 7–8, 13–15, 61 (quote). See *New World*, November 9, 1929, 4, cited in Arthur W. Thurner, "The Impact of Ethnic Groups on the Democratic Party in Chicago," PhD dissertation, University of Chicago, 1966, 344, on the Catholic resentment over the 1928 election.

31. Gems, *Windy City Wars*, 159, 191; *New World*, December 8, 1933, 13, and March 23, 1934, 13; Johnston and Curtin, *Chicago Boxing*, 68, 77; Littlewood, *Arch*, 79 (quote).

32. Littlewood, *Arch*, 49–58, 79–84; program, *Intercity Boxing: Third Annual Meeting of Golden Champions and Runner-up*, March 19, 1930, Chicago History Museum.

33. Bishop Bernard J. Sheil, ed., *C.Y.O. Survey* 2, no. 6 (June 1953), 8.

34. Program, *1st Annual Boxing Tournament* (Chicago: CYO, 1931), 1, 2, 7, Chicago Archdiocese Archives; *New World*, February 6, 1931, 9; February 20, 1931, 1, 11; November 10, 1933, 14; November 17, 1933, 15; and November 24, 1933, 14; Roger L. Treat, *Bishop Sheil and the CYO* (New York: Julian Messner, Inc., 1951), 59–78; Johnston and Curtin, *Chicago Boxing*, 71–73. For the evolution of the CYO and its forerunner at Visitation parish, see *New World*, June 6,

1930, 10, 16; June 20, 1930, 10; December 19, 1930, 65; and February 20, 1931, 1, 8, 11; as well as Gems, "Selling Sport and Religion in American Society," 303, and Ellen Skerett, "The Catholic Dimension," in Lawrence J. Mc Caffrey, et al., *The Irish in Chicago* (Urbana: University of Illinois Press, 1987), 22–60.

35. *New World*, February 2, 1934, 14, and February 9, 1934, 15; speech, 13th Annual Convention of the National Council of Catholic Men, Chicago, 1933, in Sheil Papers, Chicago Historical Society; Edward R. Kantowicz, *Corporation Sole: Cardinal Mundelein and Chicago Catholicism* (Notre Dame, IN: University of Notre Dame Press, 1983), 181–82; quote from program, *Silver Episcopal Jubilee*, 1934, n.p..

36. *New World*, February 9, 1934, 15.

37. Quote is from WMAQ radio address, December 1, 1931, in undated speeches, Box 1, file 1, 1931–1943 of Sheil Papers, Chicago History Museum; *Facts on the CYO*, n.d.; Herb Graffis, "Father of the CYO," reprint from *Esquire*, July 1942, in Sheil Papers, Chicago Historical Society.

38. McGreevy, *Parish Boundaries*, 8, 43–48.

39. *New World*, November 29, 1935, 10; a photo of fifteen different nationalities represented among the CYO boxers was included in *New World*, November 20, 1936, 12.

40. Treat, *Bishop Sheil and the CYO*, 65–119, 136; Littlewood, *Arch*, 47–52, 80–81; Lucy P. Carner, report of interview with Fr. Peter D. Meegan, February 9, 1939, Municipal Welfare Council Papers; John J. Romano, ed., *Post Boxing Record, 1937* (New York: John J. Romano, 1937), 35–44; *9th International Golden Gloves Program, Champions of Europe vs. Champions of Chicagoland*, April 10, 1940; *Chicago Tribune*, program, *37th Annual Golden Gloves Finals*, February 28, 1964, 18; *Chicago American*, October 29, 1935, 20; *New World*, February 29, 1934, 15; NBC, *This Fight Should Have Been Broadcast*, n.d. On identity construction, see Karen A. Cerulo, "Identity Construction: New Issues, New Directions," *Annual Review of Sociology* 23 (1997): 385–409; and Deborah E. S. Frable, "Gender, Racial, Ethnic, Sexual, and Call Identities," *Annual Review of Psychology* 48 (1997): 139–62.

41. *Chicago Tribune*, November 25, 1937, 37; Gems, *The Politics of Boxing*, 96; Gems, "Selling Sport and Religion in American Society," 305; quote from Bishop Bernard J. Sheil's address, 8th Anniversary Boxing Show, 1937, in Sheil Papers, Box 1, folder 5.

42. Lizabeth Cohen, *Making a New Deal: Industrial Workers in Chicago, 1919–1939* (New York: Cambridge University Press, 1990), 252–53, 261–67; Mark Naison, "Righties and Lefties: The Communist Party and Sports During the Great Depression," *Radical America* 13 (July–August 1979): 47–59; William J. Baker, "Muscular Marxism and the Chicago Counter-Olympics of 1932," *Inter-*

national Journal of the History of Sport 9, no. 3 (December 1992): 397–410; Bayor, *Neighbors in Conflict*, 40–41, 85–90; Quintin Hoare and Geoffrey N. Smith, eds., *Selections from the Prison Notebooks of Antonio Gramsci* (New York: International Publishers, 1971), 3–6, 57–59.

43. Program, Silver Episcopal Jubilee of His Excellency, the Most Reverend Bernard J. Sheil, D.D. (April 29, 1953); *Chicago Daily News*, December 5, 1944, clipping, from scrapbook, Box 3, Sheil Papers, Catholic Archdiocese of Chicago Archives.

44. "Mustafa Hamsho," BoxRec, n.d., http://boxrec.com/list_bouts. php?human_id=857&cat=boxer; "Muhammad Rachman," BoxRec, n.d., http://boxrec.com/list_bouts.php?human_id=016905&cat=boxer; "Naseem Hamed," BoxRec, n.d., http://boxrec.com/list_bouts.php?human_id=004462&cat=boxer; "Amir Khan," BoxRec, n.d., http://boxrec.com/media/index.php?title=Human:314558 (all accessed April 30, 2013).

45. "Dwight Muhammad Qawi," BoxRec, n.d., http://boxrec.com/media/index.php?title=Human:325 (accessed April 30, 2013).

46. "Nation of Islam," Southern Poverty Law Center, n.d., http://www.splcenter.org/get-informed/intelligence-files/groups/nation-of-islam; "Which Celebrities Have Converted to Islam?" Beliefnet, n.d., http://www.beliefnet.com/Entertainment/Celebrities/Galleries/Which-Celebrities-Have-Converted-to-Islam.aspx?p=3 (both accessed April 30, 2013).

47. "Anthony Mundine," Answers.com, n.d., http://www.answers.com/topic/anthony-mundine (accessed June 3, 2013); "Anthony Mundine," BoxRec, n.d., http://boxrec.com/media/index.php?title=Human:14646#Facts (accessed April 30, 2013); Michael Silk, *The Cultural Politics of Post–9/11 American Sport: Power, Pedagogy, and the Popular* (New York: Routledge, 2012), 135–36.

48. Supriya Chaudhuri, "In the Ring: Gender, Spectatorship, and the Body," *International Journal of the History of Sport* 29, no. 12 (August 2012): 1759–73); Payoshni Mitra, "Challenging Stereotypes: The Case of Muslim Female Boxers in Bengal," *International Journal of the History of Sport* 26, no. 112 (September 2009): 1840–51, quote, 1845.

49. Mitra, "Challenging Stereotypes."

Chapter Seven: Gender

1. Judith Lorber, "'Night to His Day': The Social Construction of Gender," in Paula S. Rothenberg, ed., *Race, Class, and Gender in the United States: An Integrated Study* (New York: Worth Pub., 2007), 54–64; Judith Butler, *Gender Trouble: Feminism and the Subversion of Identity* (New York: Routledge, 1990).

2. Jan Dunzendorfer, "The Early Days of Boxing in Accra: A Sport Is Taking Root," *International Journal of the History of Sport* 28, no. 15 (October 2011), 2154; Allen Guttmann, *Sports: The First Five Millennia* (Amherst: University of Massachusetts Press, 2004), 220; Jeonguk Kim, "Fighting Men and Fighting Women: American Prizefighting and the Contested Gender Order in the Late Nineteenth and Early Twentieth Centuries," *Sport History Review* 43 (2012), 105 (quote). There is an extensive and growing amount of literature on masculinity. See such early works as Elliott Gorn, *The Manly Art: Bare-Knuckle Prize Fighting in America* (Ithaca, NY: Cornell University Press, 1986); E. Anthony Rotundo, *American Manhood: Transformations in Masculinity from the Revolution to the Modern Era* (New York: Basic Books, 1993); Mark C. Carnes and Clyde Griffen, eds., *Meanings for Manhood: Constructions of Masculinity in Victorian America* (Chicago: University of Chicago Press, 1990); Peter Stearns, *Be a Man! Males in Modern Society* (New York: Holmes & Meier, 1979); Joseph and Elizabeth Pleck, eds., *The American Man* (Englewood Cliffs, NJ: Prentice-Hall, 1980); Joe L. Dubbert, *A Man's Place: Masculinity in Transition* (Englewood Cliffs, NJ: Prentice-Hall, 1979); and Gail Bederman, *Manliness and Civilization: A Cultural History of Gender and Race in the United States, 1880–1917* (Chicago: University of Chicago Press, 1995).

3. Michael S. Kimmel, *The History of Men: Essays in the History of American and British Masculinities* (Albany: State University of New York Press, 2005). There is a wealth of scholarly literature on the ramifications of the industrial process. See Thomas Dublin, *Women at Work: The Transformation of Work and Community in Lowell, Massachusetts, 1826–1860* (New York: Cambridge University Press, 1983); Bruce Laurie, *Working People of Philadelphia, 1800–1850* (Philadelphia: Temple University Press, 1980); Daniel T. Rodgers, *The Work Ethic in Industrial America, 1850–1920* (Chicago: University of Chicago Press, 1978); and Francis G. Couvares, *The Remaking of Pittsburgh: Class and Culture in an Industrializing City, 1877–1919* (Albany: State University of New York Press, 1984).

4. Ann Douglas, *The Feminization of American Culture* (New York: Alfred A. Knopf, 1977); Gerald R. Gems, Linda Borish, and Gertrud Pfister, *Sports in American History: From Colonization to Globalization* (Champaign, IL: Human Kinetics, 2008), 71–82, 165–70, 179–81, quote, 82.

5. "Carrie Nation," Alcohol: Problem and Solutions, n.d., http://www2.potsdam.edu/hansondj/Controversies/Biography-Carry-Nation.html (accessed May 3, 2013); Kim, "Fighting Men and Fighting Women," 112; Andrew M. Kaye, *The Pussycat of Prizefighting: Tiger Flowers and the Politics of Black Celebrity* (Athens: University of Georgia Press, 2004), 45, cites the *Atlanta Constitution*, December 11, 1912, 4 in the case of Worthy.

6. Barbara Holland, *Gentlemen's Blood: A History of Dueling from Swords at Dawn to Pistols at Dusk* (New York: Bloomsbury, 2003); Gorn, *The Manly Art.*

7. Kim, "Fighting Men and Fighting Women," 109; Gerald Early, *The Culture of Bruising: Essays on Prizefighting, Literature, and Modern American Culture* (Hopewell, NJ: Ecco Press, 1994), 3; Robert G. Rodriguez, *The Regulation of Boxing: A History and Comparative Analysis of Policies among American States* (Jefferson, NC: McFarland & Co., 2009), 87; Pierce Egan, *Boxiana, Vol. 1* (Scott Noble, ed., London: G. Smeeton, 1812, Nicol Island Pub., 1997), 47; Mark Kriegel, *The Good Son: The Life of Ray "Boom Boom" Mancini* (New York: Free Press 2012), 97–8, 126–38; Scott, *The Art and Aesthetics of Boxing* (Lincoln: University of Nebraska Press, 2008), 7; David L. Hudson, Jr., *Boxing in America: An Autopsy* (Santa Barbara, CA: ABC-CLIO, 2012); Benita Heiskanen, *The Urban Geography of Boxing: Race, Class, and Gender in the Ring* (New York: Routledge, 2012), 53; Oates quoted in Kath Woodward, "Rumbles in the Jungle: Boxing, Racialization and the Performance of Masculinity," *Leisure Studies* 23, no. 1 (January 2004): 5–17 (quote, 8).

8. Justin D. Garcia, "Rising from the Canvas: Issues of Immigration, Redemption, Gender, and Mexican American Identity in *Split Decision* and *In Her Corner*," in Zachary Ingle and David M. Sutera, eds., *Identity and Myth in Sports Documentaries: Critical Essays* (Lanham, MD: Scarecrow Press, 2013), 63–78.

9. Heiskanen, *Urban Geography of Boxing*, 42, cites George Bennett and Pete Hamill, *Fighters* (Doubleday, 1978).

10. Heiskanen, *Urban Geography of Boxing*, 26.

11. All quotes are derived from Kriegel, *The Good Son*, 117, 118, 142, 165, respectively.

12. Scott, *Art and Aesthetics of Boxing*, 138.

13. John Saraceno, "Gay Boxer Orlando Cruz Struggled with Coming Out," USA Today, October 18, 2012, http://www.usatoday.com/story/sports/boxing/2012/10/18/orlando-cruz-gay-boxer/1642373/; "Spiegel Interview with Orlando Cruz: 'I Couldn't Accept Being Gay Because I Was Too Afraid,'" Spiegel Online International, November 9, 2012, http://www.spiegel.de/international/world/interview-with-first-openly-gay-boxer-orlando-cruz-a-866052.html; Andy Towle, "Boxer Orlando Cruz Wins Second Match Since Coming Out While Wearing Rainbow Kilt As Sign of Gay Pride," Towleroad, March 16, 2013, http://www.towleroad.com/2013/03/boxer-orlando-cruz-wins-2nd-match-since-coming-out-while-wearing-rainbow-kilt-as-sign-of-gay-pride.html (all accessed May 4, 2013).

14. Allen Guttmann, *Women's Sports: A History* (New York: Columbia University Press, 1991), 74–75 (quote, 75).

15. Roberta J. Park, "Contesting the Norm: Women and Professional Sports in Late Nineteenth-Century America," *International Journal of the History of Sport* 29, no. 5 (April 2012): 730–49; Guttmann, *First Five Millennia*, 73. *Daily Post*, October 7, 1728, quoted in Guttmann, *Women's Sports*, 75.

16. Park, "Contesting the Norm," 733–34; the quote is from Jennifer Hargreaves, "Women's Boxing and Related Activities: Introducing Images and Meanings," *InYo: Journal of Alternative Perspectives* (September 2001), n.p. (article in author's collection).

17. Guttmann, *Women's Sports*, 76, cites the *Times*, March 24, 1807.

18. Kim, "Fighting Men and Fighting Women," 117–18.

19. Gerald R. Gems, *Windy City Wars: Labor, Leisure, and Sport in the Making of Chicago* (Lanham, MD; Scarecrow Press, 1997), 15.

20. Park, "Contesting the Norm," 740–41.

21. Guttmann, *Women's Sports*, 100–1; Park, "Contesting the Norm," 741; Kim, "Fighting Men and Fighting Women,"118; Guy Reel, *The National Police Gazette and the Making of the Modern American Man, 1879–1906* (New York: Palgrave Macmillan, 2006), 4, 136.

22. Kim, "Fighting Men and Fighting Women," 118.

23. Kate Sekules, *The Boxer's Heart: How I Fell in Love with the Ring* (New York: Villard, 2000), 57; Kim, "Fighting Men and Fighting Women," 118–19 (quote, 119).

24. Kim, "Fighting Men and Fighting Women," 119–120 (quote, 120).

25. Kim, "Fighting Men and Fighting Women," 119–120; quotes from Park, "Contesting the Norm," 741.

26. Chris Cozzone and Jim Boggio, *Boxing in New Mexico, 1868–1940* (Jefferson, NC: McFarland, 2013), 332.

27. Gail Bederman, *Manliness and Civilization*, 15.

28. Gems, Borish, and Pfister, *Sports in American History*, 189–92, 217; David L. Chapman, *Sandow the Magnificent: Eugen Sandow and the Beginnings of Bodybuilding* (Urbana: University of Illinois Press, 1994); Robert Ernst, *Weakness is a Crime: The Life of Bernarr Macfadden* (Syracuse, NY: University of Syracuse Press, 1991); John F. Kasson, *Houdini, Tarzan, and the Perfect Man: The White Male Body and the Challenge of Modernity in America* (New York: Hill and Wang, 2001).

29. Reel, *The National Police Gazette*, 112–15; quotes from Kim, "Fighting Men and Fighting Women," 108.

30. Dan Streible, *Fight Pictures: A History of Boxing and Early Cinema* (Berkeley: University of California Press, 2008), 81–90, 81 (quote); Kim, "Fighting Men and Fighting Women," 115–16.

31. Michael T. Isenberg, *John L. Sullivan and His America* (Urbana: University of Illinois Press, 1988), 248–53; Streible, *Fight Pictures*, 86; Kim, "Fighting Men and Fighting Women," 113–15 (quote, 115).

32. Kaye, *Pussycat of Prizefighting*, 44, 163; Streible, *Fight Pictures*, 174, gives a figure of 200 women at the Gans-Nelson affair, while Kim, "Fighting Men and Fighting Women," 115, states that 1,500 were present.

33. Streible, *Fight Pictures*, 85, 172–76, 231, 279; David Levinson, Stan Shipley, and Edward R. Beauchamp, "Boxing," in David Levinson and Karen Christensen, eds., *World Sport*, vol. 1 (Great Barrington, MA: Berkshire Publishing Group, 2005), 245.

34. Kim, Fighting Men and Fighting Women," 117, cites "Punish Your Insulter," *Washington Post*, August 31, 1890.

35. *Atlanta Constitution*, February 10, 1895, 6, in Kaye, *Pussycat of Prizefighting*, 163: Kim "Fighting Men and Fighting Women, 117, cites "And Now It's the Boxing Girl," *New York Times*, September 25, 1904.

36. Hargreaves, "Women's Boxing and Related Activities," n.p. (quote); Sekules, *Boxer's Heart*, 58.

37. Kim, "Fighting Men and Fighting Women," 121; quote from T. S. Andrews, *Ring Battles of Centuries and Sporting Almanac* (Tom Andrews Record Book Co., 1924), 33.

38. Irene Gammel, "Lacing Up the Gloves: Women, Boxing, and Modernity," *Cultural and Social History* 9, no. 3 (2012): 369–89 (quote, 369); Sekules, *Boxer's Heart*, 58.

39. Hargreaves, "Women's Boxing and Related Activities," cites H. C. Norris, "She Wants to FIGHT Jack Dempsey," *Japan Times and Mail*, October 3, 1926, 6.

40. Jennifer Hargreaves, "Women's Boxing and Related Activities: Introducing Images and Meanings," *Body and Society* 3, no. 4 (1997), 37.

41. See Erik N. Jensen, *Body by Weimar: Athletes, Gender, and German Modernity* (New York: Oxford University Press, 2010); David Bathrick, "Max Schmeling on the Canvas: Boxing as an Icon of Weimar Culture," *New German Critique* 51 (1990), 113–36; and Knud Kohr and Martin Krauss, *Kampftage: Die Geschichte des deutschen Berufsboxens* (Gottingen: Verlag Die Werkstatt GmbH, 2000), 235–37, for particular developments in Germany. Gammel, "Lacing Up the Gloves," 371–76 (quote, 371).

42. Gammel, "Lacing Up the Gloves, 383–85; Emily Wortis Leider, *Becoming Mae West* (New York: Farrar, Straus and Giroux, 1997), 220–21; Jill Watts, *Mae West: An Icon in Black and White* (New York: Oxford University Press, 2001), 207–8; "Victor McLaglen," BoxRec, n.d., http://boxrec.com/media/index.php?title=Human:11644 (accessed May 8, 2013); MarcD, "Clara Bow vs. Mae

West Classic Era Boxing Match, ReoCities, October 15, 2000, http://reocities. com/Area51/realm/9566/bow_west.html (accessed February 2, 2013).

43. MarcD, "Clara Bow vs. Mae West."

44. Gems, Borish, and Pfister, *Sports in American History*, 248–50; Martha H. Verbrugge, *Active Bodies: A History of Women's Physical Education in Twentieth-Century America* (New York: Oxford University Press, 2012).

45. The veracity of the match is suspect, as Hollywood gossip columnists reported the altercation took place on April Fool's Day 1927, although Bow refers to her own boxing credentials and the match in an unpublished biography. Joshua Zeitz, *Flapper: A Madcap Story of Sex, Style, Celebrity, and the Women Who Made America Modern* (New York: Crown, 2006), 235–43, 260–64, 279–81; Watts, *Mae West*, 9, 207–8; Leider, *Becoming Mae West*, 220–21 (quote, 221). See Peter Heller, *"In This Corner . . .!: 42 World Champions Tell Their Stories* (New York: Da Capo Press, 1994), 206, on West's financial assistance to Henry Armstrong in his early career.

46. Richard V. McGehee, "Boxing, Latin America," in John Nauright and Charles Parrish, eds., *Sports around the World: History, Culture, and Practice*, http://ebooks.abc-clio.com/print.aspx?isbn=9781598843019&id=A1884C_V3-1205 (accessed August 4, 2012); George Plimpton, *Shadow Box* (New York: Berkley Books, 1977), 72; Hargreaves, "Women's Boxing and Related Activities;" Levinson, Shipley, and Beauchamp, "Boxing," 245; Heiskanen, *Urban Geography of Boxing*, 91; Sekules, *Boxer's Heart*, 58.

47. Jack Hawn, "Aileen Eaton, Dynamic Boxing Promoter, Dies at 78," *Los Angeles Times*, November 9, 1987, http://articles.latimes.com/1987-11-09/ sports/sp-14600_1_southern-california-boxing (May 9, 2013); Jeffrey T. Sammons, *Beyond the Ring: The Role of Boxing in American Society* (Urbana: University of Illinois Press, 1988); quote from Mark Cram, "The Lady IS a Champ," *Sports Illustrated*, November 6, 1967, 169, http://sportsillustrated.cnn.com/vault/article/ magazine/MAG1080539/3/index.htm (accessed May 9, 2013).

48. "Jackie Kallen," AEI Speakers Bureau, n.d., http://aeispeakers.com/ speakerbio.php?SpeakerID=544; "Jackie Kallen," Jewish Virtual Library, n.d., http://www.jewishvirtuallibrary.org/jsource/biography/Jackie_Kallen.html (both accessed May 10, 2013).

49. Heiskanen, *Urban Geography of Boxing*, 136, n. 20; Sekules, *Boxer's Heart*, 14–15; Delilah Montoya, *Women Boxers: The New Warriors* (Houston: Arte Publico Press, 2006), 10; Carlo Rotella, "Good with Her Hands: Women, Boxing, and Work." *Critical Inquiry*, 25:3 (Spring 1999), 566–598; Hargreaves, "Women's Boxing and Related Activities."

50. Sekules, *Boxer's Heart*, 45, 55, 133–38; Lynn Snowden Picket, *Looking for a Fight: A Memoir* (New York: The Dial Press, 2000), 1; Heiskanen, *Urban*

Geography of Boxing, 42; quotes from Leah Hagen Cohen, *Without Apology: Girls, Women, and the Desire to Fight* (New York: Random House, 2005), 94–95.

51. Kath Woodward, "Hanging out and Hanging About: Insider/Outsider Research in the Sport of Boxing," *Ethnography* 9, no. 4 (2008): 536–61; Woodward, "Rumbles in the Jungle: Boxing, Racialization and the Performance of Masculinity," 5–17; Picket, *Looking for a Fight,* 11–35, 77, 127; Heiskanen, *Urban Geography of Boxing,* 42 (quote, 43).

52. Cohen, *Without Apology,* xiii.

53. Leslie Cove and Marisa Young, "Coaching and Athletic Career Investments: Using Organizational Theories to Explore Women's Boxing," *Annals of Leisure Research* 10, nos. 3–4 (2007): 257–71. See Garcia, "Rising from the Canvas," 74–77, on the tribulations of Marlen Esparza in her quest to make the 1912 U.S. Olympic team.

54. Montoya, *Women Boxers,* 9; Elise Paradis, "Skirting the Issue: Women Boxers, Liminality, and Change," Academia.edu, n.d., http://www.academia.edu/2211570/Skirting_the_Issue_Women_boxers_liminality_and_change (accessed February 6, 2013); Yvonne Lafferty and Jim McKay, "Suffragettes in Satin Shorts"? Gender and Competitive Boxing," *Quantitative Sociology* 27, no. 3 (Fall 2004): 249–76.

55. Sue Fox, "Dallas Malloy: She Would Not Take 'No' for an Answer," Women Boxing Archive Network, December 18, 1999, http://www.womenboxing.com/amateur.htm (accessed May 12, 2013); Heiskanen, *Urban Geography of Boxing,* 64, 91–92.

56. Montoya, *Women Boxers,* 15: Heiskanen, *Urban Geography of Boxing,* 148, n. 9, lists the International Boxing Association (IBA), International Boxing Organization (IBO), International Female Boxing Association (IFBA), International Women's Boxing Federation (IWBF), Women's International Boxing Association (WIBA), and Women's International Boxing Federation (WIBF).

57. Levinson, Shipley, and Beauchamp, "Boxing," 244; Heiskanen, *Urban Geography of Boxing,* 64, 92; Montoya, *Women Boxers,* 78; Dierdre Gogarty, Women Boxing Archive Network, n.d., http://www.wban.org/biog/dgogarty.htm (accessed May 12, 2013).

58. Montoya, *Women Boxers,* 10; Rotella, "Good with Her Hands"; Cohen, *Without Apology,* 182.

59. Montoya, *Women Boxers,* 11; Cohen, *Without Apology,* 12–13; "Ann Wolfe," BoxRec, n.d., http://boxrec.com/list_bouts.php?human_id=19247&cat=boxer (accessed May 14, 2013); quote from "Ann Wolfe," Women Boxing Archive Network, n.d., http://www.wban.org/biog/awolfe.htm (accessed May 14, 2013).

60. McGehee, "Boxing, Latin America"; "Regina Halmich," BoxRec, n.d., http://boxrec.com/list_bouts.php?human_id=5620&cat=boxer (accessed May 14,

2013); "Lucia Rijker," BoxRec, n.d., http://boxrec.com/list_bouts.php?human_id=18459&cat=boxer (accessed May 14, 2013); Montoya, *Women Boxers*, 16.

61. Picket, *Looking for a Fight*, 284–5; "Jacqui Frazier-Lyde," BoxRec, n.d., http://boxrec.com/list_bouts.php?human_id=15511&cat=boxer (accessed May 14, 2013); "Laila Ali," BoxRec, n.d., http://boxrec.com/list_bouts.php?human_id=014260&cat=boxer (accessed May 14, 2013); Edward Wong, "Women Starred, but It Was about the Men," *New York Times*, June 10, 2001, http://www.nytimes.com/2001/06/10/sports/boxing-women-starred-but-it-was-about-the-men.html?ref=lailaali (accessed May 14, 2005). Estimates of the attendance range from 6,500 to 14,000.

62. Picket, *Looking for a Fight*, 286; Stephanie Dallam, "My Sister's Story, Katie's website, n.d., http://www.kdallam.com/1/about_kd.html (accessed May 14, 2013); Rodriguez, *The Regulation of Boxing*, 60; Heiskanen, *Urban Geography of Boxing*, 53 (quote, 56). See Sekules, *Boxer's Heart*, 133–38, on the misrepresentation of women's records, as well as promoters' and managers' exploitation of fighters. Roy Dereck McCree, "The Death of a Female Boxer: Media, Sport, Nationalism, and Gender," *Journal of Sport and Social Issues* 20, no. 10 (2011):1–23 (quote, 9).

63. "Esther Phiri," BoxRec, n.d., http://boxrec.com/list_bouts.php?human_id=317544&cat=boxer (accessed May 15, 2013); Marianne Meier and Martha Saavedra, "Esther Phiri and the Moutawakel effect in Zambia: An Analysis of the Use of Female Role Models in Sport for Development," *Sport in Society* 12, no. 9 (November 2009):1158–76 (quote, 1164).

64. Jung Woo Lee, "Red Feminism and Propaganda in Communist Media: Portrayals of Female Boxers in North Korean Media," *International Review for the Sociology of Sport* 44, no. 2–3 (2009):193–211 (quotes, 202 and 205, respectively).

65. Lee, "Red Feminism and Propaganda in Communist Media," 206.

66. Paradis, "Skirting the Issue;" Cathy van Ingen and Nicole Kovacs, "Subverting the Skirt: Female Boxers' 'Troubling' Uniforms," *Feminist Media Studies* 12, no. 3 (2012): 460–63 (quote, 460).

67. Quotes from Van Ingen and Kovacs, "Subverting the Skirt," 463; Katharina Lindner, "Women's Boxing at the 2012 Olympics: Gender Trouble?" *Feminist Media Studies* 12, no. 3 (2012):464–67.

68. Christine Menneson, "'Hard' Women and 'Soft' Women: The Social Construction of Identities among Female Boxers," *International Review for the Sociology of Sport* 35, no. 1 (2000): 21–33.

69. Lafferty and McKay, "Suffragettes in Satin Shorts," 271.

70. Hargreaves, "Women's Boxing and Related Activities."

71. Cathy van Ingen, "Spatialities of Anger: Emotional Geographies in a Boxing Program for Survivors of Violence," *Sociology of Sport Journal* 28, no. 2 (June 2011): 171–88 (quote, 185).

72. Quote from Picket, *Looking for a Fight*, 69; Cohen, *Without Apology*, 48; Heiskanen, *Urban Geography of Boxing*, 11.

73. Dawn Bray, suburban survey respondent.

74. Comments by Tatiana M. and Bea M., 8 Count Boxing Gym reviews, http://www.yelp.com/biz/8-count-boxing-gym-chicago (accessed May 16, 2013).

75. Tatyana McCool interview; "Tatyana McCool 2011 National Champ," YouTube, n.d., http://www.youtube.com/results?search_query=Tatyana+McCool (accessed May 16, 2013).

76. Tiffany Perez interview.

77. "The First of Many Successful Fights to Come," CYBC Blog, n.d., http://chicagoyouthboxingclub.org/the-first-of-many-successful-fights (accessed January 16, 2013).

78. Elena Ferrarin, "Rolling with the Punches," *Fra Noi*, July 2012, 31.

79. Comment by Amy W., Ultimate Fitness Gym review, http://www.yelp.com/biz/ultimate-fitness-evanston (accessed January 26, 2013).

80. Ittzell Perez, Chicago Youth Boxing Club, www.chicagoyouth boxingclub.com (accessed January 25, 2013).

81. Hong and Luna quotes from Gym Member Testimonials, Jab Fitness Training, n.d., http://www.jabfitnesstraining.com/testimonials.html (accessed January 22, 2013).

82. Shelly Pratt interview.

Chapter 8: Conclusions

1. Hauser, *Black Lights*, cited in Benita Heiskanen, *The Urban Geography of Boxing: Race, Class, and Gender in the Ring* (New York: Routledge, 2012), 44.

2. Heiskanen, *Urban Geography of Boxing*, 2, 47–48 (quotes, 48); David L. Hudson, Jr., *Boxing in America: An Autopsy* (Santa Barbara, CA: Praeger, 2012), 152–53. The Professional Boxing Safety Act of 1996 requires minimal standards such as a medical exam, some health insurance (but not for club fighters), and that medical personnel and an ambulance be on hand at boxing sites. The 2000 Muhammad Ali Boxing Reform Act stipulates contract and fee disclosures to avoid exploitation of boxers, but few have the access or education necessary for adequate legal interpretation.

3. Teddy Atlas, commentary, ESPN2 Boxing, January 11, 2013.

4. "Jerry Quarry," BoxRec, n.d., http://boxrec.com/media/index. php?title=Human:9385 (accessed May 17, 2013); Lynn Snowden Picket, *Looking for a Fight: A Memoir* (New York: The Dial Press, 2000), 276–83; Ken Jones, "A Key Moral Issue: Should Boxing Be Banned?" *Culture, Sport, Society* 4, no. 1 (Spring 2001): 63–72, indicates 41 percent of amateurs have abnormal brain scans.

5. Hauser, *Black Lights*, 13–14, cited in Heiskanen, *Urban Geography of Boxing*, 19.

6. Both quotes from Hudson, *Boxing in America*, 108.

7. Hudson, *Boxing in America*, 116–18 (quote, 118); "Joe Grim," BoxRec, n.d., http://boxrec.com/list_bouts.php?human_id=10815&cat=boxer (accessed May 17, 2013).

8. Hudson, *Boxing in America*, 110–15; "Bruce Strauss," BoxRec, n.d., http://boxrec.com/list_bouts.php?human_id=2222&cat=boxer; "Simmie Black," BoxRec, n.d., http://boxrec.com/media/index.php?title=Human:20906 (both accessed May 18, 2013).

9. "Obie Garnett," BoxRec, n.d., http://boxrec.com/list_bouts.php?human_id=28881&cat=boxer; "Sylvester Wilder," BoxRec, n.d., http://boxrec.com/list_bouts.php?human_id=2208&cat=boxer (both accessed May 19, 2013); Michael Shapiro, "Opponents," in Joyce Carol Oates and Daniel Halpern, eds., *Reading the Fights: The Best Writing About the Most Controversial Sport* (New York: Prentice Hall, 1988), 242–49.

10. Quintin Hoare and Geoffrey N. Smith, eds., *Selections from the Prison Notebooks of Antonio Gramsci* (New York: International Publishers, 1971).

11. Hudson, *Boxing in America*, 123–54; Jones, "A Key Moral Issue." Several countries have banned professional boxing, but permit amateur competition.

12. "Biography of WBC Champion Mia St. John," Mia St. John, n.d., http://www.miastjohn.com/bio.html (accessed May 18, 2013); "Mia St. John," BoxRec, n.d., http://boxrec.com/list_bouts.php?human_id=25613&cat=boxer (accessed May 18, 2013); Kelsey McCarson, "What Gives? No TV for Women's Boxing," The Sweet Science, March 6, 2013, http://www.the sweetscience.com/news/articles/16236—what-gives-no-tv-for-womens-boxing (accessed March 9, 2013).

13. Norbert Elias, *The Civilizing Process* (New York: Urizen Books, 1978); Allen Guttmann, *From Ritual to Record: The Nature of Modern Sports* (New York: Columbia University Press, 1978); Leger Grindon, *Knockout: The Boxer and Boxing in American Cinema* (Jackson: University of Mississippi Press, 2011), 189–90, 239; R. L. Jones, "A Deviant Sports Career: Towards a Sociology of Unlicensed Boxing," *Journal of Sport and Social Issues* 21, no. 1 (February 1997): 37–52.

14. Carlo Rotella, *Good with Their Hands: Boxers, Bluesmen, and Other Characters from the Rust Belt* (Berkeley, CA: University of California Press, 2002).

15. Jones, "A Key Moral Issue."

Appendix 3: Boxing Rules

1. Anna Hodgekiss, "Headgear for amateur boxers to be banned in a bid to REDUCE head injuries," *Daily Mail*, March 15, 2013, http://www.dailymail.co.uk/health/article-2293803/Headgear-boxers-banned-bid-REDUCE-head-injuries.html (accessed May 18, 2013); "Boxing Association Reveals Changes to Olympic Rules, Scoring," SI Online, March 23, 2013, http://sportsillustrated.cnn.com/mma/news/20130323/boxing-changes.ap/ (accessed May 18, 2013).

2. "Boxing Association Reveals Changes to Olympic Rules, Scoring," SI Online.

3. "The Difference between Men's and Women's Boxing Rules," Insidewomensboxing.com, June 20, 2011, http://www.insidewomensboxing.com/2011/06/20/the-differences-between-mens-and-womens-boxing-rules/ (accessed May 18, 2013).

BIBLIOGRAPHY

Books and Articles

Abreu, Christina D. "The Story of Benny 'Kid' Paret: Cuban Boxers, the Cuban Revolution, and the U.S. Media, 1959–1962." *Journal of Sport History* 38, no. 1 (Spring 2011): 95–113.

Adelman, Melvin L. *A Sporting Time: New York City and the Rise of Modern Athletics, 1820–1870*. Urbana: University of Illinois Press, 1986.

———. "Pedestrianism, Boxing, Billiards and Animal Sports," in David K. Wiggins, ed., *Sport in America: From Colonial Leisure to Celebrity Figures and Globalization*. Champaign, IL: Human Kinetics, 2010, 45–83.

Alfonso, Barry. "Corbett, James John," in Arnold Markoe, ed., *The Scribner Encyclopedia of American Lives: Sports Figures*. New York: Charles Scribner's Sons, 2002, 193–95.

Allen, Theodore W. *The Invention of the White Race: Racial Oppression and Social Control*. London: Verso, 1998.

Altherr, Thomas L. *Sports in North America: A Documentary History, Vol. 1, Part I: Sports in the Colonial Era, 1618–1673*. Gulf Breeze, FL: Academic International Press, 1997.

Amerman, Don. "Leonard, Ray Charles ("Sugar Ray"), in Arnold Markoe, ed., *The Scribner Encyclopedia of American Lives: Sports Figures*. New York: Charles Scribner's Sons, 2002, 34–36.

Anderson, Chris, and Sharon McGehee, with Jake La Motta. *Raging Bull II*. Secaucus, NJ: Lyle Stuart, Inc., 1986.

Anderson, Dave. "Sports of the Times: Referee's Count Is What Counts." *New York Times*, February 12, 1990.

BIBLIOGRAPHY

Andrews, T. S., ed. *Ring Battles of Centuries and Sporting Almanac.* Tom Andrews Record Book Co., 1924.

——. *World Sporting Annual Record Book, 1926.* Milwaukee: n.p., 1926.

Appy, Christian G. *Working-Class War: American Combat Soldiers and Vietnam.* Chapel Hill: University of North Carolina Press, 1993.

Arnold, James R. *The Moro War: How America Battled a Muslim Insurgency in the Philippine Jungle, 1902–1913.* New York: Bloomsbury Press, 2011.

Aycock, Colleen, and Mark Scott. *Joe Gans: A Biography of the First African American World Boxing Champ.* Jefferson, NC: McFarland & Co., 2008.

——, eds. *The First Black Boxing Champions: Essays on Fighters in the 1800s to the 1920s.* Jefferson, NC: McFarland & Co., 2011.

Baker, Lee D. *From Savage to Negro: Anthropology and the Construction of Race, 1896–1954.* Berkeley: University of California Press, 1998.

Baker, William J. "Muscular Marxism and the Chicago Counter-Olympics of 1932." *International Journal of the History of Sport*, 9, no. 3 (December 1992): 397–410.

Bathrick, David. "Max Schmeling on the Canvas: Boxing as an Icon of Weimar Culture." *New German Critique* 51 (1990): 113–36.

Bayor, Ronald H. *Neighbors in Conflict: The Irish, Germans, Jews, and Italians of New York City, 1929–1941.* Baltimore: Johns Hopkins Press, 1978.

Bazzano, Carmelo. "The Italian-American Sporting Experience," in George Eisen and David K. Wiggins, eds., *Ethnicity and Sport in North American History and Culture.* Westport, CT: Praeger, 1994, 103–116.

Bederman, Gail. *Manliness and Civilization: A Cultural History of Gender and Race in the United States, 1880–1917.* Chicago: University of Chicago Press, 1995.

Beetz, Kirk H. "Tunney, James Joseph," in Arnold Markoe, ed., The *Scribner Encyclopedia of American Lives: Sports Figures.* New York: Charles Scribner's Sons, 2002, 441–43.

Benson, Peter. *Battling Siki: A Tale of Ring Fixes, Race, and Murder in the 1920s.* Fayetteville: University of Arkansas Press, 2006.

Berger, Phil. "Rocky Graziano, Ex-Ring Champion, Dead at 71." Obituary, *New York Times*, May 23, 1990. http:www.nytimes.com/1990/05/23/obituaries/rocky-graziano-ex-ring-champion-dead-at-71.html (accessedApril 1, 2013).

Berkow, Ira. *Maxwell Street.* Garden City, NY: Doubleday, 1977.

Billi, John. "U.S. Sports Firmament is Dotted with Many First Magnitude Stars of Italian Origin." *Il Progresso Italo-Americano*, November 9, 1930, 7.

Blady, Ken. *The Jewish Boxers' Hall of Fame.* New York: Shapolsky Pub., 1988.

Blum, John M., and Edmund S. Morgan, Willie Lee Rose, Arthur M. Schlesinger, Jr., Kenneth M. Stampp, and C. Vann Woodward. *The Na-*

tional Experience: A History of the United States. New York: Harcourt Brace Jovanovich, 1981.

Bourdieu, Pierre. *Outline of a Theory of Practice.* Cambridge: Cambridge University Press, 1972.

Brailsford, Dennis. "Morals and Maulers: the Ethics of Early Pugilism." *Journal of Sport History0* 12, no. 2 (Summer 1985): 126–42.

Briggs, Laura. *Reproducing Empire: Race, Sex, Science and U.S. Imperialism in Puerto Rico.* Berkeley: University of California Press, 2002.

Brodkin, Karen. *How Jews Became White Folks and What that Says about Race in America.* New Brunswick, NJ: Rutgers University Press, 1998.

Brownell, Susan, ed. *The 1904 Anthropology Days and Olympic Games: Sport, Race, and American Imperialism.* Lincoln: University of Nebraska Press, 2008.

Bunk, Brian D. "Harry Wills and the Image of the Black Boxer from Jack Johnson to Joe Louis." *Journal of Sport History* 39, no. 1 (Spring 2012): 63–80.

Burkholder, P. E, "The Gang Leader," in Ernest W. Burgess Papers, University of Chicago Special Collections, Box 128, folder 1.

Burns, Ken. *Unforgivable Blackness: The Rise and Fall of Jack Johnson.* PBS, 2005.

Burton, Lewis. "A Heavyweight Named Roland," in Thomas Hauser and Stephen Brunt, eds., *The Italian Stallions: Heroes of Boxing's Glory Days.* Toronto: Sport Media Publishing, 2003.

Butler, Judith. *Gender Trouble: Feminism and the Subversion of Identity.* New York: Routledge, 1990.

Cantwell, Robert. "The Great Dublin Robbery." SI Vault, March 19, 1979. http://sportsillustrated.cnn.com/vault/article/magazine/MAG1094742/1/index.htm (accessed January 22, 2013).

Carner, Lucy P. Report of Interview with Fr. Peter D. Meegan, February 9, 1939, Municipal Welfare Council Papers, Chicago Historical Museum.

Carnes, Mark C., and Clyde Griffen, eds. *Meanings for Manhood: Constructions of Masculinity in Victorian America.* Chicago: University of Chicago Press, 1990.

Carpenter, Harry. *Boxing: An Illustrated History.* New York: Crescent Books, 1982.

Casimir, Enver M. "Contours of Transnational Contact: Kid Chocolate, Cuba and the United States in the 1920s and 1930s." *Journal of Sport History* 39, no. 3 (Fall 2012): 487–506.

Century, Douglas. *Barney Ross.* New York: Schocken Books, 2006.

Cerulo, Karen A. "Identity Construction: New Issues, New Directions." *Annual Review of Sociology* 23 (1997): 385–409.

Chapman, David L. *Sandow the Magnificent: Eugen Sandow and the Beginnings of Bodybuilding.* Urbana: University of Illinois Press, 1994.

Chaudhuri, Supriya. "In the Ring: Gender, Spectatorship, and the Body." *International Journal of the History of Sport* 29, no. 12 (August 2012): 1759–73.

Chicago Tribune. Seventh International Golden Gloves: Champions of Europe vs. Champions of Chicagoland, program. 1938.

Chicago Tribune. 37th Annual Golden Gloves Finals, program. February 28, 1964.

Child, Irvin L. *Italian or American? The Second Generation in Conflict.* New Haven, CT: Yale University Press, 1943.

Chudacoff, Howard P. *The Age of the Bachelor: Creating an American Subculture.* Princeton, NJ: Princeton University Press, 1999.

Cincotta, John. "Alexis Arguello: Portrait of a Killer with Class" *Boxing Today,* n.d., 11–15, in Arguello file, International Boxing Hall of Fame.

Clay, Charles E. "A Bout with the Gloves," *Outing,* April 1887, 26– 31.

Cohen, Leah Hager. *Without Apology: Girls, Women, and the Desire to Fight.* New York: Random House, 2005.

Cohen, Lizabeth. *Making a New Deal: Industrial Workers in Chicago, 1919–1939.* New York: Cambridge University Press, 1990.

Couvares, Francis G. *The Remaking of Pittsburgh: Class and Culture in an Industrializing City, 1877–1919.* Albany: State University of New York Press, 1984.

Cozzone, Chris, and Jim Boggio. *Boxing in New Mexico, 1868–1940.* Jefferson, NC: McFarland, 2013.

Cram, Mark. "The Lady IS a Champ" *Sports Illustrated,* November 6, 1967, 169. http://sportsillustrated.cnn.com/vault/article/magazine/MAG1080539/3/index.htm (accessed May 9, 2013).

Cressey, Paul G. *The Taxi-Dance Hall* (Chicago: University of Chicago Press, 1932.

CYO. First Annual Boxing Tournament program, 1931. Chicago Archdiocese Archives.

Davies, Richard O. *Sports in American Life: A History.* Malden, MA: Blackwell, 2007.

Davis, Robert C. *The War of the Fists: Popular Culture and Public Violence in Late Renaissance Venice.* New York: Oxford University Press, 1994.

Dee, David. "'The Hefty Hebrew': Boxing and British-Jewish Identity, 1890–1960." *Sport in History* 32, no. 3 (September 2012): 361–81.

Demas, Lane. "The Brown Bomber's Dark Day: Louis-Schmeling I and America's Black Hero." *Journal of Sport History* 31, no. 3 (Fall 2004): 252–71.

Desch Obi, T. J. "Black Terror: Bill Richmond's Revolutionary Boxing." *Journal of Sport History* 36, no. 1 (Spring 2009): 99–114.

Douglas, Ann. *The Feminization of American Culture.* New York: Alfred A. Knopf, 1977.

Duany, Jorge. *The Puerto Rican Nation on the Move: Identities on the Island and in the United States.* Chapel Hill: University of North Carolina Press, 2002.

Dubbert, Joe L. *A Man's Place: Masculinity in Transition.* Englewood Cliffs, NJ: Prentice-Hall, 1979.

Dublin, Thomas. *Women at Work: The Transformation of Work and Community in Lowell, Massachusetts, 1826–1860.* New York: Cambridge University Press, 1983.

Du Bois, W. E. B. *The Souls of Black Folk.* New York: Penguin Books, 1989 (1903).

Duis, Perry R. *The Saloon: Public Drinking in Chicago and Boston, 1880–1920.* Urbana: University of Illinois Press, 1983.

Dunzendorfer, Jan. "The Early Days of Boxing in Accra: A Sport Is Taking Root." *International Journal of the History of Sport,* 28, no. 15 (October 2011): 2142–58.

Early, Gerald. "The Romance of Toughness," *Antioch Review* 45, no. 4 (Autumn 1987): 385–408.

———. "Battling Siki as 'Other': The Boxer as Natural Man." *Massachusetts Review* 29, no. 3 (Fall 1988): 451–72.

———. *The Culture of Bruising: Essays on Prizefighting, Literature, and Modern American Culture.* Hopewell, NJ: Ecco Press, 1994.

———. "Muhammad Ali: Flawed Rebel with a Cause," in David K. Wiggins, ed., *Out of the Shadows: A Biographical History of African American Athletes.* Fayetteville: University of Arkansas Press, 2006, 263–78.

Edwards, Anthony O. "Joe Louis: Boxing and American Culture," in David K. Wiggins, ed., *Out of the Shadows: A Biographical History of African American Athletes.* Fayetteville: University of Arkansas Press, 2006, 132–45.

Egan, Pierce. *Boxiana, Vol. 1.* Edited by Scott Noble. London: G. Smeeton, 1812; Nicol Island Publishing, 1997.

Eighth Annual Golden Gloves Tournament program, March 8, 1935.

Elias, Norbert. *The Civilizing Process.* New York: Urizen Books, 1978.

Erenberg, Lewis A. "'Rumble in the Jungle': Muhammad Ali vs. George Foreman in the Age of Global Spectacle." *Journal of Sport History* 39, no. 1 (Spring 2012): 81–97.

Ernst, Robert. *Weakness is a Crime: The Life of Bernarr Macfadden.* Syracuse, NY: University of Syracuse Press, 1991.

Espana-Maram, Linda N. "Colonial Boundaries: Filipinos in the U.S. before 1946." Paper delivered at the Organization of American Historians Conference, Indianapolis, April 1998.

ESPN. *Ali's 65: Not All Battles Are Fought in the Ring.* CD. ESPN, 2007.

BIBLIOGRAPHY

Evenson, Bruce J. *When Dempsey Fought Tunney: Heroes, Hokum, and Storytelling in the Jazz Age.* Knoxville: University of Tennessee Press, 1996.

Ezra, Michael. "Main Bout, Inc., Black Economic Power, and Professional Boxing: The Cancelled Muhammad Ali/Ernie Terrell Fight." *Journal of Sport History* 29, no. 3 (Fall 2002): 413–37.

Fanthorpe, Lionel, and Patricia Fanthorpe. *The World's Most Mysterious People.* Ontario, Canada: Hounslow Press, 1998.

Farr, Finis. "Jeff, It's Up to You!," *American Heritage,* February 1964, 64–77.

Ferrarin, Elena. "Rolling with the Punches," *Fra Noi,* July 2012, 31.

"Firpo Had the Title Within His Grasp," *New York Times,* September 15, 1923, 1.

Fisher, Rudolph. "The Caucasian Storms Harlem," in Nathan Irvin Huggins, ed., *Voices from the Harlem Renaissance* (New York: Oxford, 1995), 74–82.

FitzRoy, Charles. *Renaissance Florence on 5 Florins a Day* (London: Thames & Hudson, 2010).

Fleming, Tyler. "'Now the African Reigns Supreme': The Rise of African Boxing on the Witwatersrand, 1924–1959." *International Journal of the History of Sport* 28, no. 1 (January 2011): 47–62.

Forbes, Jack D. "The Manipulation of Race, Caste, and Identity: Classifying Afroamericans, Native Americans, and Red-Black People.," *Journal of Ethnic Studies* 17, no. 4 (Winter 1990): 1–51.

Fountain, Charles. *Sportswriter: The Life and Times of Grantland Rice.* New York: Oxford University Press, 1993.

Fox Sports Network. "Beyond the Glory." February 4, 2001.

Frable, Deborah E. S. "Gender, Racial, Ethnic, Sexual, and Call Identities." *Annual Review of Psychology* 48 (1997): 139–62.

"Frank Klaus Sees Firpo in Action," *New York Times,* September 2, 1923, 18.

Furniss, Harry. *By Ways and Queer Ways of Boxing.* London: Harrison & Sons, 1919.

Gambino, Richard. *Vendetta: The True Story of the Largest Lynching in U.S. History.* Toronto: Guernica, 1998 (1977).

Gammel, Irene. "Lacing Up the Gloves: Women, Boxing, and Modernity." *Cultural and Social History* 9, no. 3 (2012): 369–89.

Garaty, John A. *The American Nation: A History of the United States.* New York: Harper & Row, 1983.

Garcia, Justin D. "Rising from the Canvas: Issues of Immigration, Redemption, Gender, and Mexican American Identity in *Split Decision* and *In Her Corner*," in Zachary Ingle and David M. Sutera, eds., *Identity and Myth in Sports Documentaries: Critical Essays,* Lanham, MD: Scarecrow Press, 2013, 63–78.

Gavzer, Bernard. "Is It Time to Investigate Boxing?" *Parade Magazine*, October 21, 1990, 4–6.

Gems, Gerald R. *The Athletic Crusade: Sport and American Cultural Imperialism* (Lincoln: University of Nebraska Press, 2006).

———. Interview with Judge Abraham Lincoln Marovitz, December 10, 1990.

———. "Jack Johnson and the Quest for Racial Respect," in David K. Wiggins, ed., *Out of the Shadows: A Biographical History of African American Athletes.* Fayetteville: University of Arkansas Press, 2006, 59–77.

———. "The Politics of Boxing: Resistance, Religion, and Working-Class Assimilation." *International Sports Journal* 8, no. 1 (Winter 2004): 89–103.

———. "Selling Sport and Religion in American Society: Bishop Sheil and the Catholic Youth Organization," in S. W. Pope, ed., *The New American Sport History: Recent Approaches and Perspectives.* Urbana: University of Illinois Press, 1997, 300–11.

———. "Sport and the Forging of a Jewish-American Culture: The Chicago Hebrew Institute." *Journal of American Jewish History* 83 (March 1995): 15–26.

———. "Sport and the Italian American Quest for Whiteness." *Sport in History* 32, no. 4 (December 2012): 479–503.

———. *Sport and the Shaping of Italian American Identity.* Syracuse, NY: Syracuse University Press, 2013.

———. "Sport, Religion and Americanization: Bishop Sheil and the Catholic Youth Organization." *International Journal of the History of Sport* 10, no. 2 (August 1993): 233–41.

———. *Sports in North America: A Documentary History. Vol. 5: Sports Organized, 1880–1900.* Gulf Breeze, FL: Academic International Press, 1996.

———. *Windy City Wars: Labor, Leisure, and Sport in the Making of Chicago.* Lanham, MD; Scarecrow Press, 1997.

Gems, Gerald R., Linda Borish, and Gertrud Pfister. *Sports in American History: From Colonization to Globalization.* Champaign, IL: Human Kinetics, 2008.

Gilfoyle, Timothy J. *A Pickpocket's Tale: The Underworld of Nineteenth-Century New York.* New York: W. W. Norton, 2006.

———. *City of Eros: New York City, Prostitution, and the Commercialization of Sex, 1790–1920.* New York: W. W. Norton, 1992.

Gilmore, Al-Tony. *Bad Nigger! The National Impact of Jack Johnson.* Port Washington, NY: Kennikat Press, 1975.

Glenn, Mike. "George Dixon: World Bantamweight and Featherweight Champion," in Colleen Aycock and Mark Scott, *The First Black Boxing Champions: Essays on Fighters in the 1800s to the 1920s.* Jefferson, NC: McFarland & Co., 2011, 48–59.

Go, Pauline. "The Tiger King of Ayutthaya in Thailand." Ezine, n.d. http://ezine articles.com/?The-Tiger-King-Of-Ayutthaya-In-Thailand&id=581043 (accessed September 24, 2012).

Golesworthy, Maurice. *The Encyclopedia of Boxing*. London: Robert Hale, Ltd., 1960.

Gomet, Doriane. "Survival Strategy or Bloody Violence? Boxing in Concentration and Extermination Camps." Paper presented at the North American Society for Sport History Conference, Halifax, Canada, May 25, 2013.

Gorn, Elliott J. "'Good-Bye Boys, I Die a True American': Homicide, Nativism, and Working-Class Culture in Antebellum New York City." *Journal of American History* 74, no. 2 (September 1987): 388–410.

———. "'Gouge and Bite, Pull Hair and Scratch': The Social Significance of Gouging in the Southern Backcountry." *American Historical Review* 90, no. 1 (February 1985): 18–43.

———. "John L. Sullivan: The Champion of All Champions," in Stephen Wagg, ed., *Myths and Milestones in the History of Sport*. New York: Palgrave MacMillan, 2011, 224–38.

———. "The Manassa Mauler and the Fighting Marine: An Interpretation of the Dempsey-Tunney Fights," *Journal of American Studies* 19, no. 1 (1985): 27–47.

———. *The Manly Art: Bare-Knuckle Prize Fighting in America*. Ithaca, NY: Cornell University Press, 1986.

———, ed. *Muhammad Ali, the People's Champ*. Urbana: University of Illinois Press, 1995.

Gorn, Elliott J., and Warren Goldstein. *A Brief History of American Sports*. New York: Hill & Wang, 1993.

Gould, Stephen Jay. *The Mismeasure of Man*. New York: Norton, 1996 (1981).

Graham, Frank. "Tony Canzoneri: One for the Book," in Thomas Hauser and Stephen Brunt, eds., *The Italian Stallions: Heroes of Boxing's Glory Days*. Toronto: Sport Media Publishing, 2003, 44–47.

Grant, Madison. *The Passing of the Great Race or the Racial Basis of European History*. New York: Charles Scribner's Sons, 1916.

Graziano, Rocky, with Ralph Corsel. *Somebody Down Here Likes Me Too*. New York: Stein & Day, 1981.

Greenwood, Jeremy. "Roberto Duran . . . Latin Ambassador of Macho." *World Wide Boxing Digest*, clipping, 4–5, in Duran file, International Boxing Hall of Fame.

Grindon, Leger. *Knockout: The Boxer and Boxing in American Cinema*. Jackson: University of Mississippi Press, 2011.

Griffin, Robert S. "On Chuck Davey," robertsgriffin.com, October 2007.www. robertsgriffin.com/thoughts.html (accessed November 17, 2012).

Gruver, Edward. "Conn, William David, Jr. 'Billy,'" in Arnold Markoe, ed., *The Scribner Encyclopedia of American Lives: Sports Figures*. New York: Charles Scribner's Sons, 2002, 181–83.

Guglielmo, Jennifer. *Living the Revolution: Italian Women's Resistance and Radicalism in New York City, 1880–1945*. Chapel Hill: University of North Carolina Press, 2010.

Guterl, Matthew Pratt. *The Color of Race in America, 1900–1940*. Cambridge, MA: Harvard University Press, 2001.

Guthrie-Shimizu, Sayuri. *Transpacific Field of Dreams: How Baseball Linked the United States and Japan in Peace and War*. Chapel Hill: University of North Carolina Press, 2012.

Guttmann, Allen. *From Ritual to Record: The Nature of Modern Sports*. New York: Columbia University Press, 1978.

———. *Sports: The First Five Millennia*. Amherst: University of Massachusetts Press, 2004.

———. *Women's Sports: A History*. New York: Columbia University Press, 1991.

Hargreaves, Jennifer. "Women's Boxing and Related Activities: Introducing Images and Meanings." *InYo: Journal of Alternative Perspectives* (September 2001): n.p. Article in author's possession.

Harris, Othello. "Ali, Muhammad," in George B. Kirsch, Othello Harris, and Claire E. Nolte, eds., *Encyclopedia of Ethnicity and Sports in the United States*. Westport, CT: Greenwood Press, 2000, 21–23.

Harrison, John B., and Richard B. Sullivan. *A Short History of Western Civilization*. New York: Alfred A. Knopf, 1980.

Hauser, Thomas, and Stephen Brunt. *The Italian Stallions: Heroes of Boxing's Glory Days*. (Toronto: Sport Media, 2003).

Heap, Chad. Slumming: *Sexual and Racial Encounters in American Nightlife, 1885–1940*. Chicago: University of Chicago Press, 2009.

Hedin, Robert, and Michael Waters, eds. *Perfect in Their Art: Poems on Boxing from Homer to Ali*. Carbondale: Southern Illinois University Press, 2003.

Heinz, W. C. "Goodbye, Graziano," in Al Silverman, *Best from Sport*. New York: Bartholomew House, 1961, 88–95.

Heiskanen, Benita. "The Latinization of Boxing: A Texas Case Study." *Journal of Sport History* 32, no. 1 (Spring 2005): 45–66.

———. *The Urban Geography of Boxing: Race, Class, and Gender in the Ring*. New York: Routledge, 2012.

Heller, Peter. *"In This Corner . . . !": 42 World Champions Tell Their Stories*. New York: Da Capo Press, 1994.

Hennesey, Hal. "Pancho Villa: The Tiniest Giant." Magazine clipping, 40–43, 64–5 in Pancho Villa file, International Boxing Hall of Fame

BIBLIOGRAPHY

Henry, Jim. "For Wilfred Benitez, Boxing's Brutal Toll Never Ends." AOLnews, October 7, 2010. http://www.aolnews.com/2010/10/07/for-wilfred-benitez-boxings-brutal-toll-never-ends/ (accessed April 15, 2013).

Hermann, Charles H. *Recollections of Life and Doings in Chicago*. Chicago: Normandie House, 1945.

Hoare, Quintin, and Geoffrey N. Smith, eds. *Selections from the Prison Notebooks of Antonio Gramsci*. New York: International Publishers, 1971.

Hodgekiss, Anna. "Headgear for Amateur Boxers to Be Banned in a Bid to REDUCE Head Injuries." *Daily Mail*, March 15, 2013.http://www.dailymail.co.uk/health/article-2293803/Headgear-boxers-banned-bid-REDUCE-head-injuries.html (accessed May 18, 2013).

Hodges, Graham Russell. "Robinson, Walker Smith, Jr. ('Sugar Ray')," in Arnold Markoe, ed., The *Scribner Encyclopedia of American Lives: Sports Figures*. New York: Charles Scribner's Sons, 2002, vol. II, 292–94.

Holland, Barbara. *Gentlemen's Blood: A History of Dueling from Swords at Dawn to Pistols at Dusk*. New York: Bloomsbury, 2003.

Hopsicker, Peter. "'No Hebrews Allowed': How the 1932 Lake Placid Olympic Games Survived the 'Restricted' Adirondack Culture, 1877–1932." *Journal of Sport History* 36, no. 2 (2009): 205–22.

Hudson, David L, Jr. *Boxing in America: An Autopsy*. Santa Barbara, CA: Praeger, 2012.

Huggins, Mike. "The Sporting Gaze: Towards a Visual Turn in Sport History—Documenting Art and Sport." *Journal of Sport History* 35, no. 2 (Summer 2008): 311–29.

Huggins, Nathan Irvin, ed. *Voices from the Harlem Renaissance*. New York: Oxford, 1995.

Iber, Jorge, Samuel O. Regalado, Jose M. Alamillo, and Arnoldo De Leon. *Latinos in U.S. Sport: A History of Isolation, Cultural Identity, and Acceptance*. Champaign, IL: Human Kinetics, 2011.

Intercity Boxing. Third Annual Meeting of Golden Gloves Champions and Runners-Up program, March 19, 1930, Chicago History Museum.

Isenberg, Michael T. *John L. Sullivan and His America*. Urbana: University of Illinois Press, 1988.

Jackson, Ron. "The Origins of Boxing in SA." SuperSport.com, February 7, 2006. http://www.supersport.com/boxing/blogs/ron-jackson/The_origins_of_boxing_in_SA (accessed July 8, 2011).

Jacobson, Matthew Frye. *Whiteness of a Different Color: European Immigrants and the Alchemy of Race*. Cambridge, MA: Harvard University Press, 1998.

Jensen, Erik N. *Body by Weimar: Athletes, Gender, and German Modernity*. New York: Oxford University Press, 2010.

Johnson, Jack. *Jack Johnson Is a Dandy: An Autobiography.* New York: Chelsea House, 1969.

Johnson, James W. (Body). "The Fight That Won't Stay Dead." SI Vault, July 4, 1966. http://sportsillustrated.cnn.com/vault/article/magazine/MAG1078731/1/index.htm (accessed November 20, 2012).

Johnston, J. J., and Sean Curtin. *Chicago Boxing.* Chicago: Arcadia, 2005, 12.

Jones, Ken. "A Key Moral Issue: Should Boxing be Banned?" *Culture, Sport, Society* 4, no. 1 (Spring 2001): 63–72.

Jones, R. L. "A Deviant Sports Career: Towards a Sociology of Unlicensed Boxing." *Journal of Sport and Social Issues* 21, no. 1 (February 1997): 37–52.

Joplin (Missouri) *Globe,* January, 13, 1921.

Kantowicz, Edward R. "Cardinal Mundelein of Chicago and the Shaping of Twentieth-Century American Catholicism." *Journal of American History* 68 (June 1981): 52–69.

———. *Corporation Sole: Cardinal Mundelein and Chicago Catholicism.* Notre Dame, IN: University of Notre Dame Press, 1983.

Kasson, John F. *Houdini, Tarzan, and the Perfect Man: The White Male Body and the Challenge of Modernity in America.* New York: Hill and Wang, 2001.

Kaye, Andrew M. *The Pussycat of Prizefighting: Tiger Flowers and the Politics of Black Celebrity.* Athens: University of Georgia Press, 2004.

"Kid McCoy, Once Greatest Scrapper, Tells How He Used to Get the Coin in the Olden Days," *Milwaukee Sentinel,* August 1, 1915, 10.

Kim, Jeonguk. "Fighting Men and Fighting Women: American Prizefighting and the Contested Gender Order in the Late Nineteenth and Early Twentieth Centuries." *Sport History Review* 43 (2012): 103–27.

Kimmel, Michael S. *The History of Men: Essays in the History of American and British Masculinities.* Albany: State University of New York Press, 2005.

Kingsdale, Jon M. "The Poor Man's Club: Social Functions of the Urban Working-Class Saloon." *American Quarterly* 25, no. 4 (October 1973): 472–89.

Kirsch, George B., *Sports in North America: A Documentary History, vol. 3: The Rise of Modern Sports, 1840–1860* (Gulf Breeze, FL; Academic International Press, 1992).

Kirsch, George B., Othello Harris, and Claire Nolte, eds. *Encyclopedia of Ethnicity and Sports in the United States.* Westport, CT: Greenwood, 2000.

Klineberg, Otto., *Race Differences.* New York: Harper & Bros., 1935.

Kohr, Knud, and Martin Krauss. *Kampftage: Die Geschichte des deutschen Berufsboxens.* Gottingen: Verkag Die Werkstatt, 2000.

Kriegel, Mark. *The Good Son: The Life of Ray "Boom Boom" Mancini.* New York: Free Press 2012.

Lafferty, Yvonne, and Jim McKay. "Suffragettes in Satin Shorts? Gender and Competitive Boxing." *Quantitative Sociology* 27, no. 3 (Fall 2004): 249–76.

Lang, Arne K. *Prizefighting: An American History.* Jefferson, NC: McFarland & Co., 2008.

Lankford, Ronnie D., Jr. "Walker, Edward Patrick (Mickey)," in Arnold Markoe, ed., *The Scribner Encyclopedia of American Lives: Sports Figures.* New York: Charles Scribner's Sons, 2002, 471–72.

Laurie, Bruce. *Working People of Philadelphia, 1800–1850.* Philadelphia: Temple University Press, 1980.

Lee, Jung Woo. "Red Feminism and Propaganda in Communist Media: Portrayals of Female Boxers in North Korean Media." *International Review for the Sociology of Sport* 44, nos. 2–3 (2009): 193–211.

Leider, Emily Wortis. *Becoming Mae West.* New York: Farrar, Straus and Giroux, 1997.

Levine, Peter. *Ellis Island to Ebbets Field: Sport and the American Jewish Experience.* New York: Oxford University Press, 1992.

———. "'Oy Such a Fighter!' Boxing and the American Jewish Experience," in S. W. Pope, ed., *The New American Sport History: Recent Approaches and Perspectives.* Urbana: University of Illinois Press, 1997, 251–83.

Levinson, David, Stan Shipley, and Edward R. Beauchamp. "Boxing," in David Levinson and Karen Christensen, eds., *World Sport, Vol. 1.* Great Barrington, MA: Berkshire Publishing Group, 2005, 241–48.

Lewis, Franklin. "Whose Fault?" Cleveland Press, June 25, 1947, in Irving T. Marsh and Edward Ehre, eds., *Best Sports Stories: 1948 Edition.* New York: E.P. Dutton, 1948, 167–69.

Liebling, A. J. *The Sweet Science.* New York: North Point Press, 2004 (1951).

Lindner, Katharina. "Women's Boxing at the 2012 Olympics: Gender Trouble?" *Feminist Media Studies* (2012). http: //dx.doi.org/10.1080/14680777.2012.698092.

Little, Charles. "Muay Thai," in John Nauright and Charles Parrish, eds., *Sports Around the World: History, Culture, and Practice.* Santa Barbara: ABC-CLIO, 2012. http://ebooks.abc-clio.com/print.aspx?isbn=9781598843019&id=A1884C_V1-4262 (accessed August 4, 2012).

Littlewood, Thomas B. *Arch: A Promoter, Not a Poet: The Story of Arch Ward.* Ames, IA: Iowa State University Press, 1990.

Longstreet, Stephen. *Chicago, 1860–1919.* New York: David McKay Co., 1973.

Lorber, Judith. "'Night to His Day': The Social Construction of Gender," in Paula S. Rothenberg, ed., *Race, Class, and Gender in the United States: An Integrated Study.* New York: Worth Pub., 2007, 54–64.

Loudcher, Jean-Francois., "The Origins of French Boxing: Bare-Knuckle Duelling, Savate and Chausson, 1820–45." *International Journal of the History of Sport* 18, no. 2 (June 2001): 168–78.

Love, Eric T. L. *Race Over Empire: Racism and U.S. Imperialism, 1865–1900.* Chapel Hill: University of North Carolina Press, 2004.

Lussana, Sergio. "To See Who Was the Best on the Plantation: Enslaved Fighting Contests and Masculinity in the Antebellum Plantation South." *Journal of Southern History* 76, no. 4, 901–22.

Lyon, Bryce, Herbert H. Rowen, and Theodore S. Hamerow. *A History of the Western World.* Chicago: Rand McNally, 1974.

MacDonald, R. C. "Scientific Boxing under the Boston A. A. Rules," *Outing*, 21, no. 1. October 1892, 23–24.

Maeder, Jay. "Smashup Ethiopia, 1935." *New York Daily News*, June 15, 2000. http://articles.nydailynews.com/2000-06-15/news/18131296_1_addis-ababa-emperor-haile (accessed October 2, 2011).

Margavio, A. V., and Jerome J. Salomone. *Bread and Respect: The Italians of Louisiana.* Gretna, LA: Pelican Publishing, 2002.

Margolick, David. *Beyond Glory: Joe Louis, Max Schmeling, and the World on the Brink.* New York: Alfred A. Knopf, 2005.

Maselli, Joseph, and Domenic Candeloro. *Italians in New Orleans.* Chicago: Arcadia Pub., 2004.

Mason, Tony, and Eliza Riedi. *Sport and the Military: The British Armed Forces, 1880–1960.* New York: Cambridge University Press, 2010.

McArdle, David. "Can Legislation Stop Me from Playing? The Distinction between Sport Competitors and Sport Workers under the United Kingdom's Sex Discrimination Laws." *Culture, Sport, Society: Cultures, Commerce, Media, Politics* 2, no. 2 (1999): 44–57.

McCarson, Kelsey. "What Gives? No TV for Women's Boxing." The Sweet Science, March 6, 2013. http://www.the sweetscience.com/news/articles/16236—what-gives-no-tv-for-womens-boxing (March 9, 2013).

McCarthy, Joe. *Ireland.* New York: Time, 1964.

McCarthy, Karen F. *The Other Irish: The Scots-Irish Rascals Who Made America.* New York: Sterling, 2011.

McCree, Roy Dereck. "The Death of a Female Boxer: Media, Sport, Nationalism, and Gender." *Journal of Sport and Social Issues* 20, no. 10 (2011): 1–23.

McGehee, Richard V. "The Dandy and the Mauler in Mexico: Johnson, Dempsey, et al., and the Mexico City Press, 1919–1927." *Journal of Sport History* 23, no. 1 (Spring 1996): 20–33.

———. "Boxing, Latin America," in John Nauright and Charles Parrish, eds., *Sports around the World: History, Culture, and Practice.* Santa Barbara, CA:

ABC-CLIO, 2012. http://ebooks.abc-clio.com/print.aspx?isbn=978159884 3019&id=A1884C_V3-1205 (accessed August 4, 2012).

McGreevy, John T. *Parish Boundaries: The Catholic Encounter with Race in the Twentieth-Century Urban North.* Chicago: University of Chicago Press, 1996.

McKay, Brett and Kate McKay. "A History of the American Bachelor: Part II: Post–Civil War America." Art of Manliness, n.d. http://artofmanliness. com/2012/04/12/history-of-the-american-bachelor-post-civil-war-america/ (accessed November 13, 2012).

Meier, Marianne, and Martha Saavedra. "Esther Phiri and the Moutawakel Effect in Zambia: An Analysis of the Use of Female Role Models in Sport for Development." *Sport in Society*, 12, no. 9 (November 2009): 1158–76.

Melendy, Royal L. "The Saloon in Chicago (Part 1)." *American Journal of Sociology* 6 (November 1900): 289–306.

———. "The Saloon in Chicago (Part 2)." *American Journal of Sociology* 6 (January 1901): 433–64.

Mennesson, Christine. "'Hard' Women and 'Soft' Women: The Social Construction of Identities among Female Boxers," *International Review for the Sociology of Sport* 35, no. 1 (2000): 21–33.

Miles, Henry Downs. *Pugilistica: The History of British Boxing.* Edinburgh: John Grant, 1906. ebook.

Miller, Bill. "Boxing's Mosquito Fleet." Magazine clipping, 22–3, 44, in Pancho Villa file, International Boxing Hall of Fame.

Miller, Patrick B., and David K. Wiggins, eds. *Sport and the Color Line: Black Athletes and Race Relations in Twentieth Century America.* New York: Routledge, 2004.

Miller, Stephen G. *Ancient Greek Athletics.* New Haven, CT: Yale University Press, 2004.

Mirel, Jeffrey E. *Patriotic Pluralism: Americanization Education and European Immigrants.* Cambridge,MA: Harvard University Press, 2010.

Mitra, Payoshni. "Challenging Stereotypes: The Case of Muslim Female Boxers in Bengal." *International Journal of the History of Sport* 26, no. 12 (2009): 1840–51.

Montoya, Delilah. *Women Boxers: The New Warriors.* Houston: Arte Publico Press, 2006.

Mooney, Roger. "Going Home a Hero: How Ceferino Garcia Finally Realized His Dream." *Ring*, April 1994, 26–28, 60.

Moore, Katharine, and Murrray G. Phillips. "From Adulation to Persecution and Back. Australian Boxer Les Darcy in America, 1916–1917." *Journal of Sport History* 23, no. 2 (Summer 1996): 140–56.

Moore, Lucy. *Anything Goes: A Biography of the Roaring Twenties.* New York: Overlook Press, 2010.

Moyle, Clay. "Sam Langford: Heavyweight Champion of Australia, Canada, England, and Mexico," in Colleen Aycock and Mark Scott, *The First Black Boxing Champions: Essays on Fighters in the 1800s to the 1920s.* Jefferson, NC: McFarland & Co., 2011, 158–70.

Murray, Steven Ross. "Boxing Gloves of the Ancient World." *Journal of Combative Sport* (July 2010). http://ejmas.com/jcs/jcsframe.htm (accessed 12 June, 2012).

Nack, William. "Back, But Still a Long Way to Go." *Sports Illustrated* clipping, August 17, 1981, 16–17, in Duran file, International Boxing Hall of Fame.

Naison, Mark. "Righties and Lefties: The Communist Party and Sports During the Great Depression." *Radical America* 13 (July–August 1979): 47–59.

Nathan, Daniel A. "Sugar Ray Robinson, the Sweet Science, and the Politics of Meaning." *Journal of Sport History* 26, no. 1 (Spring 1999): 163–74.

———. "Sugar Ray Leonard," in David K. Wiggins, ed., *African Americans in Sports.* Armonk, NY: M.E. Sharpe, 2004, 206–7.

NBC, *This Fight Should Have Been Broadcast* (1937 pamphlet).

Nelson, Murry R., ed. *Encyclopedia of Sports in North America.* Westport, CT: Greenwood, 2009.

Nicholson, Kelly. "The Curious Case of Norman Selby." International Boxing Research Organization, October 8, 2011. http://www.ibroresearch.com/?p-5303 (accessed October 18, 2012).

Ninth International Golden Gloves Program, *Champions of Europe vs. Champions of Chicagoland*, April 10, 1940.

"N. Korean Champ Becomes S. Korean," *Korean Times*, March 18, 2007, on Empas News, January 2, 2008.

North China Herald (Shanghai), January 16, 1891; March 18, 1892.

Nossov, Konstantin. *Gladiator: Rome's Bloody Spectacle.* Oxford: Osprey Pub., 2009.

Oates, Joyce Carol. *On Boxing.* New York: Harper Collins, 2002.

Oates, Joyce Carol, and Daniel Halpern, eds. *Reading the Fights: The Best Writing About the Most Controversial Sport.* New York: Prentice Hall, 1988.

O'Connor, Daniel, ed. *Iron Mike: A Mike Tyson Reader.* New York: Thunder's Mouth Press, 2002.

"Olympic Club's New Articles," *Chicago Tribune*, March 20, 1892, 6.

O'Toole, Andrew. *Sweet William: The Life of Billy Conn.* Champaign: University of Illinois Press, 2008.

Page, Joseph S. *Primo Carnera: The Life and Career of the Heavyweight Boxing Champion.* Jefferson, NC: McFarland, 2011.

Paradis, Elise. "Skirting the Issue: Women Boxers, Liminality and Change." Academia.edu, n.d. http://www.academia.edu/2211570/Skirting_the_Issue_Women_boxers_liminality_and_change (accessed February 6, 2013).

Park, Robert E., Ernest Burgess, and Roderick D. McKenzie. *The City*. Chicago: University of Chicago Press, 1925.

Park, Roberta J. "Contesting the Norm: Women and Professional Sports in Late Nineteenth-Century America." *International Journal of the History of Sport* 29, no. 5 (April, 2012): 730–49.

Pep, Willie, with Robert Sacchi. *Willie Pep Remembers . . . Friday's Heroes*. New York: Friday's Heroes, Inc., 1973.

"Personality." *Time*, September 22, 1952, 50.

Persons, Stow. *Ethnic Studies at Chicago, 1905–1945*. Urbana: University of Illinois Press, 1987.

Peterson, Bob. "Peter Jackson: Heavyweight Champion of Australia," in Colleen Aycock and Mark Scott, *The First Black Boxing Champions: Essays on Fighters in the 1800s to the 1920s*. Jefferson, NC: McFarland & Co., 2011, 32–47.

Picket, Lynn Snowden. *Looking for a Fight: A Memoir*. New York: The Dial Press, 2000.

Pierpaoli, Alexander. "Joe Jennette and Sam McVey: Colored Heavyweight Champions," in Colleen Aycock and Mark Scott, eds., *The First Black Boxing Champions: Essays on Fighters in the 1800s to the 1920s*. Jefferson, NC: McFarland & Co., 2011, 171–99.

Pietrusza, David. *Rothstein: The Life, Times, and Murder of the Criminal Genius Who Fixed the 1919 World Series*. New York: Carroll & Graf Publishers, 2003.

Pipkin, James W. *Sporting Lives: Metaphor and Myth in American Sports Autobiographies*. Columbia: University of Missouri Press, 2008.

Pleck, Joseph, and ElizabethPleck, eds. *The American Man*. Englewood Cliffs, NJ: Prentice-Hall, 1980.

Plimpton, George. *Shadow Box*. New York: Berkley Books, 1977.

Poliakoff, Michael B. *Combat Sports in the Ancient World: Competition, Violence, and Culture*. New Haven, CT: Yale University Press, 1987.

Potter, David. *The Victor's Crown: A History of Ancient Sport from Homer to Byzantium*. New York: Oxford University Press, 2012.

Powers, Madelon. *Faces along the Bar: Lore and Order in the Workingman's Saloon, 1870–1920*. Chicago: University of Chicago Press, 1998.

Ranger, Terence. "Pugilism and Pathology: African Boxing and the Black Urban Experience in Southern Rhodesia," in William J. Baker and James A. Mangan, eds., *Sport in Africa: Essays in Social History*. New York: Africana Pub. Co., 1987, 196–213.

Reel, Guy. *The National Police Gazette and the Making of the Modern American Man, 1879–1906*. New York: Palgrave Macmillan, 2006.

Rees, Richard W. *Shadows of Difference: History of Ethnicity in America*. Lanham, MD: Rowman & Littlefield, 2007.

Regalado, Samuel O. *Viva Baseball: Latin Major Leaguers and Their Special Hunger*. Urbana: University of Illinois Press, 1998.

Restak, Richard, Stefan Bechtel, Patricia Daniels, Susan Tyler Hitchcock, Trisha Gura, Lisa Stein, and John Thompson. *Body: The Complete Human*. Washington, D.C; National Geographic Society, 2007.

Riess, Steven A. "A Fighting Chance: The Jewish American Boxing Experience, 1890–1940," *American Jewish History* 74, no. 3 (March 1985): 223–54.

———. "Closing Down the Open-City: The Demise of Horse Racing and Boxing in Chicago in 1905." North American Society for Sport History Conference, Banff, Canada, May 27, 2000.

———. "Professional Sports as an Avenue of Social Mobility in America: Some Myths and Realities," in Donald G. Kyle and Gary D. Stark, eds., *Essays on Sport History and Sport Mythology*. College Station: Texas A&M Press, 1990, 83–117.

———. *Sport in Industrial America, 1850–1920*. Wheeling, IL: Haran Davidson, 1995.

Riordan, Jim. "Sidney Jackson: An American in Russia's Boxing Hall of Fame." *Journal of Sport History* 20, no. 1 (Spring 1993): 49–56.

Roberts, Randy. *Joe Louis: Hard Times Man*. New Haven, CT: Yale University Press, 2010.

———. *Papa Jack: Jack Johnson and the Era of White Hopes*. New York: Free Press, 1983.

Rodgers, Daniel T. *The Work Ethic in Industrial America, 1850–1920*. Chicago: University of Chicago Press, 1978.

Rodriguez, Robert G. *The Regulation of Boxing. A History and Comparative Analysis of Policies among American States*. Jefferson, NC: McFarland & Co., 2009.

Roediger, David R., ed. *Black on White: Black Writers on What It Means to Be White*. New York: Schocken Books, 1998.

———. *Working Toward Whiteness: How America's Immigrants Became White, The Strange Journey from Ellis Island to the Suburbs*. New York: Basic Books, 2005.

Romano, John J., ed. *Post Boxing Record, 1937*. New York: John J. Romano, 1937.

Ross, Barney, and Martin Abramson. *No Man Stands Alone: The True Story of Barney Ross*. New York: J.B. Lippincott, 1957.

Ross, Edward Alsworth. *The Old World in the New: The Significance of Past and Present Immigration to the American People*. New York: The Century Co., 1914.

Rotella, Carlo. *Cut Time: An Education at the Fights.* Boston: Houghton Mifflin, 2003.

———. "Good with Her Hands: Women, Boxing, and Work." *Critical Inquiry* 25, no. 3 (Spring 1999): 566–98.

———. *Good with Their Hands: Boxers, Bluesmen, and Other Characters from the Rust Belt.* Berkeley: University of California Press, 2002.

Rotundo, E. Anthony. *American Manhood: Transformations in Masculinity from the Revolution to the Modern Era.* New York: Basic Books, 1993.

Rugg, George. "Corbett, James John." in George B. Kirsch, Othello Harris, and Claire E. Nolte, eds., *Encyclopedia of Ethnicity and Sports in the United States.* Westport, CT: Greenwood, 2000, 110–11.

Runstedtler, Theresa E. "African American Boxers, the New Negro, and the Global Color Line." *Radical History Review* 103 (Winter 2009): 59–81.

———. "In Sport the Best Man Wins: How Joe Louis Whupped Jim Crow," in Amy Bass, ed., *In the Game: Race, Identity, and Sports in the Twentieth Century.* New York: Palgrave Macmillan, 2005, 47–91.

———. Jack Johnson. *Rebel Sojourner: Boxing in the Shadow of the Global Color Line.* Berkeley: University of California Press, 2012.

Saeed, Amir. "What's in a Name? Muhammad Ali and the Politics of Cultural Identity." *Culture, Sport, Society* 5, no. 3 (2002): 51–72.

Sammons, Jeffrey T. *Beyond the Ring: The Role of Boxing in American Society.* Urbana: University of Illinois Press, 1988.

Sandusky (Ohio) *Register*, January 13, 1921.

Schaap, Richard. *An Illustrated History of the Olympics.* New York: Alfred A. Knopf, 1963.

Schuyler, George Samuel. *Ethiopian Stories.* Boston: Northeastern University Press, 1994.

Scott, David. *The Art and Aesthetics of Boxing.* Lincoln: University of Nebraska Press, 2008.

Sekules, Kate. *The Boxer's Heart: How I Fell in Love with the Ring.* New York: Villard, 2000.

Seutonius. *The Twelve Caesars.* New York: Penguin Books, 1978.

Shanabruch, Charles. The Catholic Church's Role in the Americanization of Ethnic Groups. PhD dissertation, University of Chicago, 1975.

Sheil, Bishop Bernard J., ed. *C.Y.O. Survey* 2, no. 6 (June 1953).

Shropshire, Kenneth. *Being Sugar Ray: The Life of Sugar Ray Robinson, America's Greatest Boxer and the First Celebrity Athlete.* New York: Basic Civitas, 2007.

Silbey, David J., *A War of Frontier and Empire: The Philippine-American War, 1899–1902.* New York: Hill & Wang, 2007.

Silk, Michael. *The Cultural Politics of Post-9/11 American Sport: Power, Pedagogy and the Popular* (New York: Routledge, 2012).

Singer, Marc. "Baer, Max." in George B. Kirsch, Othello Harris, and Claire Nolte, eds., *Encyclopedia of Ethnicity and Sports in the United States*. Westport, CT: Greenwood Press, 2000, 40.

———. "Leonard, Benny." in George B. Kirsch, Othello Harris, and Claire Nolte, eds., *Encyclopedia of Ethnicity and Sports in the United States*. Westport, CT: Greenwood Press, 2000, 284–85.

———. "Ross, Barney." in George B. Kirsch, Othello Harris, and Claire Nolte, eds., *Encyclopedia of Ethnicity and Sports in the United States*. Westport, CT: Greenwood Press, 2000, 392–93.

Silver Episcopal Jubilee of His Excellency, the Most Reverend Bernard J. Sheil, D.D. Program, April 29, 1953.

Skerett, Ellen. "The Catholic Dimension," in Lawrence J. McCaffrey, Ellen Skerett, Michael F. Funchion, and Charles Fanning., *The Irish in Chicago*. Urbana: University of Illinois Press, 1987, 22–60.

Smith, Kevin. *Black Genesis: The History of the Black Prizefighter, 1760–1870*. Lincoln, NE: iUniverse, 2003.

Spivey, Nigel. *The Ancient Olympics*. New York: Oxford University Press, 2012.

Stanley, Peter W. *A Nation in the Making: The Philippines and the United States, 1899–1921*. Cambridge, MA: Harvard University Press, 1974.

Stearns, Peter. *Be a Man! Males in Modern Society*. New York: Holmes & Meier, 1979.

Stradley, Don. "A Look at the History of Boxing in the Philippines." ESPN, June 25, 2008. http://sports.espn.go.com/sports/boxing/news/story?id=3458707 (accessed July 8, 2011).

Streible, Dan. *Fight Pictures: A History of Boxing and Early Cinema*. Berkeley: University of California Press, 2008.

Struby, Tim. "Fighting Chance." ESPN, April 30, 2001, 104–11.

Sugden, John. *Boxing and Society: An International Analysis*. Manchester: Manchester University Press, 1996.

Sullivan, Russell. *Rocky Marciano: The Rock of His Times*. Urbana: University of Illinois Press, 2002.

Sutherland, Sid. "Latin Lacks Ring Wit to Cope with Yank, the Experienced." *Chicago Tribune*, September 15, 1923, 11.

Svinth, Joseph R. "The Origins of Philippine Boxing, 1899–1926." *Journal of Combative Sport* (July 2001). http://ejmas.com/jcs/jcsart_svinth_0701.htm (accessed July 8, 2011).

Swain, Joseph Ward, and William H. Armstrong. *The Peoples of the Ancient World*. New York: Harper & Brothers, 1959, 168–70.

Tananbaum, Susan L. "Ironing Out the Ghetto Bend: Sports and the Making of British Jews." *Journal of Sport History* 31, no. 1 (Spring 2004): 53–75.

Thrasher, Frederic M. *The Gang: A Study of 1,313 Gangs in Chicago.* Chicago: University of Chicago Press, 1927.

Thurner, Arthur W. The Impact of Ethnic Groups on the Democratic Party in Chicago. PhD dissertation, University of Chicago, 1966.

Todd, Arthur J. *Chicago Recreation Survey, 1937–1940.* 5 vols. Chicago: Chicago Recreation Commission and Northwestern University, 1937–1940.

Torres, Christina Evangelista. *The Americanization of Manila, 1898–1921.* Quezon City, Philippines: Diliman, 2010).

Treat, Roger L. *Bishop Sheil and the CYO.* New York: Julian Messner, Inc., 1951.

Triem, Tony. "George Godfrey: First Colored Heavyweight Champion," in Colleen Aycock and Mark Scott, eds., *The First Black Boxing Champions: Essays on Fighters in the 1800s to the 1920s.* Jefferson, NC: McFarland & Co., 2011, 22–31.

Tucker, William H. *The Science and Politics of Racial Research.* Urbana: University of Illinois Press, 1994.

Turner, Victor W. *The Ritual Process: Structure and Anti-Structure.* Chicago: Aldine Pub. Co., 1969.

Tuttle, William M., Jr. *Race Riot: Chicago in the Red Summer of 1919.* New York; Atheneum, 1970.

Tyson, Mike. Interview, February 23, 2013, *Windy City Live* (ABC, Chicago).

van der Merwe, Floris. "Boxing, South Africa," in John Nauright and Charles Parrish, eds., *Sports Around the World: History, Culture, and Practice.* Santa Barbara, CA: ABC-CLIO, 2012. http://ebooks.abc-clio.com/print.aspx?isbn=9781598843019&id=A1884C_V1-2560 (accessed August 4, 2012).

van Ingen, Cathy. "'Dixie Kid' Aaron Brown: World Welterweight Champ," in Colleen Aycock and Mark Scott, *The First Black Boxing Champions: Essays on Fighters in the 1800s to the 1920s.* Jefferson, NC: McFarland & Co., 2011, 129–43.

———. "Spatialities of Anger: Emotional Geographies in a Boxing Program for Survivors of Violence." *Sociology of Sport Journal,*28, no. 2 (June 2011): 171–88.

van Ingen, Cathy, and Nicole Kovacs. "Subverting the Skirt: Female Boxers' 'Troubling' Uniforms." *Feminist Media Studies* 12, no. 3 (2012): 460–63.

Verney, Kevern. *African Americans and U.S. Popular Culture.* New York: Routledge, 2003.

Wacquant, Loic J. D., "The Social Logic of Boxing in Black Chicago: Toward a Sociology of Pugilism." *Sociology of Sport Journal* 9 (1992): 221–54.

———. "The Pugilistic Point of View: How Boxers Think and Feel about Their Trade." *Theory and Society* 24, no. 4 (August 1995): 489–535.

———. "Whores, Slaves and Stallions: Languages of Exploitation and Accommodation among Boxers." *Body and Society* 7, no. 2–3 (2001): 181–94.

Waltzer, Jim. *The Battle of the Century: Dempsey, Carpentier, and the Birth of Modern Promotion.* Santa Barbara, CA: Praeger, 2011.

Wamsley, Kevin B., and David Whitson. "Celebrating Violent Masculinities: The Boxing Death of Luther McCarty." *Journal of Sport History* 25, no. 3 (Fall 1998): 419–31.

Wamsley, Kevin B., and Robert S. Kossuth. "Fighting It Out in Nineteenth-Century Upper Canada/Canada West: Masculinities and Physical Challenges in the Tavern." *Journal of Sport History* 27, no. 3 (Fall 2000): 405–30.

Ward, Arch. "In the Wake of the News." *Chicago Tribune*, September 25, 1953, pt. 4, 2.

Watts, Jill. *Mae West: An Icon in Black and White.* New York: Oxford University Press, 2001.

Weinberg, S. Kirson. "Jewish Youth in the Lawndale Community: A Sociological Study." Ernest W. Burgess Papers, University of Chicago, Box 139, folder 3.

Weinberg, S. Kirson, and Henry Arond. "The Occupational Culture of the Boxer." *American Journal of Sociology* 57, no. 5 (March 1952): 460–69.

Weiss, Hedy. "Tyson Scores a Knockout," *Chicago Sun-Times,* February 17, 2013, 20A.

Weston, Stanley. "Pancho Villa: The Gigantic Runt." Clipping in the Villa file, International Boxing Hall of Fame.

Wiggins, David K. "Good Times on the Old Plantation: Popular Recreations of the Black Slave in the Antebellum South, 1810–1860." *Journal of Sport History* 4, no. 3 (Fall 1977): 260–84.

———. "Peter Jackson and the Elusive Heavyweight Championship: A Black Athlete's Struggle against the Late Nineteenth-Century Color-Line." *Journal of Sport History*, 12, no. 2 (Summer 1985): 143–68.

Wiggins, William H. "Boxing's Sambo Twins: Racial Stereotypes in Jack Johnson and Joe Louis Newspaper Cartoons, 1908 to 1938." *Journal of Sport History* 15, no. 3 (Winter 1988): 242–54.

Williams, Mary Elizabeth. "Mike Tyson's Gross Return." *Chicago Sun-Times,* July 1, 2012, 23A.

Wills, Chuck. *Destination America: The People and Cultures that Created a Nation.* New York: DK Publishing, 2005.

Winn, George, ed. *Boxing News Record.* New York: George Winn, 1939.

Winnipeg Free Press, June 6, 1879, 1; March 18, 1881, 4; March 22, 1882, 8.

Wirth, Louis. *The Ghetto.* Chicago: University of Chicago Press, 1956 (1928).

Wolff, Leon. *Little Brown Brother: How the United States Purchased and Pacified the Philippine Islands at the Century's Turn.* New York: Bookspan, 2006.

Wong, Edward. "Women Starred, but It Was about the Men." *New York Times,* June 10, 2001. http://www.nytimes.com/2001/06/10/sports/boxing-women-starred-but-it-was-about-the-men.html?ref=lailaali (accessed May 14, 2005).

Wood, William. *Manual of Physical Exercises, Comprising Gymnastics, Calisthenics, Rowing, Sailing, Skating, Swimming, Fencing, Sparring, Cricket, Base Ball, Together with Rules for Training and Sanitary Suggestions.* New York: Harper & Bros., 1867.

Woodward, Kath. "Rumbles in the Jungle: Boxing, Racialization and the Performance of Masculinity." *Leisure Studies* 23, no. 1 (January 2004): 5–17.

———. "Hanging Out and Hanging About: Insider/Outsider Research in the Sport of Boxing." *Ethnography* 9, no. 4 (2008): 536–60.

Wynn, Neil. "Deconstructing Tyson: The Black Boxer as American Icon." *International Journal of the History of Sport* 20, no. 3 (September 2003): 99–114.

Youmans, Gary B. *The Onion Picker: Carmen Basilio and Boxing in the 1950s.* Syracuse, NY: Campbell Road Press, North, 2007.

Young, A. S. "Doc." "Was Jack Johnson Boxing's Greatest Champ?," *Ebony* 18, no. 3, January 1963, 67–74.

Zang, David W. "The Greatest: Muhammad Ali's Confounding Character," in Patrick B. Miller and David K. Wiggins, eds., *Sport and the Color Line: Black Athletes and Race Relations in Twentieth-Century America.* New York: Routledge, 2004, 289–303.

Zeitz, Joshua. *Flapper: A Madcap Story of Sex, Style, Celebrity, and the Women Who Made America Modern.* New York: Crown, 2006.

Zimmerman, Warren. *First Great Triumph: How Five Americans Made Their Country a World Power.* New York: Farrar, Straus, Giroux, 2002.

Archives

Archdiocese of Chicago Archives

Bishop Bernard J. Sheil Papers, Chicago Historical Society

Bishop Charles Brent Papers

Boxing Scrapbooks

Chicago History Museum

Ernest W. Burgess Papers, University of Chicago, Special Collections

International Boxing Hall of Fame: files accessed: Alexis Arguello; Lou Ambers; Sammy Angott; Carmen Basilio; Tony Canzoneri; Johnny Dundee

(Giuseppe Carrora); Roberto Duran; Flash Elorde; Sixto Escobar; Tony
Galento; Frankie Genaro (Di Gennaro); Joey Giardello (Carmine Tilelli);
Rocky Graziano Thomas (Rocco Barbella); Emile Griffith; Fighting Ha-
rada; Kid Chocolate (Eligio Sardinias Montalvo); Kid Gavilan (Gerardo
Gonzalez); Fidel La Barba; Jake La Motta; Ray Mancini; Rocky Marciano;
Panama Al Brown; Pancho Villa (Francisco Guilledo); Willie Pep (Papaleo);
Yoshio Shirai
Italian American Renaissance Museum Archives
Leonard Wood Papers
Library of Congress
Municipal Welfare Council Papers
University of Chicago Special Collections
YMCA Archives, University of Minnesota

Internet Sources

ABC-Clio: http://ebooks.abc-clio.com/
About Boxing: http://boxing.about.com/
AEI Speakers Bureau: http://aeispeakers.com/
Aussie Box (Boxing Australia Website): http://www.aussiebox.com/
Beloved Onslaught: http://www.belovedonslaught.com/
Biography Base: http://www.biographybase.com/
Biography Channel Website: http://www.biography.com/
Boxing Biographies: http://boxing biographies.com/
Boxing Insider: http://www.boxinginsider.com/
BoxRec: http://boxrec.com
Chicago Tribune: http://chicagotribune.com/
Chicago Youth Boxing Club: http://chicagoyouthboxingclub.org/
Cyber Boxing Zone: http://cyberboxingzone.com/
East Rand Veteran Boxing Association: http://www.ervba.co.za/world-boxing-
    organisations.html
Economist: http://www.economist.com/
ESPN: http://sports.espn.go.com/
Bob Fitzsimmons: http://www.fitzsimmons.co.nz/main.html
Insidewomensboxing.com: http://www.insidewomensboxing.com/
International Boxing Hall of Fame: http:www.ibhof.com/
Irish Boxing.com: http://www.irish-boxing.com/
iSport Boxing: http://boxing.isport.com/
Jab Fitness: http://www.jabfitnesstraining.com/

BIBLIOGRAPHY

Jewish Virtual Library: http://www.jewishvirtuallibrary.org/
Los Angeles Times: http://latimes.com/
Muay Thai Fighting: http://www.muaythai-fighting.com/
National Golden Gloves Official Website: http://www.goldengloves.com/
New York Times: http://www.nytimes.com/
Sports Illustrated, MMA and Boxing: http://sportsillustrated.cnn.com/mma/
University of California Berkeley Boxing Team: http://www.ucboxingclub.org/
USA Today: http://www.usatoday.com/
Women Boxing Archive Network: http://www.womenboxing.com/

INDEX

Adelman, Melvin, 9, 139
Africa (Africans), xiii, 5–6, 15–16, 31, 39–40, 86, 93, 95, 98, 101, 103, 106–7, 113, 119, 121–23, 129, 137, 163, 168, 173–74, 210, 230, 233
African Americans, 16–17, 29, 30–31, 39, 56, 74, 75–130, 135, 139, 174–77, 200, 204, 205, 213. *See also* blacks
Ali, Laila, 206, 232,
Ali, Muhammad (Cassius Clay), xi, xiii, 80, 117, 118–24, 175, 184, 205, 206, 212, 232, 244
amateurs, 25, 39, 41, 42, 48, 57–58, 67–68, 106, 114, 141, 147, 148, 155, 160, 162, 164, 174, 183–184, 200, 229–30, 240, 241, 242, 248, 251
Ambers, Lou (Luigi D'Ambrosio), 160, 162, 166, 168
ancient boxing, 1–9, 43, 48–49
Angelou, Maya, 110, 123
Apostoli, Fred, 162
Argentina, 33, 37, 39, 40, 65, 91, 93, 182

Arguello, Alexis, 69, 172, 182–83
Armstrong, Henry, 113–14, 125, 156
art, xi, 2, 4, 10, 17, 93, 104–5, 219, 244
artists, xi, 17, 31, 55, 104–5, 106, 146, 181, 225, 244
Aryan supremacy, 68, 109–13
Asia (Asians), xiii, xiv, 6–8, 73, 86, 98, 98–100, 119, 122–23, 129, 132–35, 172–73, 184–88, 231, 243
Athletic Revolution, 118–24
Atlas, Teddy, 239–40
Attell, Abe, 61, 144, 150–51
Australia (Australians), 17, 28, 29, 30, 33, 63, 76, 78, 65–86, 141, 142, 206, 234–35

bachelor subculture, 17–18, 48–49, 51–55, 76, 215–16, 220
Baer, Max, 103–4, 106, 107, 108, 146, 147, 154, 163, 197
bantamweights, 29, 40, 79, 129, 131, 132, 134, 135, 143, 149, 150, 157–58, 162, 173, 178, 180, 184, 187, 195, 225, 232

Barry, Jimmy, 142–43, 157

Basilio, Carmen, 116–17, 162, 167–68, 170

Bassey, Hogan "Kid" (Okon Bassey Asuquo), 173

Battling Siki (Louis Amadou M'Barack Fall), 95–98, 100, 101

Belasco, Abraham, 192–93

Belcher, Jem, 14–15

Benitez, Wilfredo, 69, 175, 177

Berg, Jackie "Kid" (Judah Bergman), 152

blacks, xiii, 15–17, 29, 30, 32–34, 39, 56, 63, 68, 74, 75–129, 137, 166, 173–77, 196, 202, 205, 216, 220, 226, 257n15, 260n41, 271–72n14, 278n99. *See also* African Americans

Boston, 24, 44, 57, 60, 71–72, 78, 219

Bourdieu, Pierre, 45, 218

Bow, Clara, 225–26

boxers: bare knuckles, 1, 6, 9–25, 28, 30, 35, 39, 50, 53, 57, 58–59, 192, 211; college, 70, 138, 229, 231, 242, 243; Roman, xi; styles, 1–8, 28, 30, 40, 43–44, 56–58, 71, 80, 85, 96–97, 118, 121, 122, 132, 133, 140–41, 142, 145, 146, 154, 163, 164, 166, 169, 178, 190–92

Boxiana, xi, 256n6

boxing clubs, xiv, 17, 30, 35, 36, 39, 40, 41, 57, 58, 59, 61, 68, 71, 93, 131, 147, 150, 193–94, 220, 224, 229. *See also* gyms

Braddock, Jim, 108, 110, 111, 146–48, 154

Broughton, Jack, 11–12, 212

Brown, Panama Al, 40, 129, 131

British, 8, 21, 28, 29–31, 36, 38, 39, 40, 42, 48, 56, 57, 58, 64, 75, 78, 83, 93, 126, 142, 143, 173, 199, 205, 206, 214–15, 242, 243. *See also* English

Britton, Jack (William Breslin), 62, 145, 151

Burns, Tommy (Noah Brusso), 63, 85–86, 143

Buttrick, Barbara, 227

Byron, Lord (George Gordon), xii, 17

Callahan, Mushy (Vincent Scheer), 152

Camacho, Hector "Macho," 173, 176, 178, 212

Canada (Canadians), 24, 29, 32, 76–78, 82, 85, 86, 91, 121, 129, 173, 222, 229, 235, 242

Canzoneri, Tony, 46, 155, 159, 160

Carnera, Primo, 40, 101–4, 107, 146–47, 154, 162–63, 197

Carnival of Champions, 35, 59, 77

Carpentier, Georges, 32, 37, 64–65, 95–97, 146, 224

Castro, Fidel, 130, 179

Catholic Youth Organization (CYO), 41, 67–68, 144, 153, 201–4

Cerdan, Marcel, 166

Chambers, John Graham, 25

Charles, Ezzard, 113, 170

Chavez, Julio Cesar, 180

Chicago, 41, 45, 47, 50–51, 53, 57, 60–62, 66–68, 69, 71, 86, 89, 92, 101, 103, 107, 111, 138, 139, 140, 142, 144, 145–46, 150, 154, 156, 162, 169, 195–97, 199–204, 215, 219, 236, 237, 241

China (Chinese), 6–7, 28, 56, 74, 99, 111, 133, 183, 186

Choynski, Joe, 149–50

Clitomachus, xiii

Conn, Billy, 41, 45–46, 113, 148

Corbett, James J. "Gentlemen Jim," 28, 59–60, 70, 76, 88, 140, 141, 219, 220
Corcoran, Peter, 13
corruption, xiii, 35–36, 41, 61–62, 82, 103, 144, 162, 166, 167, 168, 191, 239, 241
Coulon, Johnny, 63
Cribb, Tom, 16–17
cruiserweights, 127, 175, 205
Cruz, Orlando, 214
Cuba, 40, 63, 91, 129, 130, 132, 133, 179, 183–84
Czyz, Bobby, 46

Dado, Speedy (Diosdado Posadas), 132–33, 225
D'Amato, Cus, 124–25
dambe, 5
Damoxenos, 3
Darwin, Charles (Darwinism), 73, 75, 76, 80, 135, 157, 159, 186, 196
Davies, Charles "Parson," 51
Davy, Chuck, 70–71
De La Hoya, Oscar, 181–82, 242
Dempsey, Jack, xii, 37, 39, 48, 64–65, 70, 92, 125, 145, 159, 224
Dempsey, Jack (John Kelly) "The Nonpareil," 28, 141–42, 220–21
Denmark (Danes), 29, 30–31, 35, 56, 83
Diagoras, 2–3
Dixie Kid (Aaron Brown), 30
Dixon, George, 29, 77–80, 144
Dobbs, Bobby, 30–31, 35
Donovan, Mike, 56, 140–41
Du Bois, W.E.B., 84, 106
Dundee, Angelo, 171, 175
Dundee, Johnny (Giuseppe Carrora), 61, 157

Duran, Roberto, 69, 175, 176, 212, 232
Duva, Lou, 170

Early, Gerald, 98, 164
Egan, Pierce, xi, 190–91
Elias, "Dutch" Sam, 191–92
Elorde, Gabriel "Flash," 133
England (English), 9–17, 22–26, 28, 29–32, 36, 42, 43, 52, 54–56, 76, 77, 78, 86, 89, 92, 109, 113, 115, 139, 141, 143, 150, 152, 189–94, 197, 199, 210, 214, 216, 224, 227, 240
Erne, Frank, 29, 30, 81, 82, 144
Escobar, Sixto, 40–41, 131–32
ethnicity, 27, 43, 49, 68, 75, 101, 137–207, 209, 214, 283n2

featherweights, 29, 40, 61, 78–79, 82, 113, 124, 130, 132, 133, 144, 149, 150, 157, 160, 162, 163, 173–74, 178, 180, 181, 183, 186–87, 197, 205, 214, 225, 230, 233
females, 6, 10, 52, 60, 80, 90–91, 140, 185, 186, 201, 206–7, 213, 214–16, 218, 220, 221, 227, 228, 230, 233–35, 237, 240. See also women
Fields, Jackie (Jacob Finkelstein), 154, 155, 197
Figg, Jim, 10, 192, 214
Firpo, Angel Luis, 37, 39, 40, 65–66, 94, 159, 171
Fitzsimmons, Bob, 28, 36, 58, 60, 69, 77, 85, 141–42, 143, 219, 220
Fleischer, Nat, 37, 96, 198
Flowers, Theodore "Tiger," 100–102, 145–46

flyweights, 40, 63, 99–100, 129, 134, 149, 157, 159, 160–61, 163, 173, 184–87, 232

Foreman, George, 121–22, 232

Fox, Richard Kyle, 26–28, 52, 216

France (French), 15, 28, 30–31, 33, 35, 36, 41, 45, 56, 58, 63–64, 68, 77, 91, 95, 134, 143, 166, 193, 203, 221, 227, 231, 235

Frazier, Joe, 47, 121, 122–23, 232

Frias, Pepe, 172

Fullmer, Gene, 116–17, 168, 173

gambling, 11, 12, 13, 14–15, 18, 21–22, 36, 39, 52, 61, 66–67, 75, 79, 82, 83, 88, 106, 113, 118, 127, 138, 145, 163, 169, 171, 190, 194, 200, 218

Gans, Joe, 29, 30, 37, 63, 80–83, 125, 144, 220, 272n18

Galento, Tony, 170

Gallico, Paul, xii, 67, 200–201

Garcia, Ceferino, 133

Gatti, Arturo, 173

Genaro (Di Gennaro), Frankie, 159

gender, 189, 209–38. See also masculinity

Germany (Germans), 15, 19, 30, 35, 40, 41, 44, 56, 63, 68, 104–6, 108–13, 138, 146, 149, 195–96, 197, 219, 221, 224–25, 232

Giardello, Joey (Carmine Tilelli), 168

gloves, 1, 3, 4–5, 7, 25, 35, 46, 51, 57, 59, 159, 192, 216, 217, 230, 251–52

Golden Gloves, 41, 67–68, 72, 106, 114, 155, 167, 171, 175, 176, 178, 197, 200, 202–3, 230, 231, 232, 240

Goldman, Israel "Charley," 150, 194–95

Gomez, Wilfredo, 177

Gordon sisters, 221, 223

gouging, 44

governing bodies, xiii, 9, 36, 40–42, 57, 119, 127, 1331, 149, 162, 172–73, 174–87, 205, 227, 228, 230–31, 233–34, 237, 239, 242, 245, 305n56

Gramsci, Antonio, 46, 241–42

Graziano, Rocky (Thomas Rocco Barbarella), 46, 124, 164–65, 166, 170, 213

Greb, Harry, 145–46

Greece (Greeks), 2–4, 9, 43, 48, 102, 110, 197, 209, 225n9. See also ancient boxing

Griffith, Emile, 132, 171, 212, 213–14

Guttmann, Allen, 9

gyms, 2, 30, 35, 48, 68, 71, 72, 144, 147, 193, 196, 197, 213, 228–29, 231, 233, 236–37, 240. See also boxing clubs

Hagler, "Marvelous" Marvin, 174–75, 176, 205

halls of fame, 37–38, 227

Harada, Masahiko "Fighting," 135

Hauser, Thomas, 239–40

Hawaii, 28, 41, 90, 100, 113, 133, 133, 134, 203

Hearns, Thomas "Hit Man," 175, 176, 228

heavyweights, xiii–xiv, 24, 25, 28, 30, 36, 37, 39, 40, 41, 46–47, 52, 57, 59–60, 63, 64, 69, 70, 75–76, 85, 87–92, 94, 95, 100, 103, 104–13, 118–29, 135, 141, 143, 146, 147,

149, 154, 157, 159, 162–63, 169–71, 176, 177, 181, 190, 192, 216, 219, 220, 241, 242

Heenan, John C. "Benicia Boy," 21–25, 50, 140

Hemingway, Ernest, xii–xiii

Herman (Gulotta), Pete, 158–59, 160

Hildreth, Helen, 221–22, 224

Hill, Harry, 52–54, 215–16

Hispanics (Latin Americans), xiii, 29, 40, 42, 47, 75, 118, 129–32, 139, 177–84, 213, 236–37, 243

Hitler, Adolf, 68, 105, 106, 110, 111,113, 154, 155

Holyfield, Evander, 126–28

Hopkins, Bernard, 127, 205

Hughes, Langston, 110, 112–13

Hyer, Jacob, 17

Hyer, Tom, 20–21

India, xiv, 39, 206–7

International Boxing Club (IBC), 41, 167, 170, 227

Ireland (Irish), 12–14, 17, 18, 19–21, 40, 41, 44, 19, 54, 56, 68, 74, 75, 93, 96, 121, 138–39, 140–49, 152, 153, 157, 197, 199, 216, 230, 234

Italy (Italians), 5, 10–11, 40, 41, 68, 74, 75, 90, 93, 94–95, 101–4, 106–7, 111, 124, 135, 138, 139, 142, 143, 156–73, 181, 197, 213, 240

Jackson, John, xii

Jackson, Peter, 28, 29, 76–77, 220

Japan (Japanese), 38, 86, 99, 111, 121, 126, 133–34, 185–86, 210, 234

Jeannette, Joe, 31–32, 35

Jeffries, Jim, 30, 37, 63, 70, 77, 85, 87–89, 141–42, 220

Jews, 74–75, 106, 110, 111, 138, 139, 149–56, 159, 165, 181, 189–98, 199, 204, 227

Johnson, Jack, xiv, 32, 37, 39, 63, 84–93, 94, 96, 98, 100, 101, 106, 116, 119, 129, 130, 143, 149–50, 220, 226, 241

Jones, Roy, Jr. 176

journeymen, 240–41

Kansas, Rocky (Rocco Tozzo), 159

Kearns, Jack "Doc," 64–65, 145

Kelly, Hugo (Ugo Micheli), 143

Ketchel, Stanley (Stanislao Kiecal), 29, 86–87, 143

Kid Chocolate (Eligio Sardinias Montalvo), 40, 129–30

Kid Chocolate (John Ebenezer Samuel deGraft-Hayford), 40

Kid Gavilan (Gerardo Gonzalez), 70–71, 132

Kid Lavigne, 30, 80

Kim, Duk-Koo, 172–73, 212

King, Don, 125–28, 242

King, Martin Luther, 117–18, 119–20

Kingpetch, Pone, 135

Korea (Koreans), 172–73, 185, 233–34, 282n144

Kreugas, 3

LaBarba, Fidel, 159–61

LaMotta, Jake, 46, 114–15, 124, 164–67, 168, 170

Langford, Sam, 31–32, 34

La Starza, Roland, 70, 170

laws, 35–36, 44, 50–51, 60–61, 64, 67, 90–91, 103, 113, 117, 199, 229, 307n2

Leon, Casper (Gaspare Leoni), 142, 157

Leonard, Benny (Benjamin Leiner), 152–54, 199, 204

Leonard, Sugar Ray, xi, 117, 175–76

Levinsky, "Battling" (Beryl Lebrowitz), 151–52

Levinsky, Kingfish, 197–98

Lewis, Lennox, 128

Liebling, A. J., xiii–xiv

light heavyweights, 29, 36, 45, 46, 64, 95–98, 118, 131, 142, 143, 145, 146, 148, 152, 154, 167, 171, 174, 176, 205, 231, 241

lightweights, 25, 29, 37, 61, 62, 69, 81, 83, 114, 130–31, 133 142, 144, 152, 155, 157, 159, 160, 162, 171–73, 175, 178, 180–81, 183, 187, 193, 212, 230, 232, 237, 241, 243

Lilly, Christopher, 18–19

Liston, Charles "Sonny," 118–19

Lonsdale, Lord (Hugh Lowther), 36

Loughran, Tommy, 146–47

Louis, Joe (Joe Louis Barrow), 39, 40, 41, 68–69, 70, 103, 106–13, 114, 116, 119, 147, 148, 154, 170, 197–98, 200, 244

Maeterlinck, Maurice, xi

Malignaggi, Paulie, 173

Mancini, Ray "Boom Boom," 171–73, 212, 213

Mandela, Nelson, 39

Mandell (Mandella), Sammy, 159

Marciano (Marchegiano), Rocky, 46, 70, 113, 135, 150, 162, 168–71, 195

Marek, Max, 200, 203

Marquez, Juan Manuel, 180–81

Martin, Christy, 230

masculinity, 18, 43–45, 49, 52, 56–57, 67, 72, 84, 108, 121, 140–41, 166,

189, 202, 209–10, 211–14, 217–19, 228–29, 243, 300n2

Maxim, Joey (Giuseppe Berardinelli), 115, 167

Mayweather (Sinclair), Floyd, 176–77

McCoy, Kid (Norman Selby), 29, 31

McCoy, Thomas, 18–19

McFarland, Packey, 62, 144–45

McGovern, Terry, 82, 143–44

McLarnin, Jimmy, 155

McVey (McVea), Sam, 31, 33, 34

Melancomas, 2

Mendoza, Daniel, 15, 189–90

Mexico (Mexicans), 29, 33, 39, 40, 42, 47, 56, 61, 92, 131, 132, 179–82, 227, 232

middleweights, 25, 29, 36, 46, 47, 48, 58, 86, 100–101, 114, 116–17, 131–33, 139, 141–43, 146, 164–68, 171, 173–78, 182, 185, 198, 205, 206, 225, 251, 241

mixed martial arts (MMA), 4, 24

Molyneaux, Tom, 16, 75

Monzon, Carlos, 182

Moore, Archie, xiii, 167, 170, 232

Morrissey, John, 21, 49–50, 75, 140

movies (films), xiv, 30, 36, 39, 45, 60, 86, 88, 89–90, 108, 109, 122, 1218, 154, 156, 165, 167, 175, 176, 188, 211, 219, 221, 223, 226, 228, 242, 243

muay thai, 7, 184

musicians, 83, 90, 106, 110, 126, 176, 182, 187–88, 198, 206, 213, 228, 244, 274n45

Musil, Robert, xii

Muslims, 205–7

Mussoloni, Benito, 68, 101, 103, 105, 111, 163

Napoles, Jose, 179
National Police Gazette, 26–27, 52,
    216, 218
Native Americans (Indians), 90, 93
Nelson, Oscar "Battling," 29, 37, 63,
    83, 220
Nevada, 35, 36–37, 60–61, 63, 64, 69,
    83, 220
New Orleans, 24, 35, 46, 59, 61, 77,
    79, 158, 160, 171
newspaper decisions, 36, 61–62, 145
Newton, Annie, 224
New York, 16, 19–20, 35, 37, 38, 41,
    45, 48, 49–50, 52–54, 61, 64, 66,
    67, 69, 71, 72, 75, 94, 98, 103, 112,
    114, 115–16, 121, 124, 130, 138,
    139, 140, 142, 143–44, 147, 148,
    150, 152, 156, 157, 160, 164, 168,
    170, 171, 177, 178, 193, 194–95,
    205, 206, 211, 216, 220, 228, 232
New Zealand, 28, 29, 141
Nigeria, 5, 6, 168, 173–74
no decisions, 61–62, 64

Oates, Joyce Carol, 47, 124, 212
O'Brien, "Philadelphia" Jack (James
    Francis Hagen), 143
O'Grady, Sean, 148–49
Olivares, Ruben, 179–80, 183
Ortiz, Carlos, 131–32
Olympics, xiv, 2–4, 41, 42, 43, 48, 67,
    90, 93, 108, 110, 118, 120, 122,
    123, 131, 134, 149, 154, 159, 160,
    168, 171, 174, 175, 176, 179, 181,
    183, 184, 186, 196–97, 199, 203,
    204, 206, 209, 214, 226, 234, 236,
    237, 243, 248–49, 251

Pacquiao, Manny, 181, 187–88
Panama, 33, 40, 41, 175–76, 183, 203

pankration, 2, 4, 43, 209
paperweight, 142, 157
Paret, Benny "Kid," 132, 212, 242
Pastrano, Willie, 171
Patterson, Floyd, 118, 119, 124
Pazienza, Vinny, 173
Pep (Papaleo), Willie, 163
Petrolle, Billy, 159
Philippines (Filipinos), 28, 38–39,
    98–100, 122–23, 132–33, 134, 181,
    186–88
Plimpton, George, xiii
Poland (Polish), 29, 41, 68–69, 75,
    113, 138, 150, 195, 197, 234
politics, 10–13, 19, 21–22, 25–26, 28,
    30, 39, 50, 56, 61, 68, 99, 102–4,
    108–13, 118–24, 130, 133–34, 139,
    144, 182, 185–86, 188, 189, 190,
    194, 197, 200, 203–4, 206, 210,
    233–34
Poole, Bill, 49–50
Puerto Rico (Puerto Ricans), 40–42,
    130–32, 137, 177–79, 214, 232,
    237

Queensberry, Marquis of (John Sholto
    Douglas), 25, 28, 57

race, xiii, 29, 30, 35, 38–39, 43, 72,
    73–135, 202, 204, 207, 209
religion, 2, 7, 9, 13, 15, 19, 39, 41,
    72, 73, 74–75, 83, 100–101, 103,
    106, 107–8, 118–19, 121, 122,
    127, 130–31, 137–38, 144, 146,
    149–56, 181, 189–207, 217,
    241
Richmond, Bill, 15–16, 75
Rickard, George "Tex," 36–38, 64–65,
    83, 87–88, 94, 129, 220
Riess, Steven, 139

Ring Magazine, 37, 117, 123, 155, 162, 163, 167, 170, 173–74, 175, 180, 182, 183, 198

Robinson, Sugar Ray (Walker Smith Jr.), xi, 69, 114–17, 166, 167, 168, 175, 244

Rome, 4–5, 57, 103, 111, 163, 209–10

Rosenbloom, Maxie, 154

Roosevelt, Theodore, 56, 84, 141

Rosario, Edwin, 178

Ross, Barney (Beryl Rosofsky), 155–56, 197, 204

Rothstein, Arnold, 144, 150

rules, 2, 4, 5–6, 7, 9, 11–12, 18, 22, 25–26, 28, 57, 59–60, 66, 190, 212, 216, 229, 230, 232, 243, 251–52

Ryan, Paddy, 26, 52, 76, 140

Saddler, Sandy, 163

Salandy, Jisselle, 232–33

Sanchez, Salvador, 180

San Francisco, 29, 59, 61, 76, 100, 140, 149, 150, 162, 187, 216, 219, 220

savate, 30–31, 221

Saxton, Johnny, 167

Sayers, Tom, 22–24

Schmeling, Max, 104–6, 108, 11–13, 146, 154, 277n89

Scotland (Scots), 15, 17, 19, 258n24

Scott, David, xii

Sheil, Bishop Bernard J., 41, 53, 201–4

Shirai, Yoshio, 134

slavery (slaves), 15–16, 75, 110, 257n15

social class, 17–19, 25, 37, 39, 41, 43–79, 119–20, 130–31, 137–39, 148, 152, 172, 188, 193 94, 199–204, 209–10, 212, 215,

217–19, 224–26, 230–31, 235–36, 241–42, 244

South Africa, 6, 15, 28, 29, 30, 36, 39, 58, 86, 89, 128

Spain (Spanish), 40, 92, 104, 107, 109, 111–12

Spanish-American War, 28, 39, 98, 129–30, 177

Stevenson, Teofilo, 183–84

Stewart, Hattie, 217–18

Sullivan (Ambrose), James "Yankee," 20–21, 49, 140

Sullivan, John L., 26, 28, 52, 54–56, 58–60, 70, 75, 76, 125, 140, 211, 216, 218, 219, 220

technology, 24, 41, 52, 64, 71, 103, 147, 186

television, xiv, 41, 71, 113, 121–22, 123, 125, 128, 132, 147, 149, 165, 170, 172, 176, 182, 188, 206, 212, 230, 239, 242

Thailand (Thais), 7, 135, 184–85, 231

Theogenes, 4

The Sweet Science, xi, xiii

Tiger, Dick (Richard Ihetu), 168, 173

Torres, Jose, 131–32, 174

training, 3, 63, 71, 72, 229, 231, 237

Trinidad, Felix, 178

Tunney, Gene, 37, 66, 70, 146, 199

Tyson, Mike, 124–29, 205, 212, 230

Uzcudun, Paulino, 40, 107

van Ingen, Cathy, 235–36

Venice, 5, 10

Villa, Pancho (Francisco Guilledo), 38–39, 99–100, 101, 132, 133, 276n66

Virgil, 5

Walcott, Barbados Joe, 29, 30

Walcott, Jersey Joe, 170

Walker, Mickey, 101, 105–6, 145–46

Ward, Arch, 67–69, 200–204, 269n62

Ward, Micky, xiv

Washington, Booker T., 83–84

weight classes, 2, 25, 37, 40, 59, 93–94, 139, 234, 242, 247–49

welterweights, 29, 30, 40, 62, 64, 114, 132, 144, 145, 150, 151, 152, 154, 155, 158, 160, 167, 171, 173–74, 179–84, 187, 192, 198, 205, 231, 232, 233, 243

West, Mae, 132, 225–27

whiteness, 74–75, 93–113, 132, 134, 135, 156, 168, 173–79

Wignall, Trevor, xiii

Willard, Jess, 63, 64, 91–92, 94, 129

Wills, Harry, 92, 100

Wolgast, Ad, 61

Wolgast, Midget (Robert Loscalzo), 160

women, 37, 39–40, 48, 56, 80, 85–86, 89–90, 91, 92, 100, 106, 109, 110, 111, 116, 126, 142, 152, 162, 198, 209–38. *See also* females

women's boxing, xiv, 10, 52, 185, 186, 206–7, 210, 214–38, 247–49, 251–52

World War I, 36, 63, 66, 75, 84, 90, 91, 92, 95, 99, 101, 103, 104, 117, 134, 142–43, 144, 150, 153, 158–59, 163, 168, 169, 199, 224

World War II, xiii, 41, 70, 93, 117, 131, 133, 134, 135, 147, 148, 153, 154, 156, 162, 163, 167, 171, 184, 185, 186, 194, 203, 204, 205, 227

writers, xii–xiii, 36, 37, 38, 39, 61, 64, 66, 67, 70, 74, 80–81, 88, 91–92, 93, 94, 96–98, 100, 101, 104–5, 107, 108–10, 117, 123, 126, 130, 145, 147, 148, 159, 160, 164, 176, 183, 190–91, 195, 198, 200–202, 212, 217, 220, 225, 227–28, 234–36. *See also* Angelou, Maya; Early, Gerald; Egan, Pierce; Fleischer, Nat; Gallico, Paul; Hauser, Thomas; Hughes, Langston; Liebling, A. J.; Musil, Robert; Oates, Joyce Carol; Plimpton, George; Scott, David; Ward, Virgil Arch; Wignall, Trevor

Zale, Tony, 165

Zarate, Carlos, 180

ABOUT THE AUTHOR

Gerald R. Gems is professor of health and physical education at North Central College in Naperville, Illinois. He is an international scholar, having presented his work in more than twenty-five countries. He is past president of the North American Society for Sport History, a Fulbright scholar, and the author of more than 160 publications. This is his tenth book.